RUSSIA

1855-1991 | From Tsars to Commissars

Peter Oxley

OXFORD
UNIVERSITY PRESS

Great Clarendon Street, Oxford OX2 6DP

Oxford University Press is a department of the University of Oxford. It furthers the University's objective of excellence in research, scholarship, and education by publishing worldwide in

Oxford   New York

Auckland   Cape Town   Dar es Salaam   Hong Kong   Karachi   Kuala Lumpur   Madrid   Melbourne   Mexico City   Nairobi   New Delhi   Shanghai   Taipei   Toronto

With offices in

Argentina   Austria   Brazil   Chile   Czech Republic   France   Greece   Guatemala   Hungary   Italy   Japan   Poland   Portugal   Singapore South Korea   Switzerland   Thailand   Turkey   Ukraine   Vietnam

Oxford is a registered trade mark of Oxford University Press in the UK and in certain other countries

© Peter Oxley 2001

British Library Cataloguing in Publication Data

Data available

ISBN 978 0 19 913418 2

20

Designed by Peter Tucker, Holbrook Design (info@holbrook-design.co.uk)

Maps by Jeff Edwards

Printed in Malaysia by Vivar Printing Sdn Bhd.

To Vera Ludmilla, b. Tver 1915,
and Jill, Tom and Rob

For their inspiration thanks to Chris Ward and my long-suffering students at TBSHS.

Acknowledgements

The author and publisher would like to thank Katharine Burn, Series Consultant, for her valuable input and advice during the development of this project.

The author and publisher would like to thank the following for their permission to reproduce the following photographs:
© Associated Newspapers/David Low/Evening Standard/Centre for the Study of Cartoons and Caricature, University of Kent, Canterbury: 240cla; © Sandra Buchanan/JVZ Picture Library: 223clb; Camera Press Ltd: 276tl; © Corbis/Bettmann: 206bl, /Wally McNamee: 277cra; Mary Evans Picture Library: 16cl, 22c, 90cl, 94clb, 105tl, 108cl, 206cla; Illustrated London News: 53cla, 64crb, 125cla, 142c; David King Collection: 11tl, 20c, 36ca, 42cl, 48tl, 55cra, 58cb, 59clb, 60bl, 61ca, 64clb, 71c, 74ca, 75tr, 79tr, 82tr, 83tl, 85ca, 88c, 92c, 97bc, 98clb, 106clb, 112clb, 123cla, 124clb, 126cl, 130tl, 131t, 146tl, 149cra, 151br, 158cra, 162cl, 165crb, 167tr, 170bl, 171t, 173ca, 174cla, 176cla, 176clb, 176cra, 177tl, 182cr, 184t, 188cl, 190cla, 200tl, 200br, 201cra, 204ca, 207tc, 212clb, 216cla, 218cra, 218bl, 219tl, 221bl, 223tl, 238ca, 245cra, 251cb, 253c, 256c, 273cla; Novosti, London: 8cl, 15bc, 17crb, 28t, 64cla, 134cla, 222bl, 242bl, 244cla, 260bl, 264ca, 272c, 292cl, 294clb; Popperfoto: 185b, 284tl, 286cr, 289br; Punch Ltd: 224cl; Society for Cooperation in Russian & Soviet Studies: 209b, 210cla, 214cla, /John Denham: 297cra; Topham Picturepoint: 238bl, 257cla, 260crb, 267crb, 268cb, 279cr, 281crb, /Zemlianichenko: 285cra.
A=above; c=centre; b=below; l=left; r=right; t=top

The author and publisher gratefully acknowledge permission to reprint from the following copyright works:
Victor Kravchenko: extracts from *I Chose Freedom* (Robert Hale, 1947), by permission of the publishers.
MacFlecknoe: untitled poem first published in the early 1930s in *New Statesman* and *Nation*, © *New Statesman* 2001, by permission of the *New Statesman*.
L J Scott: extracts from *Behind the Urals* (Martin Secker & Warburg, 1942), copyright © L J Scott 1942, by permission of A M Heath & Co Ltd, Authors' Agents.

We have tried to trace and contact all copyright holders prior to publication. If notified, by anyone we have not traced, we will be pleased to rectify any errors or omissions at the earliest opportunity.

Contents

Meeting examination criteria: a map of this book

Chapter		EDEXCEL	OCR	AQA
1	The land of the Tsars	Contextual setting	Contextual setting AS Module 2586 Russia 1825–81	Contextual setting
2	Reform and reaction – Alexander II	A2 Module 5 coursework	AS Module 2586 Russia 1825–81 A2 Module 2591 The Russian Dictatorship 1855–1956	AS Module 1 Alternative F Tsarist and Revolutionary Russia 1855–1917
3	Stemming the tide 1881–1905 The Russia of Alexander III and Nicholas II	AS Unit 1 – 5b Russia in Revolution 1905–17	AS Module 5.3.2.4 Russia 1894–17 A2 Module 2589 Lenin and the Establishment of Bolshevik Power 1903–24 A2 Module 2591 The Russian Dictatorship 1855–1956	AS Module 1 Alternative F Tsarist and Revolutionary Russia 1855–1917 A2 Module 4 Russia and the USSR 1881–1985
4	Russia on the road to democracy?	AS Unit 1 – Russia in Revolution 1905–17	AS Module 5.3.2.4 Russia 1894–17 A2 Module 2589 Lenin and the Establishment of Bolshevik Power 1903–24 A2 Module 2591 The Russian Dictatorship 1855–1956	AS Module 1 Alternative F Isarist and Revolutionary Russia 1855–1917 A2 Module 4 Russia and the USSR 1881–1985
5	1917 – A year of promise and turmoil	AS Unit 1 – Russia in Revolution 1905–17	AS Module 5.3.2.4 Russia 1894–17 A2 Module 2589 Lenin and the Establishment of Bolshevik Power 1903–24 A2 Module 2591 The Russian Dictatorship 1855–1956	AS Module 1 Alternative F Tsarist and Revolutionary Russia 1855–1917 A2 Module 4 Russia and the USSR 1881–1985
6	Why were the Bolsheviks able to stay in power?	AS Unit 10b – The Triumph of Bolshevism 1918–29	A2 Module 2589 Lenin and the Establishment of Bolshevik Power 1903–24 A2 Module 2591 The Russian Dictatorship 1855–1956	AS Module 3 Alternative F Revolutionary Russia 1917–1929 A2 Module 4 Russia and the USSR 1881–1985
7	Lenin's role in history	AS Unit 10b – The Triumph of Bolshevism 1918–29	A2 Module 2589 Lenin and the establishment of Bolshevik power 1903–24	AS Module 3 Alternative F Revolutionary Russia 1917–1929 A2 Module 4 Russia and the USSR 1881–1985
8	Which is the way to socialism? Why did Stalin come to rule Russia?	AS Unit 10b – The Triumph of Bolshevism 1918–29	AS Module 5.3.2.5 The USSR 1924–52 A2 Module 2589 Lenin and the Establishment of Bolshevik Power 1903–24 A2 Module 2591 The Russian Dictatorship 1855–1956	AS Module 3 Alternative F Revolutionary Russia 1917–1929 A2 Module 4 Russia and the USSR 1881–1985
9	Building Paradise	AS Unit 12b – Life in the Soviet Union 1928–41	AS Module 5.3.2.5 The USSR 1924–52 A2 Module 2591 The Russian Dictatorship 1855–1956	A2 Module 4 Russia and the USSR 1881–1985
10	The Terror	A2 Unit 6 6b The Soviet Union after Lenin 1924–41	AS Module 5.3.2.5 The USSR 1924–52 A2 Module 2591 The Russian Dictatorship 1855–1956	A2 Module 4 Russia and the USSR 1881–1985
11	Society and culture in Stalin's Russia	AS Unit 12b – Life in the Soviet Union 1928–41	AS Module 5.3.2.5 The USSR 1924–52 A2 Module 2591 The Russian Dictatorship 1855–1956	A2 Module 4 Russia and the USSR 1881–1985
12	Historians and Stalin	A2 Unit 6 6b The Soviet Union after Lenin 1924–41	AS Module 5.3.2.5 The USSR 1924–52 A2 Module 2591 The Russian Dictatorship 1855–1956	A2 Module 4 Russia and the USSR 1881–1985
13	Stalin – the final years	A2 Unit 4 16b Stalin and De-Stalinisation 1945–64	AS Module 5.3.2.5 The USSR 1924–52 A2 Module 2589 Stalin and the Cold War 1941–55 A2 Module 2591 The Russian Dictatorship 1855–1956	A2 Module 4 Russia and the USSR 1881–1985
14	Khrushchev and de-Stalinisation	A2 Unit 4 16b Stalin and De-Stalinisation 1945–64	A2 Module 2591 The Russian Dictatorship 1855–1956	A2 Module 4 Russia and the USSR 1881–1985 A2 Module 6 The End of the Soviet Union 1968–1991
15	Consolidation and collapse 1964–1991	A2 Unit 5 coursework		A2 Module 4 Russia and the USSR 1881–1985 A2 Module 6 The End of the Soviet Union 1968–1991
16	Continuity and change	A2 Unit 5 coursework	A2 Module 2591 The Russian Dictatorship 1855–1956	A2 Module 4 Russia and the USSR 1881–1985

Documents/Interpretations exercises*	Key skills activities**	
	p. 11 Information Technology 3.1, 3.2 and 3.3	1
pp. 28–9 Was emancipation a success?	p. 41 Communication 3.1a, 3.1b, 3.2 and 3.3	2
p. 60 Bloody Sunday	p. 63 Communication 3.1a, 3.1b, and 3.2	3
pp. 88–9 The February Revolution	p. 77 Communication 3.2 and 3.3	4
pp. 101–2 Lenin's role in April 1917 pp. 108–9 Bolsheviks and workers in 1917	p. 111 Communication 3.1b and 3.2	5
pp. 126–7 Opposition to the Reds	p. 133 Communication 3.1a, 3.1b and 3.2	6
pp. 140–1 Views of Lenin		7
	p. 160 Communication 3.1b and 3.2	8
pp. 170–1 Views of collective farms p. 181 The Five Year Plans	p. 187 Communication 3.1b, 3.2 and 3.3; Information Technology 3.1, 3.2 and 3.3	9
pp. 200–1 Images of Stalin	p. 196 Communication 3.1a, 3.1b and 3.2	10
	p. 222 Communication 3.1b, 3.2, and 3.3; Information Technology 3.1, 3.2 and 3.3	11
pp. 236–7 Stalinist politics		12
pp. 253–4 Late Stalinism	p. 246 Communication 3.1a and 3.1b p. 255 Communication 3.2, 3.3; Information Technology 3.1, 3.2 and 3.3	13
pp. 269–70 Khrushchev's achievement	p. 270 Communication 3.1a and 3.1b	14
pp. 291–3 The achievements of the USSR	p. 293 Communication and Information Technology	15
		16

* These provide examination-style questions

** See page 6

Using this book

The way in which you use this book will obviously depend on the examination specification you are following, and the particular options within it that you have chosen to study. The contents map on pages 4–5 makes clear how different chapters relate to the main AS and A level specifications, while within each chapter a clear introduction and list of key questions outline how the main issues are dealt with. Concise conclusions are offered in the end of chapter summaries.

Where there are important differences of interpretation between historians, the main text will introduce you to these controversies and suggest further reading. However, there are also specific sections that focus on major historical debates. These explore the different reasons why historians have such conflicting views, and set out criteria that you will find helpful in comparing interpretations and assessing their value.

Key Skills

Since the study of history involves information gathering (i.e. research) and processing (assessing the value and implications of different kinds of evidence) in order to reach conclusions which you then have to communicate, it can obviously contribute significantly to the practice of two of the designated *Key Skills:* Communication and Information Technology. The spread of activities within this book has, therefore, been carefully planned to provide opportunities for you to develop and demonstrate these Key Skills.

The specifications for these Key Skills at level 3 are as follows:

Communication

C3.1a Contribute to a group discussion about a complex subject.

C3.1b Make a presentation about a complex subject, using at least one image to illustrate complex points.

C3.2 Read and synthesize information from two extended documents about a complex subject. One of these documents should include at least one image.

C3.3 Write two different types of documents about complex subjects. One piece of writing should be an extended document and include at least one image.

Information Technology

IT3.1 Plan and use different sources to search for, and select, information required for different purposes.

IT3.2 Explore, develop and exchange information and derive new information to meet two different purposes.

IT3.3 Present information for two different purposes and audiences. Candidates' work must include at least one example of text images and one example of numbers.

The contents map on pages 4–5 provides a clear indication of the pages where Key Skills activities can be found and which elements of the specifications they cover. A Key Skills logo on the page itself also indicates which activity is being referred to. These Key Skills activities arise naturally out of the work that you are doing and can be used as part of your teacher-assessed portfolio of evidence, demonstrating the application of these skills.

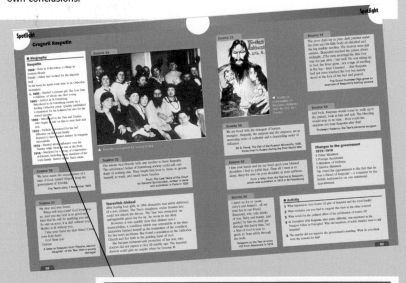

Spotlight
These sections provide opportunities for a detailed focus, either exploring significant issues within a chapter, or examining the impact of particular policies through specific case studies. They generally include a range of different kinds of source material, with structured questions and activities to help you to engage with the issues and reach your own conclusions.

Biography
These boxes provide short biographies of key individuals, helping you to assess their significance, and to place specific actions or decisions in the context of their wider careers.

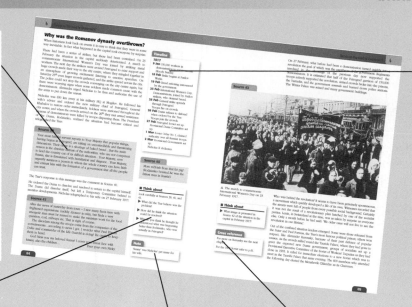

Source

A large number of sources are presented within each chapter. Primary sources give you access to the kinds of evidence on which our understanding of the period has been built, while extracts from historians' accounts give you an insight into their particular interpretation of events.

Timeline

These provide useful summaries of the main developments explained in the text. They help you to develop an overview of the particular issue or sequence of events and to locate particular incidents within a wider chronology.

Think about

Most sources are linked to a 'think about' encouraging you to reflect on the evidence or historical interpretation offered. The questions posed help you to relate the source to your developing knowledge of the topic and to assess its value and implications.

'Think about' boxes relating to the main text also help you to think critically about what you are reading: making links, drawing comparisons and predicting likely outcomes.

Note

These boxes provide additional information or reminders. They alert you to issues that may influence the judgements you may make about certain events, individuals or historical interpretations.

Cross reference

These boxes alert you to relevant sections elsewhere in the book that may extend or enhance your understanding of the text you are reading.

Facts and figures

These boxes present statistical information or specific details to exemplify and substantiate more general claims made in the main text.

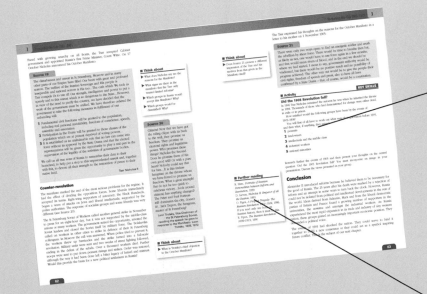

Activity

The activities include a range of exercises that will help you to make sense of all that you have read. Structured tasks encourage you to manipulate information – organising it in different ways – to complete summary charts; to analyse and compare different explanations, and to assess the consequences of particular developments. The activities take a variety of forms, including research work, decision-making exercises, role-play, discussion and debate, as well as exam-style sequences of structured questions and essays.

Further reading

Suggestions here include texts written specifically for AS and A level students as well as accessible works by prominent historians. Some include guidance as to how the books might be read and which sections may prove particularly relevant or enjoyable. Where appropriate, the place of these books in key historical controversies is also made clear.

Examination-style exercises

Each chapter includes specific assessment exercises modelled on the details provided in AS and A level specifications and specimen papers. A large number of structured *document exercises* provide plenty of opportunity for exam practice, while those chapters that deal specifically with major issues of historical controversy include similar structured exercises focused solely on issues of historical *interpretations*.

Chapter 1

The land of the Tsars

The peasants whom they met on the way were all in rags and mounted on the sorriest nags…emaciated and shaggy cows, gaunt with hunger, were greedily tearing up the grass along the ditches. They looked as if they had just been snatched from the murderous talons of some terrifying monster; and the pitiful sight of the sickly cattle in the setting of that lovely spring day conjured up like a white spectre the vision of an interminable comfortless winter of blizzards, frosts and snows …'No,' thought Arkady, 'there is no prosperity here, no sign of contentment or hard work. It just can't go on like this: this must be transformed…but how are we to do it, how should we begin?

From *Fathers and Sons*, a novel by Turgenev, 1861

◄ An 1877 painting of Alexander II, Emperor and Autocrat of All the Russias; Tsar of Moscow, Kiev, Vladimir, Novgorod, Kazan, Astrakhan, Poland, Siberia, the Tauric Chersonese and Georgia; Lord of Pskov (and over 40 other titles!)

Introduction

Winston Churchill in a broadcast in 1939 said of Russia that she was 'a riddle wrapped in a mystery inside an enigma', and many non-Russians would have agreed with him. Russia's experience and history has been very different from that of all other European countries. Indeed, it is not strictly correct to call Russia European: the greater part of nineteenth-century Russia lay in Asia. Situated as she was across two continents, and made up of over a hundred different national groups, each with their own culture and traditions, the Russia of the mid-nineteenth century was a great continental empire. These disparate areas were held together by the all-powerful figure of the Tsar (see Source 1). Many Russians were still suspicious of any new-fangled ideas from the West and believed in the superiority of their own traditional view of the world. However, more critical, and often better educated, Russians by the nineteenth century began to see their country as backward and out of step with the modern world but despaired of doing anything about it (see Source 2).

Before we can begin to study the history of this unique region, we need to have some sense of the complexity and diversity of its geography, institutions and peoples.

Key issues

- Russia's climate and geography
- Russia's mix of peoples
- Russian society
- Russia's economic development
- Russian government

The lands of Russia

The CIS today is the world's largest state. In 1855 the Russian Empire was larger still, spreading 6000 miles from the Baltic Sea in the west to the Pacific Ocean in the east and 2000 miles from north to south – and the process of conquest, which had united this huge area, was not yet quite finished. Within Russia there was an enormous diversity of climate, vegetation and physical features. These different environments in turn forced Russia's peoples to adopt a huge range of life-styles to survive in often harsh surroundings. The city of Yakutsk today suffers from extremes of climate which are typical of the centres of large continents; winter temperatures reach –60 degrees centigrade and in the summer almost 40 degrees. In northern Siberia there are only two brief months of frost-free summer when vegetation can grow. Yet the coast of the Black Sea enjoys a sub-tropical climate, where oranges and lemons grow today, as well as the vines to make Georgian wine. Around the Caspian Sea is a large desert or semi-desert area, making up about 20 per cent of Russia's total area. To the extreme north is treeless arctic tundra, where only mosses and lichens are able to grow. St Petersburg stands on the same line of latitude as Anchorage in Alaska.

Even today only one-tenth of the modern CIS is used for arable crops, and most is not farmed at all. The difficult climate and terrain in many areas made human life almost impossible 150 years ago. As a result, most of the population was concentrated west of the Ural Mountains on the more fertile East European Plain. Here too were Russia's largest cities, the capital St Petersburg and Moscow. However, only a tiny proportion of the Russian population lived in towns or cities of over 100,000 inhabitants – 1.6 per cent in 1855.

■ Think about

▶ What impression does Source 1 give of the Tsar?

▶ Why would he wish to be seen in this way?

▶ Source 2 is a novel. How does this affect its usefulness to a historian?

Definition

CIS = Confederation of Independent States, as Russia is called today after the independence of some of its former territories.

Facts and figures

St Petersburg is much closer to New York than to Vladivostok.

1	Lithuanians	4	Georgians
2	Letts (Latvians)	5	Azerbaijanis
3	Estonians	6	Armenians

Jewish Pale of Settlement

The peoples of Russia

The population of the Russian Empire rose rapidly in the second half of the nineteenth century. The census of 1897 showed the different nationalities in the Russian Empire of 126 million people. The chart below shows in millions those with over 250,000 native speakers:

Great Russians	55.6	Bashkirs	1.3
Ukrainians	22.4	Lithuanians	1.2
Poles	7.9	Armenians	1.2
White Russians	5.8	Roumanians	1.1
Jews	5.0	Estonians	1.0
Kirghiz	4.0	Mordvinians	1.0
Tartars	3.4	Georgians	0.8
Finns	3.1	Tadzhiks	0.3
Germans	1.8	Turkmens	0.3
Latvians	1.4		

Source 3

▲ The nationalities of Imperial Russia

■ **Think about**

▶ What proportion of imperial peoples were Great Russians?

▶ Which of these peoples are now independent?

Source 4

Submission may cause you to believe there is uniformity among us, but I must undeceive you; there is no other country where is found such diversity of races, of manners, of religion, and of mind, as in Russia. The diversity lies at the bottom, the uniformity appears on the surface, and the unity is only apparent.

Tsar Nicholas I quoted by the Marquis de Custine in 1043

■ **Think about**

▶ Why would this diversity make Russia difficult to govern?

▶ What was happening to Germany and Italy in the nineteenth century?

▲ Nomadic tribesmen from Turkestan at the end of the nineteenth century.

There were many more smaller national groups, each with their own language, culture, religion and traditions. The Tungus, for example, eked out a difficult life following reindeer herds as they roamed across northern Siberia in search of pasture. In the south, around the Caspian Sea, other nomads followed camel herds across the desert. These people were officially designated 'aliens' by the State and were outside its day-to-day control.

The Jews in Russia, forming the largest single Jewish community in the world, were particularly harshly treated. They were restricted to the Jewish Pale of Settlement (see map opposite) and were not allowed to live in Russia proper. They also faced restrictions in their education.

Well over 100 different languages were spoken in Russia in the middle of the nineteenth century. This created particular problems for the Tsars, since some at least of these peoples wished to have their own government rather than be ruled from St Petersburg. The government's response to national feeling was to try to stamp it out. Russian was the language of the courts and higher education. The Orthodox Church was introduced into all areas of the Tsar's dominions, Russian nobles were encouraged by land grants to settle in non-Russian territories. In 1830, when the Poles revolted against Russian rule, Tsar Nicholas I cancelled their liberal constitution and absorbed Poland into Russia itself.

■ **Activity** **KEY SKILLS**

Getting to know Russia

Divide your class into six groups. Each group should research one of the following six areas:

- The Ukraine
- The region around Archangel and Murmansk
- The Central Siberian Plateau
- The Vladivostok region
- The Moscow region
- Kazakhstan

Try to find out all you can about each region's climate, main physical features, natural vegetation, main centres of population, population density, religion, ethnicity and cultural traditions. You should also try to construct a simple timeline for the history of each region since AD 1000.

Resources, such as atlases, CD Roms and encyclopaedias, can be found in the reference sections of your school, college or local libraries. You may also find the following websites useful:

www.dur.ac.uk:
www.departments.bucknell.edu/russian/history.html;
www.interknowledge.com/russia

When you have completed your research, you must present it to the rest of your group. This can be done in an oral presentation, a class display (which you may find useful for further reference) or as an IT package. You could of course do all of these.

This could be planned to meet the requirements for the key skill of information technology. You should search for and use visual materials, maps, timelines and pictures to illustrate your points from more than one electronic source and create a new way of presenting statistical information in your report. If you prepare two presentations, one for a Y7 class as well as one for your own, you will meet the requirements for Information Technology 3.3.

The making of modern Russia

The lands making up modern Russia have had a turbulent and colourful history. The richer more fertile areas of western Russia have been fought over for centuries. The capital of the Russian state, first established by Prince Vladimir in Novgorod, moved to Kiev and then to Moscow. Mongols from the east overran much of the country in the thirteenth and fourteenth centuries. As their grip weakened, the Grand Dukes of Muscovy began to unite what is now Russian territory from their Kremlin fortress. Ivan III (1462–1505) was the first ruler to call himself 'Ruler of all Russia'. To build the Russian Empire, Russian rulers fought wars, successful and unsuccessful, with Poland, Sweden, France, China and Turkey, as well as countless lesser states.

In 1613, after years of internal division, Michael Romanov was elected Tsar (Emperor) of Russia by the National Assembly. His direct descendants were to rule until they were overthrown by revolution in 1917. The two giants of the Romanov family, Peter the Great (1682–1725) and Catherine the Great (1762–1796), ruled in the eighteenth century. In many ways their aims for Russia were similar. They both added considerably to Russia's lands by war, but also saw Russia as backward and in need of modernization along western lines. Peter built a new capital, St Petersburg, on the Baltic Sea, looking out to the west and far from Russia's traditional hinterland. Catherine the Great continued Peter's conquests, and also was influenced enormously by the progressive thinkers of Western Europe, and France especially.

In the wars against Napoleon, Russia had to suffer the indignity of the capture of Moscow by French troops in 1812. However, in 1814, victorious Russian troops marched through the streets of Paris. As long as the size of armies was the main determinant of national power, Russia would be able to play a major role in international affairs.

Timeline

1697 Kamchatka conquered
1703 St Petersburg founded
1704 Sweden defeated
1752 Winter Palace begun
1772 First partition of Poland
1781–6 The Ukraine absorbed into Russia
1784 First Russian settlement in Alaska
1801 Tsar Paul murdered
1806 Daghestan and Baku conquered
1809 Finland annexed by Russia
1812 Napoleon's army entered Moscow
1814 Russian troops entered Paris
1816–9 Serfdom abolished in the Baltic provinces
1830 Polish rebellion
1838 First Russian railway begun

Source 6

▼ The growth of Imperial Russia 1700–1914

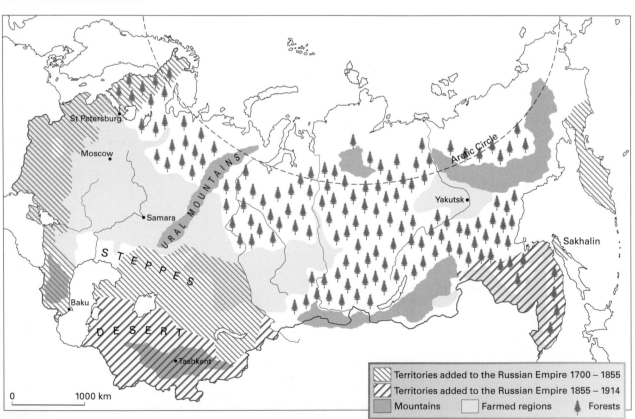

Territories added to the Russian Empire 1700 – 1855
Territories added to the Russian Empire 1855 – 1914
Mountains   Farmed regions   Forests

Note

Russia's rulers had despised constitutional government for a long time. Tsar Ivan the Terrible wrote to England's Elizabeth I in 1570:

'In your land people rule beside you, and not only people but trading peasants.'

■ Key term

Autocracy is unlimited government by one person.

■ Think about

▶ Haxthausen's book was commissioned by the Tsar. Does this make it unreliable for us today?

Quotation

He was surrounded by advisers whom he trusted. Most of his advisers were men of honour and integrity.

> I. Golovine, a Russian exile, writing in 1845

How was Russia ruled?

By 1855 in Western Europe, constitutional government had taken hold in most countries. This means that the powers of monarchs, where they existed, were constrained by a framework of law and also often by representative institutions, such as the Parliament in Britain. Russia seemed to many outsiders to be a survival from a former age. In 1832 Nicholas I (1825–1855) issued the 'Fundamental Laws' to remove any doubt about his position. They began:

Source 7

The Emperor of all the Russias is an autocratic and unlimited monarch: God himself ordains that all must bow to his supreme power, not only out of fear but also out of conscience.

Nicholas not only wanted to be obeyed, but he also expected his subjects to accept his total authority willingly. All the Romanovs had been brought up to believe that this was their God-given birthright. The motto of Nicholas' regime was 'Autocracy, orthodoxy, nationality'. Some foreign visitors were impressed by this system of government:

Source 8

A leader is absolutely indispensable in the Russian's life. The Russian selects a father if God has taken his natural father from him. …. One must keep this point clearly in mind if one is to understand the position of the Tsar. Russian society is very much like a colony of bees, in which royalty is a natural necessity. Just as the colony would cease to exist without its queen, so, too, would Russian society cease to exist without the Tsar.

August von Haxthausen, *Studies on the Interior of Russia*, 1844

However, Nicholas I could not rule a state of over 60 million people alone. His power was exercised by others acting on his behalf. These people were drawn almost exclusively from the nobility. The Imperial Council of State met regularly to advise the Tsar on policy matters and discuss proposed new laws, though in practice the Tsar often ignored it. Ministers who ran the 13 individual government departments supervised the work of the government. The legal system was overseen by the Senate, which, for example, tried serious political offences. This was made up of the highest members of the aristocracy. All who served on these bodies were appointed directly by the Tsar, and could be sacked at any time. The Tsar could accept or reject their advice as he wished. In addition, the Tsar had his own 'Personal Chancellery of his Imperial Majesty'. Divided into three sections, the first acted as the Tsar's personal secretariat, the second consisted of legal experts and the notorious Third Section controlled the political police.

A country as vast as Russia needed many administrators; in 1855 there were 114,000 of them. The provincial governors were the key figures away from the capital. Russia was divided into 50 provinces, and each province was subdivided into 20 districts. Within each province the gentry had their own assemblies, meeting every three years. These assemblies elected judges and chiefs of police in each district. Since these posts were unpaid and carried heavy responsibilities, not everyone wanted them. However, the nobility for generations had a strong tradition of service to the crown, either in government or the army. This was no longer obligatory as it had been under Peter the Great, but it was expected of a man of standing in the community. They made up the local officials and governors as well as the senior personnel in the ministries in St Petersburg, and were free of taxes as a result.

This did not mean that Russia was well governed. The Marquis de Custine in 1843 quoted Nicholas I as follows:

Source 9

Happily the machine of government is very simple in my country; for, with distances which render everything difficult, if the form of government was complicated, the head of one man would not suffice for its requirements.

■ Think about

▶ What can we deduce from Source 9 about Nicholas' views about the nature of his government?

Some nobles and many lower officials at all levels saw government service as a way to increase their income, principally by creaming off taxes and receiving bribes. So desperate was Nicholas I to get some kind of control over his administration that he forced all local governors to send in reports each year. However, when they were submitted, he was the first to acknowledge they were packs of lies! In 1849 the Ministry of the Interior alone produced 31,122,211 official papers. Every document was recorded in a ledger and then copied out in copperplate script by a clerk. It was then either filed or dispatched to another office. Keeping on top of this mountain of paperwork flooding in from all over the Empire was virtually impossible. Of these 31 million over 165,000 were marked 'urgent'! Since communications in Russia were so poor, it could take months for a report to reach St Petersburg, months for it to be considered and months more for a reply to reach the sender. Inevitably, therefore, provincial governors and local officials had a great degree of freedom to act as they wished.

Note

If anything, Russia was an under-governed society with fewer bureaucrats than the states of Western Europe.

The lack of political freedom forced any opposition to resort to violence as its only effective means of influencing the government. Violence could take the form of peasant revolts, of which there were over 1400 in the first 60 years of the nineteenth century, or acts of terrorism. Nicholas I set up the 'Third Section of the Imperial Chancellery,' a secret police force which successfully operated against dissidents opposed to the regime. Censorship was not, however, total, since some discussion of Russia's ills was permitted. Gogol's book *Dead Souls* (Source 12) was published in 1842.

Apart from the secret police, there were only a few thousand law enforcement officers in Russia. The nobility was expected to control its own districts. If law and order broke down, the army was sent in. The army, numbering about 1,400,000 men in 1855, was also a key to maintaining the Tsarist autocracy. At the time our study begins, the officers were taken from the nobility, while the ranks were forced conscripts of the tax-paying serfs. The term of service was 25 years, which meant a lifetime for most ordinary soldiers. They were taken, usually against their will, to distant parts of the Empire, leaving wives and families behind. After three years away, wives and husbands were allowed to remarry. When they were discharged, however, they returned to nothing or begged on the streets of the towns and cities. The army was used to put down internal disturbances as well as to fight wars against Russia's enemies.

Religion

Faith, and especially the Orthodox Church, was much in evidence throughout European Russia. The gilded domes and minarets of its churches still dominate the skylines of town and village today.

Every simple peasant home had a 'red corner' with its icon(s). These icons played an important part in the ceremonies of family and national life, being brought out to bless marriages and baptisms, as well as armies going off to fight. Religious celebrations also determined the nation's holidays, of which there were 90 per year according to some estimates. The Orthodox Church was not independent of the State, but was controlled by the Holy Synod, chaired by a government minister. The Tsar, Tsarevich (the Tsar's son) and their wives all had by law to be members. The Tsar had absolute power over Church finance and appointments. Priests received their meagre wages from the State, which they supplemented by working in the fields alongside their parishioners and by charges for their services. Only they could register births, marriages and deaths. The members of the many monasteries were often materially better off, and only they were allowed to rise up the religious hierarchy. The Church was a strong pillar supporting the government, emphasizing to all in society the importance of obedience to authority, whether it was political or religious. Much evidence suggests that religious belief was not just a thin veneer, but a profoundly held conviction for most Russians.

For many Russians there was a strong element of mysticism in these religious beliefs. Millions of Orthodox Christians, the Old Believers, had broken with the official Church, when it introduced new services in the seventeenth century. They said that the Orthodox Church was acting as the agent of the Antichrist. Many of these, and other Orthodox believers, fasted regularly, and consulted 'holy men' for advice about their problems. Some of these 'holy men' wandered around Russia begging, relying on the charity of believers to support them. Some claimed to have healing powers; others, called Hlysts, fasted or beat themselves or indulged in sexual orgies, believing that only after great sin could you feel real repentance.

The Orthodox Church was a strong support for the Russian status quo. By preaching blind obedience to God, it encouraged blind obedience to social superiors and ultimately the Tsars. The decorations within the churches themselves were bound by rigid rules, as shown in Source 10.

No other religious groups, however, were treated so sympathetically by the State. Jews were subject to rigorous controls, which restricted their employment and where they lived. In particular, they were subject to random but murderous attacks from their Christian neighbours called *pogroms* – often with the tacit support of the government. It was preferable, after all, to have Russians attacking Jews rather than attacking the government itself.

> **Note**
>
> Islam was Russia's second most popular religion.

Russian society

Out of the 60 million people in European Russia in 1855, 50 million were peasant serfs. Roughly half of these were privately owned by the gentry and the other half by the State. To all intents and purposes they were slaves. At the end of the eighteenth century the gentry had been confirmed in their right to physically punish or send into the army the peasants they owned. Peasants either performed *barschina* (labour) for their landlord or paid him *obrok* (cash). In return, they received a house, a garden and a share of the crops grown on the common fields. Life for the peasants was hard. They could be arbitrarily sold and brutally flogged on top of their backbreaking daily work. A General Staff report in 1860 reported that the staple diet of peasants was cabbage soup, rye bread and gruel made from wheat or millet and milk. Their houses were little better than huts, often with only one room they shared with their animals.

> **Note**
>
> While this diet may sound less than stimulating to us today, it probably compares favourably with that of many workers in Britain at the same time.

> ### ■ Think about
>
> ▶ What can we learn from Source 11 about rural life in nineteenth-century Russia?
>
> ▶ What reservations might a historian have about this as evidence?

> **Source 11**
>
> ◀ A painting of starving peasants during the 1891–92 famine.

Nicolai Gogol described a neglected village in his novel *Dead Souls*, published in 1842:

> **Source 12**
>
> The timber walls of the *izbas* (huts) were dark and old: many of the roofs were so full of holes they looked like gratings…There was no glass in the windows of the little cabins; some were stuffed with rags, or women's petticoats.

It would be wrong to generalize too much about the condition of the peasantry. Some serfs lived very comfortably, depending on the fertility of their soil and the harshness of their climate. As in medieval England, the landlord's permission was necessary for any change in a serf's life, such as getting married or leaving the village. Peasants also owed loyalty to their *mir*, village community. It was responsible for collecting the poll tax paid by all adult

Facts and figures

Village elders, usually older and more successful peasants, controlled the *mir*.

Historical debate

Not all historians accept the view that the serfs were living in such a dreadful condition. Some argue that they were better off than peasants in France at the same time, and that their position was improving before 1855. Freedom for peasants in France meant perhaps only the freedom to starve.

Source 13

Will not agriculture suffer as well? Will not many fields lie fallow, and many granaries stay empty? After all, the bread on our markets comes, for the most part, not from the free farmers but from the gentry… Freed from the surveillance of the masters… the peasants will take to drinking and villainy.

Karamzin, *Memoir on Ancient and Modern Russia*, 1811

Source 14

► Serfs gather outside their master's mansion outside Moscow to hear the news of their emancipation (freedom) in 1861 (see page 26).

■ Think about

► What can we learn from Source 14 about the relationship between social classes in mid-nineteenth-century Russia?

males, and also had to choose soldiers for the army when ordered. The *mir* was responsible for dividing up the open fields between families, and redistributing them when it became necessary, if families increased in size. Open field farming in strips and serfdom made the introduction of new farming methods unlikely. What incentive did a landlord have to try to farm more efficiently when his labour force cost him nothing? How could an individual peasant try new methods when farming was done co-operatively in the open fields? Most importantly of all, there was no incentive for serfs to produce more than they could consume themselves, for there was no one to buy it.

Thus agriculture and village life continued as it had for centuries. The limit of the serf's world was his village boundary and the nearest market. Life expectancy was poor – only about 35 years in the second half of the nineteenth century. The only escapes from the anxieties and hardship of ordinary life were in the solace of religion and the bottle. Illiteracy also made it almost impossible for peasants to change their lives and prospects.

However, the system was supported by many of the upper class. In Source 13 one member of the gentry asks himself what would happen if serfdom were to be abolished.

Life for the landlords, too, was not always perhaps as you might imagine.

Many landlords were mortgaged to the hilt to finance the life in their manor houses to which they felt entitled. According to Figes, one third of the land and two thirds of the peasants were mortgaged to the State bank or other noble banks in 1859. This forced nobles to sell off their assets little by little. Few took any real interest in their estates but left them in the hands of managers and bailiffs.

Some of the leading members of the nobility, however, like the Yusupovs, were fabulously wealthy, living in palaces in St Petersburg and Moscow and owning thousands of acres of arable land, mines and forests. Working your way up in the Tsar's service was one certain way to financial success. The royal family was generous to its servants.

Russia had only a small middle class of professional people – doctors, lawyers, university teachers. However, the interest in the Enlightenment in Western Europe encouraged a renaissance in Russian culture during the nineteenth century. Travel abroad in the early years of the century had made many writers and educated people critical of backward Russia. This growing criticism spread through some of the officer class and resulted in the Decembrist Rising in 1825. Six hundred members of the leading noble families were put on trial after this collapsed.

It did not stop the open dissatisfaction with Russia's ancient institutions, especially the autocracy and serfdom. The novelist Dostoevsky, for example, spent some of his life as a 'guest' of the Tsar in the Peter and Paul prison in St Petersburg. Nicholas I restricted passports, making foreign travel almost impossible, in order to try to stop the spread of democratic ideas. Education was similarly restricted. When Nicholas died in 1855, less than 1 per cent of the population was enrolled in schools, and there were only 3500 students enrolled in Russia's six universities. He had also introduced an increasing censorship of publications and even the examination of personal letters by his Third Section of secret police. In 1848, liberal revolutions broke out throughout Europe. Nicholas I responded to this by increasing repression. Indeed fear was perhaps the overriding theme of royal government. The standing army in 1850 was over 1 million, and this in a country nominally at peace. There remained a great distance between the monarchy and the peasantry on the one hand and the forward-looking, free-thinking educated classes on the other.

The royal family

At the apex of society stood the Tsar and his family. The whole of social life for the upper classes revolved around the royal court. The daughters of the nobility were introduced to the court. Great banquets and balls were held throughout the year in the royal palaces. The Marquis de Custine, a French traveller, described one such event in 1839:

> **Note**
>
> The Enlightenment in the eighteenth century urged an end to tradition and privilege, and its replacement by government based on reason and science.

Source 15

The interior of the grand gallery in which they danced was arranged with a marvellous luxury. Fifteen hundred boxes of the rarest plants in flower formed a grove of fragrant greenery. At one of the extremities of the hall, amid thickets of exotic plants, a fountain threw up a column of fresh and sparkling water: its spray, illumined by the innumerable wax lights, shone like the dust of diamonds.

Marquis de Custine, *Empire of the Tsar*, 1843

■ Think about

▶ How did the Marquis de Custine react to the ballroom scene?

▶ Do you think he is a trustworthy witness for us today?

The Tsar spent much of the year at the Winter Palace in St Petersburg, but also visited the Kremlin in Moscow and other palaces in the countryside and by the sea in the Crimea. The members of the royal family were educated to believe in their divine mission to rule Russia, as shown in Source 7.

The Romanov family was wealthy. G. King thought that it was certainly the richest family in the world, and estimated that the personal fortune of Nicholas II when he ascended the throne in 1894 was almost $20 billion, of which

$1 billion was held in gold. He personally owned 150 million acres. This view has been questioned by other historians who have pointed out how poor the Tsars were, in comparison with the British royal family!

The Russian economy

Peter the Great and Catherine the Great had tried desperately to modernize Russia, but seemed to have had little success. The Russian population was growing rapidly throughout the nineteenth century. In 1855 it stood at about 70 million, if all Russian territories are included. By 1897 it had risen to 126 million. Given the harsh winters and short growing period in many areas of Russia, its backward farming methods and the poor quality of much of Russia's soil, the growth of population placed an increasing strain on limited resources. Any bad harvests had a devastating effect on the rural poor. Grain, was by far the most important Russian export, accounting for about 40 per cent of total value. In the main she exported raw materials and imported finished goods from Europe and further afield. Trade was made difficult by the fact that Russia in 1855 did not have one port that was ice-free for all of the year.

In many European countries the nineteenth century was a period of rapid industrial growth. In 1800 Russia had been the world's greatest producer of pig-iron, but by 1855 Britain produced ten times more. Austria produced more cast iron. Russia faced great difficulties in matching the pace of industrialization, because it had an underdeveloped banking system, making investment difficult, and it lacked a pool of labour for new industries. This may appear odd in view of the growing population, but most of this was tied to the villages by serfdom. Most Russians were so poor that there was very little demand at home for industrial products. After bad harvests when food prices shot up, demand for manufactured goods collapsed.

Quotation

It is Russia's historic destiny to lag behind.

Mosse, *Alexander II and the Modernisation of Russia*, 1958

Facts and figures

Comparison of average income per head (in roubles in 1861)

Russia	71
UK	323
USA	450
Germany	175
France	150
Italy	183

———— The Russian frontier 1815 – 1914

• Principal cities

+++++ Railways built by 1860

⊙ Factory development before 1860

LINEN Industries expanding rapidly from 1860

▨ Centres of iron and steel production

▢ Sugar factories

Principal exports:
Wheat, rye, cereals, flour, flax, hemp, wool, animal fat, lard, seeds, wood, wood products, paper

Source 16

▶ The industrial development of Russia up to 1860

Communications and transport difficulties also hampered development. By 1860 Russia had about 1600 km of railway, compared to Britain's 15,000. The railway link between St Petersburg and Moscow was opened in 1851, after much opposition. Nicholas I's Minister of Finance said that the railways were 'a malady of our age'! Given the fact that Russia's roads were also little more than mud tracks in many areas, these transport problems were formidable, making the transport of raw materials and finished goods difficult at the best of times but almost impossible during the spring thaw and autumn rains. Russia's great rivers provided important arteries for trade, but of course they were frozen for many months.

■ Think about

▶ What can we learn from Source 17 about:

a) Russian transport?
b) Russian society?

Source 17

▲ A group of women haul a transport barge along the River Volga at the end of the nineteenth century.

Much of the industrialization that had happened by 1855 was due to the imposition of high tariffs by the government and the action of foreign companies. The most significant developments in the first half of the century had been made in textiles, where one British manufacturer controlled most of the factories in Russia. In total there were about 15,000 industrial enterprises, employing over 800,000 workers. Much of the power in factories was supplied by water, not steam.

Note

High tariffs, taxes on goods imported into Russia, made foreign goods expensive. The guarantee of high prices encouraged investors to set up businesses in Russia itself.

■ Activity

Make a list of the different difficulties Russia faced, then divide them into categories as in the chart on page 21 – military, political, economic and social. You will inevitably find some overlapping of issues! Try to be as exhaustive as possible. When you have decided on the nature of the problems facing Russia, try to suggest ways in which these problems might have been tackled. You will find this useful when you read how the new Tsar actually tried to tackle some of them.

■ For discussion

1 Which of all of these problems do you think was the most important and why?

2 Since Russia faced so many problems in the middle of the nineteenth century, and parts of that Empire are no longer ruled from Moscow today, it is easy to forget that it was an Empire of hundreds of years' standing and one that was still expanding. What glue kept the Russian peoples together?

	Problems	Possible Solutions
Military Difficulties preventing Russian military success		
Political Difficulties in the way Russia was governed		
Economic Problems facing Russian industry and agriculture		
Social Difficulties in the way that Russian people lived together in society		

Conclusion: Was Tsarist Russia a success?

Nicholas I died during the Crimean War, a war fought on Russian territory against British, French and Turkish forces. While the Russians had fought only the Turks in 1853, they had been successful. The Russian Black Sea Fleet had destroyed the Turkish navy in its own harbour at Sinope and its armies had advanced on all fronts against a weak enemy.

When British and French troops arrived in the Crimea, however, it was a different story. In a campaign, which has become a byword for incompetence and mismanagement on the British side, the heroism and patriotism of the Russian soldier could not make up for his lack of supplies and modern weaponry. In Russia, 25 million men were subject to military service but only 800,000 actually served. Most of those who did not were exempted because of poor health. Russian casualties were very high, perhaps as high as 500,000, the vast majority of which were caused by illness and disease rather than the fighting.

By December 1855 the government was exhausted of funds, the army was exhausted of supplies and recruits and there was rising popular anger with the war and the government. Nicholas I had tried hard to stamp out dissent, but it had little long-term effect. The critics had travelled in the more advanced countries of Europe, had seen their political systems and their advanced economies, and wanted to introduce them into Russia. But there were also many who regarded the West as the source of all Russia's problems – the growth of towns and cities, the spread of liberal ideas, the constant demands for change.

The new Tsar, Alexander II, was forced to ask the allies for a peace settlement, which limited Russia's power in the Near East. The internal problems facing the State were more difficult to solve, but without major changes it was clear that Russia could not play the part of a major power in European and world affairs. The past history of Russia showed that only the monarch could carry out sweeping changes, as Peter the Great had done early in the previous century. The great danger was that if there was no reform from above, there might be revolution from below, the consequences of which would be difficult to predict or contain.

How Alexander II tried to deal with the difficult situation he inherited is the subject of the next chapter.

■ Further reading

J. Cracraft, *Major Problems in the History of Imperial Russia,* 1994
C. Thubron, *In Siberia,* 2000

Chapter 2

Reform and reaction – Alexander II

▲ An engraving of the assassination of Alexander II in March 1881.

Source 2

With the help of divine Providence, which has always protected Russia's welfare… may her internal well-being be strengthened and perfected: may truth and mercy reign in her courts: and may there develop in all spheres the urge towards her enlightenment and every form of useful activity. May everybody under the protection of laws equally just for all and giving all equal protection, enjoy the fruits of his honest labour.

Alexander II's manifesto to the Russian people, 1856

Introduction

Alexander II had been well prepared for taking over from his father. The historian Lionel Kochan wrote that he was 'the best prepared heir the Russian throne ever had'. When his father was away from the capital, he regularly acted as Regent (acting Tsar). He was widely travelled, not only in Russia but also around Europe. He had had a strict military training when young, but also had a liberal tutor who had inspired in him a love for western culture. He was 37 when he succeeded to the throne and still cut a handsome figure at court.

As Tsar he undertook, over 25 years, a radical reform of many of Russia's institutions, including serfdom, local government, the army, the universities and the law. He is known to us today as the 'Tsar Liberator'. However, assassins threatened Alexander's life on so many occasions that he had to resort to a continuous armed guard and very high levels of personal security. Source 1 shows that in the end these measures were not enough and he was murdered in 1881.

His successor, Alexander III, took a different view of Russia's problems and limited some of the reforming activities of his father. He died, by contrast, naturally in his bed.

Think about

▶ What can we learn from Source 2 about Alexander II's attitudes to government?

▶ How do these compare with his father's?

Key questions

● What did Alexander II reform?
● What were the results of these reforms for the Russian people?
● Why was there increased opposition to royal authority?
● How successful were the attempts by Alexander to suppress that opposition?

The problems facing the new Tsar

In the 1830s, the Marquis de Custine said of Russia that it was:

> **Source 3**
>
> a cauldron of boiling water, tightly closed and placed on a fire which is becoming hotter and hotter; I fear an explosion.

On his deathbed, Nicholas I had apologized to his son for not leaving the Empire in the state he would have wished:

> **Source 4**
>
> I am not handing over the command in the good order I should have wished, and I am bequeathing you much worry and distress.

Think about

▶ In what sense was Russia 'tightly closed' but 'becoming hotter and hotter?'

He also famously urged him to, 'Hold on to everything!' Alexander was never to waiver from this advice. His deep concern for his people, nurtured by his study of history as a child, only strengthened his belief in his own autocratic powers.

The Crimean War, especially the capture of Sebastopol, believed by almost everyone at the time to be invincible, had revealed just how deep-seated Russia's problems were. Her communications were woeful, her munitions industries inadequate for a modern war and her administration had been revealed to be corrupt and ineffective. The State arsenals contained, for example, less than half the weapons they were supposed to have – and many of these did not work. At home, discontent had grown amongst all classes, even the nobility. Here Prince Kropotkin, a landowner and an anarchist, remembers the situation in 1855:

Source 5

The revolutions of 1848 [in Europe] had had their distant echo in the hearts of Russian peasant folk, and from 1850 the insurrections of revolted serfs began to assume serious proportions. When the Crimean War broke out, and militia was levied [raised] all over Russia, these revolts spread with a violence never before heard of. Several serf-owners were killed by their serfs, and the peasant risings became so serious that whole regiments with artillery were sent to quell them.

Kropotkin, *Memoirs of a Revolutionist*, 1862

Russia was seen by many to be hopelessly backward. Clearly there was an urgent need for some kind of restructuring, or *perestroika*, as it has been called in more modern times. Alexander had one great asset on his side. A contemporary, Nikolai Dobriulov, recalls the atmosphere a short time after his accession:

Source 6

A time of widespread euphoria and enthusiasm. Every breast swelled, and everyone's speech flowed sonorously and smoothly like a river that had been freed of ice. What a glorious time it was!

■ **Think about**

▶ Why was there such enthusiasm on Alexander II's accession to the throne?

▶ Why might a historian be cautious about this source?

Many now saw the need for change. But what change? And how was it to be realized? How would the nobility and gentry, those traditional supporters of autocratic power, receive reform?

Slavophiles and Westernizers

Debate had ranged for many years about the best way forward for Russia. Russian writers and artists divided into two quite distinct schools, which came to be called Westernizers and Slavophiles. The view of the Slavophiles is typified by the commentator K. Aksakov writing in 1855:

Source 7

[In 1612] the people called for political power, elected a Tsar, and entrusted their fate to him; they then peacefully laid down their arms and dispersed to their homes. Russia's history contains not a single instance of a revolt against authority and in favour of political rights for the people...

Under Peter there began that misfortune which is still with us today. In the West there is this constant enmity and rivalry between State and people, who fail to understand the relationship that exists between them. In Russia we have never had that enmity and rivalry. The Russian people remained true to their outlook and did not encroach upon the State; but the State encroached upon the people, forcibly changing their ways and customs, even their costume...Thus was destroyed the ancient union between the land and the State.

Let us re-establish the ancient union between government and people, state and land, upon the lasting foundation of truly basic principles.

■ **Think about**

What is Aksakov's attitude to:

▶ the Russian people?

▶ Peter the Great?

Note

The Decembrists were idealistic young officers of noble birth, who wanted to set up a republic in Russia. They planned to kill the new Tsar in 1825.

■ **Think about**

How do Sources 7 and 8 differ in:

▶ their view of what was wrong with Russia?

▶ their attitude to the West?

The Westernizers took a different view. Here the Decembrist Fonvisin, one of those from wealthy families who rose up against the Tsar in 1825, reflects on the causes of the uprising:

Source 8

During the campaigns in Germany and France our young people became acquainted with European civilization, which made a strong impression on them so that they could compare everything they had seen abroad with that which presented itself at every turn at home – the slavery of the vast majority of Russians who had no rights, the cruel treatment of subordinates by their superiors, all manner of the abuse of power, everywhere arbitrary rule – all this excited the discontent and outraged the patriotic feelings of educated Russians.

The differences between these two groups was to be a feature of Russian history for the whole of the period covered by this book, though it will change in character after 1917.

The end of serfdom

For those wanting change, the reign got off to a promising start. Alexander immediately stopped all army recruitment and eased censorship. He also released all those Decembrists, still in prison or exile, who had tried to overthrow his father in 1825. A similar amnesty was given to those Poles who had rebelled in 1830–1831. The restrictions on foreign travel were also quickly lifted. In 1859, 26,000 passports were granted to travel abroad.

For many critics, the abolition of serfdom was the most urgent need. To them it was the principal handicap to Russia's development into a modern state, the equal of the other European powers. They believed:

● Serfdom prevented the growth of Russian industry, obstructing the free flow of labour and restricting enterprise.

● It also prevented the introduction of modern methods of agriculture, leaving Russia poor and lagging behind the rest of Europe.

● Defeat in the Crimea had shown that the army needed urgent reforms. This too was difficult as long as serfdom survived, for serfs serving 25 years in the ranks formed the mass of the soldiers.

● Abolition was the only way to stop the rising number of peasant revolts. There had been 1467 of these since 1800.

However, not everyone agreed with this view of serfdom.

■ **Think about**

▶ What view does Karamzin have of the peasants?

▶ Why does he think serfdom should be preserved?

Source 9

Freed from the surveillance of the masters…the peasants will take to drinking and villainy – what a gold mine for taverns and corrupt police officials, but what a blow to morals and the security of the State. In short, at the present time, the hereditary nobility, dispersed throughout the State, assists the sovereign in preserving peace and order; divesting them of this supervisory authority, he would, like Atlas, take all of Russia upon his shoulders. Could he bear it? The collapse would be frightful.

Karamzin, *Memoir on Ancient and Modern Russia*, 1811

Nicholas I had recognized serfdom as a 'flagrant evil' and set up nine different secret committees to investigate how it could be ended. The future Alexander II served on one of these committees, but none achieved anything. The reason for this was the extraordinary difficulty and complexity of the problem. The gentry complained that they would be ruined if peasants were given land when they were freed. The peasants knew that freedom without land would be meaningless, leaving them at the mercy of the landlords as before. How would law be maintained if owners lost the control of their serfs, a matter which clearly concerned Karamzin in Source 9?

In March 1856, after making peace with his enemies in the Crimean War, Alexander made a dramatic announcement to the Moscow gentry:

Source 10

To refute any groundless gossip on so important a subject [freeing the serfs] I consider it necessary to inform you that I have no intention of doing so immediately. But of course, and you yourselves realize it, the existing system of serf owning cannot remain unchanged. It is better to begin abolishing serfdom from above than to wait for it to begin to abolish itself from below. I ask you, gentlemen, to think of ways of doing this.

■ Think about

▶ Alexander was an autocrat. Why then was he asking the gentry to end serfdom?

The following year he created the Secret Committee on Peasant Affairs, followed by a number of Editing Commissions, to work out the details of the scheme. The whole process was opposed by the *krepostniki* – defenders of serfdom – who included members of the royal family, the leaders of the Orthodox Church and many leading figures in noble families. The process was long and tortuous, and inevitably resulted in a compromise between the different powerful interests. Alexander himself played a very prominent role in pushing the process forwards to fruition, occasionally chairing discussions himself.

The Great Emancipation Statute was announced to the Russian people from pulpits throughout the country in February 1861. It affected only privately owned serfs. The State serfs had to wait a few more years.

Here are the key terms:

- The serfs were freed. This meant they could marry whomsoever they wished, own property and set up their own businesses.
- The land at the moment remained the property of the gentry, though they had to grant use of their home and a portion of arable land to each peasant.
- Each serf was guaranteed a minimum size of allotment, which differed according to area. Assessors apportioned these later.
- 75 per cent of allotments were less than 4 dessyatinas, when, in a **good** soil area, 5 dessyatinas were regarded as usually the minimum to feed a peasant family. On average, peasant families now farmed 20 per cent less land than before emancipation.
- Landowners were compensated by the State immediately, on a very high valuation of the land.
- The freed serfs were to pay back to the State redemption taxes for 49 years, including interest at 6 per cent. Only when these were paid would they have legal title to their land. Alternatively, they could continue to work 30 or 40 days per year on the lord's land to pay off the redemption of the land.
- The local *mir* (village council) was made responsible for paying the redemption taxes.

Facts and figures

A dessyatina is a measurement of land, roughly equal to 2.7 acres

- Labour services, limited to 40 days per male 'soul', were to be continued for two years, after which they could be converted into a money payment.
- The separation by a peasant of his land from the commune could only be done with the consent of the *mir*, until the redemption tax was paid. The *mir* was very powerful, as D.M. Wallace recorded in 1877:

Source 11

The Heads of Household must often meet together and consult in the Village Assembly…They cannot begin to mow or plough the fallow field until the Village Assembly has passed a resolution on the subject. If a peasant becomes a drunkard…every family in the village has a right to complain, not merely in the interests of public morality, but from selfish motives, because all the families are collectively responsible for his taxes…If a peasant wishes to go away for a short time, in order to work elsewhere, he must obtain a written permission, which serves him as a passport during his absence.

- The State peasants received better treatment but had to wait a few more years until 1866 for their freedom. They were allotted plots of land on average over twice the size of the private serfs.
- The Household serfs came out worst of all. They received no land, just their freedom.

Emancipation was both praised and criticized at the time. Because of the shortcomings of the emancipation deal, there was civil unrest in all but one of the provinces affected by the reform. There were 647 incidents of peasant rioting in the four months following the publication of the Emancipation Edict. Troops were used in 449 cases. In Bezdna a peasant, Anton Petrov, said he had found by examining the Emancipation Edict closely that the Tsar really had granted freedom for all the peasants, and he urged them to seize it for themselves. When thousands gathered to support him, the army was sent in. Soldiers fired repeatedly on the crowds, killing 70. Petrov was arrested and executed.

The peasants now had less land than they had before, and were having to pay a redemption tax higher than the land was worth. The landowner often reserved the best land for himself. When the growth of population is taken into account, and the redistribution of land which inevitably followed this increase, land shortage became an ever increasing problem, leaving peasant families helpless if the harsh Russian climate was worse than usual.

A sign of the economic difficulties facing many peasants was the growing amount of redemption and poll tax arrears, a feature for the next 20 years. There was also little incentive for a peasant family to invest in their land, if it could in part be taken from them and reallocated when the village population expanded. Most peasants continued to farm in the same inefficient ways as before.

Nor were many landowners happy with the emancipation. Almost two-thirds of landowners were already mortgaged to the banks before emancipation. The redemption money therefore, in many cases, went to pay off existing debts. By 1905 the nobles owned 40 per cent less land than in 1861, mainly perhaps because they found their estates unprofitable and slowly sold off land to their peasants and others. Anton Chekhov's plays, written after emancipation, portray a gentry class facing financial, and therefore social, ruin.

■ Think about

▶ According to Wallace in Source 11, what powers does the *mir* have over the freed serfs?

■ Think about

▶ What does the Bezdna incident tell us about the Russian peasantry at the time?

Note

However, the peasant birth-rate grew noticeably at this time. This is usually seen at other times as a sign of optimism in the future. Some peasants went east into Siberia and claimed larger plots of free land.

■ Research

Chekhov's *The Cherry Orchard* is the classic work illustrating this point.

To some of the intelligentsia, the limited nature of the reform proved that the Tsar's government was incapable of meeting the needs of ordinary Russians. Ironically, therefore, it caused more revolutionary and terrorist activity.

This did not, however, cause the cautious Tsar Alexander to abandon his reforms. Known liberals replaced almost all the conservatives in the government in the early 1860s.

Document exercise: was emancipation a success?

Source A

The sovereign has betrayed the hopes of the people; the freedom he has given them is not real and is not what the people dreamed of and need…

We do not need a Tsar, or an emperor, or the Lord's anointed, or a robe of ermine covering up hereditary incompetence; we want to have as our head an ordinary mortal, a man of the soil, who understands life and the people who have elected him.

To the Younger Generation, a pamphlet written by the Radicals Mikhailov and Shelgunov in September 1861 after the Emancipation Edict

Source B

The same enthusiasm was in the streets. Crowds of peasants and educated men stood in front of the palace, shouting hurrahs, and the Tsar could not appear without being followed by demonstrative crowds running after his carriage…

When I saw our peasants, fifteen months after the liberation, I could not but admire them. Their inborn good nature and softness remained with them, but all traces of servility had disappeared. They talked to their masters as equals talk to equals.

Prince Kropotkin, *Memoirs of a Revolutionist, c. 1876.*
A serf-owner describing the reaction to the Emancipation Edict

Source 12

▲ A peasant in 1906 is ordered off land belonging to the estate-owner.

■ Think about

▶ Why might a peasant have tried to farm land which does not belong to him?

Compare the horses.

▶ What does this photograph suggest about peasant prosperity 40 years after emancipation?

After several postponements, the peasant reform became law on 19 February 1861. It was solemnly proclaimed in all churches on the eve of the Great Lent, but it fell singularly flat – it satisfied nobody, not even the *krespotniki*…The peasants received the reform with complete disbelief; they even suspected the authenticity of the Imperial Manifesto…Soon spokesmen for the peasants…trudged by the hundreds along the interminable Russian roads to see the Tsar and to tell him of the injustice and hardship suffered by his people.

Apostles into Terrorists by Vera Broido, 1977.
She spent her 'childhood with Russian revolutionaries'

The peasant reform safeguarded many traces of feudalism. There can be no doubt that the reform defrauded the peasants. Some of the peasants' land was reduced…The most onerous conditions of all were the terms of redemption…Thanks to them, the peasants lost the largest quantity of land…The allotments obtained by the private peasants through the reform were for the most part entirely inadequate given the prevailing system of land tenure.

Zaionchkovsky,
The Abolition of Serfdom in Russia, 1978

■ Examination-style questions

1 Comprehension in context
What was the attitude of the author of Source A to the emancipation?

2 Comparing the sources
How and why do Sources B and C differ in their view of the popular reaction to the proclamation of the Emancipation Edict?

3 Assessing the sources
What reasons might a historian have to be cautious about the reliability of Source C?

4 Making judgements
Using the sources and your own knowledge, do you agree with Zaionchkovsky in Source D that 'the reform defrauded the peasants?'

Alexander's other reforms

Army reforms

Russian defeat in the Crimea had been the catalyst for fundamental change. Alexander moved quickly to reform the army. Recruitment was suspended in 1856. Military colonies were abolished altogether. Every man over 20 was made liable to conscription, if medically fit. The length of service for conscripts was reduced to six years, followed by nine years in the reserve and five in the militia. The military reserve was, as a result, raised from 210,000 to 553,000 by 1870 and the training and discipline of soldiers was made both more humane and more efficient.

Local government reforms

Alexander was personally committed to the maintenance of his autocratic rule. But he also recognized that there had to be changes in the governmental system. The abolition of serfdom necessitated some reform, since the gentry had lost much of the legal basis of their control of the peasantry. Central government could not fill the void. Russia was an undergoverned society, having many fewer civil servants than Britain. It was essential that local people, therefore, filled administrative roles.

In 1864 new bodies were created in Russia, called *zemstva* (singular, *zemstvo*). The members were chosen by three electoral colleges, representing the peasants, townspeople and the gentry. Townspeople and gentry elected their colleges, but village elders chose the peasant representatives. There were to be *zemstva* for both districts and provinces, and each assembly elected a 'board' to supervise its work. The responsibilities of these new bodies were restricted to public health, prisons, roads, agriculture, the relief of famine and to some areas of education.

In the towns and cities in 1870, municipal councils, *dumas*, were set up with similar responsibilities. Larger cities were given a different status, with commandants to run them. Only those who paid trade taxes or were on a property register were granted the vote.

Neither *zemstvo* nor *duma* had control of the police, which remained under the Minister of the Interior. What was the relationship between these new bodies and the government in Moscow? This was not precisely defined, but provincial governors had the power to countermand all *zemstvo* decisions. The *zemstva* were also permanently short of money to attend to the problems that were their responsibility. They did, however, provide new opportunities for many people who had not been involved in political life before.

Reform of the law

> ### Source 13
>
> A man of the humble class who falls into the hands of the law is more afraid of the process of the law itself than of any punishment. He looks forward with impatience to the time he will be sent to Siberia; his martyrdom ends with the beginning of his punishment.
>
> *My Past and Thoughts*, Alexander Herzen, a Russian exile, 1851

> ### ■ Think about
>
> ▶ How does Herzen in Source 13 show his sympathy for men 'of the humble class'?

Before the reforms, the poor's chances of justice were indeed remote. The accused were presumed guilty unless proven innocent. There were no juries or lawyers in court, and the judges sat in closed session examining only written evidence. Inevitably, the police heavily influenced the judges. The process of law was also painfully slow. In November 1864 the Tsar published the reforms of the legal system:

> ### ■ Think about
>
> ▶ Why did these features of the law mean there was little chance of justice for the peasantry?

> ### Source 14
>
> …to establish in Russia courts of justice that are swift, fair, merciful, and equal for all our subjects, to raise the authority of the judiciary, to give it the independence that befits it.

The most striking reform was the introduction of juries in criminal cases. These were selected from lists of propertied people, prepared by the *zemstva*. A hierarchy of courts was set up from magistrates' courts, which dealt with minor offences, to the Senate, the final court of appeal. Judges were well paid, and therefore less likely to take bribes. Courts were now open to the public.

However, as we will see later, political cases were in future to be removed from the jurisdiction of these courts. The police of the Third Section were still active and were able to arrest people as they wished. Nonetheless, the new courts enjoyed great freedom of expression and many of the rising intelligentsia found a new and exciting career in the law. Some court cases became famous.

Censorship and the Press

In Nicholas I's reign censorship was severe. All books and newspapers had to be submitted in advance to the censor for his approval. This situation eased under Alexander. When the emancipation of the serfs was being considered, the Press openly discussed the question.

In 1863, censorship became a responsibility of the Ministry of the Interior and, in 1865, it produced a new set of rules to guide writers and editors. Editors no longer had to get prior approval for their texts. Instead they were submitted after printing but before release. The Ministry of the Interior maintained the power to suspend and close publications and fine their publishers. Later in 1873 it was also given the power to forbid certain topics from discussion.

The censors made some major mistakes, by allowing seditious books to be printed. The publication of Chernyshevski's *What is to be Done?* was perhaps the most glaring error. This book urged its readers to:

> **Source 15**
>
> Come up out of your godforsaken underworld, my friends, come up. It is not so difficult.

Educational reforms

In this new atmosphere of toleration and reform since the death of Nicholas I, there was a rapid growth of private schools. These, however, were uncontrolled and taught 'dangerous' subjects such as history, as well as literacy and numeracy. New regulations (1863) allowed private schools, but prescribed a common curriculum of religion, reading and writing (in Russian only), and arithmetic. They were subject to regular inspection, and inspectors could order changes in the curriculum. Pupils had to pay for the gymnasia (like grammar schools) which gave entry to university if the final exams were passed. In these schools Greek and Latin were stressed rather than science. In 1870 the first schools to offer girls non-vocational education were authorized. Much of the improvement in literacy was due to the efforts and money of the *zemstva*. By 1914 they ran almost half of all primary schools. It is important to also note the contribution of the army in reducing illiteracy. From 1874 to 1894, between 2 and 3 million men learned the basics of reading and writing in the armed forces.

There were also sweeping reforms of universities. Scholars were able to travel abroad to study, and the curriculum was broadened to include philosophy and western European law. There was no more surveillance of students when off

Facts and figures

Number of newspapers licensed

1845–54	6
1855–64	66

1855–64 The number of licensed periodicals grew from 19 to 156

■ Think about

▶ Why was history seen as dangerous?

Facts and figures

Number of primary children in school

1856	450,00
1878	over 1,000,000

Literacy in 1897	21%

the campus. A new breed of liberal professors was appointed to succeed many of the conservatives in place during Nicholas' reign. The State also exempted the poor from fees and, by 1859, two-thirds of all students at Moscow University were exempt. Soon professors and students were engaged in fundamental discussions about the future of Russia.

When a more conservative line was introduced in 1861, it provoked student riots in St Petersburg and the mass resignation of professors. A new University Statute two years later gave back to universities much of their power to run themselves and to appoint their own deans and professors, subject to confirmation by the Minister of Education.

Economic development

Industrial development was noticeable but slow under Alexander II. The industrial workforce expanded from 860,000 to about 1,320,000 by 1887. There were some marked economic successes. Perhaps most notable were the Nobel brothers, who set up the Naphtha Extraction Company in 1879 to exploit the oil reserves at Baku in the Caucasus.

	1865	1870	1875	1887
Tons of oil	8912	27,200	83,200	244,000

In coal production the advance had also been considerable.

	1860	1872	1880	1887
Tons of coal	300,000	1,000,000	3,212,000	4,428,000

New industrial areas were beginning, especially in the Ukraine and the Urals. Much of this had been instigated by foreign investment. The town of Yusovka was named after one such Welsh entrepreneur, Hughes. The textile industries around Moscow also grew, as did the St Petersburg industrial region. The growing railway system in the 1860s and 1870s (see p. 47) was largely constructed from imported materials. The Russian railway network grew from 2,200 to 14,200 miles; not much by international comparisons, particularly when the size of Russia is taken into account, but none the less a significant advance.

There was a growing market in the countryside for manufactured goods because of Russia's growing population.

	1861	1870	1880	1887
Pop. in millions	74	84.5	97.7	113

It must be remembered, however, that the peasant market was a very fragile one, largely dependent on the quality of every harvest. Also, transport difficulties meant that much of the market was almost inaccessible.

The nationalities

The nineteenth century throughout Europe saw a rising tide of national consciousness. As Russians were a minority in the Empire, nationalism had obvious dangers for the Tsar and his regime. A reawakened interest in folk traditions and in native languages caused a growing sense of the differences between the various national groups and the Russian population. In the

(see p. 47)

> ## Quotation
>
> The government's liberality turned universities into a powder keg. Staff spoke out and students began to organize. The lectures of the former and the associations of the latter appeared to be serving not only academic and economic purposes but also the promotion of political instability.
>
> Saunders, *Russia in the Age of Reaction and Reform*, 1992

Ukraine, the first journal in the Ukrainian language, *Osnova*, was published and societies (*hromady*) were established to set up schools throughout the Ukraine and celebrate Ukrainian culture.

Alexander II allowed a relaxation of central control in some regions, especially in Poland and the western provinces of Russia. Warsaw was granted its own archbishop and medical school. An Agricultural Society was set up in 1857, which became a debating chamber for political ideas. An attempt was made to kill the Russian-appointed Polish Prime Minister. When the perpetrators were caught and publicly hanged, there was a storm of protest. Russian troops arrested whole congregations of Catholics in church, but only sparked off rebellion in January 1863. The rebellion was finally crushed in 1864 after a fierce guerrilla war, and then less liberal policies were pursued.

The Finns proved to be more amenable – at least they did not revolt – and were rewarded with their own currency and Diet (parliament). Alexander II is still regarded as a founder of modern Finland today.

Of all the groups in Russia, the Jews had fared worst at the hands of the Russians. They had been confined to the Pale of Settlement for centuries and subject to random attacks. Of the 5.2 million Jews living in the Empire, about 2 million lived in the Ukraine. Most were artisans or traders. Alexander removed some of the restrictions placed on them, allowing them into higher education and the government service. Some Jews were also allowed to settle outside the Pale. Many other restrictions were simply no longer enforced.

The end of the reforms

These reforms together were the most far-reaching changes made since Peter the Great. They did, however, almost grind to a halt. Reforming ministers were replaced with more conservative figures in the later 1860s. Perhaps Alexander's enthusiasm for reform was over, his mind perhaps changed by the first serious attempt on his life in 1866. Perhaps all along he had only seen reforms as limited measures, necessary to meet the needs of the crisis facing the country in 1855. Perhaps his infatuation with his new mistress, Catherine Dolgoruky, was uppermost in his thoughts!

One area that saw very little reform was the financial policies of the government. The poll tax, from which the gentry were exempt, remained a heavy burden on the peasants. In fact it increased by 80 per cent over Alexander's reign. The Finance Minister, Reutern, was able to centralize the accounting system so that the budget was more easily assessed and understood. He had to abandon a plan to stabilize the value of the rouble.

The growth of opposition

Despite the reforms, the political climate in Russia grew more threatening for the regime. The new openness encouraged by the reforms aroused expectations which the Tsar would never be able to satisfy. In particular, radical demands for a constitution (a written set of rules for government defining the powers of everyone, including the Tsar) and a national assembly were never granted. Students, who found their organizations banned and their favourite authors arrested, formed the basis of opposition in the 1860s.

Cross reference

See the map on page 10

■ Activity

Look at the problems facing the regime which you identified at the end of Chapter 1.

1 How far do you think Alexander solved these problems?

2 How did his reforms match up to your own ideas?

3 Would your own ideas have been more effective?

4 If so, why were they not adopted by the Tsar?

5 Discuss your own ideas with your group.

Debate – Does Tsar Alexander II deserve his reputation as a great reformer?

Study abroad

Many students went abroad to complete their studies. Switzerland was a magnet for these people, partly because of its political toleration but also because of the presence of well-known Russian dissidents, such as Mikhail Bakunin and Peter Lavrov. Bakunin, in particular, held considerable sway over the young, because he preached that the regime could be overthrown quickly by violence. He believed self-governing communities, such as the peasant communes, should replace the structures of the State. When students returned to Russia, they set up new subversive organizations and distributed pamphlets, many written by the exiles.

The literature of opposition

The 1860s were a hotbed of new ideas in the freedom allowed by the censors. This is caught well by Dostoevsky in his novel *The Devils*:

Source 16

They talked of the abolition of censorship, and of phonetic spelling, of the substitution of the Latin characters for the Russian alphabet… of splitting Russia into nationalities, united in a free federation, of the abolition of the army and navy, of the restoration of Poland … of the peasant reforms and of the Manifestos, of the abolition of the hereditary principle and of the family, of children, of priests, of women's rights.

In 1862 perhaps the most influential novel of all was published, *Fathers and Sons* by Turgenev. It featured a new kind of man, the 'nihilist'. Turgenev described his character Bazarov thus:

Source 17

A nihilist is a man who does not bow before any authorities, who does not accept a single principle on trust.

Men and women such as Bazarov were dangerous indeed in nineteenth-century Russia, where autocracy and the Orthodox faith relied on unquestioning acceptance of the status quo. At the same time, Bakunin's *Catechism of the Revolutionary*, written in 1868 in Zurich, Switzerland, urged a selfless dedication to revolutionary violence:

Source 18

Merciless towards himself, he must be merciless towards others. A single cold passion for the revolutionary cause must suppress within him all tender feelings for family life, friendship, love, gratitude, and even honour…Day and night he must have one single purpose: merciless destruction.

Free thinking led to a commitment to the cause of reform, and some of its believers came to believe the cause was worth more than their own lives. The scene was set for a major confrontation between the Tsar and his opponents.

■ Biography

Mikhail Bakunin

1814 Born into a gentry family.
1840 Emigrated.
1848–49 Involved in Dresden uprising and extradited to Russia.
1861 Escaped from prison.
1868 Founded Alliance for Social Democracy.
1873 Wrote *Statism and Anarchy*.
1876 died.

He advocated attempts to stir up rebellion among the peasants.

He believed that future society should consist of self-governing communities.

■ Further reading

Fyodor Dostoevsky's novels provide an interesting insight into Russia in the middle of the nineteenth century.

You may also like to look into his political ideas. They underwent an interesting and perhaps unexpected change.

■ Think about

▶ Sources 16 and 17 are taken from novels of the period. Does this reduce their value to the historian?

The first attempt on the Tsar's life

In April 1866 Dmitri Karakozov, a disillusioned student, decided to kill the Tsar. He had joined a student group called 'Hell' at Moscow University. Karakozov was an idealistic landowner and had given away his possessions to his peasants when they were freed. He shot at the Tsar who was taking a walk in the Summer Gardens, but missed, was arrested and executed. Prince Kropotkin described the result:

Source 19

After Karakozov had shot at Alexander II in April 1866, the State police had become omnipotent. Everyone suspected of radicalism…had to live under the fear of being arrested any night, for the sympathy he might have shown to someone involved…

Kropotkin, *Memoirs of a Revolutionist, c. 1876*

'Going to the People' – The Narodniks

In the 1870s some idealistic young members of the gentry and intelligentsia were still determined to change the political system. Since they were in such a small minority and the State was so strong, between one and two thousand students and former students decided the future lay in the hands of the peasants and went into the countryside to share the lives of the peasants, win their respect and rouse them into action (Source 20).

The police reacted with waves of arrests in Moscow and St Petersburg. The students in the countryside were also not able to evade arrest for very long. The movement was smashed in a few months. They had found bridging the gap between liberal student and the ignorant conservatism of the peasant difficult, many being denounced by stewards and the local gentry.

Not all were arrested. Some escaped to continue the campaign by setting up 'Land and Liberty'. In 1876, this organization successfully freed Kropotkin from prison (where he had been sent in 1874) and began a demonstration outside Kazan Cathedral in the heart of St Petersburg. But from this point the revolutionary opposition was to remain in the hands of only a few until the next century.

'Guests' of the Tsar

The Tsar's prisons were so full that the government had to build new facilities, such as the House of Preliminary Detention in St Petersburg. A prominent dissident G. Plekhanov, quickly renamed this The House of Slow Strangulation. They were brutal places; political prisoners were usually kept in solitary confinement. Prisoners often had a long wait here while their cases were investigated, before they were brought to trial – sometimes four years. They were usually allowed books, and limited exercise. Some walked round their tiny cells, others practised Russian country dances if their cells were too small. Ingenious methods of communicating with one another were developed, the most common being tapping the walls or water pipes.

Arrest might begin with prison, but it often ended in internal exile. Perhaps as many as 150,000 travelled the great road to Siberia during Alexander's reign. The journey to Siberia was usually on foot and in leg-irons and took months.

Definition

Narodniks is derived from the Russian Narodya, which means 'people' in English.

Source 20

It was found that many young men had abandoned their studies, donned peasant clothes, procured false documents and, in the guise of simple unskilled labourers, 'went to the people' – to use their own phrase…Many persons no longer young, fathers and mothers of families, secure in prosperous and respectable social positions, not only did not oppose [the propagandists], but often offered them substantial sympathy, help and support.

From an official report by the Minister of Justice, Count Pahlen, 1875

■ Think about

▶ What evidence does Source 20 provide that 'Going to the People' was more than a spontaneous movement of the young?

Those serving hard labour sentences were often sent to special mining settlements. Those sentenced to exile could find themselves in better conditions, living in a larger town and making a living teaching or in business. Political exiles were often in demand because they could usually read and write. They could mix with other exiles – a fruitful way of discussing revolutionary theory and strategies. The difficulties of climate and transport, and the immense distances involved, meant that escape was difficult. When attempts were made, they were often not reported because it was certain they would be caught.

> **■ Think about**
>
> ▶ What was the purpose of the prison system?
>
> ▶ Does it seem to have been working under Alexander II?

▼ Prisoners being fitted with leg-irons at Sakhalin Island in the late nineteenth century.

Source 21

The Political Trials

The government set up a special department of the Senate to try political cases, and in 1877 there were a number of prominent trials. The 'Trial of the 50' lasted five weeks, open to the public and reported in the government press. Some of the accused chose to defend themselves, giving them the right to the last speeches in the court. Here are some excerpts from P. Alexeev's closing address:

> **■ Think about**
>
> ▶ What impression does Source 21 give of the prisoners? Locate Sakhalin Island on the map on page 10. How did the prisoners travel to Sakhalin Island?

Source 22

Are we, the workers, really…deaf, dumb, and blind…unaware of how all around us other people get rich? Are we really such dullards as not to see…why our work is priced so low and where their wealth comes from?…
[But we get] no help or sympathy except from our educated young people. They alone stretched out a brotherly hand to us. They alone…understood why the peasants were groaning all over the Russian Empire…They alone…will walk shoulder to shoulder with us toward that day (he raised his arm) when the millions of working people will raise their strong arm and …. despotism, sheltering now behind soldiers' bayonets, will crumble into dust! (There were shouts of silence from the judge as he finished.)

> **Facts and figures**
>
> The 50 were members of the 'Pan-Russian Social-Revolutionary Organization' based in Moscow.

> **■ Think about**
>
> ▶ What impression do you think this speech created in court?

They were sentenced to prison and periods of exile outside European Russia. The Imperial Chancellor criticized the Minister of Justice:

You have merely persuaded everybody that they were no children, no silly boys and girls, and no drunken peasants either...but men and women of mature intellect and strong, unselfish character, who...knew full well what they were fighting for.

The 'Trial of 50' was followed by the 'Trial of 193' who had 'gone to the people' in the early 1870s. This time the trial was secret. Most defendants refused to plead before the court, but their lawyers still had a field day at the State's expense, emphasizing the youth of the accused and the evils of Tsarist society. Of the 193 on trial, 90 were acquitted and only 28 were sentenced to hard labour. The judge made a plea for leniency to the Tsar. It fell on deaf ears.

Violence intensifies

The terrorists at large now turned their attentions on the Tsar and his closest associates. In January 1878 Vera Zasulich shot Trepov, the Chief of Police of St Petersburg in his office, though he survived. Despite admitting her guilt, the defence made such play of the inhumanity of the victim that the jury acquitted her to public rejoicing. The Tsar ordered her immediate re-arrest, but the order arrived too late and she was whisked away by supporters to the safety of asylum abroad.

Later that year the head of the Third Section was assassinated. However, Land and Liberty, which planned these actions, itself split between those wanting the terrorist campaign to continue, and those led by Plekhanov who wanted them to concentrate on winning over the workers to the cause of the new ideas of Marxism. Plekhanov's group was called Black Repartition. Those believing in terrorist tactics called themselves The People's Will.

In 1881 they achieved their main aim – they assassinated the Tsar as he returned from military manoeuvres on 1 March. Members of the group had lain in wait along the Nevsky Prospekt, but quickly moved to the banks of the Catherine Canal when the Tsar's route was changed. A first bomb killed a Cossack guard. Alexander stepped out of his carriage to lend help to the casualties and was killed by a second bomb, which also killed its thrower.

Would the assassination of the Tsar push the regime into following the route of constitutional change, or would the Romanovs instead turn their backs on any more concessions to the demands of liberals and terrorists?

Spotlight

The People's Will

The People's Will (*Narodnaya Volya* in Russian) was one of Russia's most notorious and successful terrorist organizations. It was formed out of the remnants of the Land and Liberty opposition group, which had split over whether terrorist tactics should be used against the regime. Some members had believed that the only way forward was in the political education of the peasants and workers, which would be a long drawn out process. The People's Will believed that, because normal political life did not exist in Russia, terrorism was the only method likely to be effective in bringing about change in the near future.

In response to the increasing violence in 1879 Alexander II appointed Temporary Governor-Generals within the most rebellious districts, who had sweeping powers. They could deport suspects, try those accused of political offences before military courts, and suspend newspapers and other publications, 'whose tendency they consider harmful'. In a way this measure pushed opposition into the hands of the terrorists.

On 26 August 1879, the Executive Committee of The People's Will sentenced Alexander II to death. There were eight assassination attempts. In 1879 they blew up the wrong train, the Tsar having passed earlier than expected over the prepared explosives. In 1880 Khalturin succeeded in exploding a bomb in the Winter Palace, killing 12 and wounding many more soldiers and civilians but not the Tsar – who was late for dinner!

Source 24

The programme of the People's Will 1879

1 Popular representation through a National Assembly
2 Local self-government with the election of all officials
3 The *mir* to administer local and economic affairs
4 Ownership of the land by the people
5 The control by the workers of all mines and factories
6 Freedom of conscience, speech and association
7 Universal franchise
8 The replacement of the army by a territorial militia

Organization

The People's Will did not try to widen its membership, but consisted of a few dedicated revolutionaries. The Executive Committee consisted of 37 members. It was, however, supported by others, but these knew only the identity of their own contact. It organized a group of young officers, and another of workers. They lived under assumed names and moved around to avoid the secret police.

Source 25

The leaders of The People's Will

A.D. Mikhailov – an engineering student
Vera Figner – a medical student for 3 years in Zurich
Pesnyakov – a St Petersburg worker
Khalturin – son of a peasant, carpenter
Zhelyabov – son of a serf who was educated by his master and sent to Odessa University
Perovskaya – daughter of a Governor-General of St Petersburg; at 17 she joined a student group in St Petersburg.

Source 26

The mad villains who killed your father will not be satisfied by any concession, and will only burst into a frenzy. They can be repressed; the evil seed can be uprooted, only by a battle to the death with them, by blood and iron. Perish in battle, but conquer. It is hard not to conquer.

A letter to the new Tsar Alexander III in March 1881 from Pobedonestsev, his former tutor

Source 27

A few days ago, during a nocturnal search of a house in St Petersburg, a printing press was accidentally discovered…Leaflets of the revolutionary publication *The People's Will* were being printed. There were five people in the apartment, including two women; all of them tried to defend themselves with revolvers but were nevertheless seized, except for one who succeeded in shooting himself…

Never before has so much unlimited arbitrary power been granted to the administration and the police. But it is hardly possible to put an end to the revolutionary underground activity…It is hard to root out the evil when not in a single layer of society does the government encounter either sympathy or true support.

The diary of D. A. Miliutin, a government minister, for 22 January 1880

The fate of the leaders of The People's Will:

Kvyatkovsky and Presnyakov were executed on 4 November 1880.

A.D. Mikhailov, sentenced to life imprisonment, died in The Peter and Paul Fortress in St Petersburg in 1884.

Five leaders of the group who carried out the assassination of Alexander II were hanged on 3 April 1881.

Vera Figner, the last active member of the Executive Committee that planned Alexander II's death, was sentenced to death in 1884. Her sentence was cut to life imprisonment and she was released after 20 years of solitary confinement.

The Younger People's Will

The Younger People's Will was formed in 1884. It demanded a Constituent Assembly and was prepared to use terrorist tactics to force the government to grant its demands. It produced its own newsletter, *The Bulletin of the People's Will*. One leader was arrested in October 1884 with a book of members and addresses. The secret police then made arrests in 32 cities. However, in the south, especially in Kiev and Odessa, the organization escaped and continued. In 1886 one of this surviving group was arrested and turned informer. The existing membership was arrested and the movement smashed.

Source 28

There is something higher than natural human feelings and that is duty towards one's native land…The bloody tragedy of the Catherine Canal…was inevitable…Sire, the revolutionary movement does not depend on a few individuals; it is a function of the national organism…created by the discontent of the people, by the desire of the country for new social forms. The whole people cannot be exterminated, nor can its discontent be subdued by repression; that only strengthens it.

Open letter to Alexander III from *The People's Will*, March 1881

Source 29

The years in prison fused together, made known to each other, a great mass of people. Having got into prison before they could properly be called revolutionary, being caught in the mesh often quite by chance…having spent several years in solitary confinement…the majority…emerged as fully fledged protesters.

From the Declaration of A. Kvyatkovsky

The terrorist section of The People's Will

This was formed by a small band of students, who determined to kill Alexander III. Three bombs were made containing strychnine pellets. On 26 February 1886 three assassins stood at various points along Nevsky Prospekt, but the Tsar failed to appear. They were spotted by police agents and put under surveillance. When they arrived on Nevsky Prospekt on 1 March they were arrested along with their known associates. Fifteen were charged with treason, though only five were executed. One of these was Alexander Ulyanov, whose brother became better known as Lenin, leader of Communist Russia.

■ **Activity**

Was the government winning the battle against the terrorists?

Look at the text on pages 33–37 and the Spotlight on pages 38–39.

1 What kind of people joined terrorist groups in Russia at this time?
2 What continuity can you see in the programmes of the different terrorist groups?
3 What success did the police have in dealing with the terrorists?
4 Why did the police find dealing with them difficult?

In Source 25 Pobedonostsev said, 'They can be repressed…It is hard not to conquer.'

In Source 27 The People's Will claimed that repression only strengthened opposition.

5 Who do you think was nearer to the truth?

■ **Activity**

Why did opposition to Alexander II increase?

Some of the reasons why people were discontented with the regime had little to do with the actions of the Tsar. There were, for example, a series of very poor harvests during his reign, especially between 1879 and 1881. He was unlucky that there was a world agricultural depression after 1875, which meant low prices for Russian grain sold overseas.

However, much of what the Tsar had done in his early years was designed to improve the lot of his subjects and to make the Russian state less oppressive. It is your task to draw together what you have read in order to explain why this most reforming of Tsars faced such violent opposition, resulting eventually in his own assassination in 1881. You will need to read carefully through the preceding pages.

Draw up a table, based on the one below, to assess the nature of Alexander's reforms. Summarize the actions made by his government and explain why and by whom these reforms were either opposed or thought to be inadequate.

	Actions taken	Which groups opposed? Why?
Serfdom		
The armed forces		
Civil rights		
Good government		
Justice and the law		
Education		
Popular representation		
Dissent		
Economic backwardness		

D. Saunders ends his book *Russia in the Age of Reaction and Reform 1801–1881* with this statement:

'Terrorism made compromise impossible.'

1 Is it possible that the responsibility for the Tsar's failure to continue the reforms he had begun ultimately lies with the opposition?

2 Was it their idealistic refusal to accept anything less than total success for their cause that is ultimately to blame?

■ **Activity**   **KEY SKILLS**

Were Alexander II's policies mistaken?

1 What were the likely results of greater democracy in Russia's multinational Empire?

2 What were the likely results of more open discussion of Russia's institutions and criticism of the regime?

3 If the Tsar's first priority was to preserve the Empire, what policies made best sense?

Look back at what you learned about Russia in Chapter One. Consider what happened to the USSR once multi-party democracy was allowed at the end of the twentieth century. Add to your knowledge by reading a book in the Further Reading list or any other source in your school library or on the Internet. Present a short talk to members of your group, using at least once image (eg spidergram, table etc) and use this as the basis of a group discussion for all in the group.

Assessment

You should now be in a position to answer any examination question on this subject, such as:

1 Describe the main reforms carried out by Alexander II.

2 Why did these reforms result in more opposition to Alexander's rule?

Conclusion

Alexander's accession to the throne was greeted warmly by many, if not all, his subjects. He introduced a series of reforms to many of Russia's main institutions. Many of these reforms improved the lot of his subjects, though they did not provide the wholesale changes to autocracy and society that the radicals hoped for. His death came at a critical moment when he was about to sign a measure to introduce more public consultation about the work of central government. Would his death further the cause of reform or would it bring about a reaction against the changes he had made?

■ **Further reading**

V. Broido, *Apostles and Terrorists*, 1977, carries many details of individual cases.
W.E. Mosse, *Alexander II and the Modernisation of Russia*
J.N. Westwood, *Endurance and Endeavour: Russian History 1812–1992*, 1993
D. Mackenzie-Wallace, *Russia 1877,* the result of many years as *Times* Correspondent in Russia.
L. Kochan and R. Abraham, *The Making of Modern Russia*, 1983

Chapter 3

Stemming the tide 1881–1905
The Russia of Alexander III
and Nicholas II

To the Russian Tsar has been granted a special significance distinguishing him from other rulers of the world. He is not only the sovereign of his people, but he is ordained by God as the guardian and defender of the Orthodox Church, which…has abjured [given up] any activity save spiritual, leaving all cares concerning its earthly welfare… to the consecrated leader of the orthodox people

From an editorial in *Moscow News*, 1882

◄ A Marxist view of Russia in 1901. The layers in the illustration, from the top, say:
   "The royal family"
   "We rule you"
   "We mislead you"
   "We shoot you"
and the bottom layer says
   "We work for you and feed you"

Introduction

The assassination of Alexander II unsurprisingly had a dramatic effect on the rest of his family. His son Alexander III moved the family home away from the Winter Palace in St Petersburg to the altogether more cramped and less magnificent palace at Gatchina, 30 km outside the capital. There he remained, receiving guests only on two days per week and surrounded by guards.

The reign of Alexander III, and that of his son Nicholas II after him, is looked upon by most historians, until 1905 at least, as a time of repression that saw the undoing of many of the reforms carried out by his father. This was certainly a time of great economic and social change for the Russian people, but Sources 1 and 2 suggest that perhaps in other ways change was very limited indeed. In the West the social and economic changes of the industrial revolution had led to great pressures on political systems, as for example in Great Britain. Would the Russian autocracy be able to preserve its authority as Russia plunged into her own industrial revolution?

Key questions

- To what extent and why did Alexander III and Nicholas II until 1905 turn their back on the reforms of the 1860s?
- How successful were their attempts to assert imperial authority?
- How was Russia changing economically and socially?
- What kinds of opposition challenged imperial authority?
- Why did the Russian people revolt in 1905?

Turning back the clock?

The new Tsar

Alexander III was deeply suspicious of the direction in which his father had taken Russia. Even before his father's death he was receiving advice like this from the Procurator of the Holy Synod, K. P. Pobedonostev:

> ### Source 3
>
> All the officials and learned men here sicken my heart, as if I were in the company of half-wits or perverted baboons. I hear from all sides that trite, deceitful and accursed word: constitution…But I also meet and talk with some Russian men…Their hearts are seized with fear; above all else they fear that basic evil, a constitution. Among the common people everywhere the thought is spreading: better a Russian revolution and ugly turmoil than a constitution. The former could soon be suppressed, with order restored throughout the land; the latter is poison to the entire organization.
>
> *From a letter to the future Alexander III, 4 December 1879*

The new Tsar's first task was to review a proposal which was to have been finally approved by his father on 4 March 1881. Alternatively called either 'an innocuous [harmless] scheme' or a 'constitution', the proposal would have appointed committees to discuss legislation and the administration of the country, a kind of consultative assembly. It would have involved *zemstva* leaders and other public figures; many saw it as the first step towards some kind of representative parliament.

However, three days earlier, on 1 March, Alexander II was assassinated, and his son announced to his Council of Ministers, 'I give you advance notice that the

■ Think about

▶ What is the message of the cartoon (Source 1)?

▶ Which groups of people in Russia might have accepted this view in *c.*1900?

▶ How is the view of the monarchy and the Church different from that suggested in Source 2?

Note

The Procurator of the Holy Synod was in effect Minister for the Russian Orthodox Church, though he was not a priest. The Tsar was the head of the Church as he was head of state.

■ Think about

▶ Why did Pobedonostev think a constitution would be 'poison to the entire organization'?

▶ What does he claim is the people's view of a constitution?

▶ What does he think should be done with the growing opposition in Russia?

question has not yet been decided.' There followed intense debate between liberals and conservatives in the State Council. At the end of April the battle was over. The reforms were abandoned.

This was the new Tsar's manifesto to his people, written at the end of April 1881:

Source 4

Acknowledging the will of Providence and the law of Imperial succession, We accepted this burden in a terrible hour of public grief and horror, before Almighty God, trusting that, foreordained as it was that We should assume power at such a dangerous and difficult time, he would not refrain from granting Us his assistance. We trust also that the fervent prayers of Our devoted people, known throughout the whole world for their love and devotion to their sovereigns, will draw God's blessing upon Us and the labour of government to which We have been appointed…Consecrating Ourselves to Our great service, We call upon all Our Faithful subjects to serve Us and the state in fidelity and truth, for the eradication of the vile sedition disgracing the Russian land, for the strengthening of faith and morality, for the proper upbringing of children, for the extermination of falsehood and theft, and for the introduction of truth and good order in the operations of the institutions given to Russia by her benefactor, Our beloved father.

The Manifesto of Alexander III, 1881

■ Activity

1 What clues are there in this manifesto to the Tsar's attitude to his future role?

2 How far would this manifesto satisfy the terrorists who killed his father?

3 Compare what the Tsar said with Sources 12 and 14.

When Nicholas II succeeded to his father's throne in 1894 his manifesto contained similar sentiments, including the famous sentence:

Source 5

I shall adhere as unswervingly as my father to the principle of autocracy.

Undoing the reforms

Many of the other reforms that were Alexander II's legacy also were affected:

- All police were centralized under the control of the Ministry of the Interior. Special courts still dealt with serious political offences.
- Judges were given clear advice on sentences and verdicts.
- Elected Justices of the Peace were abolished. 'Land Captains', who had total authority in local court cases and administration, including tax collection, replaced them. These were drawn exclusively from the ranks of the gentry.
- Conditions in prisons were made severe, though violent attacks on the regime were reduced.
- Newspapers who had been warned three times had to submit their papers to the censor a day before publication.
- A committee of government ministers was set up with powers to close any publication deemed 'harmful,' and put a life ban on editors and publishers.
- Libraries and reading rooms faced restrictions on the books they were allowed to stock.
- Universities lost some of their ability to run their own affairs. The election of officers was replaced by a system of appointments. Students also found themselves subject to inspectors inquiring into their non-academic activities.

- Peasant representation in the *zemstva* was reduced, and the peasant representatives were appointed and no longer elected. Provincial governors were given 'supervision over the correctness and legality of *zemstvo* institutions' by a new statute in 1890.
- Lower-class children were effectively banned from secondary education

Despite these policies, the State did not turn its back on reform altogether. The introduction of Land Captains can be seen as a reforming measure, a desperate effort to bring about efficient local government. Tax collections had become even more corrupt than before, and arrears were constantly rising. The taxes paid to the *zemstva* were always most in arrears. Absenteeism at all levels from the new assemblies was also a chronic problem.

Three other important steps were taken by Alexander III's government to improve the quality of rural life. In 1886 the poll tax, paid only by peasants, was abolished. In 1883 the Peasants' Land Bank was created to help peasants to buy land from the landlords. This was so successful that peasants had purchased one-third of all landlord estates by 1904. Since the gentry were also selling land to townspeople, this gave concern to the government who saw the gentry's social and political position under threat. Accordingly the State set up the Nobles' Land Bank offering loans at cheaper rates than to the peasants. It held mortgages on a third of all gentry land in 1904, and many noble accounts were in arrears.

One thing in rural life did not change – the backward methods of most agriculture. Plots for most peasants were becoming smaller as the land was redistributed as the rural population increased. The *mir* was still an obstacle to the introduction of new methods, requiring the agreement of the entire village to introduce change. Russian crop yields were far below those of Western Europe.

The 1891 famine

This was the first real test of the reforms to local government. Famine hit 17 of Russia's 39 provinces. There had been an early winter followed by a long hot and dry summer, which ruined almost all the crops. Food shortages were normal in many years, but this was an altogether more drastic situation. According to Professor Hutchinson, this was 'the defining event of the decade.' It was made worse by the inevitable outbreak of cholera and typhus the following year.

The government was partly responsible for the severity of the famine, or so many believed. In an effort to raise much needed revenue, the government had heavily taxed consumer goods. To afford what they needed, the peasants were forced to sell more and more grain, leaving them with no reserves of seed-corn for them to use in a bad year.

■ Think about

▶ Why did Alexander III want to give financial help to the gentry?

■ Think about

▶ What does Source 6 tell us of government priorities?

▶ How do you think it was received by the general public?

Source 6

We ourselves will not eat but we shall export.

This was the slogan people attributed to the Minister of Finance, Ivan Vyshnegradskii. Perhaps this explains why the government was slow to act, despite reports reaching it of hardship since the spring of 1891. Censors prevented newspapers carrying reports of the famine. The government postponed a ban on grain exports until the situation was acute in August 1891.

The result was that many blamed the government for the famine. It was not until November that the government gave way and appealed to the public to engage in voluntary assistance schemes. The young heir to the throne, Nicholas, was put in charge of the Special Committee on Famine Relief. Alexander III announced two State lotteries to raise money to buy in emergency supplies for the peasants.

The public appeal saw an astonishing response from the intelligentsia. The *zemstva* led the way. Prince Lvov, the future Prime Minister of Russia's first republican government, organized famine relief in his own province of Tula. Tolstoy, Russia's most famous writer, organized soup canteens and the playwright Chekhov went back to being a doctor in Moscow to organize treatment for the cholera victims.

■ **Think about**

▶ You might like to look at the famines of 1920–1922 and 1933–1934. In what ways were the causes similar?

▶ How did the governments respond to the crises?

▶ Who coped with the crises best?

Source 7

Never, neither in Russia, nor any other state, has the concern of the central government for helping the population ruined by crop failure been so great and achieved so much as at the present time.

From a Report of the Committee of Ministers, 25 Feb 1892

However, the peasant S. Semenov wrote this about the famine:

Source 8

With every day the need and the misery of the peasants grew. The scenes of starvation were deeply distressing, and it was all the more disturbing to see that amidst all this suffering and death there were sprawling huge estates, beautiful and well-furnished manors, and that the grand old life of the squires, with its jolly hunts and balls, its banquets and its concerts, carried on as usual.

■ **Think about**

▶Why was the famine such a public relations disaster for the government?

▶What conclusions do you think those involved in dealing with the famine drew?

Despite all their efforts, over 350,000 died either from starvation or disease. It did, however, demonstrate that, in a crisis, all sections of the community had been able to work together: *zemstvo* leaders, Land Captains, peasant elders, local gentry and the national government.

Economic growth

Industrial growth at the end of the nineteenth century

The economy, already growing as we have seen under Alexander II, developed dramatically, with an average growth rate of 8 per cent per annum at the end of the century. This was the highest growth rate of any of the world's major economies. Russia became the world's fourth largest industrial economy. The person given most credit for Russia's continued and more rapid growth is Count Witte, who became Minister of Finance in 1893. Short of capital inside Russia, he turned to Western Europe for investment. He was dramatically successful, increasing foreign investment from 98 million roubles in 1880 to 911 million roubles in 1900. The result was an increase in annual production.

(Figures in millions of tons)			
	Coal	Pig iron	Oil
1880	3.2	0.42	0.5
1890	5.9	0.89	3.9
1900	16.1	2.66	10.2
1910	26.8	2.99	9.4

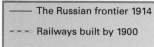

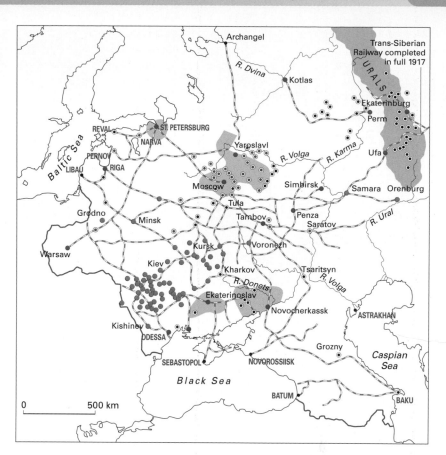

	The Russian frontier 1914
---	Railways built by 1900
●	Important manufacturing centres
⊙	Heavy industry, principally iron, steel and metalworks
⊙	Textiles
●	Manufactured food, principally sugar
▦	Areas with the greatest influx of workers from other regions
RIGA	Ports with flourishing import and export trades by 1900

Principal exports in 1914:
Cereals, timber, petroleum, eggs, flax, butter, sugar

Principal imports in 1914:
Raw cotton, machinery and metal goods, tea, coal, iron, lead, copper

Source 9

▶ Economic growth in Imperial Russia before the First World War.

Railways

Many of the 'westernizers' saw the railway as an important way to modernize the country. It would unite the country, open up trade with Europe, China and the USA, develop Siberia's mineral resources and also be a stimulus to the growth of Russian industry. The figures below (in kilometres) show the considerable progress that was made.

	1840	1860	1880	1900
Russia	27	1,626	22,865	53,234
France	496	9,167	23,089	38,109
Great Britain	2,390	14,603	25,060	30,079
Germany	469	11,089	33,838	51,678

The centrepiece of Russia's railway expansion was the Trans-Siberian Railway, linking Russia and the Far East. Huge sums of government money were invested in the enterprise. The vast distances involved meant that European standards of safety and construction had to be abandoned, and trains could only travel slowly around its sharp curves and up its steep inclines. It was hoped that the line would quickly pay for itself in passenger and freight charges. By 1905 almost two-thirds of Russian railways were owned by the State.

The urban poor

This 'industrial revolution' also brought profound social changes. Millions of peasants moved into the developing industries. By 1913, according to Robert Service, the working class in the cities and towns had reached almost 11 million. Russia's two 'capital cities' grew most dramatically.

Facts and figures

	Populations of	
	Moscow	St Petersburg
1881	753,500	928,000
1890	1,038,600	1,033,600
1900	1,345,000	1,439,600
1910	1,617,700	1,905,600

Source 10

◀ Living conditions in an early twentieth century workers' hostel.

As in Britain during the industrial revolution, the workers from the countryside moved into slums on the outskirts of the cities. Here they found unsurfaced roads, tenements or worse still barrack blocks. Some workers lived and slept by their factory machines. In 1904 the average St Petersburg apartment housed 16 people, about six people per room. Running water was available in only one-third of St Petersburg houses. Cesspools, piles of human manure and a polluted water supply were a constant threat to the health of the poor.

Wages were low and employment insecure. Things were much worse for women than men. In Moscow there was a daily market where labourers were hired just for the day.

Source 11

One workday at the factory lasted eleven and a half hours, plus a one-and-a-half-hour lunch break. In the beginning I would grow so terribly tired so that as soon as I got home from work and ate dinner, I would fall into my filthy sack and sleep like a dead man, despite the myriad bedbugs and fleas…We rented the apartment communally as an artel (collective) of about fifteen men…I was put in a tiny, dark, windowless corner room; it was dirty and stuffy …All fifteen men ate from a common bowl with wooden spoons. The cabbage soup contained little pieces of meat.

From *A Radical Worker in Tsarist Russia* by S.I. Kanatchikov, describing his living conditions on arrival in Moscow in 1895. He later joined the Bolsheviks. This memoir was published in Moscow between 1929 and 1934

■ **Think about**

▶ How reliable do you think Kanatchikov is as a source about the lives of the poor at this time?

Russia was badly hit by the world depression of 1899, leaving a dangerous situation in urban areas. Most of the new workforce were born in the countryside and had left for the cities and mines to find a better life. They were obviously very susceptible to the propaganda of the revolutionary groups which also developed at the same time (see pp. 55–56).

In the past the Russian Orthodox Church had shaped the peasants' view of the world. This influence was, if not entirely shattered, seriously weakened when they moved into the cities. No longer was daily life governed by the accidents of weather. Nor would traditional village society mould a man's views. Literacy was also much higher in the towns than the country, leaving workers open to many new influences.

■ **Think about**

▶ If you are also studying Britain at this time, did the same happen there?

Government finances

Autocracy needed sound finances. Towards the end of Alexander's reign (1877–1878) Russia was once more plunged into war with Turkey. As in 1854–1855, the government was forced to print more paper money, causing a depreciation of the rouble and inflation averaging about 30 per cent a year. Over 30 per cent of government expenditure was being spent on the armed forces, but another third simply disappeared on debt interest, leaving little left for education or social welfare. The government desperately needed to sell more grain overseas to restore international confidence. The famine of 1891 was the result.

Vyshnedgraskii, Finance Minister 1887–1892, began rescuing the government finances from their parlous state. He was able to reduce imports and raise more revenue by imposing tariffs on imported goods. He also built up Russia's gold reserves and balanced the budget. All this was put in jeopardy by the famine which overwhelmed large parts of the country in 1891. A more stable rouble was essential for international trade and for investment. There was little point in saving if inflation was running at 30 per cent! After his resignation, his work was continued by his successor Count Witte, who finally introduced a new gold currency into which paper money could be converted. He modestly later claimed it was, 'One of the great successes in the peaceful cultural development of mankind.'

Was Russia becoming a modern industrialized state at the end of the nineteenth century?

The number of factory workers in 1914, at the outbreak of the First World War, was still only 2.5 million, just 1.88 per cent of the total population. Although figures suggest that they were more concentrated in larger enterprises, like the Putilov Works in St Petersburg for example, this did not mean that Russian factories were particularly efficient. Much industrial production took place away from large factories in small workshops in the countryside and the towns. Most of the workers in the new industries had been born and brought up in the countryside and perhaps looked back with some nostalgia to a rural past. At the turn of the century many went back to their villages every year to help with the harvest and haymaking. When food was scarce during the First World War and afterwards, many went back to their villages to live.

Industry depended hugely on State intervention and orders – especially the railways and the armaments industry. Foreign credit also played a disproportionate role in Russian development. From 1885 onwards, military spending was never less than 50 per cent of the government's expenditure. The internal market was too weak, it has been argued, to sustain industrial growth. The economy before the First World War was not producing what the peasants, making up 80 per cent of the total population, wanted. A 'command economy' of a kind was therefore in existence long before the days of Lenin and Stalin. It was an economy designed to protect the territorial integrity of the Empire in an increasingly threatening world. The needs of ordinary Russians in this situation were bound to be secondary.

> **Note**
>
> A 'command' economy is one where the government decides what is produced, not 'demand' i.e. what consumers want.

The intelligentsia and the middle class

As cities and commerce grew, there was also a relative growth in the professional and managerial middle classes. The work of the *zemstva* had also led to an expansion in this group, employing as they did educated teachers, administrators, doctors and experts. The number of banks and other financial institutions mushroomed. Many of these people had become used to some kind of involvement, at a low level, in public service and decision-making. They were confident about themselves and their future. As the work of the *zemstva* expanded, so did the expectations of their leaders and employees for wider political consultation at a national level. The intelligentsia had changed since the beginning of the nineteenth century. Nobles no longer constituted the great majority of students at university; these were now drawn from almost all classes, including wealthy peasants.

Despite this, the intelligentsia had little in common with the peasants or the workers, but were equally ignored by the political establishment. In Britain in the nineteenth century they had been included in the political system. In Russia this was denied to them, pushing them as well as the poor towards radical and revolutionary politics. It is noticeable that the intelligentsia and the prosperous middle classes throughout modern Russian history, as we have seen already with The People's Will, provided leaders for the revolutionary groups. The refusal of both Alexander III and his son Nicholas II to sacrifice any of their autocratic power meant that even moderate liberal-minded people were driven to support the calls of the men of violence. When violence began, it would be difficult to stop.

The nationalities question

In the last chapter we noticed that, as in many parts of Europe, some of the non-Russian peoples of the Empire were becoming more conscious of their national traditions and heritage. Fundamentally the Tsars could react to the growing sense of national consciousness in one of two ways:

- They could recognize and give to each developed nationality some form of autonomous structure.
- They could try to control and suppress manifestations of national culture and consciousness wherever they occurred.

Russification

The Tsars after 1881 took the latter course. Some have argued that this reaction to national dissent was crude. Where there was any talk of greater autonomy, the Tsars withdrew what local self-government they already had. In truth this was a policy that Alexander II had already begun in troublesome areas. In 1866, once the Polish rebellion had been crushed, the Kingdom of Poland became the Vistula Provinces, and subject to the same laws as the rest of Russia. The Russian language became the only language allowed in schools. The emancipation statute for Poland had been decidedly less advantageous to the Polish gentry, who had been sympathetic to nationalist ideas.

In the Ukraine in 1863 the Minister of the Interior, Valuev, said that the Ukrainian language, 'has not existed, does not exist and shall never exist'. He promptly banned virtually all publications in Ukrainian, or as he called it, the 'Little Russian dialect'. In 1876 all existing books in Ukrainian were ordered to be removed from schools, and, as in Poland, only Russian was to be used in schools. This repression of everything Ukrainian was continued by his successors.

The death of Alexander II was the occasion for widespread attacks on Jewish settlements. These continued throughout Alexander III and Nicholas II's reigns. The most notorious of these outbreaks occurred in Kishinev in 1903. Jewish houses and businesses were broken into, women were raped and men beaten

■ **Think about**

The Tsars had excellent advisers. Why did they not contemplate constitutional reform?

Cross reference

For a full table of nationalities in Russia see page 10.

Quotation

I am always happy when they beat the Jews.

Attributed to Alexander III

and murdered. In all, 47 died. The Cossacks who arrived to restore order joined in the attacks. The government was blamed for this and many other such outrages. Though it probably had nothing to do with these attacks, the government set the tone for the public's view by its own actions. The Minister of the Interior at the time, Plehve, and both Alexander III and his son, were strong anti-Semites. His reign was marked by many more restrictions on the Jewish people. According to Figes, there were 1400 different statutes regulating their life. They were, for example, forbidden by law to own land or take commissions in the army.

Was Russification successful?

The Tsars would not have accepted this as a valid question. If they could not tolerate a free press or responsible organs of local government, how could they give recognition to demands for more regional or national self-government? Russification was to them an essential policy. To them autocracy, nationality and orthodoxy were integral to each other. If concessions were made on any front, it would jeopardize the whole structure of the regime. The alternative was to grant a constitution to all Russian people and begin what the Romanovs felt was the slippery slope to becoming a figurehead monarch without any real power, a monarchy on the British model perhaps. It would also be to betray a sacred trust from their forefathers.

Ignoring national differences or trying to minimize them seemed to them the only policy.

The implications of this were profound. A large standing army would need to be maintained in the frontier regions not only to protect Russia's frontiers but to secure it from possible enemies within.

■ Activity

How many of Alexander II's reforms were discarded after his death?

To assess the changes made by Alexander III and his son you will need to go back to Chapter 2 or the table you made of the reforms between 1855–1870. Make out another table like the one below and work out for yourself whether Alexander III did reject all his father's reforms.

	Actions taken under Alexander III	What was left of Alexander II's reforms?
Serfdom		
Civil rights		
Good government		
Justice and the law		
Education		
Popular representation		
National rights		
Dissent		

1 How accurate is it to label Alexander II as a great reformer and Alexander III as a great reactionary?

2 Does the evidence above suggest that Russia had found a basis for future stability?

The rising tide of opposition

The Romanovs seemed to face difficult dilemmas at almost every turn. The pressure to maintain Russia as a major European and world power forced the regime to try to modernize the economy and follow the western example, to some extent at least. However, industrialization and modernization meant new social forces were being created which threatened to overwhelm the regime itself. An educated and freethinking middle class, able to travel and read the works of western authors, was one such force. An industrial workforce, concentrated in the urban areas in squalid conditions, was another potential source of opposition. In the 1880s and 1890s the industrial workers were preoccupied with making a living and had not developed a political consciousness of their own.

Populism

The opposition groups we studied in Chapter 2, Land and Liberty, The People's Will etc., are loosely lumped together by historians as 'Populists', the term originating from those who 'went to the people' in the 1870s. Radical intellectuals dominated these early groups, who argued passionately about how the regime could be changed. All, however, believed in a society based on the village communes, where all land was held in common. As the number of industrial workers increased, the Populists also attracted some support at the factories. The chosen method of most of the Populists was terrorism and assassination. This continued after the Tsar's assassination.

Immediately after Alexander II's death, 150 members of the People's Will were arrested. The secret police had repeated successes in penetrating the organization, even at the highest level. There were few successful terrorist attacks. The most notable exception was the shooting in 1882 of Governor Strelnikov in broad daylight. Khalturin, who had planted the bomb in the Winter Palace in 1880, and his associate were immediately captured, tried before a military tribunal and hanged four days later. In 1883 Vera Figner, the movement's most active leader, was betrayed to the police. She spoke these words in her final speech to the military court in 1884:

> **Note**
>
> Populists are 'Narodniks' in Russian.

Source 12

All my experience had convinced me that the regime could only be changed by violence. Without the liberty of the Press the dissemination of ideas through the written word is impossible. If some social institution had shown me some other way of achieving Russia's liberty perhaps I would have adopted it. I would certainly have tried it … I do not attach any great importance to supporting a republic or a constitutional monarchy, but I do believe it to be essential that conditions should be created in which the individual should have the possibility of developing to the full all his talents and devoting them without reservations to the service of society.

> ■ **Think about**
>
> ▶ Which groups in Russia were likely to be sympathetic with this statement by Vera Figner?

Figner's arrest did not bring an immediate end to terrorist activity. None the less after Alexander Ulyanov's failed attempted assassination of the Tsar in 1887, the interest in new attempts seemed to wane. The secret police were too effective and the waste of life too high perhaps. There had also been very little support for the attacks amongst the general public. The terrorists were, for example, always short of money. Famine in 1891–1892 also meant many were preoccupied in relief work where their efforts could see some tangible results.

By the later 1890s, after the disappointment of a new Tsar, Nicholas II, who seemed just as unbending as his father, the few surviving Populists began to re-emerge in a slightly different guise. Groups of Socialist Revolutionaries were set up in Moscow, the Ukraine and Minsk. A new publication *Revolutionary Russia* appeared on the streets. In 1902 these different groups formed themselves into a political party 'The Party of Socialist Revolutionaries' (SRs). This party was of course illegal on its foundation so its headquarters was established in Switzerland, where *Revolutionary Russia* was now published. This new party did not abandon terrorist activities, but it also saw the need for propaganda campaigns to raise the political understanding of the masses.

The SRs had their own Combat group, which continued its activities. In 1902 Sipyagin, Minister of the Interior, was killed by a young volunteer. He entered the Minister's office, disguised in military uniform, and shot Sipyagin without making any attempt to escape. He was sentenced by a military tribunal and hanged. In 1904 the Combat group had its greatest success when it blew up the new Minister of the Interior, Plehve, who had become the Tsar's closest adviser.

Marxism

The SRs were not the only revolutionary organization to be formed. The ideas of Karl Marx, a German exile living in England, were becoming popular, not only in Russia but also throughout Europe. You will already know that a party claiming to follow his ideas took over and dominated Russia for over 70 years. It would be a mistake to think, as you read this, that this outcome was in any way foreseeable.

Karl Marx based much of his thinking about history, economics and philosophy on his research into the history of France and Great Britain. The French Revolution particularly interested him. Like many other political thinkers of the nineteenth century, Marx was a socialist. He believed that an economic and political system that allowed a few individuals to become rich while others went poor was unfair. However, Marx's ideas went further than this. He believed that he had in his research discovered the law which governed the development of society. Hence he regarded himself as a 'scientific socialist', unlike many other 'ideal' socialists at the time.

The force driving history was, he believed, the struggle between different classes in society (see quotation 1 on page 54). A person's class was decided by his relationship to 'the means of production', that is by whether he owned or managed land or factories or whether he worked for other people. Marx's view of history led him to think that the course of history was predictable. Marx did not claim to be able to foresee specific events or individual actions, but he did believe that he knew the broad lines along which most societies would develop. History, for Marx, reflected the march of human progress. For him progress meant the growth of human production to the point where all basic needs would be fully satisfied. Only when material needs were satisfied would everyone reach fulfilment and happiness.

The first humans were hunter-gatherers. At that time there was no property or means of production, and everyone was roughly equal. When farming was developed, this equality was shattered. Whoever owned the land producing the food on which people depended would also dominate and control society. This would eventually end with feudalism, where peasants were virtually slaves to the landowners.

■ Biography

Karl Marx (1818–1883)

Born 1818 in Trier, Germany
Studied law in Bonn and Berlin

1841
Journalist in Cologne

1843 Studied the French Revolution in Paris

1845
Expelled from Paris. Settled in Belgium

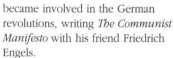

1848–9
became involved in the German revolutions, writing *The Communist Manifesto* with his friend Friedrich Engels.

1849 settled in Britain, where he wrote his major work *Das Kapital* (Money).

1883 died in exile.

Note

An example of an 'ideal socialist' was Fourier. He planned ideal communities, which he called *phalasteries*. These apparently included a platform complete with piano in the middle of the fields to entertain the workers.

Within feudal society itself, however, would develop a new class of people, capitalist entrepreneurs, who would eventually overthrow it when industry and trade expanded with the industrial revolution. This created new means of production, machines; power now passed away from landowners to capitalist factory owners, the 'bourgeoisie' as Marx called them. Those who worked on their machines he called the 'proletariat'. They became a new slave class.

Marx thought that competition between factories would grow more intense, and successful companies would buy out or put out of business those who were less efficient. This process would continue until production was in the hands of monopolies. Political power also would be in the hands of the owners of these monopolies. The proletariat would be more and more exploited as the bourgeoisie struggled to make maximum profits, until finally they would be driven to revolt against their exploiters.

Then would follow a period which Marx called the 'dictatorship of the proletariat', when the new ruling class would use the power of the State to destroy all traces of bourgeois society (quotation 2). Once this had been achieved, all people would be on the same level, private property would not exist and the State would no longer be necessary. People would live side by side in harmony, taking from society what they needed and putting into society their talents and their labour (quotation 3). A classless, Communist society would have been reached. An important point to note is that Marxists were internationalists, believing national borders would disappear after a successful Communist revolution (quotation 4).

Why were these ideas so appealing in the nineteenth century? One of the great attractions was the theory's seeming scientific character, but it had almost a religious aspect too. It taught that the exploited would eventually inherit the good things of life, almost a heaven on earth. Marx himself was an atheist. He believed that religion had been developed to persuade the poor to accept their position on earth, rather than try to change their situation by force (see quotation 5). After the famine of 1891–1892 Marxism attracted more support from intellectuals who could see little future in a peasant revolution.

Quotation

Quotations from the works of Karl Marx

1 'The history of all hitherto existing society is the history of class struggle.'

2 'The class struggle necessarily leads to the dictatorship of the proletariat.'

3 'From each according to his abilities, to each according to his needs.'

4 'The workers have nothing to lose but their chains. They have a world to gain. Workers of the world, unite!'

5 'Religion...is the opium of the masses.'

■ Activity

Marxists and Populists

Read through the last few pages and then fill in the table below.

	Populists	Marxists
How did they believe power would be achieved?		
Which groups held the key to future power?		
What was their vision of the future Russia?		

1 How did the ideas of the Populists and Marxists differ?

2 In what ways were their ideas similar?

3 Whose ideas seem to have been more relevant to conditions in Russia at the end of the nineteenth century?

Russian Marxists

In Russia the ideas of Marx came at a convenient time. The Populists had put their faith in the peasantry and in terrorist violence but so far without success. Marxism suggested another way forward. The proletariat held the key to the future, and Marxists believed that if they directed their efforts at guiding, instructing and leading the new working class they would eventually be rewarded with the overthrow of the Russian autocracy.

> Lenin (seated behind table) and fellow revolutionaries in 1897.

■ Think about

▶ What impression does Source 13 give of these Russian revolutionaries?

■ Biography

Lenin

1870 Born in Simbirsk, in the Urals. His father was a schools inspector and a noble.

1891 Gained a first class law degree as an external student.

1895 Visited Plekhanov in exile.

1897 Sent into exile in Siberia.

1898 Married N. Krupskaya.

1898–9 Wrote the Development of Capitalism in Russia.

1900 Went into exile abroad.

1900–3 Edited the newspaper *Iskra*, (*The Spark*).

■ Think about

▶ Why might a follower of Marxism believe that a proletarian revolution was unlikely in Russia for a long time?

Source 13

The first Marxist group, the Liberation of Labour, was set up in 1883 by G. Plekhanov, whom we last saw breaking away from Land and Liberty in 1879 in opposition to their terrorist tactics. Plekhanov went overseas to escape the attentions of the secret police. Marxists in Russia set up the grandly named 'Union of Struggle for the Emancipation of the Working Class' in 1895. Seventeen intellectuals wrote pamphlets and helped to organize a strike, until they were arrested. Amongst them was Vladimir Ulyanov (Lenin), the younger brother of Alexander, executed after the unsuccessful 1887 plot to kill the Tsar. In 1898 the Russian Social Democratic Labour Party (RSDLP) was founded in Minsk, though its most prominent members were again arrested shortly after its formation.

Bolsheviks and Mensheviks

In 1903 the RSDLP held its first Congress in Brussels. They were so harried by the Belgian police that they moved to London. Their main task at the meeting was to decide a party programme. This was quickly agreed but the party divided when they came to discuss party membership.

Lenin proposed that the party should be limited only to dedicated revolutionaries, people who would eat, drink and sleep the revolution. Another prominent member of the *Iskra* editorial board, Martov, argued that membership should be open to anyone who accepted the party programme and was willing to follow the instructions of the party leaders. Lenin won the debate, and his group was afterwards called the 'Bolsheviks', the majority. Martov's group was called the 'Mensheviks', the minority.

This disagreement, seemingly trivial, arose because of a profound difference in their beliefs of the role of the party. For Lenin the party was to be a group prepared to seize power as soon as possible; for Martov the main purpose of the party was to spread propaganda and raise the level of consciousness of the proletariat. This was because he did not believe that Russia was ready for a Marxist revolution for many years.

The division became permanent over the following years. In effect the two groups grew into two different political parties. This table explains the differences in their interpretation of Karl Marx's writings.

	Mensheviks	Bolsheviks
The future revolution	The time for a Marxist revolution was a long way off. The economic conditions were not yet right in Russia. The proletariat was too small.	Lenin believed that a dedicated party could lead a small proletariat into power. He argued that capitalism in Russia was well enough developed. The bourgeois and proletarian revolutions could be combined.
Membership	Membership should be open to as many as possible. It could include affiliated trade unionists and other sympathizers.	Only genuine totally reliable revolutionaries should be allowed in.
Decisions in the party	Decisions should be made by members after open debate and free votes.	Party leaders should make these, and all members must accept them. This was called 'democratic centralism'.
Role of the party	The party's role was to educate the workers to appreciate their role in the future. It should support all forms of workers' protest and their struggle for better conditions.	The party should plan for revolution. It could act as 'the vanguard of the proletariat' and seize power on behalf of the future generations of workers. Lenin had no confidence that the proletariat were really revolutionary in Russia.

Of the two groups the Tsarist secret police regarded the Mensheviks as the greater threat because they were more involved in inciting and supporting working-class discontent. As you will see, neither group had any significant support in 1905.

Opposition from intellectuals

In 1902 a new opposition journal *Liberation* appeared. Edited by a young radical, Struve, it set out to build a common front between all the groups opposed to the autocracy of the Tsars. In 1904 members of many different groups met in St Petersburg and set up the Union of Liberation. The resolution laid out in Source 14 was passed at its first meeting.

■ **Think about**

▶ Why would this programme have been supported by many in Russia?

▶ Why did the Bolsheviks refuse to support it?

Source 14

The Union of Liberation assumes as its first and principal task the political liberation of Russia. The Union regards political freedom even in its most minimal dimensions as utterly incompatible with the absolutist character of the Russian monarchy, and for that reason it will struggle above all for the liquidation of autocracy and the establishment in Russia of a constitutional regime…It recognizes above all…the principle of a universal, equal, secret, and direct vote…As regards the national question, the Union recognizes the right to self-determination of the various nationalities living in the Russian state.

Within the *zemstvo* movement there were also rising demands for more representation and participation in central government, if only to escape the arbitrary interference in their affairs.

■ **Think about**

▶ What are the author's main areas of complaint?

▶ Why is Source 15 particularly valuable to a historian studying opposition to the government of this period?

Source 15

Because of the unrestrained abuse of power by officialdom, senseless bureaucratic whims, regulations bordering on the ridiculous, the absence of any sound policy discussed in advance, capricious interference in affairs, and especially appointments by the empress, the grand dukes and duchesses, the Russian people are sinking deeper into oppression and misery…the ground for anarchy is becoming ever more propitious [favourable].

The diary of A.A. Polovtsev, member of the State Council, September 1902

Popular violence

There was a significant rise in the political temperature in the capital. Serious student disorders since 1899 culminated in February 1901 in the assassination of the Minister of Education. There were waves of strikes, especially in St Petersburg. The Obukhov factory was the centre of a series of disputes in 1901, which were only defeated by mounted Cossack troops and armed policemen. Peasant protests after 40 years of relative quiet broke out again in 1902 after a poor harvest. This resulted in attacks on landowners and their property in the Poltava and Kharkov districts.

Any impartial observer of the political scene realized that the political situation was deteriorating and that some measures were needed by the government to stem the tide.

The 1905 Revolution

The Russo-Japanese War 1904–1905

Instead of turning its attentions to solving the growing problems within, the government seemed deliberately to pick a quarrel with the Far Eastern neighbour Japan. There had been disputes between the two countries for many years over Korea and Manchuria. Russia had a long-term objective to expand her influence in the Far East, perhaps to make up for her loss of influence in Europe. The building of the Trans-Siberian Railway, almost complete in 1904, now gave her the means to do this. In 1904, as the Russians had predicted, the Japanese attacked Port Arthur.

Note

Nicholas II was personally involved in foreign policy. He allowed Russian forces and settlers into new areas in Manchuria and Korea. When the Japanese made an attempt to settle their differences with Russia, Nicholas rejected their proposals. The Japanese were almost forced into war.

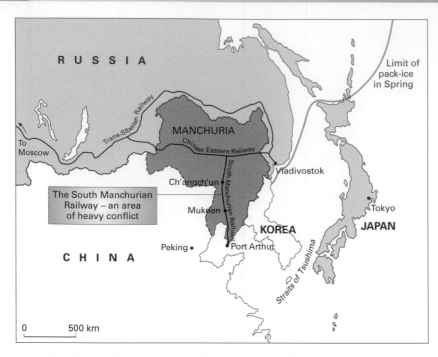

◀ The Russo-Japanese War, 1904–1905

Russia had believed that Japan would be easy prey for the Russian armies and navies. Nicholas called the Japanese 'little yellow monkeys' but they defeated Russia in every single major confrontation.

▼ A Russian postcard produced at the beginning of the Russo-Japanese War.

In April Russia's army was driven back from the Yalu River. It suffered further defeats in May and June 1904. The Japanese captured Port Arthur after a long heroic siege in January 1905. The main Russian army was defeated in February at Mukden. The final humiliation came in the straits of Tsushima in May with the total destruction of Russia's main battlefleet, which had sailed half way round the world from the Baltic Sea.

■ Think about

▶ What does Source 17 tell us about the reasons why the Russians were confident of success in the war against Japan?

Quotation

This statement was commonly believed to have been made by Plehve: 'We need a small victorious war to avert a revolution.'

Facts and figures

The Assembly of Russian Factory and Mill Workers was set up to distract workers away from more radical politics, under the aegis of Zubatov, Chief of the Moscow Secret Police. Every meeting began with the Lord's Prayer, finishing with a singing of the national anthem.

However, the organization became more and more radical, attracting supporters from other movements. By November it had 7000 members.

■ **Biography**

Father Gapon

Educated at the St Petersburg Theological Academy, Gapon believed that there was some kind of mystical union tying the Tsar and the people together. He preached in the workers districts of the capital, and was recruited by Zubatov to win over the workers from opposition groups.

● In 1903 he set up workers' tearooms and clubs.
● In January 1905, he helped to organize the Putilov strike.
● After 'Bloody Sunday' he fled to Finland.
● In 1906 he was assassinated by former opposition comrades on his return to Russia.

Russia was forced to seek peace in the summer of 1905. The Treaty of Portsmouth gave Korea and Port Arthur to the Japanese and Russian forces left Manchuria. Once again, fighting on territory Russia regarded as its own, Russian forces had proved inferior, not in terms of their personal courage, but with regard to their leadership and communications and supply. The regime, as we have seen, was in a shaky position before the war. This series of military disasters convinced many it was time for a change.

Growing discontent

In July 1904 terrorists had a major success. They succeeded in the murder of Plehve, Minister of the Interior and the man who most people blamed for the war with Japan. The Tsar appointed a new minister, Prince Sviatopolk-Mirskii, a man with more moderate views. To assuage public opinion he announced the lifting of some restrictions on the *zemstva* and an extension of press freedom. New newspapers appeared, carrying reports of public meetings and openly discussing political reform. In November the first Congress of *Zemstvo* Activists met in St Petersburg, bringing together many of the Tsar's liberal critics. As pressure on the Tsar for reform grew, Nicholas II issued a manifesto, promising, rather vaguely, broader participation in public affairs and a review of restrictions on national rights. It changed nothing immediately and only increased the popular mood of dissatisfaction. To avoid censorship, different societies held public banquets to call for constitutional government. The intelligentsia in Russia was taking the lead in pressing the regime to make fundamental reforms.

Bloody Sunday 9 January 1905

Five men were sacked from the Putilov factory in St Petersburg. Other workers went on strike demanding their reinstatement. The news spread through the capital like wildfire and by Friday 7 January 105,000 workers throughout the city had downed tools in sympathy. On Sunday 9 January 1905 a large demonstration was organized by Father Gapon, head of the Assembly of Russian Factory and Mill workers. The march had been officially banned by the police, but Gapon continued to make the preparations. The Governor-General stationed thousands of troops around the city centre and on the bridges to stop any marchers. When they met, the crowds carried icons and headed for Palace Square outside the Winter Palace to present a list of grievances and to ask for radical reforms. You can read a section of their petition in Source A on the next page.

Marchers had gathered at different points throughout the city to march on the Winter Palace. It was a bitingly cold day. Father Gapon at the head of one group wore a white cassock and carried a cross. The group carried icons as well as portraits of the Tsar and Tsarina. They sang hymns and the national anthem. As the groups neared the heart of the city they met lines of armed troops who tried to disperse them, first by peaceful persuasion but then by shooting into the crowds. In Source B on page 60 you can read an official police report on the events.

However, some marchers reached Palace Square on which stands the Winter Palace, where they faced artillery and more armed soldiers. One report says that children and women were placed in the front of the column to deter the soldiers from firing again. They opened fire. In the various 'incidents' perhaps 200 were killed and 800 wounded, according to modern historians.

Although some of the demonstrators dispersed, others gathered together in various points of the city and set up barricades. The army and police quickly broke these down.

Document exercise: Bloody Sunday

Source A

From the petition of Father Gapon and his followers

SIRE, We the workers and inhabitants of St Petersburg, of various estates, our wives, our children, and our aged, helpless parents, come to THEE, O SIRE to seek justice and protection. We are impoverished; we are oppressed, overburdened with excessive toil, contemptuously treated…We are suffocating in despotism and lawlessness. O SIRE we have no strength left, and our endurance is at an end. We have reached that frightful moment when death is better than the prolongation of our unbearable sufferings.

Source B

The official report of the head of the Okhrana on the events of 9 January 1905

When a crowd of several thousand had assembled…Father Gapon said prayers…Despite pleas by local police officers and cavalry charges, the crowd did not disperse but continued to advance. Two companies opened fire, killing ten and wounding twenty…Towards 1 p.m. people began to gather in the Alexander garden…The cavalry made a series of charges to disperse the crowd, but as this had no effect a number of volleys were fired into the crowd. The numbers of dead and wounded is not known as the crowd carried off the victims…In all some 75 people were killed and 200 wounded. It appears that among the dead are numbered women and children.

Source C

Source D

Maxim Gorky, a socialist, who was present, describes one death

The dragoon circled round him and, shrieking like a woman, waved his sabre in the air…swooping down from his dancing horse…he slashed him across the face, cutting him open from the eyes to the chin. I remember…the murderer's face…his teeth clenched in a grin and the hairs of his moustache standing up on his lip. Brandishing his tarnished shaft of steel he let out another shriek and…spat at the dead man.

■ Examination-style questions

1 Comprehension in context
What is the attitude of the petitioners in Source A to the Tsar?

2 Comparing the sources
Do Sources B and D give the same impression of the army's actions on 9 January 1905? Explain your answer by careful reference to the sources.

3 Assessing the sources
What reservations might you have about the reliability of both Sources B and D?

4 Making judgements
Use these sources and your own knowledge. Why did Bloody Sunday inspire such strong protest throughout Russia?

◀ A peaceful demonstration in St Petersburg just before the Bloody Sunday massacre.

The October Manifesto

'Bloody Sunday,' as the events of 9 January 1905 were immediately known, caused a storm of protest across the country. That 'innocent' women and children, who were simply trying to hand in a loyal petition to the Tsar, should be gunned down in cold blood shocked the nation. The prestige of the royal family, the peculiar mystique of the Tsar as the Father of the Nation, was smashed and gone for ever.

Source 18

▶ A Russian cartoon published immediately after Bloody Sunday, entitled 'Death stalks the barricades'.

■ **Think about**

▶ What was the cartoonist trying to convey in Source 18?

▶ Who do you think he held responsible for the deaths?

Timeline

1905

2 Jan Port Arthur captured by Japanese forces.

3 Jan Putilov strike begins.

9 Jan Bloody Sunday. A flood of strikes spreads across Russia.

4 Feb SRs assassinate Grand Duke Sergei.

5 Feb Tsar proclaims his ministers will draw up proposals for an elected duma.

Feb/March Russian army defeated at Mukden.

May Union of Unions set up.

May Russian Baltic Fleet destroyed at Tsushima.

June All-Russian Union of Peasants set up.

Sept Isolated mutinies in army garrisons.

8 Oct Railway strike begins.

13 Oct St Petersburg Soviet set up.

17 Oct The October Manifesto issued.

Nov St Petersburg general strike and Soviet leaders arrested.

Dec Lenin arrives in Russia. Moscow rising crushed.

Strikes swept the country – St Petersburg, Moscow, Warsaw – all the major urban centres in the Empire. The Minister of the Interior was sacked, General Trepov was made Governor-General of St Petersburg with sweeping powers. Peasant revolts broke out in western Russia and spread to some central and northern districts. The assassination of the Tsar's uncle, Grand Duke Sergei, made such a profound impression that Nicholas announced that he would create a consultative assembly. This concession was too little, too late.

In May the Union of Unions came into being. Springing from the Union of Liberation it united many different professional groups. In June a Union of Peasants was set up and finally with the mutiny of the battleship *Potemkin* in the Black Sea the discontent spread to the armed forces. The Tsar met with *zemstvo* leaders, but only gave vague promises for the future. City duma representatives met and demanded a constituent assembly and full civil rights for all. Eventually the Tsar published a cautious scheme for a consultative assembly, but which excluded most townspeople and all workers.

Once again it failed to satisfy anyone. Peasant violence was spreading alarmingly; in the Volga region houses of the gentry were burnt down and they were thrown off their land. In October a strike broke out on the Russian railways. In the capital there was a general strike, which resulted in workers setting up their own council, or soviet, to co-ordinate their actions in future. Its executive committee comprised 22 workers and 3 representatives from each of the Bolsheviks, Mensheviks and SRs. A Moscow Soviet soon followed. By mid-October the whole of Russia was paralysed by a general strike, which was actively supported by the Union of Unions. The Tsar's opponents from all classes were now united.

Faced with growing anarchy on all fronts, the Tsar accepted Cabinet government and appointed Russia's first Prime Minister, Count Witte. On 17 October Nicholas announced his October Manifesto:

Source 19

The disturbances and unrest in St Petersburg, Moscow and in many other parts of our Empire have filled Our heart with great and profound sorrow. The welfare of the Russian Sovereign and His people is inseparable and national sorrow is His too…The oath which We took as Tsar compels Us to use all Our strength, intelligence and power to put a speedy end to this unrest which is so dangerous to the State…However, in view of the need to pacify the country, we have decided that the work of the government must be unified. We have therefore ordered the government to take the following measures in fulfilment of our unbending will:

1 Fundamental civil freedoms will be granted to the population, including real personal inviolability, freedom of conscience, speech, assembly and association.
2 Participation in the Duma will be granted to those classes of the population which are at present deprived of voting powers…
3 It is established as an unshakeable rule that no law can come into force without its approval by the State Duma and that the elected representatives will be given the opportunity to play a real part in the supervision of the legality of the activities of government bodies.

We call on all true sons of Russia to remember their duty to their homeland, to help put a stop to this unprecedented unrest and, together with this, to devote all their strength to the restoration of peace to their native land.

Tsar Nicholas II

Counter-revolution

The manifesto marked the end of the most serious problems for the regime. It had the effect of dividing the opposition forces. Some liberals immediately accepted its terms. Right-wing supporters of autocracy, the Black Hundreds, began a wave of attacks on Jews and liberal intellectuals, supported by the police authorities. The response of socialist groups and some liberals was very different (see Source 20).

The St Petersburg Soviet of Workers called another general strike in November to press for an eight-hour day, but it was not supported by the middle-class unions or many workers. The government seized the opportunity, arrested the Soviet leaders and closed the Soviet itself by military force. The Bolsheviks called on workers in other cities to strike in defence of their St Petersburg colleagues. In Moscow the call was answered. When police tried to prevent it, the workers threw up barricades and the strike turned into a full-scale revolution. Military units were sent and two weeks of street fighting followed, ending in the defeat of the rebels. Over a thousand workers died. Further troops were sent to put down peasant risings and strikes. Order was restored, although the way it had been done left a bitter legacy of hatred and mistrust. Would this provide the basis for a new political settlement in Russia?

■ Think about

▶ What does Nicholas say are the reasons for the Manifesto?

▶ What signs are there in the manifesto that the Tsar only wanted limited reforms?

▶ Which groups in Russia would accept this Manifesto? Why?

▶ Which groups would be dissatisfied? Why?

Source 20

Citizens! Now that we have got the ruling clique with its back to the wall, they promise us freedom. They promise us electoral rights and legislative power. Who promises these things? Nicholas the Second. Does he promise them of his own good will? Or with a pure heart? Nobody could say that for him…It is this tireless hangman on the throne whom we have forced to promise us freedom. What a great triumph! But do not be too quick to celebrate victory…Look around citizens; has anything changed? The Peter and Paul Fortress still dominates the city, doesn't it?…Isn't Trepov, the hangman, master of St Petersburg?

Leon Trotsky, Vice-Chairman of the St Petersburg Soviet, recalling the speech he gave in response to the Manifesto. Leon Trotsky, *1905*, 1972

■ Think about

▶ What is Trotsky's chief objection to the October Manifesto?

The Tsar expressed his thoughts on the reasons for the October Manifesto in a letter to his mother on 1 November 1905:

Source 21

There were only two ways open: to find an energetic soldier and crush the rebellion by sheer force. There would be time to breathe then but, as likely as not, one would have to use force again in a few months; and that would mean rivers of blood, and in the end we should be where we had started. I mean to say, government authority would be vindicated, but there would be no positive result and no possibility of progress achieved. The other way out would be to give the people their civil rights, freedom of speech and press, also to have all laws confirmed by a State Duma – that, of course, would be a constitution.

■ **Think about**

▶ Does Source 21 present a different impression of the Tsar and his motives from that given in the Manifesto itself?

■ **Activity**   **KEY SKILLS**

Did the 1905 Revolution fail?

In 1906 Tsar Nicholas remained the autocrat he was when he inherited the throne in 1894. Thousands of those who had demonstrated for change were either dead, in exile or in prison.

How satisfied would the following groups have been by the events of 1905–1906?

You will first of all have to work out what were their grievances before 1905, and then what, if anything, they gained.

1 peasants

2 landowners

3 intellectuals and the middle class

4 industrial workers

5 national minorities

Research further the events of 1905 and then present your thoughts on the central question 'Did the 1905 Revolution fail?' You must incorporate an image in your presentation. Discuss the views presented in your group.

Conclusion

Alexander II introduced reforms because he believed them to be necessary for the good of Russia. The 25 years after his death were marked by a rejection of reform and an attempt in some ways to turn back the clock. However, Russia could not be isolated from political and intellectual developments in the rest of the world. Ideas derived from Bakunin, Marx and from the liberal democratic parties of Britain and France found a growing number of supporters in the universities, the *zemstva* and amongst the industrial workers. As Russia experienced the most rapid expansion in its trade and industry of any western nation, these groups gained an increasingly important economic position. They demanded a political voice.

The events of 1905 had shocked the nation. They could serve to bind it together to build a new consensus or they could act as a symbol inspiring future conflict. This is the subject of our next chapter.

■ **Further reading**

R. Hare, *Portraits of Russian Personalities between Reform and Revolution*, 1959
D. Lieven, *Nicholas II: Emperor of all the Russias*, 1993
O. Figes, *A People's Tragedy: The Russian Revolution 1891-1924*, 1996. If you read only one book on Russian history, then it must be this.
R. Pipes, *The Russian Revolution 1899-1919*, 1990

Chapter 4

Russia on the road to democracy?

◀ Tsar Nicholas II rides past crowds in front of the Kremlin in May 1913, as part of the celebrations to mark the 300th anniversary of his Romanov dynasty.

Source 2

▲ An anti-government cartoon, printed just after the 1905 Revolution. The caption says 'In this world there is a Tsar. He has no pity. His name is Hunger.'

Source 3

▲ Tsar Nicholas II and his family before the First World War.

Introduction

The introduction of the October Manifesto gave the Tsar an opportunity to build a consensus of support with at least some of those who had joined together to protest and demand change. Nicholas talked about conciliating the 'well-intentioned' elements in the opposition. The fundamental question underlying the years 1905–1917 was, however, the same as before. It was clear that he had made limited concessions in the face of overwhelming opposition. Would Nicholas II be content to become a fully constitutional monarch on western lines, and allow not only popular representation and consultation, as promised in October, but also popular control over the affairs of state? Or, as memory of the crisis faded, would the Tsar seek to reassert his prerogative powers? Would the genuine respect for the Tsar and his family shown during the 300th anniversary of Romanov rule over Russia (Source 1) help this coming together of people and monarch, or would the government be unable to solve the problems shown in Source 2 and the voices of violence and revolution gain the upper hand?

For some historians, Russia until 1914, was proceeding both politically and economically down the road of gradual change towards constitutional and democratic government. In Britain these developments had taken centuries to achieve and had involved a civil war in which the King, Charles I, was executed. Russia was not given as long. Another war intervened in 1914, but this time a war on such a scale that even modern economies and democratic political systems creaked and collapsed under its strain.

Key questions

- How did the nation react to the October Manifesto?
- Was the government able to build a satisfactory working relationship with the Duma?
- Were the revolutionaries as serious a threat after the October Manifesto?
- Was Russia becoming an economic and political success before 1914?
- How did the Russian armed forces perform in the First World War?
- Why was there a revolution in February 1917?
- Why did the Romanov dynasty fall?

How was the October Manifesto received by the Russian people?

The day after the proclamation of the October Manifesto, Witte was named as Chairman of the Council of Ministers. It was due to his prompting that the Tsar had made these concessions: now it was Witte's task to make them a success. The first signs were promising. The representatives of some of the liberal groups welcomed the Manifesto as a solution to Russia's political difficulties. The general strike quickly came to an end, despite the promptings of Lenin (who was shortly to arrive in Russia) and of others to continue the struggle. In November the government announced an end to redemption dues, hoping by this to win the peasants back to what it regarded as their fundamental loyalty to the Tsar.

However, some rejected the October Manifesto as simply empty words. They no longer had any confidence in the regime. Trotsky, as the head of the St Petersburg Soviet, called for a new strike and for everyone to withdraw their money in gold from the banks to bring the government to its knees. It was poorly supported – and Witte felt strong enough to arrest the entire Soviet and throw them in prison. Trotsky was soon to be put on trial and faced execution.

Think about

▶ What image does Source 1 present of the Tsar's relationship with his people?

▶ What impression does Source 3 give of the Tsar?

Timeline

1906 Witte, Russia's first Prime Minister, replaced by Prince Goremykin
The First Duma elected
Stolypin becomes Prime Minister
1907 Second Duma elected
Stolypin's house bombed
Third Duma elected after changes in the electoral system
1908 Education reforms
1911 Stolypin assassinated
1912 Lena Goldfields massacre
Fourth Duma elected
1914 Duma suspended when war is declared in August

In Moscow things were different. The workers here did carry out an effective general strike, backed by some of the revolutionary groups, including Lenin's. There was general fighting with barricades thrown across the city streets. Loyal troops crushed the rising with artillery. By a combination of firmness and an apparent willingness to introduce fundamental reform, perhaps the regime could build a new stability.

Witte had hoped that he would be able to put together a government which would incorporate some of the government's critics and thus draw the teeth (reduce the force) of the opposition. However, when talks began, the price the liberals demanded included a constituent assembly with powers to rewrite the constitution. This was unacceptable to both Witte and the Tsar. The new Cabinet consisted, therefore, largely of traditionally minded bureaucrats. The Union of Liberation was split for ever by these developments. Some liberals supported the Manifesto changes, and set up a political party, the Union of October 17, henceforward known as 'Octobrists'. The majority, however, wanted to press on with the full programme of the Union of Liberation. They now set up the Constitutional Democratic Party (Kadets for short) and continued to campaign against the government.

> **Note**
>
> Political parties became legal after the October Manifesto.

Was the government able to build a satisfactory working relationship with the Duma?

Before the Duma could meet for its first session, Nicholas II published The Fundamental Laws, which made quite clear to all his own views of the changes that had been made:

Source 4

1. The Russian State is one and indivisible.
4. The Russian language is the general language of the State, and its use is compulsory in the army, the navy and State and public institutions.
5. Supreme Autocratic Power belongs to the Emperor of all Russia.
9. The sovereign emperor ratifies the laws. No law can come into force without his consent.
15. The sovereign emperor appoints and dismisses the Chairman of the Council of Ministers and individual ministers.

Extracts from The Fundamental Laws 23 April 1906

> **■ Think about**
>
> Compare the Fundamental Laws with the October Manifesto in the previous chapter.
>
> ▶ How and why do they differ?

The voting system for the new Duma was complex, and quite deliberately so. For the Tsar and his ministers, its chief function was to minimize the numbers of representatives from the discontented classes and prevent any direct link between the voters and those elected. Voting was carried out by class as you can see in Source 5; each voter elected representatives, and these then elected others to electoral colleges or curia. This system gave proportionately more influence to landed gentry and propertied townspeople than to peasants, and even less to industrial workers – in fact one gentry vote was equal to 3.5 townspeople's votes, 15 peasant votes and 45 workers' votes.

Source 5

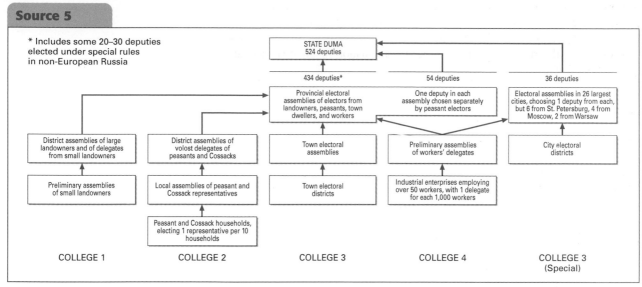

* Includes some 20–30 deputies elected under special rules in non-European Russia

▲ The new system of government

In the new system of government there was also a State Council, which was to act as an upper chamber. Half its members were appointed by the Tsar, the other half were elected by the *zemstva*, academic institutions, gentry assemblies, the clergy and other groups. The Tsar's ministers were confident that the electoral college system for the State Duma would produce an amenable lower house. They expected that the peasants, guided by the Orthodox Church, would return to their traditional loyalty to the Tsar and become an obstacle to further unrest. Any legislation, of course, also needed the Tsar's personal approval.

The Duma elected was far from compliant. The peasant deputies were both radical and irrepressible. The resignation of Witte just before the first session of the Duma and his replacement by Goremykin, a man with conservative credentials and not associated with reform as Witte had been, did not make relationships between the government and Duma any easier. The Cabinet Goremykin chose was without any known progressives. Over 20 parties were represented in the First State Duma when it met and they were in bitter mood. The results of the four Duma elections, for the larger political groups only, were as follows:

■ Think about

▶ What were the main changes between the 1st and 2nd Dumas?

▶ How were the 3rd and 4th Dumas different from the 1st and 2nd?

Source 6

Party	1st Duma April – July 1906	2nd Duma Feb – June 1907	3rd Duma Nov 1907 – June 1912	4th Duma Nov 1912 – Feb 1917
Bolsheviks	–	–	19	15
Mensheviks	18	47	–	-
Trudoviks*	102	104	13	10
SRs	34	37	–	-
Kadets	182	91	54	53
Octobrists	17	42	154	95
Progressists**	–	–	28	41
Right-wing groups	9	10	147	154
National groups	60	93	26	22

*The Trudoviks were a Labour group, who came into existence because the SRs refused to stand in the Duma elections, though as you can see some were none the less elected.

**The Progressists were a moderate liberal party.

When the first session of the Duma opened, the representatives expected to debate the most important issues of state, especially the future constitution and the question of land. When these were not offered by the government as topics for discussion, the Duma felt betrayed and immediately demanded from the Tsar universal suffrage, a Cabinet responsible to the Duma and major land reform, amongst other things. The Prime Minister Goremykin replied as follows:

Source 7

Ministers will pay special attention to the questions raised by the State Duma of the immediate satisfaction of the pressing needs of the rural population...The preparation of a law on universal primary education, the imposition of taxation on the more prosperous sections of society.

The Council of Ministers regards the solution of the peasant-land question proposed by the Duma through the use of Crown, Cabinet and Church lands and the compulsory expropriation of private land as completely unacceptable.

Other suggestions made by the Duma dealt with the introduction of a government responsible to, and having the confidence of the Duma, the abolition of the State Council and the removal of the limits placed on the Duma's competence. The Council of Ministers does not feel that it has the right to consider these proposals: they imply a huge change in The Fundamental Laws, which cannot be dealt with at the instigation of the Duma.

Response of Goremykin to the proposals of the First Duma, 13 May 1906

■ Think about

▶ Why was this reply unsatisfactory to the Duma?

▶ Does this mean that the government had no intention of reaching an agreement with the Duma?

This is how the Duma replied to Goremykin's rebuff:

Source 8

The declaration of the Chairman of the Council of Ministers clearly indicated that the government had absolutely no desire to satisfy the demands of the people and their expectations of land, rights and freedom, which were set out by the State Duma in its reply to the throne...By its refusal to fulfil the people's demands, the government is displaying obvious contempt for the true interests of the people and is clearly willing to countenance new upheavals in the country, already rent by poverty, a lack of basic rights and the continued rule of arbitrary power, left unpunished...[The Duma] believes...that the present ministry should resign immediately and be replaced by a government enjoying the trust of the State Duma.

Reaction of the First Duma to Goremykin's Declaration, 13 May 1906

Although the Duma was to continue sitting for a further two months, the gap between the ministers and the Duma seemed unbridgeable. An outbreak of violence and assassination gave the government the excuse to close the Duma and order new elections. The response of some 200 of the Kadets and Trudoviks was strong and principled. They adjourned to Vyborg in Finland and issued the declaration in Source 9.

Source 9

Citizens, stand firmly for the trampled rights of the people's representatives, stand firmly for the State Duma. Russia must not remain a single day without popular representatives. We have the means of achieving this: the government has no right either to collect taxes from the people or to mobilize men for military service without the consent of the people's representatives…And so, until the convocation of the people's representatives, do not give a single kopek to the Treasury or a single soldier to the army.

The Kadets' call for civil disobedience, 10 July 1906

The appeal provoked little response. Most of those who signed it were arrested and barred from standing in the elections. There were no riots or demonstrations in defence of the closed Duma, though the government had taken the precaution of surrounding the Tauride Palace, where it met, with dependable troops.

A Second Duma was elected. Despite substantial government interference in the campaign, particularly against the Kadets – two leading Kadets were assassinated during the elections – it proved to be no more amenable than its predecessor. After three months it too was dissolved by the Tsar. Evidence was forged which seemed to suggest that Social Democrat deputies to the Duma were involved in plotting to kill the Tsar. When the Duma refused to expel them, Nicholas declared this compelled him to close the Duma.

For the Third Duma elections the Tsar decreed, in direct contravention of The Fundamental Laws he had published only a year earlier, a substantial change in the electoral law. He increased substantially the number of deputies elected by the gentry electoral college, and reduced that for the peasants and workers. The government now had a working majority, and pressed on with land reform and social insurance schemes. However, the cost was that Russia now had a Duma which was seen to be totally unrepresentative of the Russian people.

■ Think about

Look back at Source 6.

▶ How successful was the harassment of the Kadets?

▶ Which parties benefited most from the government's activities?

▶ Would this make the Duma more amenable?

■ Think about

▶ This change in the electoral law was immediately condemned as a *coup d'etat* by Kadets and parties on the left.

▶ Would this strengthen or weaken the hands of those groups in Russia who wanted to reach a compromise between the Tsar and his critics?

■ Activity

How had the political situation changed?

Sources 10 and 11 are excerpts from the political programmes of two parties who were represented in the First and Second Dumas. The first is that of the SRs, a party grown from revolutionary roots. The second is that of an extreme right-wing group opposed originally to the very idea of constitutional government.

Read these sources and answer the questions which follow on page 70.

Source 10

The Political Programme of the Socialist Revolutionary Party (SRs) November 1905

Political Objectives

The establishment of a democratic republic with wide autonomy for regions and both rural and urban settlements; the recognition of their undoubted right to self-determination; the appointment by election, removal at any time and legal responsibility of all officials; equality of languages…

Economic Objectives

1. The establishment of a legal maximum to working hours, a minimum wage and state insurance.
2. Socialization of all privately owned land and its transfer to democratically organized communes.

Source 11

Programme of The Union of the Russian People
2 September 1906

The Union of the Russian People aims to unite all true Russians, loyal to their sworn oath in the name of Faith, Tsar and Fatherland. The Union will support the following proposals both inside and outside the Duma:

The AUTOCRACY of the Russian TSARS...has remained unchanged...after 17 October and should always remain so for the good and enlightenment of Russia.

The Unity and Indivisibility of Russia.

All Jews should immediately be declared foreigners.

The transfer to land shortage peasants of Crown lands on advantageous terms for them. As the quantity of Crown lands is not sufficient for this purpose...land should be bought by the State from private landowners.

The Union will work for a reduction in the working day...and State insurance against death, sickness and old age.

■ Questions

Consider the attitudes in Sources 10 and 11 to the following:

(a) Land.

(b) Industrial workers.

(c) National rights.

(d) The position of the Tsar.

1. On what policy issues did they agree/disagree?

2. What evidence does this programme give that even the right-wing Union of Russian People had been affected by the events of 1904–1905 in Russia?

3. Which of the two programmes do you think was most realistic given the circumstances of the time?

4. Which of the two parties showed a greater willingness to compromise? Why?

Stolypin's reforms

In July 1906 Nicholas appointed his Minister of the Interior, Peter Stolypin, as Prime Minister. He was known as a firm, even ruthless, administrator, but one who recognized the new realities of the political situation. He believed that the best way to strengthen support for the regime was by careful reform. He had hoped to attract liberals by new measures. As we have seen in the Second Duma, this hope was not at first realized. However, by Tsarist decree and with a majority in the Third Duma he was able to begin a programme of reform.

The land

On his appointment he faced new waves of terrorism – his own house was destroyed and his children injured in one attack. He was not deflected from his determination to change the political atmosphere of the countryside. Stolypin believed the key to building a coalition of support in the Duma, and also in the country, lay in solving the peasant question. Firstly the peasants made up the vast majority of the electorate, and secondly their numbers were growing rapidly. The Russian population was the fastest growing in Europe, increasing

■ Biography

P. Stolypin
1862 Born. Father a general and writer.
1885 Graduated from St Petersburg University.
1885 Began work with the Ministry of the Interior.
1902 Governor of Grodno.
1903 Governor of Saratov.
1906 Minister of the Interior.
1911 Assassinated.

Cross reference

The Peasants Land Bank was set up at the end of the last century. See page 45.

from 133 million to 161 million in just the decade 1900–1910. Stolypin persuaded the Tsar to introduce a number of reforms:

● All State and Crown lands were made available to the Peasants Land Bank for purchase by enterprising peasants.
● Peasants were allowed by imperial decree to withdraw from their commune (*mir*) without needing its consent first.
● Peasants who left the *mir* were later able to have all their land together, rather than have to farm in strips like the rest of the village.
● He declared an end to the redistribution of land as the population grew, making all the land the hereditary property of the head of the family.

Source 12

▼ The wreckage of Peter Stolypin's house after the bomb attack which injured his children.

Source 13

The number of peasant households leaving the *mir*. There were about 12 million households in total.

1907	48,271
1908	508,344
1909	579,409
1910	342,245
1911	145,567
1912	122,314
1913	134,554

By his reforms, Stolypin hoped to create a new class of well-to-do peasants. He called it his 'bet on the sober and strong'. They would be able to leave the commune (*mir*), extend their landholdings and build up their own independent consolidated farms. This meant that they would be able to try new agricultural techniques and grow what crops they wished. An end to redistribution meant that there was now encouragement for every peasant to improve his land. Stolypin believed that these new independent farmers would provide stable support for the imperial government. His policies met with some success, as Source 13 shows.

By the outbreak of the First World War almost 2 million peasant families had left their communes, but the war quickly put an end to further departures. Many peasants themselves opposed the idea; they appreciated the security of the *mir*. Those who did leave the *mir* were often those with little land, who took their land in order to sell it and move away with the proceeds. During the same period, 3 million peasants also left their communes to take up land in Siberia, with government financial help.

Other reforms

In 1908 the Duma agreed to a programme of educational reform. As a result, the number of primary schools almost doubled between 1905 and 1914. *Zemstva* expenditure on health, poor relief and agricultural advice and support almost doubled between 1906 and 1912. After Stolypin's death his proposal to reintroduce elected magistrates was approved.

Stolypin's programme of reforms in other areas met powerful opposition. Tsar Nicholas was always deeply suspicious of change, as was the extreme right in the Duma and a substantial number of the State Council. Stolypin's attempt to bring about religious toleration, especially for Jews, was passed by the Duma after a struggle but was vetoed by the Tsar. A plan to extend the *zemstva* into non-Russian areas was rejected by the State Council. Both were felt to be a threat to the nationality principle which they believed held Russia together. In Poland, which would have been the chief beneficiary, this was particularly resented. Similarly, a proposal to extend participation in local government by setting up a new layer of lower level *zemstva* was never accepted.

The Tsar's uneasy relationship with his Prime Minister came to an end when Stolypin was shot at a gala performance at the Kiev opera in October 1911.

Stolypin's death was greeted with enthusiasm by both the extreme left and the extreme right. Perhaps this indicates that his policies were those best-suited to Russia at that moment in history. Perhaps it also shows that those policies would never have been allowed to work for long.

From then on Nicholas seems to have decided that if a Prime Minister was essential, it would be better to have one who had no interest in working with the Duma, and would follow the advice of the Tsar and the State Council. The culmination of this trend was the reappointment in 1914 of Goremykin, now aged 74, a man who had no commitment to the post. Nicholas was back in charge.

Were the revolutionaries less successful after the October Manifesto?

Stolypin conducted a vigorous campaign against terrorists and revolutionaries. So many were arrested and executed that the hangman's noose came to be nicknamed 'Stolypin's necktie'. The figures given below show the extent of terrorist violence after the October 1905 Manifesto, but also the effectiveness of the police response.

Source 14

Year	Numbers of Terrorists' Victims		Death Sentences	
	Killed	Wounded	Sentenced	Executed
1905	233	358	72	10
1906	768	820	450	144
1907	1231	1312	1056	456
1908	394	615	1741	825

The main revolutionary parties were divided during much of this period and lost support. Perhaps the majority of the population just wanted to get on with the difficult task of living. The SRs organized peasant risings in 1907 which failed to spread into the general insurrection they had expected. This, and the discovery in 1908 that a police spy was the head of their terrorist group, discredited terrorism as a sensible way forward. However, the party also opposed standing in elections for the Duma. It was not clear how the SRs would bring about a change in the existing political situation.

The RSDLP was locked in all kinds of internal party struggles. There were attempts made by Trotsky and others to unite the two factions of the party, the Bolsheviks and Mensheviks. They all came to nothing. There were hot debates as to whether they should be concentrating on trade union activities to raise the level of consciousness of the workers and win their support. Lenin urged against this as a distraction from the real issue of preparation for the seizure of political power. However, membership of the RSDLP declined drastically, from about 150,000 at its height in 1905 to perhaps as little as 10,000. In the Fourth Duma the two factions together were able to muster only 13 seats. The leadership continued to be in exile, and its disagreements must have seemed rather irrelevant to many of its former supporters in the industrial areas of Russia. Foreign Marxists looked on with amazement:

> **Note**
>
> Although Bolshevik membership declined, the workers in St Petersburg and Moscow voted consistently for the Bolsheviks before 1914.

> **Source 15**
>
> [They are a] handful of fighting cocks living abroad...and to expect anything of these cocks is a pure delusion.
>
> Rosa Luxemburg, a German Marxist writing to a colleague in 1916

This was a difficult time for Lenin personally. He mistakenly supported a suspected police agent as a leading member of the Bolshevik faction. The secret police supported the agent Malinovsky, helping him to be elected to the Fourth Duma, and through Malinovsky encouraged Lenin in his divisive attacks on the Mensheviks. Lenin found himself in a minority within his own Bolshevik section on more than one occasion. He did see that the success of Stolypin's reforms would help to strengthen the Tsarist state at least in the short run. He also expected that the reforms would aid the cause of revolution eventually by dividing peasants into two clear groups – rich 'kulaks' who benefited from Stolypin's reforms, and poor 'muzhiks', who would have little or no land and would, therefore, be a revolutionary force in the countryside.

Strikes

If the socialist political parties were making no discernible advances, in the industrial areas, there were other important developments. The government had legalized trade unions after the 1905 revolution. Ironically this coincided with a fall in the numbers of strikers. Many workers must have watched the crushing of the Moscow strike in 1905–1906 and the arrest of the St Petersburg Soviet with dismay. No doubt this was an important reason why fewer took strike action after 1905. The government played its part by using the police to interfere in union activities.

Facts and figures

Numbers of people who took strike action

1905	2,863,000
1906	1,108,000
1907	740,000
1908	176,000
1909	64,000
1910	47,000
1911	105,000
1912	725,000
1913	887,000
1914	1,337,000

Workers also saw a steady increase in their living standards thanks to a boom in Russian industry, much of this inspired by a vast increase in military spending by the government and supported by foreign credit. The industrial workforce grew quickly over these years. More peasants arrived in the cities and towns of Russia, finding inadequate accommodation, squalid slum areas, long working hours and poor wages.

Source 16

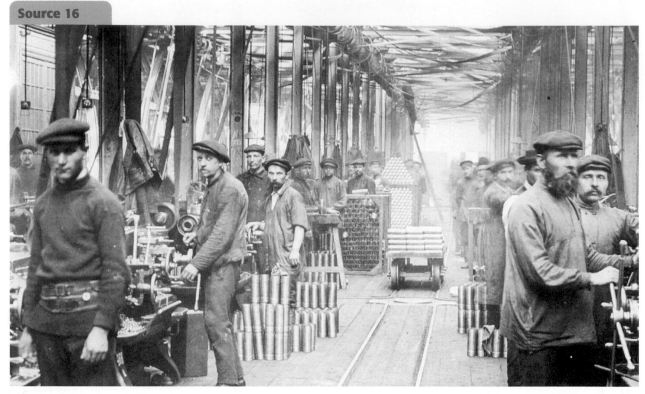

When the factories had full order books, workers knew that the strike weapon was more effective. The number of strikes rose rapidly. According to the Ministry of Trade and Industry's own published statistics over two-thirds of the strikes before the outbreak of the First World War were political and not economic. Clearly workers were regaining a little of the confidence they had lost in 1905.

The government by its own heavy-handed approach contributed to the political demands of the strikers. In 1912 there was a serious strike in the Lena goldfields, where working conditions were truly appalling. The employers refused to grant the strikers' demands for better wages and working conditions. They called on police to arrest the strike leaders. The confrontation ended with troops firing on the unarmed demonstrators, killing 200 and wounding perhaps twice that number.

▲ Workers in a munitions factory meet the demands caused by increased military spending by the government.

■ Think about

▶ Does Source 16 support the view that working conditions were a major source of discontent in pre-war Russia?

▶ What questions would a historian want to ask about this photograph?

Source 17

■ Think about

▶ What impression would photographs like these have in Russia?

▶ Why did the events of 1912 remind Russians of 1905?

▶ Victims of the massacre of strikers at the Lena goldfields by government forces in 1912.

It created, just like Bloody Sunday, a storm of protest throughout the country. Inevitably moderate and radical opinion both reflected on whether anything had really changed in Russia since 1905.

Clearly the government had not yet reached a new *modus vivendi* or way of living together with many elements in society. If workers were denied the right to trade unions, and their political representation was effectively prevented by Stolypin's strict electoral law, what way forward was there for workers who wanted to improve their lot? At the same time those members of the middle class who had supported the Kadets in their demands in 1905 found that they were in a similar position. The Duma and State Council were dominated by deeply conservative landowners, who saw almost any criticism of government policy or any radical change as a threat to the stability of the regime, their own privileged positions and the Empire.

There was a real danger that the forces of reform would be thrown together, very reluctantly as before in the 1905 revolution. The leader of the Octobrists, a party which you will remember accepted the October Manifesto as a sensible way forward for Russia, expressed his fears:

Source 18

What is to be the issue [outcome] of the grave crisis through which we are now passing? What does the encroachment of reaction bring with it?

Whither is the government policy, or rather lack of it, carrying us? Towards an inevitable and grave catastrophe! In this general forecast all are agreed; people of the most sharply opposed political views...

Are we not...in danger of being plunged into a period of protracted, chronic anarchy which will lead to the dissolution of the Empire?

Speech by Guchkov to the Octobrist Party, 8 November 1913

■ Think about

▶ Why did Guchkov regard the situation as a 'crisis?'

Was Russia an economic and political success at the outbreak of the First World War?

A whole host of economic indicators showed that Russia was making enormous economic progress.

	1900	1910	1913
Pig Iron (millions poods)	179.1	185.8	283.0
Coal (millions poods)	986.3	1,526.3	2,200.1
Railways (thousands km)	53.2	66.6	70.2
Cotton consumption (millions poods)	16.0	22.1	25.7
Imports (millions roubles)	626.3	1,084.4	1,084.4
Exports (millions roubles)	716.2	1,449.0	1,520.0
Budget revenue (millions roubles)	1,704.1	2,780.9	3,417.3
Budget expenditure (millions roubles)	1,559.1	2,473.1	3,094.2

Note. A pood is a Russian measurement equal to 16.39kg

Savings accounts grew from 4,988,000 to 8,992,000 between 1905 and 1913. The National Debt (the money owed by the government – in Russia mainly to foreign banks) dropped from 9,014,000 to 8,835,000 roubles. The average annual growth rate between 1907 and 1914 was over 6 per cent, which surpassed that of any other Western European country. However, to continue this development Russia needed both domestic harmony, which we have seen was under threat, and, even more importantly, peace with her neighbours. The assassination of Archduke Franz Ferdinand and the events which followed were to shatter both.

■ Think about

▶ Which groups in society would have savings accounts?

Was Russia on the road to peaceful and successful reform before the First World War?

Here is what two historians have written on the subject:

Source 19

Pre-revolutionary Russia needed a few decades more of peace to be transformed into a society no longer conspicuously backward as compared to the West, and no longer endowed with dangerous tensions. Russia was well on the way towards entering the family of nations enjoying the advantages of modern civilization.

Timasheff, *The Great Retreat*, 1946

Source 20

Social strife was continual. National resentments among the non-Russians were on the rise. Political opposition remained strident and determined. The monarchy was ever more regarded as an oppressive, obsolescent institution which failed to correspond to the country's needs.

Robert Service, *A History of Twentieth Century Russia*, 1997

■ **Activity**

There is a huge gulf between the two historians in Sources 19 and 20. Go back through this chapter and collect evidence under the following headings. Look for evidence both for and against each of these propositions:

1 Were the peasants contented in 1914?

2 Were the workers contented?

3 Was the middle class contented?

4 Was there less political opposition, violent and non-violent?

5 Did economic growth have a strong basis?

6 Had the Tsar built a new stable political basis for the regime?

Which of the views expressed by the two historians above do you think best describes Russia at the outbreak of the First World War?

What do you think were the chances of Russia making a peaceful transition to a west European style democracy?

Prepare notes on each of the propositions and then produce a summary of evidence which supports and undermines the two different views expressed in Sources 19 and 20. You should now write a report or essay explaining your own answer to the main question. You will need to incorporate a visual image in your report.

Why did Russian forces perform so badly in the First World War?

The public reaction to the outbreak of war

The war began with a display of patriotic feeling. When the Tsar appeared on the balcony of the Winter Palace soldiers and civilians fell to their knees and sang 'God bless the Tsar'. Would this emotional attachment be strengthened by a victorious war against the Central Powers, Turkey, Germany and Austria-Hungary – a war which Russia was entering in defence of fellow Slavs in Serbia?

The Duma met a week after the declaration of war and gave the government almost a unanimous vote of confidence. Only 22 socialists walked out of the chamber and refused to support the war. Lenin denounced it from abroad:

■ **Think about**

▶ What happened in front of the Winter Palace in 1905?

■ **Think about**

▶ What is Lenin urging Russian soldiers to do in this source?

▶ Why do you think this appeal did not have much success with the soldiers in the Russian, or for that matter any other, army?

> ### Source 21
>
> The slogans of social democracy at this time must be: First, all-embracing propaganda extending to the army and to the theatre of war, propagating socialist revolution, and the necessity of using weapons not against one's own brothers, the hired slaves of other countries, but against the reactionary and bourgeois governments and parties of all nations…a ruthless struggle against the chauvinism and 'patriotism' of the petty bourgeoisie and bourgeoisie of all countries without exception.
>
> **Written by Lenin in September 1914**

Virtually no one in Russia supported Lenin's call. The first years of the war were a barren time for the would-be revolutionary. Patriotism made a stronger claim on workers everywhere than the summons to class war.

Military problems

Russian forces quickly found out that they would not find it easy against the modern German army. Their surprisingly quick advance into the east of the German Empire was brought to an abrupt stop at the battle of Tannenberg and later at the Masurian Lakes where a whole army was surrounded. The Russians lost over 4 million men in the first 12 months of the war.

Timeline

1914
7 August Russian victory at Gumbinnen
18 August Russian defeat at Tannenburg
2 September Russian defeat at Masurian Lakes
1915
February Russian advance into East Prussia repelled
4 March Russia seizes Memel from Germans
7 June Russian defeat at Rawa Ruska
August Tsar Nicholas assumes command of Russian forces
September Russian forces evacuate Vilna
1916
February Russia captures Erzerum from Turkey
June The Brusilov Offensive – halted after early success
1917
4 June Russian offensive against Austrians begins
July Russian forces in retreat
20 August Russians evacuate Riga
5 December Peace talks open with Germany and her allies at Brest-Litovsk

Source 22

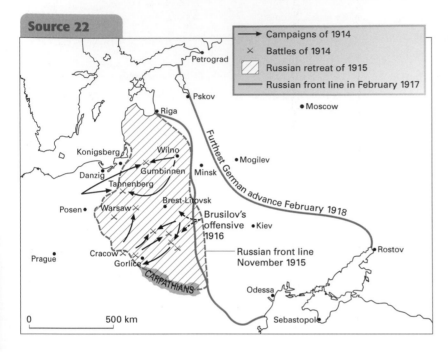

Key:
→ Campaigns of 1914
× Battles of 1914
▨ Russian retreat of 1915
— Russian front line in February 1917

▲ The Eastern Front in the First World War

The heroic efforts of their badly trained and equipped soldiers were no match for German superior tactics and artillery. A British historian who spent much of the war in Russia wrote:

Source 23

The most impressive thing of all is the extraordinary endurance of the men in the trenches. It is a common sight for a man to be five to eight days in the trenches in pouring rain, almost, or sometimes altogether without food, then perhaps to rush on to the enemy, to fall and see half his comrades fall, but the rest still going forward, to lie perhaps through the night, and then to the hospital to lose a limb: and yet…such men are not only patient and affectionate to all who do anything for them, but really cheerful and contented.

Sir B. Pares, *The Fall of the Russian Monarchy*, 1939

They did, however, make some early gains against the Austro-Hungarian army in Galicia. By the end of 1915 the Russian army was in headlong retreat. Difficulties of transport produced other problems, as Sir B. Pares goes on to recount (Source 24).

■ **Further reading**

N. Stone, *The Eastern Front*

Source 24

The normal monthly wastage exceeded in quantity the supplies received from the rear. The greatest lack was still of rifles. Unarmed men had to be sent into the trenches to wait till their comrades were killed or wounded and their rifles became available.

▶ A priest blesses the wounded at a Russian field hospital during the First World War.

■ **Think about**

▶ What does Source 25 suggest about the organisation of the Russian army's medical care?

■ **Think about**

▶ Why did this simple decision threaten 'the dynasty with serious consequences?'

Note

One historian has suggested that the Russians were producing more shells than the Germans in the autumn of 1916. The problem was getting the shells to the guns.

As Russia's difficulties mounted in August 1915 the Tsar made a crucial decision. He decided to take over the command of the armed forces himself. The Duma chairman Rodzianko and his ministers begged the Tsar not assume leadership of the army. The ministers expressed it most bleakly in this appeal to the Tsar:

Source 26

Sire, we make bold once more to tell you that, to the best of our understanding, your adoption of such a decision threatens Russia, yourself, and your dynasty with serious consequences.

In 1916 the Russian Command was under heavy pressure from their allies to launch an attack to relieve the pressure in France. For a short while the Russians won their most spectacular victories of the war, when General Brusilov's campaign against the Austro-Hungarian forces drove the enemy forces back. However, German troops stemmed the retreat and it was not long before Russian forces were on to the defensive again.

Nevertheless, the shortage of shells had been partially overcome and it is now generally accepted that the Russian army was probably in better shape in the summer of 1916 than it had been in 1914. The Chief of Staff General Alexeev enjoyed the full confidence of the army and the government. The revolution in February 1917 was not, therefore, simply a result of military defeat, though it provided the essential backdrop for the coming events.

Why was there a revolution in February 1917?

Political resistance intensifies

The shock of the 1905 revolution, as we saw earlier, had persuaded some liberals, the Octobrists, to give support to the regime. However, as Russian defeats mounted in 1914 and 1915 this support dwindled. There were scandals about shell shortages and munitions supplies. The Octobrist leader Guchkov had set up the Central War Industries Committee in 1915 to co-ordinate war production. Two other organizations were also set up after the outbreak of war, the All-Russian Union of Towns and the All-Russian Union of *Zemstva*. They involved themselves in relief for the wounded and in supplies for the soldiers. The leaders of all three organizations became increasingly vocal in their criticism as they encountered time and time again gross incompetence from administrators and stubborn inflexibility from the government.

In 1915 moderates in the Duma joined together to form 'The Progressive Bloc', comprising about two-thirds of Duma members. They agreed a programme, were supported by the Union of Towns, the Union of *Zemstva* and the War Industries Committee and even won the support of a majority in the Council of Ministers. Here was a real chance of a government of national unity, as was formed in Britain in 1917.

Astonishingly the Tsar's response to these developments was to suspend the Duma in August 1915. Since many conservatives as well as those in the centre and on the left of politics had supported the Progressive Bloc, by this one decision Nicholas managed to alienate responsible people right across the political spectrum. Had the war gone well, perhaps the Tsar would have been able to maintain his position. At the Duma opening on 1 November 1916, Miliukov attacked the government:

Note

The Progressive Bloc originally comprised the Mensheviks, the Social Revolutionaries, many Kadets and Progressive Nationalists.

■ Think about

▶ How was the situation facing the Tsar similar to that of 1905?

▶ Had Nicholas learned any lessons from what happened then?

Source 27

As before, we are striving for complete victory; as before, we are prepared to make all the necessary sacrifices; and as before, we are anxious to preserve our national unity. But I say this candidly: there is a difference in this situation. We have lost faith in the ability of this government to achieve victory (Voices: 'That's true')…Today we see…that with this government we cannot legislate, any more than we can with this government lead Russia to victory…We are telling this government, as the declaration of the Bloc stated: We shall fight you; we shall fight with all the legitimate means until you go…When the Duma insists that the rear must be organized for a successful struggle, while the government persists in claiming that organizing the country means organizing a revolution and deliberately prefers chaos and disorganization, then what is this: stupidity or treason?

By the end of 1916 the opposition was gathering in an ominous way for the government. As in 1905 when political discontent merged with anger at military defeat and economic and social grievances, there developed a critical situation.

Facts and Figures

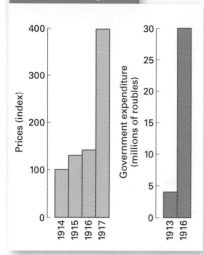

Economic discontent

The living standards of the population suffered a rapid decline after the outbreak of fighting in 1914.

- **Inflation**

  Rising prices destroyed the buying power of wages. To meet the heavy costs of war the Tsar's government, as in almost every other combatant state, resorted to printing more paper money. Wages also increased but at only half the pace.

- **Food shortages**

  Russia enjoyed good harvests in 1914, 1915 and 1916. Grain stocks were high in the autumn of 1916, but they were not getting through to the cities and towns. As prices for other goods escalated and they were in ever shorter supply, there was little incentive for peasants to sell their produce. Instead they began to hoard it or feed it to their animals. The second reason was a serious breakdown in rail communications. The army commandeered a large number of the trains and wagons. On top of that the rail network was in poor condition, much of it was only single track and the advancing enemy forces had captured some key main lines.

- **Fuel shortages**

  There were in addition, in the capital in particular, shortages of coal and other fuels. Not only did this affect people in their homes, but also factories, which in February 1917 were forced to close or operate on short time. The winter of 1916–1917 was especially harsh, freezing railway lines further interfering with the distribution of food and fuel to the armed forces and the urban population. Bakeries in Petrograd in February 1917 were closed, because they had no fuel to power their ovens

Nicholas and Alexandra

The strongest influence on Nicholas was certainly his wife, Alexandra. A convert to the Orthodox faith, she believed totally in the Tsar's divine mission to rule as autocrat. While he was away at the front, Nicholas, who was thought by everyone to be weak-willed, became more and more dependent on his wife, who had been left in control of the government in his absence. She wrote often, but in a vein that did nothing to encourage compromise with those of different views. Source 28 gives examples of some of her comments to Nicholas during the political crisis in August 1915.

Alexandra had become very unpopular. She had chosen to live in a palace outside the capital at Tsarskoye Selo and was not often seen in public. The fact that she was of German birth also did not endear her to her Russian subjects. There were serious anti-German riots in Moscow in 1915. 'Down with the German Woman' was chanted in the streets. She was blamed for bringing about Russian defeats.

Worse still amidst the growing political uncertainty, the court was also caught up in scandalous rumours surrounding the mysterious figure of Grigorii Rasputin. According to these rumours the Tsarina, now in charge of the government, was being manipulated by this bearded ex-peasant and reputed holy man from Siberia. Others said that she and Rasputin, and other ladies, took part in orgies at court.

Source 28

Russia, thank God, is not a constitutional country, tho' those creatures try to play a part & meddle in affairs they dare not. Do not allow them to press upon you – it's fright if one gives in & their heads go up.

Our souls are fighting for the right against evil. It is all much deeper than appears to the eye – we, who have been taught to look at all from another side, see what the struggle here really is & means – you showing your mastery, proving yourself the *Autocrat* without whom Russia cannot exist.

Note

The Germanic-sounding St Petersburg was renamed Petrograd in 1914, in a wave of anti-German hysteria.

Gregorii Rasputin

■ Biography

Rasputin

1869 – Born in Pokrovskoe, a village in western Siberia.

Family – father had worked for the imperial mail.

In his teens he spent some time in an Orthodox monastery.

c. 1890 – Married a peasant girl. She bore him 4 children, of whom one died young.

1903 – Arrived in St Petersburg.
Introduced to St Petersburg society by a leading Orthodox priest. Quickly established a reputation for his holiness but also for his sexual appetite.

1905 – Introduced to the Tsar and Tsarina, who began to rely on him to treat their sick son.

1912 – Publicly denounced for his bad influence on the royal family.
Reputed to have treated Aleksei by telegram successfully.

1915 – Exerted strong influence over the Tsarina while Nicholas was at the front.

1916 – Murdered by a group of conservative noblemen, including some members of the royal family. Buried on the Tsar's estate.

Source 29

▲ Rasputin surrounded by society ladies.

Source 30

'We have made the acquaintance of a man of God, named Grigorii from the government of Tobolsk.'

The Tsar's diary, 1 November 1905

Source 31

My dear and true friend,
When will you come? God loves you so. And you say God is so good and kind that he will do anything you ask. So visit us soon, it is dull without you. Mother is ill without you…
I kiss your hand my dear friend I kiss your holy hand.
God bless you
Tatyana

A letter to Rasputin from Tatyana, second daughter of the Tsar, then a young teenager

Source 32

The salons vied fiercely with one another to have Rasputin. The unbalanced ladies of Petersburg society could talk and think of nothing else. They taught him how to dress, to groom himself, to wash, and much more besides.

From *The Last Years of the Court*
by General Spiridovitch, written in exile
and published in Paris in 1928

Tsarevitch Aleksei

After having four girls, in 1904 Alexandra was safely delivered of a son, Aleksei. The Tsar's daughters, under Russian law, could not inherit the throne. The Tsar was overjoyed; 'an unforgettable great day for us', he wrote in his diary.

However, it was quickly clear that Aleksei was a haemophiliac, a condition which was untreatable at the time. Alexandra blamed herself as the transmitter of the condition for her son's problems. She found consolation in the Orthodox Church and her faith in the guiding hand of God.

She became tremendously protective of her son, who doctors did not expect to live till middle age. The imperial doctors could give no respite when he became ill.

Source 33

◀ A cartoon commenting on Rasputin's influence over the Tsar and Tsarina.

Source 37

The poor child lay in pain, dark patches under his eyes and his little body all distorted and the leg terribly swollen. The doctors were just useless…[Rasputin] reached the palace about midnight…[The next morning] the little boy was not just alive – but well. He was sitting up in bed, the fever gone…not a sign of swelling in the leg – later I learned … that Rasputin had not even touched the boy but merely stood at the foot of the bed and prayed.

The Grand Duchess Olga gives an example of Rasputin's healing powers

Source 34

We are faced with the strangest of human triangles…Rasputin, the empress and the emperor; set in ascending order of authority and a descending order of influence.

Sir B. Pares, *The Fall of the Russian Monarchy*, 1939. Pares lived in Russia during the First World War

Source 35

I kiss your hands and lay my head upon your blessed shoulders. I feel so joyful then. Then all I want is to sleep, sleep for ever on your shoulder, in your embrace.

From a letter from the Tsarina to Rasputin, which was published in 1912 in St Petersburg

Source 36

I stand up for yr. cause, Baby's and Russia's…all my trust lies in our Friend [Rasputin], who only thinks of you, Baby and Russia. And guided by him we shall get through this heavy time, but a Man of God is near to guide yr. boat safely through the reefs.

Telegram to the Tsar at army HQ from Alexandra in 1916

Source 38

And look, Rasputin would come in, walk up to the patient, look at him and spit. The bleeding would stop in no time…How could the empress not trust Rasputin after that?

Professor Federov, the Tsar's personal surgeon

Changes in the government 1915–1916

4 Prime Ministers
3 Foreign Secretaries
3 Ministers of Defence
6 Interior Ministers
'He owed his appointment to the fact that he was a friend of Rasputin' – a comment by the British Ambassador on one ministerial appointment.

■ Activity

1 What impression does Source 33 give of Rasputin and the royal family?

2 What evidence can you find to support this view in the other sources?

3 What would be the political effect of the publication of Source 35?

4 In December 1916 Rasputin, after some difficulty, was murdered in the Yusupov Palace in Petrograd. Why did members of noble families want to kill Rasputin?

5 The murder did not improve the government's standing. What do you think were the reasons for this?

Why was the Romanov dynasty overthrown?

When historians look back on events it is easy to think that they were in some way inevitable. In fact what happened in the capital took everyone by surprise.

There had been a series of strikes, but these had been contained. On 23 February the situation in the capital suddenly deteriorated. A march to commemorate International Women's Day was joined by striking metal workers. The next day the strikers went around Petrograd to raise support and huge crowds made their way to the city centre, where they mingled together in an atmosphere of growing excitement listening to emotive speeches. On Saturday 25th even larger crowds gathered, and the strike spread across the city. The police could not stop the crowds converging on the city centre again, but there were worrying signs when some soldiers made common cause with the demonstrators. Alexandra urged Nicholas to be firm and authorize the use of the army to put down the unrest.

Nicholas was 650 km away at his military HQ at Mogilev. He followed his wife's advice and ordered the new military chief of Petrograd, General Khabalov to restore order immediately. Soldiers were stationed throughout the city centre and when the crowds arrived on the 26th they met armed resistance. Dozens of demonstrators were killed by troops dispersing them. The President of the Duma, Rodzianko, realized the situation had become critical and telegraphed the Tsar:

Source 39

Your most faithful servant reports to Your Majesty that popular risings, having begun in Petrograd, are taking on uncontrollable and threatening dimensions. Their cause is a shortage of baked bread…But the main reason is the absolute distrust of the authorities, who are not competent to lead the country out of its difficult situation…Your Majesty, save Russia; she is threatened with humiliation and disgrace…Your Majesty, urgently summon a person in whom the whole country can have faith and entrust him with the formation of a government that all the people can trust.

The Tsar's response to this message was the comment in Source 40.

He ordered the Duma to dissolve and resolved to return to the capital himself. The Duma did dissolve itself, but left a Temporary Committee behind to monitor developments. Nicholas telegraphed to his wife on 27 February 1917:

Source 41

After the news of yesterday from town – I saw many faces here with frightened expressions. Luckily Alexeev is calm, but finds a very energetic man must be named to make the ministers work for the food question, coal, railways etc. That is right of course.

   The disorders among the troops come from the companies of the convalescents…according to news I got. I wonder what Paul [Grand Duke and commander of the Life Guards] is doing? He ought to keep them in hand.

   God bless you my beloved Sunny! I cover your sweet face with kisses, also the children…   Ever your own Nicky

Timeline

1917

9 Jan 150,000 workers in demonstration to commemorate Bloody Sunday.

18 Feb Strike begins at Putilov Works.

19 Feb Bread rationing announced by the government.

23 Feb International Women's Day. Demonstrations, joined by Putilov strikers, who demand bread.

25 Feb General strike spreads through Petrograd. Troops fire on crowds.

26 Feb Duma refuses to disband when ordered by the Tsar. Troops join the crowds.

27 Feb Petrograd Soviet set up. Provisional Duma Committee set up.

1 Mar Soviet Order No 1, claimed authority over all Russian troops.

2 Mar Provisional Government set up. Nicholas II abdicates.

Source 40

More rubbish from that fat pig! (Rodzianko boasted he was the fattest man in Russia!)

■ Think about

Look carefully at Sources 39, 40, and 41.

▶ What did the Tsar believe was the problem?

▶ How did he think the situation could be resolved?

▶ Why do you think he thought he understood what was happening better than Rodzianko, who was actually in Petrograd?

Note

'Sunny' was Nicholas' pet name for his wife.

On 27 February, what before had been a demonstration turned quickly into a revolution the goal of which was the overthrow of the government. Regiments involved in the shootings of the previous day now supported the demonstrators. It is estimated that half of the Petrograd garrison of 150,000 troops actively supported the revolution. Armed crowds broke into the prisons, the barracks, and the government arsenals and burned down police stations. The Winter Palace was seized and many government buildings.

Source 42

▲ The march to commemorate International Women's Day on 23 February 1917.

■ **Think about**

▶ What image is presented in Source 42 of the situation in the capital in February 1917?

Cross reference

For more on Kerensky see the next chapter.

For the 1905 Soviet refer to p.61.

Who was behind the revolution? It seems to have been genuinely spontaneous, a movement which quickly developed a life of its own. Witnesses recorded that the streets were full of people from every possible social background. Certainly it was not the result of a revolutionary plan hatched by one of the socialist parties. Lenin, in Switzerland at the time, was as taken by surprise as everyone else. Only a month before he had said: 'We older ones will not live to see the revolution in our lifetime'.

Out of the confused situation leaders emerged. Some were those released from the Peter and Paul Fortress, the Tsar's most famous political prison; others won respect, like Alexander Kerensky, because of their past defence of popular causes. As the crowds milled round the Tauride Palace, where they had gone to greet the expected new Duma government, groups of socialists set up a Provisional Executive Committee of the Soviet of Workers' Deputies as they had done in 1905. It called for immediate elections to a new Soviet which was to meet in the Tauride Palace that same evening. The 600 members who attended the following day elected the Menshevik Chkeidze as its Chairman.

Elsewhere in the Tauride Palace the Duma leaders of the 'Temporary Committee', looked on with alarm. Figes sums up the situation:

Source 43

By 28 February, then, two rival centres of power had emerged: in the right wing of the Tauride Palace there was the temporary Committee of the Duma, which had the closest thing to formal power but no authority in the streets; while in the left wing there was the Soviet, which had the closest thing to power on the streets but no formal authority.

Figes, *A People's Tragedy*, 1996

The Duma leaders were reluctant to declare themselves the new government without the approval of the Tsar. However, on 1 March the Temporary Committee met with the Soviet leaders and agreed a programme. With great reluctance the Duma leaders took up the burdens of government. The following day the new Cabinet was announced to the world.

And what of the Tsar? Nicholas never made it to the capital. Disloyal troops blocked the line. From his train on 1 March he sanctioned the formation of a Duma government and then, when his own generals and members of the new government urged it, on 2 March he signed his abdication in favour of his brother Grand Duke Michael. He rejected his son's accession to the throne because of his haemophilia. When the Grand Duke rejected the throne, the 300 years of Romanov rule had come to an end.

■ Activity

Why did Nicholas abdicate?

1 Look carefully at the timeline on page 84. What were the key moments, from January 1917 onwards, which brought about the fall of the Romanov dynasty?

2 Nicholas was never short of advice. Historians going through the archives have been impressed by the excellent quality of much of the advice Nicholas and other Tsars received. This did not only come from his bureaucrats and ministers.

Source 44

'Your majesty, if I may be permitted to say so, has but one course open to you – namely, to break down the barrier that separates you from your people and to regain their confidence.' Drawing himself up and looking hard at me, the Emperor asked: 'Do you mean that *I* am to regain the confidence of my people or that they are to regain *my* confidence?' 'Both, sir,' I replied, 'for without such mutual confidence Russia will never win the war.'

Report by the British Ambassador, Sir George Buchanan, of his audience with the Tsar, 30 December 1916

Why did the Tsar not accept this advice?

What do the events of February tell you about the Tsar's character and his beliefs?

3 Many individuals played a part in the crisis. Make out a table like the one below and add how each did, or did not, contribute to Nicholas' abdication.

Individual or group	Explanation of their role in the crisis
Tsar Nicholas	
Tsarina Alexandra	
Lenin and the Bolsheviks	
Ordinary soldiers	
Army leaders	
The Russian peasantry	
Workers	
The Duma leaders	

4 Who do you think played the key role in the crisis? If his/her/their decisions/actions had been different, how might events have developed differently?

When in February do you think the Tsar's abdication became the only possible solution to the political crisis? Why?

5 In 1905 the regime had survived a similar crisis. Why did it not survive this one?

Make out a table like the one below and fill it in with details from both crises. How was the situation in 1917 different from that in 1905?

	1905	1917
The war		
The armed forces' attitude to the regime		
The attitude of the liberal opposition		
The prestige of the royal family		
Social and economic discontent		
The Tsar's actions		

Document exercise: The February Revolution

Source A

This is a hooligan movement, young people run about and shout that there is no bread, simply to create excitement, along with workers who prevent others from working. If the weather were cold they would all probably stay at home. But all this will pass and become calm, if only the Duma will behave itself.

Letter from the Tsarina to Nicholas II, 26 February 1917

Source B

▲ The distribution of revolutionary newspapers to a crowd in February 1917.

Source C

The industrial proletariat is on the verge of despair and it believes that the smallest outbreak due to any pretext will lead to uncontrollable riots and tens of thousands of victims.

Report by the Okhrana (Tsarist secret police), October 1916

■ Examination-style questions

1 Comprehension in context

To whom does the Tsarina in Source A attribute responsibility for the political situation?

2 Comparing the sources

Does Source B support the Tsarina's view of the situation? Explain your answer by careful reference to both sources.

3 Assessing the sources

What value would a historian studying the situation in Russia put on Source C?

4 Making judgements

Do these sources give a sufficient explanation of the political situation in February 1917?

Conclusion

■ Further reading

D. Lieven, *Nicholas II: Emperor of all the Russias*, 1993

O. Figes, *A People's Tragedy: The Russian Revolution 1891-1924*, 1996.

R. Pipes, *The Russian Revolution 1899-1919*, 1990

R. Kowalski, *The Russian Revolution 1917-21*, 1997

S. Smith, *Red Petrograd: Revolution in the factories*, 1985

Ed D. Kaiser, *The Workers Revolution in 1917*, 1988

The dynasty which had ruled Russia for over 300 years collapsed in a few days. Although there was a mounting number of strikes before the outbreak of war in 1914, none the less there was something like stability at the centre of politics.

The war changed all this. It drove all the potential opposition groups together. In October 1905 some of the liberals had accepted the Tsar's semi-constitutional Manifesto. In 1917 the liberals en masse deserted the Crown – in fact they had deserted it in 1915 when the Progressive Bloc had presented their programme and Nicholas had rejected it. Even former monarchists had lost all faith in the Tsar's capacity to deal with the deteriorating military and economic situation.

It was also the war that created the severe food and fuel shortages in the capital and brought hundreds of thousands onto the streets. Military discipline had shown some signs of breaking down even before the February crisis. As the Russian army had suffered 50 per cent losses by the end of 1916, this is not surprising. When their loyalty was put to the test at the end of February, at least half of the Petrograd soldiers, many of them fresh recruits, made a conscious decision for political change.

Note

Figes suggests that Nicholas was much happier once the heavy responsibilities of state were taken from his shoulders.

In the last analysis, the responsibility must fall on the shoulders of the last Romanov. As we have seen, Nicholas had been urged from many quarters to make a compromise with the Duma opposition long before 1917. Even at the height of the crisis in February 1917, if the Tsar had appointed a government acceptable to moderate opinion, the regime would probably have been saved – in the short term at least. His firm belief, supported by his wife, that the future of Russia and the Romanov autocracy were one and the same made compromise impossible. Perhaps a wiser and more flexible man would have seen that even his most cherished principles had to be abandoned or amended in the circumstances. For Nicholas II, 300 years of history and tradition as well as his own upbringing and personality prevented him from making that imaginative leap.

Chapter 5

1917 – A year of promise and turmoil

My memories of the first few weeks of the Provisional Government are among the happiest of my political career. There were eleven of us in the government, of whom ten belonged to the liberal and moderate parties…From the very first Cabinet meeting we talked with such complete and immediate agreement among ourselves about what had to be done. We all shared a feeling of duty which transcended our loyalty to any party…In the first month of the Revolution each of us was guided, rightly or wrongly, by only one consideration: the higher interests of the nation.

Alexander Kerensky, *Memoirs*

◀ A Russian poster, probably from October 1917. The banner above the field-gun reads 'All Power to the Soviets'. The Winter Palace is in the background.

Introduction

■ Think about

▶ What impression does Source 1 seek to give of the October Revolution?

Although it had ruled Russia for over 300 years, the Romanov dynasty collapsed in just a few days. Its passing was mourned by few of its former subjects. There was no serious attempt to reinstate Nicholas II, not even by Nicholas himself! The whole country seemed to breathe a sigh of relief, and looked forward to the better future they believed Russia's new government would bring. There was, in the words of historian Christopher Read, 'a nationwide honeymoon. For the only time in its history, the Russian Empire was unitcd'. Kerensky, the sole socialist member of the new Provisional Government, wrote of the new atmosphere of hope in Russia in his memoirs (Source 2).

Despite the good intentions of Kerensky and his colleagues, it proved difficult to create a new order which satisfied all Russians. The new Provisional Government had to face those same problems, exacerbated by Russia's involvement in the war, that the Tsarist government had failed to solve, as well as to meet the eager expectations of 160 million people. In fact the Provisional Government proved quite unable to deliver what was expected. It was increasingly seen as a product of the old regime and as unrepresentative of the Russian people. Perhaps it would have been impossible for any government to succeed in the circumstances it inherited. The government lasted only a few weeks before being replaced by another, and then another. The 'honeymoon' was soon over and its authority gradually slipped away. As early as 9 March, only one week after the Provisional Government's formation, the Minister of War wrote to one of his generals:

Source 3

The Provisional Government has no real power of any kind and its orders are carried out only to the extent that this is permitted by the Soviet of Workers' and Soldiers' Deputies…The Provisional Government exists only as long as it is permitted to do so by the Soviet.

Russia was then plunged into anarchy and lawlessness. National groups demanded more self-government, workers took over their factories, peasants seized the landed estates, soldiers disobeyed their officers, and thc crime rate shot up in the cities. In this period of confusion and turmoil the Bolsheviks, a tiny group of no more than 23,000 in February, grew stronger and stronger until in October they were able to seize power in Petrograd and create the first Marxist government in world history.

Key questions

● Who ruled Russia after the abdication?
● How did the government try to address Russia's problems?
● Why did the government lose support?
● Why were the Bolsheviks able to seize power in October 1917?

What kind of government ruled Russia in March 1917?

On 2 March the new Provisional Government was announced to the people of Russia. It had been agreed by the Provisional Committee of the Duma and members of the Petrograd Soviet of Workers' and Soldiers' Deputies. All the ministers had been elected to the Duma in 1912 and had been involved in earlier attempts to persuade the Tsar to introduce reforms. Most of them were members of the Provisional Committee set up when the Tsar dissolved the Duma on 26 February.

The members of the Cabinet were:

P.N. Miliukov
Foreign Minister
Born in 1859, he was a wealthy history professor with a long tradition of liberal opposition to the Tsar. He had founded the Kadets in 1905 and had led the criticisms of Rasputin and the Tsar's governments during the war.

A.I. Guchkov
Minister for War and Navy
A rich Moscow industrialist, freemason* and monarchist. He had founded the Octobrists in 1905. He chaired the War Industry Committee to improve the war effort in 1915. He tried to replace Tsar Nicholas with Grand Duke Michael, and was threatened with execution by workers in Petrograd.

Prince G.E. Lvov
Prime Minister and Interior Minister
Born in 1861, he was a wealthy landowner with an estate near Moscow. The Lvovs were one of the oldest Russian noble families. He had worked for over 20 years in the *zemstvo* movement, becoming chairman of the Union of *Zemstva*. He was deeply religious, a freemason* and a leader of the Progressive Bloc from 1915 onwards. He was known for his concern for the peasants.

V.N. Lvov
Procurator of the Holy Synod
A nobleman and landowner, he was a member of the Octobrist Party. He had very conservative views and was suspicious of giving more power to 'the people'.

N.V. Nekrasov
Transport Minister
A little-known freemason,* he was a member of the Kadet Party. He had been Vice-President of the Duma and a member of the Provisional Committee of the Duma. He had a reputation for being concerned about the industrial workers.

A.A. Maniulov
Education Minister
A little-known member of the Kadet Party. He was a professor and a freemason.*

Source 4

▲ The Provisional Government with the Winter Palace in the background.

A.I. Shingarev
Agriculture Minister
A wealthy but little known provincial doctor and member of the Kadet Party. He was a freemason.*

A.I. Konavolov
Trade and Industry Minister
A clothing millionaire, he had founded the Progressive Party in 1912. He was a Vice-President of the Central War Industry Committee. He was a freemason.*

A.F. Kerensky
Justice Minister
His father was Lenin's headmaster. He studied law and joined the Socialist Revolutionaries in 1905. A brilliant orator he won a reputation for defending political cases in court. He was a freemason.*

M.I. Tereschenko
Minister of Finance
Was a little-known wealthy Ukrainian businessman and a freemason.* He was only 29 in 1917 but had been a Vice-Chairman of the Central War Committee. He was an expert on ballet.

Note
*Freemasons were members of a society which met for discussion and for self-help.

The programme of the Provisional Government

The Provisional Government wanted to create a government of national unity. To try to rally the people behind them, they immediately put forward these eight principles which they said would guide their work.

1   Immediate amnesty for all political prisoners, including terrorists.
2   Immediate freedom of speech and assembly and the right to strike.
3   Immediate abolition of religious, national or social privileges.
4   Immediate preparations for a Constituent Assembly for which everyone could vote.
5   Abolition of all police units and their replacement by a local militia with elected officers.
6   Elections for all local councils and *zemstva* for which everyone could vote.
7   All military units that had joined the Revolution were to keep their weapons and would not be sent to the front.
8   Maintenance of military discipline.

The new government quickly began to tackle some of these issues. Within a few days all police departments had been abolished and all provincial governors and their deputies had been sacked. Political prisoners in hundreds were released and flocked to Petrograd and Moscow. Trotsky was given a free passage from America! Political meetings happened everywhere. Newspapers and pamphlets flooded the cities. Wartime Russia became 'freer than any other country even at peace' (R. Service). A committee of legal experts was appointed to produce a plan for elections to the Constituent Assembly.

> **Note**
>
> ## The Constituent Assembly
>
> Free elections, in which all adults voted, would choose representatives to this body. This would then decide a new constitution for Russia. It would be the first body to truly represent the Russian people. Opponents of the Tsar had been calling for it for many years.

■ Activity

In pairs look at the ministers in the Provisional Government on the previous page.

1 From what classes in society did they come?

2 What experience of government did they have?

3 Why had these men become the government of Russia?

Look back at the last chapter or your notes.

4 Draw up a list of all the main difficulties faced by the Tsar's government in 1917.

5 Which of them were most serious? Try to put them in some kind of rank order.

Look carefully at the programme of the new government above. It was, in fact, based on ideas put forward first by the Petrograd Soviet. The Provisional Government accepted them after a few changes had been made.

6 Which of the difficulties confronting the Tsar's government were not mentioned in the new government's statement?

7 Can you suggest some reasons why not?

8 Which actions taken by the new government in the first few days actually made the task of government more difficult?

9 Can you suggest a programme which would have won the government stronger support?

The collapse of central authority in Russia from March to October

In this section we shall learn how the already difficult position of the Provisional Government in March became steadily worse as the year wore on.

The atmosphere in Petrograd

Early in 1914 the Tsarist minister Durnovo had written:

Source 5

In the event of defeat [by Germany]…social revolution cannot be overlooked…It will start with all disasters being attributed to the government…which will result in revolutionary agitation throughout the country.

Precisely this had now happened. The agitation, however, did not stop when the Tsar abdicated. Instead Russia, and Petrograd in particular, became a hotbed of political activity. Two million people joined trade unions, banned by the Tsar, in 1917. A visiting American commented that 'Russia had become a nation of one hundred million orators'.

Source 6

◀ Striking waiters demand an end to demeaning tips!

■ Think about

▶ What impression does Source 6 give of striking workers in Petrograd in the spring of 1917?

The Petrograd Soviet

The strongest threat to the authority of the Provisional Government was the Petrograd Soviet. It was also the closest since the two bodies met in different wings of the same building, the Tauride Palace. The Soviet elected an Executive Committee led by the Menshevik Chkheidze as Chairman with another Menshevik, Skobelev, and the SR, Alexander Kerensky, as Vice-Chairmen. Fearing a counter-attack by Tsarist forces, on 1 March the Soviet immediately passed Soviet Order Number One, which included the following instructions to the soldiers:

1   All military units were to elect committees from their members.
2   All military units were to elect representatives to the Petrograd Soviet.

Quotation

Newspapers

This was a period in which the press played a significant role in political struggles…In Petrograd alone the moderate socialists published no less than 500 different pamphlets with a total run of 27 million.

Kolonitskii,
Critical Companion to the Russian Revolution (ed. E. Acton), 1994

Timeline

March–June

1 Mar Petrograd Soviet Order Number One.

2 Mar Provisional Government set up. Nicholas II abdicates.

12 Mar Leading Bolsheviks Stalin and Kamenev return to Petrograd.

3 Apr Lenin returns to Petrograd.

4 Apr Lenin's *April Theses*

20–21 Apr Demonstrations in Petrograd against the war

4 May Trotsky returns to Russia.

5 May Mensheviks and Bolsheviks begin reunion talks. Mensheviks and SRs join a new government.

3–24 June First All-Russian Congress of Soviets meets in Petrograd, dominated by SRs and Mensheviks.

18 June Russian (Kerensky) offensive begins.

3 The orders of the Petrograd Soviet should take priority over the orders of the Provisional Government.

4 All weapons were to be controlled by the military committees and not to be given to officers.

This order showed the distrust of the Provisional Government felt by many workers and soldiers in the capital from the very start. One worker had shouted at Foreign Minister Miliukov, as he announced the new Provisional Government, 'Who elected you?' In this atmosphere of suspicion began the period of so-called Dual Authority, with the Provisional Government and the Soviet working side by side. As news of the Tsar's fall spread, soviets were elected all over Russia. Many of these later sent representatives to the Petrograd Soviet. The Soviet could now claim to be more representative than the Provisional Government itself.

The return of political exiles, spring 1917

Soon the government's amnesty brought exiled or imprisoned leaders of left-wing parties back to the capital. They were given rapturous public receptions. Most important in terms of later events was the return of Lenin. Their return increased the political temperature in the cities.

The key political issues

The reputation of any government is built on its policies. The Provisional Government faced many problems; the most urgent were its own lack of authority, the peasants' clamour for land, dissatisfaction amongst the urban workers and the war with the Central Powers. On these issues, as we have seen, the government's early declaration had been silent, but they did begin to address them.

1. The Provisional Government's lack of authority

This was a difficult problem to tackle. The government had not been elected, as its members were well aware. The election by all Russians of a Constituent Assembly might have provided Russia with a strong, legitimate government. The government promised elections, but delayed them because there was no accurate electoral register. Most Russians knew that the Provisional Government would be replaced after elections and saw the delay as an attempt by 'the bourgeois ministers' to hang on to power. The biggest challenge to its authority was the existence of the soviets, especially the Petrograd Soviet.

2. The land question

This question, as you have read before, had been central to Russian politics for many years. Now the revolution had at last occurred, the peasants expected their land. The government set up a committee to advise on future policy. This committee recommended that only the expected Constituent Assembly could make policy.

3. Urban discontent

The February Revolution had sprung out of poverty. Inflation shot up in 1917. Wages could not keep pace, despite the activities of unions and factory committees. The grant of an eight-hour day, the government hoped, would appease the workers and restore factory discipline, which had broken down completely during the Revolution.

■ **Think about**

Legitimate, in this context, means ruling by consent.

▶ Why was legitimacy important to the Provisional Government in 1917?

Facts and figures

According to the Russian historian Stepanov, the cost of living in Petrograd rose by over 1400% between 1913 and October 1917.

Real wages fell by between 10% and 60% between January and October 1917.

Unable to collect taxes, the government printed huge amounts of paper money. This made the problem still worse.

4. The war

The Petrograd Soviet in March called for a 'peace without annexations or indemnities'. It agreed a policy of 'revolutionary defensism' – a war of defence to preserve the Revolution's gains but without costly attacks on the enemy. The Provisional Government agreed on 27 March a similar 'Declaration of War Aims'. However, Miliukov, Foreign Minister, also promised the Allies that the government would honour its promises to them to continue the war to 'decisive victory'. There was a storm of protest in Petrograd. Angry demonstrations of armed soldiers and workers fought with supporters of the war on the streets of the capital. The threat of open civil war forced Miliukov and Guchkov, Minister for War, to resign. Prince Lvov set up a new government. Recognizing the importance of the Petrograd Soviet, he invited six Soviet leaders into the government.

The first coalition government, May 1917

Prince Lvov	Prime Minister	Kadet
	Interior Minister	
Tereschenko	Foreign Minister	Kadet
Kerensky*	Minister of War	SR
Chernov*	Agriculture	SR
Tsereteli*	Posts and Telegraphs	Menshevik
Skobelev*	Labour	Menshevik
Shingarev	Finance	Kadet
Nekrasov	Transport	Kadet
Konavolov	Industry	Progressive
Maniulov	Education	Kadet
V. Lvov	Church Minister	Centrist
Peshekhonov*	Minister of Food	Popular Socialist
Pereverzev*	Justice	SR
Godnev	State Controller	Octobrist
Prince Shakhovskoi	Welfare	Kadet

* denotes Soviet leaders

> ■ **Think about**
>
> ▶ What advantage might Prince Lvov have seen in inviting the Soviet leaders into a coalition government?

Tsereteli was given only a minor post because he was in effect 'Minister for the Petrograd Soviet'. It was his job to ensure that the government's policies were explained to the Soviet and to win its support. In fact Prince Lvov consulted with an inner circle of ministers and only Tsereteli of the new ministers was included in this group. The entry of the Mensheviks and SRs into the Cabinet can, with the benefit of hindsight, be seen as a gamble. It gave them a share of responsibility for righting the problems of Russia. If they failed to do so, it would open them to the criticism that they had sold out the workers to the bourgeoisie. In fact the policy of the new government seemed little different from that of the 'bourgeois ministers.'

> ■ **Think about**
>
> ▶ Why were the Bolsheviks especially likely to benefit from any failure of the coalition government?

1. It delayed again national elections to a Constituent Assembly.
2. It failed to address the immediate demands of peasants for land. Even though an SR was Minister of Agriculture, the government continued to delay settling the land problem until a Constituent Assembly had been elected.
3. It tried to limit the activities of the workers' committees, which now controlled some of the factories.
4. It continued an unpopular war (see opposite). It tried unsuccessfully to reintroduce military discipline into the army. Soldiers' and sailors' committees were now active at the front and behind it. The Petrograd garrison was particularly 'independent'.

Lenin summed up its policies:

Source 7

Wait until the Constituent Assembly for land. Wait until the end of the war for the Constituent Assembly. Wait until total victory for the end of the war.

> ■ **Think about**
>
> ▶ What is Lenin suggesting in Source 7 about the Provisional Government?

In June a huge demonstration was organized by the Soviet to demonstrate public support for their new involvement in the government. According to Figes, however, most posters carried the Bolshevik slogan 'All Power to the Soviets'.

The 'Kerensky' Offensive, June 1917

Support for the Provisional Government was now dwindling rapidly. The economy was in ruins; unemployment mounted. Soviets had sprung up throughout Russia, many of which ignored the government. Workers' committees were demanding control of factories. Here is how the socialist writer Gorky, living in Petrograd, described the city in June 1917:

> ■ **Think about**
>
> ▶ Why is Gorky's view of the situation in Petrograd especially valuable to the historian?

Source 8

This is no longer a capital, it is a cesspit. No one works, the streets are filthy…There is a growing idleness and cowardice in the people…Although I am a pacifist, I welcome the coming offensive in the hope that it may at least bring some organization to the country.

> ■ **Think about**
>
> ▶ What does Source 9 reveal about Kerensky and his view of his own importance?

Kerensky believed that only a successful war would stop the complete disintegration of Russia. The Russian armies were inadequately equipped and morale was low. Despite the growing doubts of General Brusilov and desertions before the battle (numbered conservatively at 170,000 by official figures) the offensive against the Austrians began. After initial success, the armies were badly defeated. Russian losses may have been as high as 400,000 men. Some regiments mutinied and deserted. Russia took one more step towards chaos.

Source 9

▶ Kerensky photographed sitting at the Tsar's desk in the Tsar's study in the Winter Palace.

On 3 July Prince Lvov wrote in a letter to his parents:

Source 10

Without doubt the country is heading for general slaughter, famine, the collapse of the front...and the ruin of the urban population...Armies of migrants, then small groups...will roam around the country fighting each other with rifles, and then no more than clubs.

■ Think about

▶ When you read on, you will see how well Prince Lvov understood Russia. Does this make his actions as Prime Minister incomprehensible?

The July Days

On 3 July the Kadet Ministers resigned from the government. Protests against the war and the government were becoming more serious. Mass demonstrations packed the streets of Petrograd, supported by sailors from Kronstadt, the nearby naval base. It is possible that the Bolsheviks planned the whole affair to test the political situation; certainly the demonstrators chanted the Bolshevik slogans, 'Peace, Bread, Land' and 'All Power to the Soviets'. The demonstrators called on the Petrograd Soviet to take power, but the Mensheviks and SRs, who controlled it, refused. The demonstrating troops and sailors were given no clear leadership from Lenin, who probably thought the rising was premature.

Source 11

▼ Troops loyal to the Provisional Government fire on demonstrators in Petrograd in July 1917.

The government was saved when loyal troops arrived on 5 July and cleared the streets. It banned Bolshevik newspapers and ordered the arrest of many of the party's leaders. Although Lenin escaped to Finland, 800 leading Bolsheviks were imprisoned. The government published documents, seized from Bolshevik Party headquarters, showing they were receiving money from Germany. It discredited the Bolshevik leaders as traitors and spies. Apparently the Bolsheviks' challenge for power was over for good.

■ Think about

▶ What impression does Source 11 give of the ease or difficulty of dealing with the demonstrators?

On 8 July Kerensky became Prime Minister. He still had support from the Kadets, and could hope to build a new alliance between the moderate socialists in the Soviet and the government. However, moving into the Tsar's apartments in the Winter Palace did not do much to support his image as 'a man of the people'.

The Kornilov *coup*

Not everyone thought that Kerensky had done enough to suppress the threat from the Left. Many army officers wanted decisive action against mutinous troops and those back home who were urging them to take up arms against the government. At the end of August the new Commander-in-Chief of the Army, General Kornilov, suddenly ordered troops to march on the capital 'to hang the German supporters and spies' and to close down the Soviet. The truth about these events is uncertain. The historian Richard Pipes thinks that 'the available evidence points to a "Kerensky plot" engineered to discredit the General'. The effects of the affair were clear for all to see. To meet the threat Kerensky and the Soviet armed the workers of Petrograd, many of them by now committed Bolsheviks, to protect the capital.

Kornilov's army was unable to advance because the railway workers refused to move his trains, and he quickly gave himself up. Kerensky had been unable to command the support of any troops in the capital. The attempted *coup* showed the workers and soldiers that there was still a real threat to the Revolution from right-wing army officers.

Lenin watching these events from Finland now began to demand that his party plan to seize power

Growing turmoil in Russia

Inside and outside Petrograd the economic and political situation continued to deteriorate.

1   The Provisional Government had still taken no positive steps to satisfy the demands of the peasants for land. Peasants increasingly began to seize land for themselves.
2   The elections to the Constituent Assembly, promised in February, were finally fixed for November.
3   Bolshevik propaganda was also increasingly influential among the armed forces, most of whom now wanted peace. Petrograd was full of deserting soldiers. The command structure of the army had collapsed.
4   The government faced demands for self-government from many of Russia's nationalities. It granted this to the Ukraine in July and also to Finland. This encouraged other areas to expect the same.
5   The earlier rash of strikes, caused by the growing desperation of the industrial workers, ended in the summer. They now looked to political action to secure a better life.

■ Biography

General Kornilov

Kornilov was a career soldier. He had fought in the war against Japan. He had been captured by the Austrians in the First World War, but had escaped. Kerensky made him Commander-in-Chief after the failure of the June Offensive in 1917.

Timeline

July – November

3 July July Days demonstrations begin.
5 July Bolskevik press closed down and Lenin goes into hiding.
8 July Kerensky becomes PM.
21 Aug Germans occupy Riga.
26 Aug Kornilov sends troops against Petrograd.
8 Sept Bolsheviks take control of Petrograd Soviet.
7 Oct Lenin's secret return to Petrograd.
10 Oct Bolsheviks decide to plan 'revolution'.
24 Oct Petrograd Soviet Military Revolutionary Committee begins seizure of power.
26 Oct Provisional Government arrested – Kerensky escapes.
30 Oct Kerensky's forces defeated at Pulkovo.
2 Nov Bolsheviks in control of Moscow.

Why were the Bolsheviks able to seize power in October 1917?

We have seen how the Provisional Government's authority, never strong, slowly ebbed away. With hindsight we know that the Bolsheviks formed a new government in Petrograd in October. In February this was impossible for anyone to foresee. That they did was due not only to their own efforts, but also the failure of other socialist groups to capitalize on their opportunities.

What was the Bolshevik situation in February 1917?

Source 12

We of the older generation may not see the decisive battles of this coming revolution.

So said Lenin in Switzerland in January 1917. His wife was even making plans to begin compiling an encyclopaedia! The swiftness of events in Petrograd in February took Lenin, like everyone else, by surprise. The Bolsheviks had very little involvement in the events themselves. They had probably only 10,000 members in Russia at the start of the year. Of all the parties in Russia in February, the Bolsheviks seemed the least likely to take power. Most of their leaders were scattered across the world. Trotsky, the organizer of the October Revolution, was not even yet a Bolshevik. However, of these 10,000, almost one-third was in Petrograd, and the Bolsheviks did have a clear sense of how they differed from other left-wing parties.

How did the Bolsheviks react to the February Revolution?

You will recall that the Soviet in March showed a willingness to work with Lvov's government. At first Bolsheviks in Petrograd were unsure what their reaction to the new Provisional Government should be. *Pravda* carried an article urging critical support, exactly the same position as that adopted by the Mensheviks. For most Marxists, what had occurred in February was the bourgeois phase of historical development. This would have to establish itself, probably for a long time, before the proletariat and its organizations were strong enough to take over the government. There was a strong call from the Mensheviks for the two branches of the RSDLP to join together after their long hostility. Some Bolsheviks also favoured this approach. At the time it seemed to them most important that the new democracy should be a given chance to survive.

Note

Pravda was the main Bolshevik newspaper in 1917.

Cross reference

The Russian Social Democratic Party (RSDLP). See more on p.55.

■ Think about

▶ Why did the Germans help Lenin and his friends back into Russia?

How did Lenin's return to Russia affect the Bolsheviks?

On 3 April 1917 Lenin returned to Petrograd. He had travelled part of the way in a train provided by the Germans. In Churchill's words 'They transported Lenin in a sealed truck like a plague bacillus into Russia'. He immediately condemned the stand taken by the Bolsheviks in Petrograd. In his *April Theses* he urged the party to reject any co-operation with the Provisional Government, which he labelled as 'parliamentary-bourgeois,' and to campaign for 'All Power to the Soviets'. Lenin claimed that the soviets would be the basis of a new revolutionary government. He also demanded an immediate end to the 'imperialist' war. 'Peace, Bread, Land' was a slogan which he used to highlight the three problems most important to the mass of Russian people.

At once this identified the Bolsheviks as the main left opposition group to the February Revolution. They were heavily criticized by others on the left. Lenin was called variously a 'madman' and a 'has-been'. Nor did everyone in his own party accept this hectoring interference from someone who had just arrived in Russia after more than 11 years in exile. Much would now depend on whether the Provisional Government in partnership with the Petrograd Soviet could live up to the people's expectations.

Document exercise: Lenin's role in April 1917

Source A

1. The country is passing from the first stage of the revolution – which…placed power in the hands of the bourgeoisie – to its second stage, which must place power in the hands of the proletariat and the poorer sections of peasants.
2. No support for the Provisional Government; the utter falsity of all its promises should be made clear.
3. The masses must be made to see that the Soviets of Workers' Deputies are the only possible form of revolutionary government, and that therefore our task is… to present a patient, systematic, and persistent explanation of their errors, an explanation especially adapted to the practical needs of the masses.

Lenin's *April Theses*, 4 April 1917

Source B

In agreement with the Petrograd Soviet of Workers' and Soldiers', the Provisional Government published a programme of governmental work.

The All-Russian Conference of the Soviets of Workers' and Soldiers' Deputies recognizes that this programme includes the basic political demands of Russian democracy…

The Conference appeals to democracy to support the Provisional Government without assuming responsibility for all the work of the government, as long as the government steadfastly confirms and expands the gains of the Revolution and so long as its foreign policy is based on the renunciation of ambitions of territorial expansion.

A Resolution of the All-Russian Conference of Soviets, 5 April 1917

Source C

In yesterday's issue of *Pravda* Comrade Lenin published his 'theses'. They represent the personal opinion of Comrade Lenin and by publishing them Comrade Lenin did something which is the duty of every outstanding public man – to submit to the judgement of the revolutionary democracy of Russia his understanding of current events. As regards Comrade Lenin's general line, it appears to us unacceptable inasmuch as it proceeds from the assumption that the bourgeois-democratic revolution has been completed and it builds on the immediate transformation of this revolution into a Socialist revolution. The tactics that follow from such analysis are greatly at variance with the tactics defended by the representatives of *Pravda* at the All-Russian Congress.

Kamenev, a prominent Bolshevik,
in an article headed 'Our Differences', *Pravda*, 8 April 1917

■ Examination-style questions

1 Comprehension in context
Study Source A. What did Lenin mean by the 'first' and 'second' stages of the revolution?

2 Comparing the sources
Study Sources A and B. How and why do they differ in their attitude to the Provisional Government?

3 Assessing the sources
Study Source C. How useful is this source in helping us to understand the position of Lenin within the Bolshevik Party?

4 Making judgements
Using the sources and your own knowledge, how dominant does Lenin's authority in the Bolshevik Party appear to have been in April 1917?

The First All-Russian Congress of Soviets

Over 1000 delegates from soviets throughout Russia met in Petrograd for the first time in June 1917. The Bolshevik breakthrough had not yet occurred, though the elections showed that their support was growing. The most dramatic moment occurred when Lenin declared to everyone's astonishment that the Bolsheviks were ready to take over the government alone!

The other socialist parties

The entry of the Mensheviks and SRs into government with the 'bourgeois ministers' left a huge vacuum on the left of politics. By opposing the new coalition government, the Bolsheviks now appeared to be the only party to stay loyal to the working class – and their support grew because of it. As inflation soared, workers' demands grew more radical, encouraged and led by Bolsheviks in the factory committees. S. Smith describes the deteriorating situation as follows:

Source 13

By midsummer 1917 the crisis in Russian industry was leading to factory closures and rising unemployment. Between March and July 568 factories…employing some 104,000 workers shut down operations…The number of metalworkers who registered with a union as unemployed rose from 37.4 per day in July to 71.3 in October.

As the economic crisis deepened, so the class conflict accelerated.

S. Smith, *Red Petrograd*, 1983

Smith shows how unions and factory committees were involved in struggles to stop factory closures and redundancies. More and more workers came to recognize that only a Bolshevik government would really change things in their favour. The Bolsheviks released a flood of propaganda aimed at different groups. They printed a special version of *Pravda* especially for the troops at the front, which was widely read. The SRs meanwhile were in no hurry for a second revolution; they knew they would win an outright majority in the Constituent Assembly whenever it was elected. The Mensheviks believed that their Marxist understanding of history showed that any revolutionary attempt too soon would be bound to fail.

Facts and figures

All-Russian Congress of Soviets, June 1917

SRs	285
Mensheviks	248
Bolsheviks	105

Quotation

The effect of strikes

All the time strikes became more organized, more large-scale and more militant. Strikes were a politicizing experience…making hundreds and thousands of workers aware of political matters and making the policies of the Bolshevik Party attractive.

S. Smith, *Red Petrograd*, 1983

The July Days

These were armed demonstrations supported by tens of thousands of ordinary soldiers, sailors and workers but were not backed by the Bolshevik leadership. The government's counter-attack against the Bolsheviks threw Lenin into despair as well as exile. In Finland he began to make arrangements for publishing his work after his expected death. However, even with their leaders absent from the political scene, the Bolsheviks began to attract more support.

Growing Bolshevik support in the soviets

The Petrograd Soviet began to approve Bolshevik proposals for the first time in August. Bolshevik influence in the factories and the armed forces rapidly recovered from the setback of July. In the elections in August to the Petrograd City Duma (Council) the Bolsheviks increased their vote from 19 per cent to 33 per cent. Whole Menshevik branches switched allegiance to the Bolsheviks. A Menshevik newspaper explained this was because the government had 'not given the masses any concrete results' (C. Read *From Tsar to Soviets*, 1996).

The Bolsheviks had also recognized the importance of winning peasant support by adapting their own policy of land nationalization to one of 'Land to the Peasants'. Since most soldiers were peasants, this was essential. The change caused a split amongst the SRs, traditionally the peasants' voice. A breakaway group, known as the Left SRs who had grown increasingly disillusioned with the Provisional Government, now supported the Bolsheviks. The Bolsheviks were no longer isolated.

The Kornilov *Coup*

Kornilov's *coup* played into Bolshevik hands. The Provisional Government's weakness now was evident to everyone. Workers turned to the one party who had refused to co-operate with the failed regime. In the new soviet elections in August and September the Bolsheviks won control of both the Petrograd and Moscow Soviets for the first time. But they were still reluctant to seize power. In October Lenin returned in secret to Petrograd. He argued for an immediate rising. After much debate the Bolshevik Central Committee was won over. The rising was organized by the new Military Revolutionary Committee (MRC) of the Petrograd Soviet, chaired by Trotsky who had joined the Bolsheviks in the summer. Two prominent Bolsheviks, Kamenev and Zinoviev, disapproved of the planned rising and wrote an article in a socialist newspaper warning of its coming. Kerensky at last decided to act. On 24 October he sent troops to close down Bolshevik newspapers and to guard the Neva bridges against workers from the suburbs. This proved to be the catalyst for the *coup*. It provided the MRC with the ideal opportunity to present the *coup* as an act of self-defence against the counter-revolutionary Kerensky.

Facts and figures

Approximate Bolshevik Members in 1917

February	23,600
April	100,000
October	300,000

■ Historical debate

For some historians (e.g. S. Smith) the Bolsheviks were the beneficiaries of growing worker radicalism. For others (e.g. R. Pipes) the Bolsheviks almost tricked workers into supporting them.

Note

After the split among the SRs, the remaining group were variously known as the Right SRs or the Majority SRs.

Note

The Military Revolutionary Committee was set up by the Petrograd Soviet in October. It was supposed to guard against any further right-wing threats to the revolution, like those of Kornilov. In fact it carried out the October Revolution.

Cross reference

The bridges across the river Neva linked the central government and bourgeois districts with the northern industrial districts.

(See map p. 107)

Alexander Kerensky

Does Source 14 or Source 15 present the 'real' Kerensky?

Source 14

The democrat Kerensky was invited into the new government in order to create the impression of popular representation, in order to have a democratic windbag who would make impressive but meaningless proclamations to the people, while the Guchkovs and Lvovs continued with their anti-popular activities.

Lenin writing in 1917

Source 15

The only man in the Cabinet who had any power.

Bruce Lockhart

The most influential member of the government and a strong man...and alone among his colleagues he enjoyed evident support on the part of the masses.

Sir George Buchanan, British Ambassador in Petrograd

Western views of Kerensky before he became Prime Minister

Quotation

Kerensky wrote in his Memoirs later:

'That [The February Revolution] was the historical moment which gave birth to "my Russia", an ideal Russia which took the place of that Russia which had been defiled and polluted by Rasputin and the universally hated monarchy.'

What does this passage tell us about Kerensky's political talents?

■ Think about

Russian joke from autumn 1917.

What is the difference between Russia today and at the end of last year?

Then we had Alexandra Fedorovna (Tsarina), but now we have Alexander Fedorovich (Kerensky).

▶ What does this joke tell us about public perceptions of Kerensky in the autumn of 1917?

Kerensky's image in the press

Press quotes:
'Knight of the revolution'
'First love of the revolution'
'The hero-minister'
'The leader of freedom'
'Leader of the Russian Revolution'

Kerensky's rise to prominence

Kerensky made his name representing defendants in political cases. He was a prominent member of the commission that investigated the massacre at the Lena goldfields in 1912 (see pp. 74–75).

He joined the Social Revolutionaries and became an outspoken critic of the Tsar's regime.

During the February 1917 crisis, Kerensky took the lead in the movement to force the Tsar's abdication. He called on the Duma to reject the Tsar's attempt to dissolve it. He spoke to workers and soldiers in the capital, urging them to force changes in the government. He won their trust and was elected vice-chairman of the Executive Committee of the Petrograd Soviet. He occupied a unique position in Russian politics in March 1917, being a member both of the Provisional Government and the Executive Committee of the Petrograd Soviet.

Source 16

When the Petrograd Soviet was discussing whether to join the Provisional Government on 2 March, Kerensky entered. The historian R. Abraham describes the scene:

Kerensky entered still clad in the worker's jacket and breeches that suggested an affinity with his audience. This time...he vaulted on the Chairman's desk and burst into speech.

'Comrades, do you trust me?'

'We trust you, we trust you,' came a score of voices.

'I am speaking from the depths of my heart, Comrades, I am ready to die, if that will be necessary...In view of the fact, Comrades, that I accepted the duties of Minister of Justice before receiving your mandate, I renounce the title of Vice-Chairman of the Soviet. But for me life without the workers is unthinkable, and I am ready to accept that title for myself if you think it necessary.'

Kerensky as a public speaker. Abraham, *Alexander Kerensky*, 1987

Source 17

▲ A German view of Kerensky in July 1917.

According to Kolonitskii, medals were produced in his honour, depicting Kerensky on one side surrounded by flowers, while the reverse bore the slogan 'the glorious, wise, true and beloved leader of the people – 1917.' And yet a few months later his reputation lay in ribbons. Perhaps later events help us to understand.

1. The June Offensive
Kerensky's attempt to identify himself with Napoleon was dashed by this dramatic defeat. Ordinary soldiers lost faith in their hero.

2. Rising prices
Workers became even more radical. The workers in Petrograd could not eat the fine words of their Prime Minister. Why was his government not delivering the people's expectations?

3. Kerensky's public image took a huge battering
Stories even went round that he dressed in women's clothes! He was certainly using drugs, probably to help him sleep.

4. Land
Still Kerensky's government refused to introduce land reform.

Why was Kerensky seen like this in the autumn of 1917?

Source 18

2. All basic social reforms and all questions relating to the form of government are to be left to the Constituent Assembly.
3. In matters of war and peace, the government is to be guided by the principles of complete union with the Allies.
4. Steps are to be taken to develop a strong army by restoring strict military discipline and putting a definite stop to interference by soldier committees in questions of tactics and strategy.

Kadet ultimatum to Kerensky, 15 July

Source 19

'What was to be done next?' since it was clear that there was no time to be lost. I had the idea to proceed at once to the… Provisional Government and demand…that posters should be printed immediately and that same night be pasted across the city. They were to declare that the Provisional Government:
1 would demand…an armistice
2 would order the transfer of all landed estates into the control of local land committees
3 would hasten the Constituent Assembly.

Kerensky declared that it did not need to take advice from outside and that it would act alone and itself deal with the rising.

Fedor Dan, a leading Menshevik, remembers the final Menshevik and SR attempt to stop the Bolshevik Revolution in October

■ Activity

Interpreting Kerensky
Kerensky has aroused strong passions amongst historians. Here are some possible views of the man:

1 Kerensky allowed himself to be manipulated by the rich and powerful.

2 Kerensky was a man of fine words, but in 1917 words were not enough to unite Russia.

3 Kerensky was a weak man who dithered when faced with problems.

4 Kerensky tried to keep the nation together but began to lose touch with the needs of ordinary people.

5 Kerensky was overwhelmed by problems that would have been too much for anyone in his position.

Try to find from this chapter evidence which supports each of these statements.

Which of the statements do you think best describes Kerensky in 1917?

Compare your views with those of others in your group.

The October Revolution, 23–25 October

It took three days to take over the capital, though no soldiers made a serious attempt to fight for Kerensky. Troops from the Petrograd garrison and Red Guards from the industrial suburbs took over the railway stations, public buildings, and eventually the Winter Palace. When the battleship *Aurora* fired blanks at the Winter Palace, the members of the Provisional Government gave themselves up. Kerensky, however, escaped out of the capital to try to raise an army. There were only five deaths during the three days and normal life continued. Shops were open and the opera performed as usual.

Some historians have shown that the October Revolution in fact was not a highly planned affair. Few Red Guards were involved and the *Aurora* fired blanks because it had no live ammunition on board! Kerensky was able to telephone out of the Winter Palace during the rising and the American John Reed was given a conducted tour of the Winter Palace while the *coup* was under way. Later Trotsky claimed 500 loyal troops could have prevented the Revolution. Kerensky, however, could not find them anywhere in the capital, although most of the garrison in the capital did not take part in the Revolution.

> **Note**
>
> The soviets and factory committees began to organize protection squads from August onwards, known as Red Guards. They were not all Bolsheviks by any means.

> **Source 20**
>
> ◀ A painting of the fall of the Winter Palace, painted several years after the event.

> **■ Think about**
>
> ▶ What impression of the capture of the Winter Palace does Source 20 give?
>
> ▶ How reliable do you think it would be for a historian today?

The Second All-Russian Congress of Soviets, 25 October

The meeting of the Soviet Congress in Petrograd was the reason for the timing of the Revolution. Lenin wanted this organization to give his government the stamp of legitimacy after the rising. If the MRC had not itself seized power, there was every prospect that the Congress would itself have done so. At the first meeting he presented his new entirely Bolshevik government for approval by the delegates, who had been elected by soviets all over Russia. With 399 Bolsheviks out of the 670 members, this approval was not absolutely guaranteed, since some Bolsheviks favoured a coalition government. However, the Menshevik and Right SR delegates, in protest against the seizure of power, walked out, leaving the Bolsheviks in charge of the Soviet Congress and the future of Russia. As they left, Trotsky shouted after them: 'Go where you belong – to the rubbish bin of history!'

> **■ Think about**
>
> ▶ Had the new Bolshevik government a better claim to legitimacy than the Provisional Government?

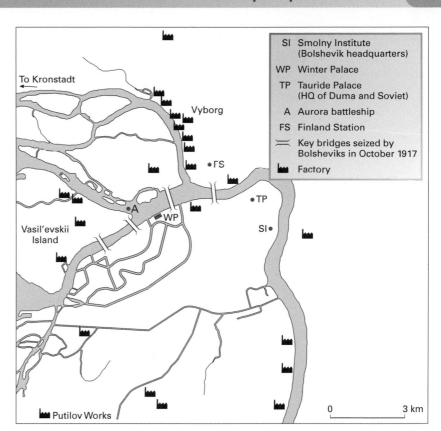

Source 21

▶ Petrograd in 1917

The great events of Russia in 1917 were largely acted out in the capital Petrograd, formerly St Petersburg. It was then by far the largest city in the Russian Empire with a population of almost two-and-a-half million. It highlighted more than anywhere else in the Empire Russia's great social and political divisions. In the central districts were the Tsar's fabulous Winter Palace and the mansions and palaces of the rich and of government ministers. Around this area lay the slums of the industrial districts. Social deprivation was at its worst – appalling housing, inadequate sanitation, dirt roads and the ravages of disease. Most of the new proletariat worked in large factories of over 1000 employees; the giant Putilov Works alone employed more than 30,000. Out of these conditions grew a strong sense of class solidarity – a sense of shared troubles.

■ Think about

▶ On what points do these two interpretations differ on the roles played by the Bolsheviks and the workers in the capital in 1917?

Interpretation A

A small clique of activists somehow smuggled themselves into power in the Russian capital without the consent or assistance of the…masses. By sleight of hand and outside financing a cadre of loyalists managed to take over an empire and frustrate the desires of millions.

Kaiser, *The Workers' Revolution in Russia*, 1987

■ Historical debate

Historians have disagreed about the role played by the Bolsheviks and by the workers themselves in the events of 1917.

Interpretation B

The masses were not enticed into revolt by superior leaders. Their extreme radicalism was not the product of manipulation and brainwashing by the Bolsheviks…The goals for which they strove were their own…The masses were motivated by something deeper than poverty, envy and desire for revenge. They sought to assert their human dignity.

Acton, *Critical Companion to the Russian Revolution*, 1994

Document exercise: Bolsheviks and workers in 1917

Source A

Report by a Bolshevik member at the Putilov Works, Summer 1917

The mass of workers in the factory are in a state of turmoil because of the low rates of pay, so that even we, the members of the works committee, have been seized by the collar, dragged into the shops and told 'Give us money!'

Source B

◀ Workers taking over a factory in December 1917.

Source C

A worker's speech to the Central Executive Committee of the Petrograd Soviet, July 1917

The Soviet had just called for an end to the July Days demonstrations, calling the demonstrators 'counter-revolutionaries'.

Our demand – the general demand of the workers – is all power to the Soviets of Workers' and Soldiers' Deputies. We demand the retirement of the ten capitalist ministers. Our comrades, the socialist ministers, entered into an agreement with the capitalists, but these capitalists are our mortal enemies. The land must pass immediately to the peasants! Control of production must be instituted immediately! We demand a struggle against the starvation that is threatening us!

Source D

Declaration of the Izhora Works, March 1917

All measures of the Provisional Government that destroy the remnants of the autocracy and strengthen the freedom of the people must be fully supported by the democracy. All measures that lead to conciliation with the old regime and that are directed against the people must meet with decisive protest and counteraction.

Source E

Resolution by workers at two metal foundries, April 1917

The government cannot and does not want to represent the wishes of the whole toiling people, and so we demand its immediate abolition and the arrest of its members. We recognize that power must only belong only to the people itself i.e. to the Soviet of Workers' and Soldiers' Deputies, as the sole institution of authority enjoying the confidence of the people.

Source F

Bolshevik Proclamation 5 July 1917

Comrades! The object of this demonstration was to show to all the toiling and exploited masses the strength of our slogans, their weight, their significance and their necessity for the liberation of the peoples from war, hunger and ruin. The object of the demonstration was achieved…Comrades! For the present political crisis, our aim has been accomplished. We have therefore decided to end the demonstration.

Source G

Leon Trotsky speaking to the Second Congress of Soviets 25 October, immediately after the Revolution

What is taking place is not a conspiracy but an insurrection…The masses gathered under our banner, and our insurrection was victorious.

■ Examination-style questions

1 Comprehension in context
What does Source D suggest about the attitudes of Petrograd workers to the Provisional Government in March 1917?

2 Comparing the sources
Does Source E suggest an attitude similar to or different from that in Source D?

3 Assessing the sources
Why would Sources A and B be useful to a historian studying the revolutions of 1917?

4 Making judgements
Using the sources and your own knowledge explain whether Trotsky's version of the October Revolution in Source G is correct?

■ Activity

1 What evidence can you find to support each interpretation on page 107?

2 Which interpretation seems to you to fit the evidence best?

Why did the Provisional Government lose support?

The events of 1917 are complicated. It is important to understand the order of events as well as their significance.

This summary outlines seven of the most important problems facing the Provisional Government.

1. The soviets

The Provisional Government lacked authority. The Duma members had been elected in 1912 under a very unrepresentative electoral system. It was difficult for the new government to claim it represented the nation. The Duma Committee on 1 March asked for the Petrograd Soviet's approval **before** the new government was announced. The Petrograd Soviet was set up before the Provisional Government. It led the opposition to the Tsar and could claim to represent the majority of people in the capital. Soviet Order Number One, published on 2 March, was clearly a challenge to the government's authority. Petrograd was controlled from the first by the Soviet, not by the government. It even appointed a Soviet committee to monitor the government's actions.

Soviets and committees sprang up throughout the country, which showed no respect for the authority of any other body. These soviets, unlike in 1905, included soldiers' deputies and could not be dispersed as easily as in 1905–1906.

2. The war

The problems brought on by the war had been a major factor in the collapse of Tsarism. Russia was committed by treaty to support her allies, but there was little enthusiasm amongst her soldiers to launch new offensives. The Soviet on 14 March appealed for a democratic peace and an end to the fighting. The last Russian offensive in 1916 had ended in defeat.

3. Peasant committees

These took control over their villages. There was no clear pattern at first in what they did, except that they cut rents and increased wages. The peasants expected to benefit from land reform soon. As in the cities the peasants now had the guns of the deserters returning to the villages.

4. The armed forces

Mao Tse-tung, the Communist leader of China in the 1940s said 'Political power comes from the barrel of a gun'. In Russia soldiers and sailors set up committees which undermined or destroyed the authority of the officers. Some unpopular officers, such as Admiral Viren in Kronstadt, were killed. They called for a negotiated peace and demanded fairer treatment and better conditions. In Petrograd many units were strongly influenced by socialist political groups.

5. Unrest in the factories

The workers were mainly concerned with the problems of everyday living. Factory committees demanded an eight-hour day, better working conditions, more food in the shops, and better pay. Socialist agitators were active in mining and industrial centres.

6. Inflation

Prices had increased rapidly since the war began. The government had been forced to print more money to meet the costs of the war. Prices had risen particularly quickly during the winter of 1916–1917. This badly eroded living standards in the cities.

7. The national question

The collapse of the Romanov dynasty encouraged many national groups to present demands for more self-government. The Finns and Ukrainians were the first to do this. Was the future of the Empire at stake?

■ Activity

Draw up a large chart with three columns like the one below.

Use the information in the summary above to add more detail to your first column so that you have a clear understanding of what each problem was.

Nature of problem	Action taken	Results
1. The soviets		
2. The war		
3. Land		
4. The armed forces		
5. Unrest in the factories		
6. Inflation		
7. The national question		

Now use the information in this chapter to help you fill in the second and third columns.

In column two you need to make notes on what the Provisional Government did to address these problems. So, for example, the **action taken** in response to the soviets might be that:

'The Provisional Government tried to establish links with the Petrograd Soviet. It invited a Menshevik Chkeidze to join the government, though he refused at first. Kerensky was for a short time the Chairman of the Soviet as well as a minister.'

In column three make notes on how these actions affected, or failed to affect, the situation in Russia. The **result** of the actions taken in relation to the soviets might be:

'The prestige of the Petrograd Soviet continued to grow.'

■ **Activity**   **KEY SKILLS**

Could 1917 have turned out differently?

The Russian Revolution, whatever historians' attitudes to it may be, is certainly one of the most significant events of the last century and therefore a favourite topic for examiners. It may add to your understanding of this key moment in world history to discuss the following:

1   Did the Provisional Government ever have any real prospect of success?

2   Do you think any of the following would have prevented a Bolshevik government:
   a) Early elections to the Constituent Assembly – in March or July?
   b) An early armistice with the Germans?
   c) A Soviet take-over of the government in May or July?
   d) Lenin's imprisonment in July?

3   If you think any of these things would have prevented the later seizure of power by the Bolsheviks, why weren't they done at the time?

4   What were the greatest assets of the Bolshevik Party in 1917?

5   When do you think a Bolshevik government became probable rather than possible?

Prepare a presentation to your group by carrying out further reading from sources in your library or the Internet. Incorporate a visual image in your report – it does not have to be a picture.

Conclusion

The Provisional Government has been criticized for failing to act decisively to tackle the many difficulties it faced. It did not bring the war to an end and did nothing to meet the expectations of the peasants and workers. Kerensky, a socialist, has in particular been portrayed as a vain and indecisive Prime Minister.

According to some historians, the Bolsheviks played the decisive role in organizing the masses and undermining the Provisional Government. They also emphasize the important influence that Lenin had on events, persuading the Bolsheviks to oppose the Provisional Government in March and to overthrow it in October.

More recently research has emphasized the activity of the workers, soldiers and sailors in Petrograd and Kronstadt in 1917. They set up their own organizations and pressed for reforms. They were not simply manipulated by the Bolsheviks. In fact the Bolsheviks were divided as to how to exploit the critical situation in the capital.

The other socialist parties also had a decisive part to play. Both the SRs and the Mensheviks proved reluctant revolutionaries. Their decision to co-operate with, and finally join, the Provisional Government left a vacuum on the left of politics. It was this vacuum that the Bolsheviks were able to exploit.

Even so, events could easily have turned out differently. Lenin's failure to back the July Days put the party at risk when Kerensky's government for once took firm measures and arrested many of its leaders. If in October the Bolshevik opponents of revolutionary action had won the day, the second Congress of Soviets would probably have set up a very different socialist coalition government. As in February events in the capital decided the whole future of Russia. It was the growing Bolshevik dominance here that enabled them to dismiss Kerensky's creaking Provisional Government.

■ **Further reading**

Most of the books recommended in the previous chapter.
R. Abraham, *Alexander Kerensky: First Love of the Revolution*, 1987
D. Volkogonov, *Lenin Life and legacy*, 1994
R. Service, *Lenin a biography*, 2000

Chapter 6

Why were the Bolsheviks able to stay in power?

Source 1

ПРОЛЕТАРІИ ВСЕХ СТРАН СОЕДИНЯЙТЕСЬ !

ГОД ПРОЛЄТАРСКОЙ ДИКТАТУРЫ.
ОКТЯБРЬ 1917 – ОКТЯБРЬ 1918

Source 2

A revolution is a rising of the people…But what have we here? Nothing but a handful of poor fools deceived by Lenin and Trotsky…Their decrees and their appeals will simply add to the museum of historical curiosities.

From the *Dielo Naroda*, a Petrograd newspaper, Saturday 28 October 1917

Source 3

The insane attempt of the Bolsheviks is on the eve of collapse. The garrison is divided…The Ministries are on strike and bread is getting scarcer. The Bolsheviks are alone.

Soldier Section of the SR Party, Saturday 28 October 1917

◀ A poster celebrating the first year of the 'proletarian dictatorship'. The words at the top read 'Workers of the world unite!'

Think about

To a partly illiterate population symbols were important.

▶ What symbols can you make out in the poster, Source 1?

▶ What do they represent?

▶ What image does it present of Communist Russia?

▶ Why was the image of the Bolsheviks important in those early days?

Introduction

In the last chapter we learned how the Bolsheviks were able to build support after the Tsar's abdication and then to seize control of the capital in October 1917. This chapter is devoted to the problems faced by the new government and its struggle to consolidate its position.

Key questions

● How did Russia become a one party state?
● Why was there a civil war in Russia?
● Why were the Bolsheviks able to win the Civil War?
● How did the Bolsheviks change Russia in the first few years of government?

How did the Bolsheviks establish their dictatorship?

On 26 October the Bolsheviks controlled little except Petrograd. Sources 2 and 3 show how unlikely many thought it was that the Bolsheviks could hang on to power. Even in the capital itself, loyal troops had to be used to overcome strikes by civil servants and bank employees. Fighting immediately broke out in Moscow and, after more than a thousand had died, the city was taken by the Bolsheviks. How would this party of only 300,000 members establish control over the vast expanses of the rest of Russia?

The approval of the Second All-Russian Congress of Soviets was critical for the government's future. The Provisional Government had failed to convince many Russians of its right to rule. Now the Second Congress of Soviets gave a seal of approval to the new regime. The October Revolution was also presented to the Russians as a rising by the Petrograd Soviet, in which many parties were represented. It was not immediately seen as a Bolshevik take-over. This made the new regime more acceptable to all those who had come to look on the Petrograd Soviet as the only organization to represent ordinary Russians. The Bolsheviks liked to present themselves as the leaders of a nation-wide movement, of workers and poor peasants, as Source 1 suggests.

More soviets continued to be set up in towns and cities across the country; many of these, but by no means all, soon had Bolshevik majorities. Most soviets, following the example of Petrograd, organized military revolutionary committees. These quickly seized power in their areas, often coming to blows with representatives of the old order and the bourgeoisie. Upon these fragile new bodies Bolshevik power now depended. In fact, huge parts of the former Russian Empire remained outside Bolshevik control for years, as you will read below.

Sovnarkom – a one party government

The Bolsheviks expected the October Revolution to mark the start of a new age, a complete break with Russia's past and a new beginning for the whole world. They, therefore, abandoned the bourgeois title 'Ministers' for the more proletarian 'People's Commissars'. The Cabinet now became Sovnarkom, the Soviet of People's Commissars. This body in theory was approved by, and authorized to make decrees by, the Congress of Soviets. Lenin appears to have been carried away with optimism in the first few weeks. However, he believed that only the Bolsheviks were capable of building this new world, and he, therefore, refused to invite other socialist parties into his government. Some leading figures in the party protested at this narrow view of politics.

Source 4

It is our view that a socialist government must be formed from all parties in the Soviet...We believe that, apart from this, there is only one other path: the retention of a purely Bolshevik government by means of political terror.

Statement issued by Kamenev, Zinoviev, and others in October 1917

While 'political terror' was abhorrent to many western liberals and some of his own party, for Lenin and many of his Marxist comrades it was not something to be avoided. Instead it was an inevitable stage in building socialism. Marx after all had said that the revolution would be followed by the 'dictatorship of the proletariat'. Lenin believed the Bolsheviks, as the 'vanguard of the proletariat', had a right, indeed an obligation, to establish that dictatorship. The Russian Revolution had to succeed to inspire the wider revolutionary movement he expected to sweep across Europe. Lenin, however, relented a little and in January some Left SRs briefly joined the government, but only after pressure from within his party and the mainly Menshevik Union of Railway Workers.

Note

The Union of Railway Workers was able to cut the fuel and food supplies to the cities if it wished. These were already in very short supply.

The army

Control of the army was vital to the survival of the new government. Lenin knew that the officer class was unlikely to support a workers' government. However, the High Command under General Dukhonin was already weakened by the soldiers' committees, which the troops had elected after the Tsar's abdication. The Bolsheviks' biggest asset was the desperate desire of almost all the troops for a quick end to the war, and this the Bolsheviks had promised to do.

Lenin ordered Dukhonin to sign an immediate armistice with the German forces. When he refused, Ensign (junior officer) Krylenko, a reliable Bolshevik, was sent with a train of loyal troops to the Army HQ at Mogilev to replace him. When his train arrived, Krylenko found Dukhonin's body at the station, murdered by his own troops. An armistice was quickly signed. Many officers now left the front and either returned to civilian life or fled to non-Bolshevik areas of Russia to join opposition groups. Only a small group of 600 Cossacks under General Krasnov were willing to fight for Kerensky in October, and they gave up when Bolshevik agitators arrived.

The Bolsheviks had survived their first emergency.

Cheka

All dictatorships rely to some extent on force or the threat of force. In December 1917 Sovnarkom set up its own secret police, Cheka, the All-Russian Extraordinary Commission for Combating Counter-Revolution and Sabotage, headed by the fanatical Bolshevik Dzerzhinsky. Lenin 'knew' all history was driven by class struggle and therefore he expected opposition to the new government from its class enemies, the bourgeoisie. These, therefore, must be hunted down. Cheka also arrested opponents on the left, including several hundred anarchists in April 1918, and even more SRs in July after they tried an unsuccessful coup. The growing size of the organization showed its important role in maintaining the Bolsheviks in power. In March 1918 Cheka had 120 employees; by 1921 this had risen to 143,000 (even 250,000 according to other estimates). They were not restricted by the law, executing supposed enemies without trial. In 1918 alone it has been estimated Cheka killed 50,000 people. The first labour camps were set up to contain so-called political prisoners.

Quotation

This is no time for speechmaking. Our revolution is in serious danger...We have no need for justice now. Now we have a battle to the death.

Felix Dzerzhinsky, December 1917

On the altar of this sacred ambition have been shed rivers of blood. Now the People's Commissars have ordered the murder of this democracy.

Maxim Gorky, 1918

■ Think about

▶ What proportion of the votes cast in the elections was for socialist parties?

The death of the Constituent Assembly

In November, elections were held all over Russia to the Constituent Assembly. The long delayed elections had been arranged by the Provisional Government before its overthrow and were the first test of support for the new 'soviet' government. Since most voters were peasants, the Bolsheviks cannot have expected to emerge as the largest party. In fact the results for the larger parties were as follows:

	% of the votes
Socialist Revolutionaries	40.4
Bolsheviks	23.2
Mensheviks	2.9
Other Socialists	15.0
Kadets	4.6
National parties	7.7
Cossacks	2.2

Over 47 million of the 80 million electorate voted. It was the most representative body Russia had ever seen.

The Bolsheviks had criticized the Provisional Government for delaying the elections, but they had now produced a non-Bolshevik Assembly. On its first day, 5 January 1918, the Assembly elected the SR leader, Chernov, as its President and also approved some of Lenin's government's early decrees. (You can read about these below.) The next day, however, Bolshevik sailors prevented it meeting again. There were no popular demonstrations in the Assembly's favour either in Petrograd or anywhere else. Lenin justified the closing of the Assembly with these words:

■ Think about

▶ How true was it that the Soviets were 'the only organization of the all the exploited working classes?'

▶ Was the Constituent Assembly really 'an expression of the old regime?'

Note

A federation is an association of self-governing states which form a larger political unit.

Source 5

The Russian Revolution created the Soviets as the only organization of all the exploited working classes in a position to direct the struggle of those classes for their complete and economic liberation…The Constituent Assembly, elected on the old register, appeared as an expression of the old regime when the authority belonged to the bourgeoisie.

At the end of January the closure of the Constituent Assembly was approved by the Third All-Russian Congress of Soviets, which, of course, had a Bolshevik majority. This body also announced the setting up of The Russian Soviet Federative Socialist Republic (RSFSR). In July Lenin announced a new constitution for the new state.

How did the Bolshevik government try to change Russia?

It would be entirely wrong to think that the new government was completely preoccupied with the struggle to survive. It began a far-reaching programme of reforms. If it had not been able to offer the prospect of a better future to its supporters and millions of ordinary Russians, then it is difficult to see how the government could have survived. Decrees passed during the first few weeks after the October Revolution included:

1   The Decree on Peace
    The first decree passed by the Second All-Russian Congress of Soviets

invited 'all belligerents to open negotiations without delay for a just and democratic peace…a peace without annexations and indemnities.'

2 The Decree on Land
This abolished the landlords' right of property, also confiscating large estates from monasteries, churches and the nobility. Land was to be redistributed by the peasant soviets.

3 The Decree on Nationalities
This allowed the right of self-government to any national group.

4 Housing in the cities was removed from private owners. Committees began to relocate poor families into the houses of the wealthy.

5 Civil marriage and divorce was introduced and made easier.

6 A Commissariat of Public Education took all education out of the hands of the Church.

7 All titles were abolished. Comrade now became the title used by all.

8 An Institute for the Protection of Mothers and Children was formed.

9 Some larger factories were nationalized without compensation.

The Treaty of Brest-Litovsk, March 1918

Lenin had wanted an immediate peace treaty with Germany and her allies. An armistice was signed on 2 December, but the terms the Germans demanded for a permanent peace were so harsh that many in Sovnarkom refused to accept them. Lenin argued that the government had no choice but to sign the treaty whatever the cost, since Russia could not continue to fight. He knew that most Russians expected an end to the war. However, Trotsky, the Commissar for Foreign Affairs, persuaded the Central Committee to adopt his own strategy of 'No peace, no war'. He hoped that dragging out the talks would enable Russian Communist soldiers to mix with members of the German army. This, he expected, would inspire the German army to mutiny and take the revolution back to Berlin.

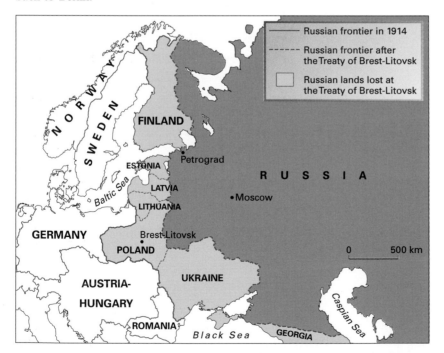

> **Think about**
>
> ▶ Why was the Decree on Peace the first to be passed by the new government?

> **Think about**
>
> ▶ Who stood to lose from these decrees?

> **Quotation**
>
> It is a question of signing the peace terms now or signing the death sentence of the Soviet Government three weeks later.
>
> **Lenin to the Central Committee**
> **23 February**

> **Source 6**
>
> ◀ Russian land lost as a result of the Treaty of Brest-Litovsk

The German army quickly grew tired of this tactic, ended the armistice and in February renewed their armed advance towards Petrograd. When bombs fell on Petrograd, the government was forced to move the capital to Moscow. Only then was Lenin able to persuade the party to accept the German terms – by threatening to resign. The terms were extremely harsh, as the map opposite shows. Russia lost one third of her European land and half of her industrial capacity. The loss of the Ukraine's grain was also a terrible blow.

Many patriotic Russians took up arms to oppose a government they regarded as having betrayed 'Mother Russia'.

The suppression of opposition, October 1917 – July 1918

Decrees of Sovnarkom soon banned all the bourgeois parties and their newspapers. Later this was extended to all other political parties. Although the Right SRs enjoyed the support of many Russian peasants, their support lay in the countryside and was difficult to organize. The Left SRs walked out of the government after the Treaty of Brest-Litovsk and were suppressed after their rising in July. The new government also used Cheka and loyal troops to prevent anti-government demonstrations. The Bolsheviks took control of many local soviets – sometimes by persuasion and sometimes by force. Opposition groups were either disbanded by force or went underground.

By July 1918, a Bolshevik dictatorship was in place.

Why was there a civil war in Russia?

Although the new government had established itself securely in many cities, from the summer of 1918 onwards the Communist government became more and more concerned about its survival as opposition gathered in other areas.

1. The collapse of the Russian Empire

> **Source 7**
>
> By the spring of 1918, the largest state in the world fell apart into innumerable overlapping entities. In a few months Russia reverted politically to the Middle Ages.
>
> **Pipes, Russia under the Bolshevik Regime, 1919–1924, 1994**

As we have seen in the previous chapter, Russia began to split apart before the collapse of the Provisional Government. Lenin had decreed in November 1917 that territories were free to leave Russia. As a result many territories declared themselves independent of the RSFSR. Within Great Russia soviets took over large areas and often pursued their own policies. The Central Siberian Region Soviet in Irkutsk even rejected the peace with Germany. Volga Tatars and Bashkirs later set up their own republics. There were thirty-three sovereign governments in Russia in June 1918. Many patriotic Russians wanted to stop the disintegration of their country and keep 'Russia, one and indivisible' (General Denikin). Some fought the Civil War to achieve self-government; others fought to prevent it.

2. Political opposition

The policies and the actions of the Bolsheviks in their first few months in power (see pp. 115–117) made them many enemies. Because of these policies a number of opposition groups developed. The Union for the Defence of the Motherland and Liberty – founded in January 1918 – organized three armed revolts in July 1918 and the murder of Count Mirbach, the German ambassador.

Facts and figures

Lenin was shot by the SR Dora Kaplan in August 1918. Cheka carried out arrests of many suspects in Petrograd afterwards.

Timeline

Declarations of Independence after the Revolution

Finland	6 Dec 1917
Lithuania	11 Dec 1917
Latvia	12 Jan 1918
Ukraine	22 Jan 1918
Estonia	24 Feb 1918
Transcaucasia	22 Apr 1918

Other opponents flocked to join the groups gathering on the edge of Bolshevik-controlled territory. Fellow socialists, Mensheviks and SRs, joined these when they were banned from the Executive Committee of the Soviets in June 1918.

3. Allied opposition

On 10 November 1917 the *Morning Post* in London called for direct military action against the Bolsheviks. They had given Russia's former allies good reasons to oppose them:

On 23 November Trotsky published the 'secret treaties' signed by the Tsar with the Allies during the war. They showed the Allies had planned to seize territory when Germany and her allies were defeated; they were not fighting for democracy as they pretended.

The Bolsheviks seized all foreign property and cancelled the Tsar's vast debts to the Allies.

In March 1918 the Treaty of Brest-Litovsk finally ended Russia's involvement in the First World War, leaving France and Britain to face renewed attacks on the Western Front. They were willing to send help to any group which offered to reopen the Eastern Front against the Germans. The French sent 7 million francs to Kaledin, leader of the Don Cossacks in January 1918.

4. The breakdown of law and order

The situation in the capital and other cities worried and alarmed many ordinary citizens. The British Ambassador wrote in December 1917:

Source 8

The Russian idea of liberty is to take things easy, to claim double wages, to demonstrate in public, and to waste time in talking and passing resolutions in public meetings.

A Frenchman, De Robien, wrote:

Source 9

Violence or the threat of it seemed everywhere that winter, as mobs of armed soldiers roamed Petrograd's streets.

Many Russians from all backgrounds were horrified by the growing lawlessness in the country and longed for a government strong and determined enough to restore law and order.

5. Food requisitioning

In the summer of 1918 the food situation in the cities was desperate. The Ukraine, Russia's 'bread basket' was lost. Peasants had no incentive to sell their produce because there were few products in the shops for them to buy, and the money they gained quickly lost its value as inflation soared. Lenin's solution was to send requisition squads of workers, soldiers and Cheka into the countryside to look for the grain, which they said *kulaks* (so-called rich peasants) were hoarding. In May 1918 Lenin demanded 'the ruthless and terroristic struggle against the peasant and other bourgeoisie who are holding back surpluses'. He urged villages to set up committees of poor peasants to

Quotation

Sated and self-satisfied, their money-boxes stuffed with huge amounts which they made out of the state during the war, the peasant bourgeoisie is obstinately deaf and indifferent to the cries of the starving workers and peasant poor.

Lenin on kulaks

■ **Activity**

Who provided the opposition?

What reasons would the following groups have to oppose the Bolsheviks?

(a) Members of the Orthodox Church
(b) Landowners and industrialists
(c) Members of other socialist parties
(d) Russian patriots
(e) Peasants
(f) Democrats

seize surplus food from their better off neighbours. These strategies were not very successful and made many more enemies for the Bolsheviks.

The Civil War

> ### Source 10
>
> When an empire as vast and diverse as Russia disintegrates, and its segments fly in all directions, no coherent structure remains; and where no coherence exists, the historian can pretend to provide it only at the risk of distorting reality.
>
> Pipes, Russia under the Bolshevik Regime, 1919–1924, 1994

Fighting broke out as the Bolsheviks seized power on 25 October 1917. Kerensky escaped and marched on Petrograd with General Krasnov and a few Cossacks. At the same time more Cossacks and young trainee officers seized the Kremlin in Moscow. Both these threats were quickly defeated. However, the Bolshevik seizure of power accelerated the move into anarchy already sweeping through the whole country. The fighting which followed continued until 1922 and plunged an already impoverished people into more hardship and misery.

It is impossible to describe the events of the Civil War years in full. For example, the Ukrainian capital, Kiev, changed hands 16 times during the war. Here is a brief outline of the main events which you can use with the map on page 121.

It is possible to divide the Civil War broadly into four distinct phases.

Phase one – early resistance

Kerensky's attempts to rally an army after the seizure of power failed in November 1917.

In the spring the Bolsheviks crushed resistance from Cossack armies in the Urals and the Don.

Later the Bolsheviks also defeated the Volunteer Army, which had gathered under General Kornilov in southern Russia. In April 1918, Lenin optimistically talked of the Civil War being at an end.

Phase two – war with the SRs

In May 1918 the Czech Legion, travelling to Vladivostok for shipping to Europe, rebelled. The 40,000 Czechs were captured members of the Austro-Hungarian army. Before the Treaty of Brest-Litovsk they had fought in the Russian army trying to win independence for Czech lands. After Brest-Litovsk arrangements were made for them to leave Russia and join the allied armies in Europe. When a few were arrested after a brawl, they quickly became a focus for opponents of the regime, especially SRs who had been denied posts in the Soviet government. Komuch, a government based on members of the Constituent Assembly, was set up at Samara. The Czechs travelled along the Trans-Siberian railway towards Moscow. The Red Army sent to confront them collapsed and fled.

In July Nicholas Romanov, formerly Tsar Nicholas II, was executed at Ekaterinburg in the Urals.

In August Trotsky arrived by train at Svyazshk. There, retreating Red officers and one in ten of the soldiers were shot on Trotsky's orders.

In September the Directory government was set up at Ufa, backed by the Czechs, SRs and other anti-Bolshevik groups.

Red forces counter-attacked the Directory's forces and forced the White armies back beyond the Ural mountains. The Directory was ended when Admiral Kolchak made himself military dictator in November 1918.

Phase three – war with the Whites

From December 1918 until the ejection of Baron Wrangel from the Crimea in 1920 the Reds fought the Whites, who represented the traditional conservative forces in Russia: landowners, businessmen and army officers. Their forces gathered all around the Russian heartland.

In March 1919 Kolchak's army began to advance west along the Trans-Siberian Railway. In April Trotsky's forces forced them to retreat. In May 1919 General Denikin with an army of Cossacks and others began to advance on Moscow from the south.

In August the Red Army was forced to abandon Kiev, capital of the Ukraine.

In October Yudenich began to advance towards Petrograd from Estonia, but was defeated outside Petrograd. Also in October Denikin's forces were defeated at Orel and forced to retreat.

In the winter Red armies advanced on all fronts.

In January 1920 Kolchak abdicated.

In February Estonia signed a peace with Sovnarkom

In April a Polish army attacked Russia with initial success.

In June the Red Army counter-attacked the Poles and advanced towards Warsaw. Lenin talked of taking socialism into Europe 'on the point of Russian bayonets'. In the same month Denikin's successor, Baron Wrangel, advanced in the south but was quickly pushed back into the Crimea.

A Polish counterattack in August forced a Red retreat. Finally, in October 1920, the Treaty of Riga ended the Russo-Polish War.

In November the last White forces left southern Russia pursued and shelled by Red forces.

Phase four – war with the Greens

The Greens were largely movements of peasants who resented Bolshevik policies. They demanded greater autonomy from Moscow. Some were led by anarchists, like Makhno in the Ukraine and Antonov in Tambov. This period began before the Whites were defeated and ended in 1921. Overlapping with all these were movements for national independence.

Note

The ex-Tsar, his family and servants were taken into a basement and killed to avoid their capture by White forces. Those killed included their pet spaniel. The bodies were recently reburied in the Cathedral of St Peter and St Paul in St Petersburg.

Note

The Poles wanted to seize more territory while the Russians were busy fighting each other.

▶ The Civil War.

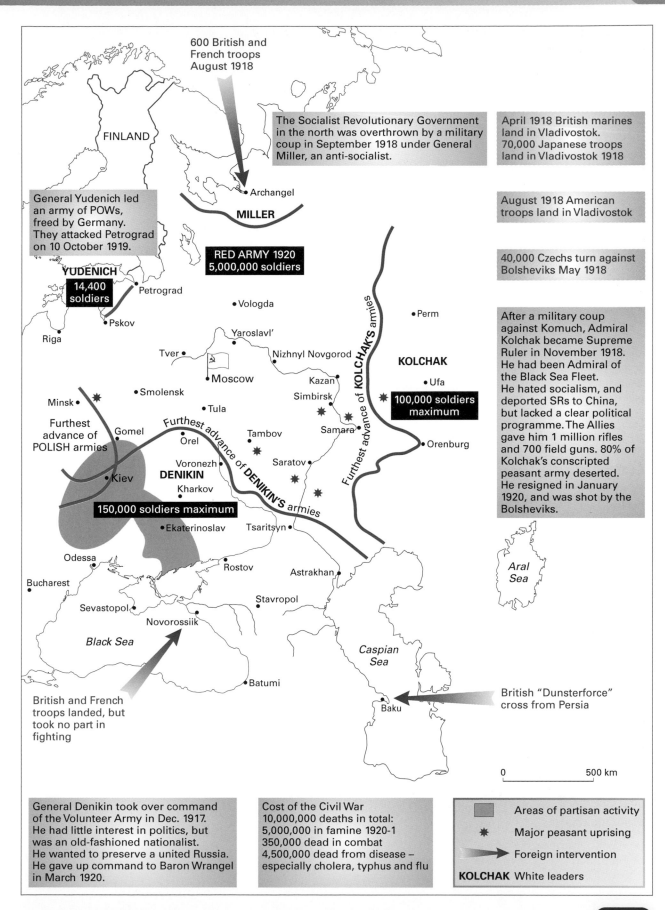

600 British and French troops August 1918

The Socialist Revolutionary Government in the north was overthrown by a military coup in September 1918 under General Miller, an anti-socialist.

April 1918 British marines land in Vladivostok. 70,000 Japanese troops land in Vladivostok 1918

FINLAND

Archangel

MILLER

August 1918 American troops land in Vladivostok

General Yudenich led an army of POWs, freed by Germany. They attacked Petrograd on 10 October 1919.

RED ARMY 1920 5,000,000 soldiers

40,000 Czechs turn against Bolsheviks May 1918

YUDENICH
14,400 soldiers

Petrograd

Pskov

Riga

Vologda

Yaroslavl'

Tver

Nizhnyl Novgorod

Moscow

Smolensk

Tula

Kazan

Simbirsk

Samara

Perm

Furthest advance of KOLCHAK'S armies

KOLCHAK

Ufa

100,000 soldiers maximum

Minsk

Furthest advance of POLISH armies

Gomel

Orel

Tambov

Furthest advance of DENIKIN'S armies

DENIKIN

Kharkov

Kiev

150,000 soldiers maximum

Voronezh

Saratov

Orenburg

Ekaterinoslav

Tsaritsyn

Odessa

Rostov

Astrakhan

Bucharest

Stavropol

Sevastopol

Novorossiik

Black Sea

Batumi

Aral Sea

Caspian Sea

Baku

After a military coup against Komuch, Admiral Kolchak became Supreme Ruler in November 1918. He had been Admiral of the Black Sea Fleet. He hated socialism, and deported SRs to China, but lacked a clear political programme. The Allies gave him 1 million rifles and 700 field guns. 80% of Kolchak's conscripted peasant army deserted. He resigned in January 1920, and was shot by the Bolsheviks.

British "Dunsterforce" cross from Persia

British and French troops landed, but took no part in fighting

0   500 km

General Denikin took over command of the Volunteer Army in Dec. 1917. He had little interest in politics, but was an old-fashioned nationalist. He wanted to preserve a united Russia. He gave up command to Baron Wrangel in March 1920.

Cost of the Civil War
10,000,000 deaths in total:
5,000,000 in famine 1920-1
350,000 dead in combat
4,500,000 dead from disease – especially cholera, typhus and flu

Areas of partisan activity

✳ Major peasant uprising

➡ Foreign intervention

KOLCHAK White leaders

Spotlight

Did the people support the Communists in the Civil War?

Historians have disagreed strongly about this in the past. What do you think?

Note

*On August 31 Lenin was shot and wounded by Fanya Kaplan, an SR. At the same time the head of the Petrograd Cheka was killed.

Facts and figures

Membership of the Communist Party

March 1919	250,000
October 1919	350,000
March 1920	612,000

In the summer of 1919 100,000 'margarine (i.e. pretend) socialists' were expelled from the party.

Source 11

As many as 2 million Red soldiers were 'lost' in the course of 1919 due to illness, desertion and, much less significant, battle casualties.

Mawdsley,
The Russian Civil War, 1987

Facts and figures

The outnumbered and almost surrounded People's Army of Ekaterinburg marched 1000 miles over the Ural Mountains to escape White attacks. Near the Black Sea another People's Army of 16,000 marched for weeks without food, crossing deserts and climbing crags while fighting off attacks to reach safety.

■ Think about

▶ Why were members of the Red Army made to swear the oath in Source 15?

Source 12

Now it is the time for our turn…Out of the way with the sentimentalists who are afraid to shed innocent blood!…Each drop of Lenin's blood must be paid for by the bourgeoisie and the Whites in hundreds of deaths…It is time to be pitiless.

A Bolshevik newspaper, 31 August 1918*

Source 13

By July Bolsheviks were almost the only party left in the Soviets: the other parties had either been expelled or walked out. The last Soviet elections in the spring of 1918 suggest falling support for the Bolsheviks. In Petrograd the Bolsheviks won only 48 per cent of the votes; in Kronstadt they won 29 per cent, a pattern repeated throughout all provincial capitals, where data is available.

Soviet election statistics for 1918, according to Faber

Source 14

You must get out of the city for the time being. After the seizure of Kazan by the Czech-White-Guard bands, the city has become a nest of counter-revolution. This nest has to be destroyed. In the event of further resistance, the counter-revolutionary parts of the city will be razed to the ground. Our gunners operating on land and on the river, and also our airmen, will do their utmost to avoid damaging the homes and districts of the poor…It is necessary to remove your children from the town as soon as you can…Within a few days the working population will be able to return to a city cleansed of vermin, along with the Soviet troops.

A warning to the working population of Kazan by Trotsky,
War Commissar, in August 1918

Source 15

1. I, a son of the working people and a citizen of the Soviet republic, assume the title of a soldier of the Workers' and Peasants' Red Army.
2. Before the working class of Russia and of the whole world I pledge myself to bear this title with honour, to study the art of war conscientiously, and to protect, like the apple of my eye, all public property from damage and robbery.
3. I pledge myself to observe revolutionary discipline strictly and unflaggingly, and to obey without question all orders given by commanders appointed by the Workers' and Peasants' Government.

The oath of the Red Army, agreed in March 1918

Source 16

Urgent. You must organize a picked guard. Exercise pitiless mass terror against the kulaks, the priests and the Whites. Imprison suspects in concentration camps outside the towns. Telegraph back implementation.

Telegram to Penza from Lenin, 19 August 1918

Source 17

Source 18

The country was divided into a number of areas often no larger than one city or even a single village, ruled by different parties and all sorts of adventurers. Often one came across neighbouring villages surrounded by trenches fighting each other for the land of their former landlords. It is not true that the Bolsheviks are only supported by Russian soldiers...the industrial workers are with them, so is a considerable part of the demobilized soldiers. The attitude of the peasants is difficult to ascertain. Villages that have been visited by Bolshevik groups are as a rule anti-Bolshevik but in other areas Bolshevik propaganda seems to have been successful.

A German report from the Ukraine, March 1918

Source 19

More than 170 [artists] shared in the preparation of decorations for the first October anniversary in Petrograd...A multitude of self-taught also took part in decorating the city...The industrial workers asked for...architects, painters and sculptors to set up Palaces of Labour, workers' clubs, monuments to revolutionary leaders and war memorials. They wanted everything changed, including postage stamps and official seals.

Zhadova Malevich, Suprematism in Russian Art, 1978

Source 20

The most cultured, the most politically developed sections...do not show any capacity for raising their sights to think of the state as a whole. Their economic mental outlook has not carried them very far beyond the outskirts of their villages or rural districts.

A secret Soviet report from 1921 on public opinion amongst the peasants of Tambov

◀ The cinema carriage of an Agitprop train with Bolshevik propaganda painted on the outside.

Note

Agitprop was a government organization which advertised the Bolshevik cause in the countryside. The trains carried theatre and music groups as well as printing presses.

Source 21

The Cheka reported uncovering 142 counter-revolutionary organizations in just 20 provinces in 1918, and facing 245 insurrections. Most early victims were from the old elite. Petrograd was the worst: the killing of 500 hostages was announced in September, and the total may have been twice that.

Mawdsley, The Russian Civil War, 1987

■ Activity

Collect together evidence from the sources under three headings – opposition, apathy and support – according to what they show about Russian attitudes to the Communists. You may be able to put some evidence under more than one heading. What kinds of people opposed and supported the Communists?

1 Do you think that most of the Russian people supported the Reds?

2 Why have historians disagreed about the level of public support for the Communists during the Civil War?

Why did the Communists win the Civil War?

Most historians now accept that the Reds held many advantages, although a glance at the map on page 121 may lead you to think otherwise. Many of the reasons why they were victorious in the wars you will have encountered earlier in this chapter. Here is a summary of the key points.

1. The Red Army

This did not exist in March 1918, but in 1920 it was 5 million strong. In 1918 the Communists introduced conscription into the areas they controlled, and although they suffered heavy desertions, they had almost limitless human resources to draw upon. It has been estimated that the largest combined total of White forces facing the Reds at any one time was no more than 500,000, and they were divided between different armies.

Greater numbers alone do not win wars, though they certainly help. Trotsky also reintroduced ranks and military discipline into the Red Army. To remedy his lack of experienced officers (the White forces had plenty), against much opposition within his party, Trotsky recruited 50,000 former Tsarist officers. To ensure their loyalty on the battlefield, he also appointed Bolshevik political commissars to supervise the officers and maintain the troops' morale. Trotsky also created a large force of Red cavalry, which played an important role in disrupting enemy lines of communication and countering the Cossack forces in the south.

■ Think about

▶ Why did many Communists oppose the use of former officers?

Source 22

◀ A Civil War recruitment poster for the Red cavalry. It reads 'To Horse Proletarians!'.

■ Think about

▶ Why did the Red Army have few cavalry at the start of the Civil War?

▶ Do you think this would have been an effective recruitment poster?

Quotation

The main base of Bolshevik support came not from the people at large… but from the Communist Party apparatus, which grew by leaps and bounds during the Civil War: at its conclusion, the party numbered between 600,000 and 700,000 members… Membership offered privileges and security in a society in which extreme poverty and insecurity were the rule… Their numbers were small - with their dependants perhaps 3 million - but in a country in which virtually no organised life above village level had survived, such a cadre, subject to party discipline, represented an awesome force.

Pipes, Russia under the Bolshevik Regime, 1994

2. Munitions and manpower

The Communists found themselves in control of the Russian heartland with much of its industry and population. This was reorganized to produce materials and men for the war effort. (See below for more discussion of the economy.) The Allied blockade meant that without home-produced weapons, the Red armies would have been badly equipped. White armies had to rely on the Allies for much of their weaponry.

3. Commitment to the cause

Some Red soldiers deserted, but other units, especially of workers were fanatically loyal. The propaganda of the Bolsheviks presented the war as a struggle against the evil forces of Tsarism, the bourgeoisie, superstition and foreign capital. No steps were spared to spread Soviet propaganda wherever Red troops went. The political commissars in the Army began this work, but it was reinforced by Agitprop trains, river steamers and theatre groups.

4. The Red Terror

The Bolsheviks imposed strict controls within their areas. Suspects were arrested and harshly dealt with. The Cheka ensured discipline. Some sources say 50,000 were shot in 1918 alone. It was not unknown for Cheka squads to follow unreliable forces into battle to shoot any deserters.

5. Control of the railway centres

Armies and munitions had to cover vast distances. The main battles were fought along the railway lines. The Communists controlled the hub of the railway system, which gave them a decisive advantage enabling them to move forces and munitions from one front to the other. The same crack troops were to be found fighting against Kolchak, Denikin and Yudenich, all within six months.

6. Trotsky's leadership

For three years Trotsky lived largely on his armoured train steaming from front to front. He travelled 65,000 miles during the course of the war. His train carried printing presses, a map room and a car as well as munitions and soldiers. With his dedication to the cause he inspired uncertain officers and men, and his ruthlessness against waverers became legendary.

Why did the Whites lose the Civil War?

1. Allied help

This was essential to maintain the White armies in the field, but it meant that it was easy for Communists to portray them as puppets of the Allies. Lenin was thus able to appeal to Russian patriotism to recruit men for the Red Army. The foreign forces in Russia were rarely involved in the fighting and withdrew quickly, France as early as April 1919.

2. White divisions

Unlike the Bolsheviks, the Whites had no sense of common purpose. In political terms they stretched across the political spectrum from socialists to conservatives, many of whom wanted to return to the society of Tsarist times. Many of their forces were fiercely territorial and would not advance from their own area. This handicapped Kolchak's forces in Siberia, as well as Denikin's in the Don region.

3. Lack of co-operation

Because of their mutual suspicions and differing goals, the White forces did not co-operate in their military planning. Geographical distance also made this difficult. The leaders of Kolchak's forces and Denikin's forces had to hold their meetings in Paris! The Red Army was able to defeat them one after the other, as in 1919.

Source 23

▲ Trotsky in 1920 as head of the Red Army.

Facts and figures

Trotsky's famed ruthlessness was shown in a famous incident in summer 1918. At Svyazhsk the newly arrived Trotsky confronted 200 deserters who had commandeered a riverboat to escape from advancing White forces. Trotsky ordered the decimation of the regiment – i.e. the execution of one man in ten. His orders were carried out on the quayside.

4. Lack of commitment

Desertions affected all armies, but the White forces found it more difficult to recruit and keep their ordinary soldiers than the Reds. Peasants had doubts about their policy on land, for their leaders seemed to be drawn from the former ruling classes. In Denikin's words:

Source 24

For them it was a question of returning to the past – and they tried to restore it both in form and spirit.

Document exercise: opposition to the Reds

Source A

◀ A Bolshevik poster from 1919.

Source B

Extracts from the Komuch Programme, 25 July 1918

1. The land has once and for all passed into the possession of the people and the Committee will not permit any attempts to return it to the landlords.
2. The existing laws about the protection of labour preserve their force....
4. Workers and peasants are requested to defend their interests only by legal means, in order to avoid anarchy and chaos.
5. Dismissal of workers and stoppage of the work of undertakings, if not justified by the conditions of production..., are forbidden under pain of severest liability to punishment.
8. The rights of trade unions, as defined by law, preserve their force....

Note

Komuch was the Committee of Members of the Constituent Assembly set up by SRs in Samara.

Note

Denikin was Commander of the Volunteer Army in the Don region of Russia.

Source C

Statement by Denikin, 14 December 1919

I order the Special Conference to adopt the following positions:
1. United, Great, Indivisible Russia. Defence of the Faith. Establishment of order.
2. Struggle with Bolshevism to the end.
3. Military dictatorship. Reject all pressure from political parties…
6. Aid the press which is with us, tolerate the dissenting press, annihilate the destructive press.

No class privileges, no preferential support, administrative, financial or moral.
7. Restore the morale of the front and the military rear…by field courts martial and by the use of extreme repressive measures.
8. Strengthen the rouble…The burden of taxation should fall mainly on the well-to-do.

Source D

The Programme of the Antonov Movement

The overthrow of the government of the Communist-Bolsheviks. Political equality of all citizens, without class distinctions; convocation of the Constituent Assembly on the basis of equal, universal, direct and secret ballot..; freedom of speech, press, conscience, associations and assembly; the actual implementation of the law on the socialization of the land; …partial denationalization of factories and plants, with large-scale industry remaining in the hands of the State; freedom of production for domestic (cottage) industry; free self-determination for the nationalities.

Note

Antonov led the Union of Toiling Peasants in rebellion in Tambov 1920–1. He was a 'Green' leader.

Source E

In terms of their psychology and world-view, their customs and their habits, they were so far removed and alienated from the changes that had taken place in the country that they had no idea how to act in the new revolutionary era. For them it was a question of returning to the past —and they tried to restore the past both in form and spirit.

General Denikin describing the landlords after the Civil War

■ Examination-style questions

1 Comprehension in context
  (a) What does Source A suggest about the opposition to the Bolsheviks?
  (b) Why did the Bolsheviks wish to present their enemies in this way?

2 Comparing the sources
  (a) Do Sources B and D support the Bolshevik view of the Whites?
  (b) What differences can you see between the political programmes presented in Sources B, C and D?

3 Assessing the sources
Why might a historian have reservations about Source E?

4 Making judgements
How do these sources help historians to understand why the Bolsheviks emerged victorious in the Civil War? Use the sources and your own knowledge to help you answer the question.

The economics of survival

The reorganization of the economy was important to the survival of the regime during the Civil War. Everything had to be used to meet the demands of the war effort. Marxists also believed that Russia had to become fully industrialized before a Communist classless society could be achieved. Lenin, after seizing power, seems to have been optimistic about this at first, announcing:

'In six months we will build communism in Russia.'

Events did not prove his optimism justified.

State Capitalism, 1917–18

Immediately after the October Revolution the government introduced what it called 'State Capitalism'. Lenin did not believe it was possible to achieve socialism immediately in backward Russia, but he confidently expected that the events in Petrograd would be the spark to set off revolutions throughout industrialized Europe. Until that time, bourgeois experts and managers were still needed to run industry and trade, at least in the short term. To co-ordinate and plan the economy, Sovnarkom set up Vesenkha, the Supreme Council of National Economy. This body nationalized the banks, shipping, railways and some larger factories.

Workers, however, were impatient for change and seized control of many more factories, even though the government passed decrees in January and April 1918 to try to stop them. Lenin was not confident that the workers would yet have the expertise to manage industrial enterprises.

After Brest-Litovsk in March 1918, Russia found itself cut off from the grain supplies of the Ukraine; White armies controlled many other rich farming areas. This created extreme food shortages: bread rations fell to 50 grams per day in the cities. There were acute shortages of all foods and also many consumer items. Workers in hundreds of thousands left the cities and industrial areas to seek food in the countryside. The government also faced the prospect of a long civil war. In this situation, to survive, its economic policy was abandoned.

> **Quotation**
>
> Down with Lenin and horsemeat
> Give us the Tsar and pork
>
> **Slogan chanted by workers
> in March 1918**

War Communism, 1918–21

The government decided to take direct control of economic life. In June 1918 a decree nationalized all industries. All production was to be concentrated on the war effort. Factory committees lost the ability to manage their workplaces; instead party officials and appointees took over this role. Production collapsed as the transport of goods and raw materials was totally disrupted by the Civil War. The Allies blockaded Communist territory and prevented it receiving foreign trade. Without work or food, the population of Moscow and Petrograd was halved. Of the 2.6 million workers in Russia in 1917, only 1.2 million were left at their posts in 1920.

> ■ **Think about**
>
> ▶ Why is this policy called War Communism?

Source 25

	1913	1921
Industrial production index	100	31
Farming production index	100	60
Coal (million tons)	29	9
Oil (million tons)	9.2	3.8
Electricity (million Kwhs)	2039	520
Pig iron (million tons)	4.2	0.1
Bricks (millions)	2.1	0.01

> **Quotation**
>
> [Red Square] where Lenin had addressed a crowd was no more than a white desert surrounded by dead houses.
>
> **V. Serge remembers
> Moscow in January 1919**

Source 25 shows it was not only industrial production that collapsed. The shortage of food was even more serious. Peasant communities fiercely resisted the grain requisitioning of 1918 (see pp.118–119) – some by force. Many reacted by refusing to grow more crops than they needed for their own consumption. They also refused to join the State collective farms the government had set up. This produced a crisis of food supply. Requisition squads entered the villages again in 1919 and 1920, confiscating not just the peasants' surplus – this was not enough to feed the army and the cities – but also seed grain and the food the peasants needed for themselves and their families.

The value of money during this period totally collapsed. Inflation between 1917 and 1922 ran at about 1,000,000 per cent! Workers were paid in goods not worthless money. Some Communists, eg Bukharin, actually welcomed this development. They saw it as marking the end of capitalism. Inflation removed any incentive to work hard or produce goods or food for sale.

The situation in Russia at the end of the Civil War

By the end of 1920 the Civil War had been won, peace had been made with Poland and foreign troops had left Russian territory. Just when the Communist government should have been celebrating its victory it found itself thrown again into another series of conflicts. There were hundreds of peasant risings in 1920 and 1921. These were the Greens (see page 120). Requisitioning had turned millions of peasants against the regime. 'By March 1921 Soviet power in much of the countryside had ceased to exist,' according to Figes. At the same time a wave of strikes threatened the regime in the cities and industrialized areas. These strikes in Petrograd turned into mass demonstrations, in which soldiers and sailors joined. The Communists had won the Civil War but their methods had lost them the support of the people.

Famine!

A drought in 1920 was followed by a severe winter. When another dry spell followed in the summer of 1921, Russia was hit by famine on a terrifying scale. Peasants had either eaten any reserves or seen them confiscated by the requisition squads. A combination of government policy and climate caused the worst famine for thirty years.

In 1920 Ukraine grain production fell to 20 per cent of its pre-war total. Perhaps five million died not only of famine but also of disease, as typhus and cholera followed in its wake. Millions more tramped across the country in search of food. Reports of cannibalism reached foreign reporters. Corpses, especially of children, were stored to be eaten by their own families. Deaths would have been even greater had it not been for the American Relief Administration. Herbert Hoover raised money from the American people and used it to distribute food and seed in the worst famine areas. An estimated 14 million people were kept alive in this way. Throughout the famine Lenin's government had not been swift to act, and accepted American help with great reluctance.

■ **Think about**

▶ Why were some Communists pleased to see the collapse of the value of the rouble?

Facts and figures

By 1920 in Petrograd two-thirds of adults ate in communal canteens.

■ **Think about**

▶ Why was the work of the American Relief Administration deeply embarrassing for the Communists?

Source 26

◀ Victims of the famine of 1921.

The Kronstadt Mutiny, 1921

The most serious and disturbing threat came from Kronstadt. The naval base here had a special significance in Communist mythology. Its sailors had taken to the streets of Petrograd to demonstrate for a soviet government in the July Days and had played a key role in the Bolshevik seizure of power in October 1917. When demonstrations began in Petrograd in 1921, they quickly spread to Kronstadt on 28 February. Within hours the garrison called for an end to the Communist dictatorship. Communist Party members in the base supported the demands to hold new soviet elections, release political prisoners and end the grain requisitioning. Most of those based at Kronstadt were peasants and knew only too well what Communist rule had brought to their villages.

Source 27

In carrying out the October Revolution, the working class hoped to achieve its liberation. The outcome has been even greater enslavement of human beings... By means of State-run trade unions, the workers have been chained to their machines so that labour is not a source of joy but a new serfdom. To the protests of the peasants, expressed in spontaneous risings, and those of the workers, whom the very conditions of life compel to strike, they have responded with mass executions and an appetite for blood that by far exceeds that of Tsarist generals.

Declaration by the Kronstadt 'Rebels',
8 March 1921 in The Kronstadt Pravda

■ Think about

▶ What was the main criticism of the Communist government made by the Kronstadt 'rebels'?

Lenin and the government acted swiftly. Trotsky was sent to crush the rebellion. It was a bloody affair. The first attacks failed, but eventually 50,000 Red Army troops recaptured the island base after an advance across the ice.

Source 28

▲ Red soldiers, many of them dressed in white camouflage, advance across the ice to recapture the Kronstadt naval base after the mutiny there. Dead and wounded men can be seen on the ice after earlier attacks.

■ **Think about**

▶ What questions would a historian wish to ask about this photograph?

■ **Think about**

▶ Why was Lenin heard in silence?

10,000 Red soldiers were killed in the attack. Captured rebels were treated savagely, many being executed and others being sent to the first Soviet concentration camp, inside the Arctic Circle.

The New Economic Policy, 1921

While the Kronstadt mutiny was at its height, the Communist Party was holding its Tenth Party Congress in Moscow. It was clear to everyone that the government faced a national emergency. Drastic action was needed if the Communists were to retain power. The peasants held the key, as Lenin realized. On 15 March Lenin explained to the party that it had to rebuild a smychka (alliance) with the peasants. 'Let the peasants have their little bit of capitalism as long as we keep the power,' he said. He spoke for three hours, and his speech was heard virtually in silence.

The New Economic Policy comprised:

1. The end of the requisitioning of grain
2. The payment by peasants of a tax in kind (i.e. grain) to the government. This was eventually set at 10 per cent of their crop.
3. The reintroduction of a free market, in which peasants were to be able to sell any extra surplus.
4. The legalization of small businesses
5. Heavy industry, transport, banking, 'the commanding heights' of the economy, were to remain under State control.

Walter Durranty, an American reporter in Moscow, described how Lenin later justified this new policy to a meeting of party delegates:

Source 29

'The real meaning of the New Economic Policy is that we have met a great defeat in our plans and that we are now making a strategic retreat,' said Lenin in one of the frankest admissions of failure ever made by a leader of a great nation…

'Before Lenin spoke,' says the official newspaper *Izvestia*, 'there had been a somewhat acrid discussion, which many Communists cannot fail to regard as an objuration (denial) of their dearest ideals. But, as usual, Lenin's logic vanquished opposition. His statement is clearly intended to close the discussion definitely.' 'Our defeat in the economic field, whose problems resemble those of strategy, though even graver and more difficult,' said the Soviet chief, 'is more serious than any we suffered from the armies of Denikin or Kolchak. We thought the peasants would give us sufficient food to ensure the support of the industrial workers, and that we should be able to distribute it. We were wrong, and so we have begun to retreat. Before we are utterly smashed, let us retrace our steps and begin to build on a new foundation.'

Moscow 22 October 1921. Walter Durranty, *Russia Reported –
a collection of reports for The New York Times*, later published in 1934

■ Think about

▶ Why did Lenin regard this policy as a 'great defeat'?

This new policy eventually put an end to armed resistance in the countryside. Those groups, which had already rebelled, were put down ruthlessly by Marshal Tukhachevski. Farmers and workers returned to work and the immediate crisis was lifted. Better weather and grain donated by Americans also helped to ensure better harvests in 1922 and 1923. In 1922 the government introduced a new currency to replace the old, devalued rouble. At least people would now have some incentive to sell food and other goods again.

However, many members of the party were unhappy about this change of direction. Only Lenin's enormous personal authority and a tight control of the proceedings at the Congress ensured its acceptance. Despite the controversial nature of the changes, only four short speeches were allowed after Lenin had finished speaking.

The Decree on Party Unity, March 1921

Acceptance of the NEP was made easier by an earlier decision of the 10th Party Congress to ban the formation of any subgroups/factions within the Communist Party. The rising discontent amongst workers and peasants during the Civil War had caused the formation of two distinct pressure groups in the party. The most important was centred around Shliapnikov and Kollontai, both commissars in the government, and called itself 'The Workers' Opposition'. It called for more worker involvement in the running of their factories and a greater role for independent trade unions. Together with the 'Democratic Centralists' they called for a greater involvement in policy-making for ordinary party members.

Quotation

Marxism teaches that only the political party of the working class, i.e. the Communist Party, is capable of uniting, training and organising a vanguard of the proletariat… that will alone be capable of withstanding the inevitable traditions and relapses of narrow craft unionism.

Lenin, *Left-wing Communism*, 1920

Under the decree, opposition to decisions by organized party groups was now formally banned. Another decree finally made the Communists the only legal political party in the country.

Cross reference

Chapter Seven introduces the debate between historians about Lenin's role in these events.

■ **Activity**   **KEY SKILLS**

Why did the Communists stay in control of Russia, 1917–22?

This is a very common focus for examination questions and you should be sure that you understand the different reasons.

In pairs collect together evidence on the following topics:

The divided opposition to Communist rule after 1917

The policies of Lenin's government

The attitudes of different groups to the government's policies

The flexibility of the Communist government

The Communist Party – was it a united or divided party?

The apparatus of repression

The roles of Trotsky and Lenin

Prepare a presentation to your group on which of these factors or group of factors was most important and then debate your own conclusions with those of other groups.

Prepare your presentation group by carrying out further reading from sources in your library or the Internet. Incorporate a visual image in your report – it does not have to be a picture.

Conclusion

The Bolsheviks had won the Civil War, but it was largely a war of their own making. If they had not insisted on a one-party dictatorship, but instead taken other socialist groups into coalition in 1917 or 1918, there would have been no war on such a grand scale. In the end most Russians probably did not care about the war, despite the announcement of some radical social and economic policies by the Bolshevik government. They simply wanted to be left alone. A combination of ruthlessness, propaganda, geography and some support from the industrial proletariat and the soldiers in the Red Army enabled the Communists to win the Civil War. The Whites were outnumbered and divided. Despite Allied help, the longer the fighting went on the more hopeless their position became.

By the end of 1921 peace had been restored across the whole of the country. However victory had its price. The Communists found they had lost the support of the population, and the country was in ruins. A Communist vision of the future also seemed further away than ever with the introduction of the NEP. The party had accepted this reluctantly, and Lenin had tried to restrict party debate by the decree on party unity.

Nor was Russia firmly under Communist control. Very few peasants were Communists and in the backward regions poor transport and lack of telephones meant that the government in Moscow was very remote indeed. Robert Service in his *A History of Twentieth Century Russia* suggests that there was only one Communist group for every 1200 square kilometres of Russian countryside during the period of the NEP. This issue was to return to the centre of politics later.

■ **Further reading**

G. Leggett, *The Cheka*, 1981
S. Fitzpatrick, *The Russian Revolution*, 1987
R. Sakwa, *The Rise and Fall of the Soviet Union 1917–91*, 1991
D. Volkogonov, *Lenin Life and legacy*, 1994
C Read, *From Tsar to Soviets*, 1996
R. Service, *Lenin a biography*, 2000
W. Lincoln, *Red Victory*, 1989
C. Mawdsley, *The Russian Civil War*, 1987

Lenin's role in history

Source 1

Source 2

On 21 January Vladimir Ilych drank some broth thirstily and felt slightly better, but then he started gurgling in his chest…His eyes looked less and less conscious…He occasionally moaned quietly, a tremor ran through his body. At first I held his hot damp hand, but then just watched as the towel turned red with blood, and the stamp of death settled on his deathly pallid face.

In these words Krupskaya recounted the death in January 1924 of her husband Lenin, creator and leader of the world's first Communist state

◀ A statue of Lenin outside the Finland station in St Petersburg.

Source 3

My own housekeeper, a girl of about 20, the daughter of a small real estate agent ruined by the Revolution, stood in line from midnight until 5 o'clock this morning to pay her last respects to a man she had never seen, and who had altered her whole life for the worse. She hardly knew why she went. She just repeated: 'Lenin was the greatest man in the world and wished everyone to be free, happy and peaceful – I must see him.' I walked down with her to the Theatre Square, a huge open space swept by the north wind from straight across the snowbound steppes of the Arctic Ocean. The temperature was below 18 below freezing, yet there was in the immense concourse tens upon tens of thousands of men, women, even young children, waiting with the unfathomable patience of the Slav.

W. Durranty described for the *New York Times* on 6 January 1924 the mood in Russia when the news of Lenin's death was published. Durranty, *Russia Reported*, 1934

■ Think about

▶ What is happening in the photograph?

▶ When do you think it was taken?

■ Think about

▶ In what ways had Lenin altered 'her whole life for the worse' in Source 3?

Introduction

The public grief displayed in Source 3 is shown in many other contemporary accounts. However, *The Times* in England wrote:

Think about

▶ What are the main criticisms made of Lenin's achievements?

▶ Is this prejudiced view of any value to a historian studying Lenin?

> ### Source 4
>
> This is not the place to describe in detail the terrible achievements of Bolshevism – the shameful peace with Germany, the plundering of the educated and propertied classes, the long-continued terror with its thousands of innocent victims, the Communist experiment carried to the point of suppressing private trade, and making practically all the adult population of the towns servants and slaves of the Soviet Government…Never in modern times has any great country passed through such a convulsion as that brought about by Lenin's implacable effort to establish Communism in Russia, and thence to spread it throughout the world.

Lenin has both passionate advocates and bitter critics. You will find both in the assessment exercise at the end of this chapter. In this chapter we will consider Lenin's place in history.

Key questions

- What was Lenin's contribution to the events of 1917?
- What was the nature of the Bolshevik government?
- What was Lenin's legacy?

How important was Lenin in the October Revolution of 1917?

Cross reference

Look back at Chapter 5 for more detail about the events of 1917.

Historians from the West and East are largely agreed on the centrality of Lenin to the events of 1917. This is how Leon Trotsky summed up the October Revolution:

> ### Source 5
>
> If neither Lenin nor I had been present in Petersburg, there would have been no October Revolution: the leadership of the Bolshevik Party would have prevented it from occurring – of this I have not the slightest doubt.

It is not difficult to present a case for this point of view. Here are three strong arguments in its favour.

Quotation

History will not forgive us if we do not take power now.

Lenin, September 1917

Think about

What do these three interventions by Lenin tell us about:
▶ his position in the Bolshevik Party?

▶ his own personality?

- Lenin's arrival in Petrograd in April 1917 certainly transformed the Bolshevik attitude to the Provisional Government. *Pravda* had given it a cautious welcome and Stalin and others had announced they were prepared to work with it. Lenin's April Theses, calling for the overthrow of Lvov and his ministers, were received badly at first but soon Lenin persuaded the party that they should prepare for revolution.
- Similarly it was Lenin's return to Petrograd from hiding in Finland that inspired the October coup. Indeed, he threatened to resign if the coup was delayed any longer. Even then, as we have seen, some senior Bolsheviks did their best to prevent it.
- Perhaps most important was Lenin's adaptation of Marxism to fit Russian circumstances. Marx forecast proletarian revolutions in industrialized

societies. Russia was a peasant country with a tiny proletariat. Lenin's insistence that a party of professional revolutionaries could seize power, 'telescope' together the bourgeois and proletarian revolutions, and establish a Communist regime in backward Russia was what made the October Revolution possible. Without Marxism-Leninism there would have been no Bolsheviks.

However, there is another way of looking at these events. Research over the last 20 years has stressed that the working class in Petrograd and elsewhere was not simply the plaything of the Bolsheviks but genuinely revolutionary in its own right. More than one historian has pointed out that there would have been a workers' revolution at the end of 1917 without Lenin.

Cross reference

See pages 53–54 for more details about Marxism.

Source 6

The common ordeal, suffered during months of feverish political agitation and organization, greatly intensified class-consciousness...Increasingly they directed their demands to the government itself – to halt speculation, arrest profiteers, punish hoarding, control prices, ban lock-outs, and support factory committees and trade unions against employers' sanctions...As summer wore on, the workers, like the soldiers, demanded with growing impatience a government responsive to their immediate needs.

Acton, *Russia*, 1986

This would probably have ended with a coalition of all socialist parties. What Lenin did from this point of view was to hi-jack this revolutionary fervour and use it to set up what was to become a Bolshevik one-party state. In other words, by his dogmatic insistence on his own analysis of the Russian situation, Lenin prevented the development of democratic socialism in Russia.

For other western anti-Marxist historians, Lenin's rise to power was largely accidental, the result of blunders by other politicians and the growing chaos of 1917 Russia. They also believe that Lenin came to power by false pretences. Throughout 1917 he had demanded a Constituent Assembly, but he closed it down when it finally sat in January 1918. He also called for 'all power to the soviets', but set up a government which was a narrow Bolshevik regime. Lenin in other words was both duplicitous and lucky.

What was the nature of the Bolshevik Government?

Was Lenin a dictator?

Source 7

At that time Lenin was a real dictator. They obeyed him not for fear, but with pleasure. He was their leader. He gave instructions, they merely carried them out. Lenin decided there must be a Red Army. Trotsky carried out the idea. Lenin outlined the functions of Cheka; Dzerzhinsky put these instructions into practice. Lenin put forward the watchwords of the economic policy, and the Commissars eagerly applied them...As in the beginning, so to this day Lenin has inspired the policy and kept the peace within the Communist ranks.

The Times, 1923

■ Think about

▶ Was the one-party state Lenin's creation?

▶ What was the position taken by the other socialist parties in the Second All-Russian Congress of Soviets?

▶ Which other socialist group joined the government in 1917?

▶ Why did it leave?

Source 8

At the hour when many of us, including myself, were doubtful as to whether it was admissible for us to sign the Brest-Litovsk peace, only Comrade Lenin maintained stubbornly, with amazing foresight and against our opposition, that we had to go through with it to tide us over until the revolution of the world proletariat.

Trotsky

Trotsky's comments give us some idea of Lenin's enormous personal authority in the Bolshevik government. It has led some historians, like *The Times* in 1923, to describe this period as 'Lenin's dictatorship'. However, closer examination shows this to have been very far from the case. Lenin was unable to persuade Sovnarkom to sign an immediate peace treaty with Germany in November 1917. Only when the capital itself was threatened by the German advance did it reluctantly agree to accept Lenin's view – and that only after he again threatened to resign. If there was a dictatorship, it was the dictatorship of the party leadership not simply that of Lenin.

Why was Lenin's government so ruthless?

The archives of the former USSR are full of invocations to the Bolsheviks to be ruthless towards their enemies. Many thousands who were innocent of any crime or opposition died at the hands of the Bolsheviks.

Source 9

If we can't shoot a White Guard saboteur, what sort of great revolution is this? Haven't you seen what the bourgeois garbage is writing about us in the press? What sort of dictatorship is this? All talk and no action? This is *impossible!* The terrorists will think we're milksops. We have an extreme war situation. We must encourage energy and widespread terror against the counter-revolutionaries.

Lenin

Of course during all wars, and especially in civil wars, there are bound to be casualties. Faced with foreign intervention as well as armed resistance in Russia itself, the regime, fighting for its very existence, carried out savage reprisals against suspected oppositionists. The normal rules of law and justice disappeared. But during the war, terror was used by both sides. Baron Wrangel, a White leader in the Crimea, ordered the execution of 300 prisoners of war, while the Green leader Antonov allowed his army of peasants to bury alive captured Communists.

For the Bolsheviks, however, the political terror did not end with the Civil War. They had a 'higher' idea than 'bourgeois morality': Lenin called it 'revolutionary justice'. He said:

Source 10

To us all is permitted, for we are the first in the world to raise the sword not in the name of enslaving and oppressing anyone, but in the name of freeing all from bondage.

Quotation

For years Lenin had laboured to build up an obedient following of men who would stop at nothing in the party interest... he had a natural asceticism of character which power did not corrupt, and could do evil without losing sight of the ultimate good.

Schapiro, *The Communist Party of the Soviet Union*, 1960

In 1922, when a new criminal code was being drafted, Lenin wrote:

Source 11

The law should not abolish terror; to promise that would be self-delusion or deception; it should be substantiated and legalized as a matter of principle, and its sphere of application be as broad as possible.

The only test of right and wrong now became whether or not an action furthered the cause of the revolution. 'Bourgeois morality', in Lenin's view, was designed to protect the interests of the propertied and exploiting classes. For the so-called vanguard of the proletariat there could be no such ideological shackles.

It is interesting to contrast the often brutal nature of the regime with what Lenin himself wrote in autumn 1917 when in hiding after the July Days. He put together a short book called *State and Revolution* in which he reflected on the nature of a future Communist society.

Source 12

In September 1917, in his meandering utopia of *State and Revolution*, Lenin had envisaged socialism as leading to the position where 'the need for violence against people in general, for subordination of one man to another, and of one section of the population to another, will vanish altogether since people will become accustomed to observing the elementary conditions of social life *without violence* and *without subordination.*'...By the time of his death Lenin's regime had accustomed the Russian people to violence and subordination, and the habit, once acquired, would outlive more than one generation.

Shukman, *Lenin and the Russian Revolution*, 1967

Historians' views of Lenin's regime are fundamentally determined by their sympathy with Lenin's aims and motives. Those who share his aims tend to excuse his methods as being necessary in the difficult times he faced. Christopher Hill, a Marxist historian, wrote glowingly of Lenin and his regime and excused his harsh policies:

Source 13

Lenin possessed a second quality, which symbolises the achievements of the Revolution as a whole. It is the quality, which on Maurice Baring's first visit most impressed him as typical of the ordinary Russian – humaneness. The attempt to overthrow the Bolsheviks after the Revolution produced cruelties indeed; but the revolutionary process abolished a regime of despair and created a new world of hope...

    Gorky...says of him: 'I never met anyone in Russia...nor do I know anyone who hated, loathed and despised all unhappiness, grief and suffering as Lenin did.'

Hill, *Lenin and the Russian Revolution*, 1947

■ **Think about**

Shliapnikov, a leader of the Workers' Opposition in 1921, congratulated Lenin's government on becoming 'the vanguard of a non-existent class'.

▶ What did he mean by this?

■ **Think about**

▶ What criticism of Lenin does Shukman make in this extract?

▶ Is it fair to criticize Lenin for what others did after he was dead?

▶ Is there any real contradiction between Lenin's Marxist vision of a free Communist society and the need to follow ruthless policies until it was achieved?

■ **Think about**

▶ Do you agree that Lenin's regime was humane?

Those who find his methods and aims unacceptable disagree:

> ### Source 14
>
> Lenin had destroyed any possible allies when he got rid of the Mensheviks and SRs. His papers are full of instructions on ways to 'root out' all Russian socialists who did not accept Bolshevik authority…Unshlikht [a Cheka leader] reported…'Mass operations have to be conducted against these bodies on a state-wide scale'.
>
> Volkogonov, *The Rise and Fall of the Soviet Empire*, 1998

■ Think about

▶ Why was Volkogonov keen to stress the actions of Lenin against the Mensheviks and SRs?

What was Lenin's legacy?

> ### Source 15
>
> The October Revolution was achieved in response to Lenin's compelling rational leadership, not under his whip. The people followed Lenin because they believed in him, not because they feared him. Lenin raised and unified the aspirations of the people.
>
> Khrushchev, *Khrushchev Remembers*, 1971

Khrushchev, successor and harsh critic of Stalin, as you will read later, was a strong defender of Lenin's role in history. Like Hill, in Source A on page 140, Khrushchev believed that October 1917 was a turning point in world history, opening up a new chapter for oppressed peoples everywhere. However, since the collapse of the Communist system, Russian historians have been more critical:

> ### Source 16
>
> As early as 1918 the Bolsheviks began organising concentration camps, and those who were spared the bullet began filling them…Soon the entire secret map of the country would be pitted by evil pock-marks of the camps, through which millions would pass in the 70 years of the Leninist regime.
>
> Volkogonov, *Lenin: Life and Legacy*, 1994

Note

Lenin was effectively removed from politics after his first stroke in May 1922. He suffered further strokes in December 1922 and March 1923.

■ Think about

▶ What examples can you find of Lenin altering course/changing his mind.

Note

Lenin and the government now also had to face up to the failure of international revolution.

Many western historians similarly hold him responsible, as does the Russian Volkogonov, for creating all the features of the regime, which brought millions to death, imprisonment and transportation under Stalin. Under Lenin, they argue, all the components of Stalinism were in place. Lenin had demanded a one-party government; Lenin set up Cheka; Lenin tried to put an end to inter-party debate in 1921; Lenin created the centralized and all-powerful bureaucracy; Lenin promoted Stalin to all his posts etc.

There is a problem for historians; as with every person in the past, it is difficult to understand precisely what he intended. For being a pragmatic politician meant that many of Lenin's statements and policies seem to be contradictory. The other complicating factor is the short period of time he was actually able to direct policy. By the summer of 1921 he was increasingly absent from the helm of the state, and after Christmas 1922 he was totally incapacitated. This meant that throughout virtually all his time in office he had to grapple with emergencies, which threatened the security of the government. How would he have governed in a period of greater calm and tranquillity?

This is further complicated by the documents he dictated after his strokes. His *Political Testament*, his last articles in *Pravda* and his liaison with Trotsky over the Georgian question (see p.145) suggest to some historians that, taken together with the NEP, Lenin had come to a new programme, a *perestroika* of the Communist system. (According to American historian M. Lewin, he was still 'thinking beautifully'.) These suggest Lenin was contemplating more local autonomy for the republics, greater openness in the party, less power for the bureaucracy, and that village communes and co-operatives might be used to build a socialist society in the countryside.

Perhaps given these constraints any judgement on Lenin is bound to be provisional and uncertain.

Document exercise: views of Lenin

Source A

I come back continually to this feature of the Russian Revolution, that it uplifted the poor and the downtrodden and improved their lot in the everyday things of life. This is what most impresses in contemporary records of the revolution, and this is what is likely to be its most widespread and lasting effect. For the everyday things of life still mean most to the poor and downtrodden, and they are still the majority of the population of the world.

Hill, *Lenin and the Russian Revolution*, 1947

Source B

Lenin was realist enough to know that his regime was not popular...he held both Russian workers and peasants in contempt...The main base of Bolshevik support came not from the people at large, the 'masses,' but from the Communist Party apparatus, which grew by leaps and bounds during the Civil War: at its conclusion, the party numbered between 600,000 and 700,000 members...They joined because membership offered privileges and security in a society in which extreme poverty and insecurity were the rule...

Toward outsiders, people not belonging to his order of the elect, Lenin showed no human feelings whatever, sending them to their deaths by the tens of thousands, often to serve as an example to others.

Pipes, *Russia under the Bolshevik Regime 1919–24*, 1994

Source C

I am amazed and alarmed at the slowing down in the operation against Kazan; what is particularly bad is the report of your having the fullest possible opportunity of destroying the enemy with your artillery. One should not take pity on the city and put off matters any longer, as merciless annihilation is what is vital once it is established that Kazan is enclosed in an iron fist.

Lenin to Trotsky, 21 August 1918

Note

Lenin had set up model collective farms after 1917 to act as examples to the peasantry.

Quotation

We lack enough civilisation to enable us to pass straight to socialism. We must reduce our state apparatus to the utmost degree.

Lenin in *Pravda* March 1922

Source D

Lenin is no more. We have lost Lenin…Medicine has proved itself powerless to accomplish what was passionately hoped for, what millions of human hearts demanded…And now Lenin is no more. These words descend upon our consciousness like gigantic rocks falling to the sea. Is it credible, can it be thought of?

How shall we advance, shall we find the way, shall we not go astray? For Lenin, comrades, is no longer with us!

Trotsky speaking at Tiflis Station, 22 January 1924

Source E

In the face of large well-equipped 'White' armies supported by several Western countries, a strict centralism and absolutism became imperative. …No democratic procedure would have made solutions possible, but only authoritarian ones: orders, appointments and dismissals…

If in the end Lenin's regime came to be based on a force, the bureaucracy, which he abhorred, it was only the result of a situation in which a program of development is imposed by a new regime on a backward country whose vital social forces are either weak, indifferent or hostile…

At the end of his life, Lenin saw all these problems more and more clearly…He would have to live on to prove that he could have changed anything substantially.

Lewin, *Lenin's Last Struggle*, 1968

■ Examination-style questions

1 Comprehension of a source
Study Source A. What does Hill in this source think was Lenin's most important achievement?

2 Comparison of sources
Study Sources A and B. How does Pipes differ from Hill in his view of Lenin and his achievement?

3 Understanding of the factors affecting historical interpretations
Study Sources A and B. Why may the date they were written be an important factor in determining the authors' views of Lenin?

4 Utility of sources in supporting a historical interpretation
Study Sources A, B and C. Which author, Hill or Pipes, would be able to make best use of Source C?

5 Evaluation of sources
Study Source D. What is the value and limitation of Source D to a historian of Russia in the 1920s?

6 Comparison of historical interpretations
Study Source E. Is Lewin more likely to agree with the views of Hill or those of Pipes? Refer to all three sources in your answer.

7 Understanding a source in context
Why was Lenin still important to the Communist Party after his death?

8 Understanding the nature of historical debate
Why have historians found it difficult to agree about Lenin's impact on Russian history? Use all the sources and your own knowledge to answer the question.

■ Further reading

C. Hill, *Lenin and the Russian Revolution*, 1947
O. Figes, *A People's Tragedy: The Russian Revolution 1891-1924*, 1996.
R. Pipes, *The Russian Revolution 1899-1919*, 1990
M. Lewin, *Lenin's Last Struggle*, 1968
D. Volkogonov, *Lenin Life and legacy*, 1994
R. Service, *Lenin a biography*, 2000

Chapter 8

Which is the way to socialism? Why did Stalin come to rule Russia?

Source 1

▲ Lenin and Stalin sitting together in 1922.

Source 2

Stalin, one of the most remarkable men in Russia and perhaps the most influential figure here today…During the last years Stalin has shown judgement and analytical power not unworthy of Lenin. It is to him that the greatest part of the credit is due for bringing about the new Soviet Union.

From an article for the *New York Times*, written in Moscow on 16 January 1923 by W. Durranty in *Russia Reported*, 1934

Source 3

Certainly Stalin was a shrewd tactician, but his intellectual equipment was second-rate. He was so preoccupied with the mechanics of the power-struggle that he could seldom be bothered to waste time on substantive [important] issues.

From *Stalin, the Red Dictator* written by Boris Bazhanov, Stalin's secretary 1923-6

Source 4

Stalin is too rude and this defect, although quite tolerable in our midst and in dealing amongst us Communists, becomes intolerable in a General Secretary. That is why I suggest that the comrades think about a way of removing Stalin.

From Lenin's *Political Testament*, 1923

Introduction

As Lenin had been removed from the centre of politics since May 1922, all prominent Bolsheviks must have wondered how Russia would be governed once he was gone. No one surely would be able to equal his personal authority in the party as the inspiration behind the October Revolution. Today with the benefit of hindsight we know Stalin emerged as the dominant figure. How and why this happened is a matter of dispute and debate. Lenin's own attitude to Stalin had not been consistent. He had appointed him to many key positions in the government and the party. Moshe Lewin described Stalin as Lenin's 'Chief of Staff'. Yet a year before his death Lenin condemned Stalin, Source 4, and called for his dismissal. Those who had come into contact with Stalin formed very different impressions of his abilities.

The focus of this chapter is the period between 1922 and 1929. It was a time of intense debate within the party at all levels.

■ Think about

▶ What does Source 1 suggest about the relationship between Lenin and Stalin?

▶ How do Sources 1 and 2, 3, and 4 differ in their view of Stalin?

Key questions

- Why had the relationship between Lenin and Stalin deteriorated?
- Where did real political power lie in the Soviet Union?
- Who of the main rivals was best placed to lead the Communist Party after Lenin's death?
- What political differences divided the Communist Party in the 1920s?
- Why did Stalin become so dominant in the party and government?

Who should lead the party after Lenin?

The Triumvirate

Many in the party saw Trotsky as the biggest threat to the future of communism in the RSFSR. All Bolsheviks were students of Marx, who had based many of his own ideas on the events of the French Revolution. This had ended with a military government under Napoleon. In the troubled times of the early 1920s, many Marxists dreaded the same happening in Russia – and as head of the Red Army Trotsky was the only figure in a position to establish such a military dictatorship. In 1922, to prevent his taking power after Lenin's death, Zinoviev, Kamenev and Stalin formed an informal alliance in the Politburo – the triumvirate or *Troika*. Zinoviev was Chairman of the Petrograd Party, Kamenev chaired the Moscow Party, while Stalin was General Secretary of the Party. Between them they hoped to control the decisions of the party.

Note

In December 1922 the Russian Socialist Federal Soviet Republic, set up in January 1918, was replaced by the Union of Soviet Socialist Republics (the Soviet Union).

Who did Lenin wish to succeed him?

When Lenin died he left a Politburo of six, soon to be increased to seven. But like many other great leaders before and since, he failed to make any precise arrangements about how Russia should be ruled and by whom. He did, however, write what has become known as his *Political Testament*, though it was called at the time 'A Letter to Congress'. This important document was dictated to his secretary in December 1922 after his second stroke, and he added a postscript the following month. In it Lenin reviewed the most prominent figures in the Communist Party.

Source 5

I think that the prime factors in the question of stability are such members of the C.C. [Central Committee of the Communist Party] as Stalin and Trotsky. I think that relations between them make up the greater part of the danger of a split, which could be avoided, and this purpose, in my opinion, would be served, among other things, by increasing the C.C. members to 50 or 100…Comrade Stalin, having become Secretary General, has unlimited authority concentrated in his hands, and I am not sure that he will always be capable of using that power with sufficient caution. Comrade Trotsky, on the other hand…is distinguished not only by his outstanding ability. He is personally perhaps the most able man in the C.C., but he has displayed excessive self-assurance and shown excessive preoccupation with the purely administrative side of the work. These two qualities of the outstanding leaders of the present C.C. can inadvertently lead to a split, and if our party does not take steps to avert this, the split may come unexpectedly. I will not give further appraisals of the personal qualities of other members of the C.C., [but] recall that the October episode with Zinoviev and Kamenev was no accident, but neither can the blame for it be laid upon them personally, any more than non-Bolshevism can upon Trotsky. Speaking of the young C.C. members, I wish to say a few words about Bukharin and Piatakov. They are, in my opinion, the most outstanding figures [among the youngest ones] and the following must be borne in mind about them: Bukharin is not only a most valuable and major theorist of the party; he is also considered the favourite of the whole party, but his theoretical views can be classified as Marxist only with great reserve…[Piatakov] is unquestionably a man of outstanding will and outstanding ability, but shows too much zeal for…the administrative side of the work to be relied upon in a serious political matter.

25 December 1922

Postscript
Stalin is too rude and this defect, although quite tolerable in our midst and in dealing amongst us Communists, becomes intolerable in a General Secretary. That is why I suggest that the comrades think about a way of removing Stalin and appointing another man in his stead who in all other respects differs from Comrade Stalin in having only one advantage, namely that of being more tolerant, more loyal, more polite and more considerate to the comrades, less capricious etc. This may appear to be a negligible detail. But I think from the standpoint of what I wrote about the relationship between Stalin and Trotsky it is not a detail, or it is a detail which can assume decisive importance.

4 January 1923

■ Think about

▶ What was Lenin's biggest fear for the future of the Communist Party?
▶ What are the main criticisms Lenin made of Trotsky and Stalin?
▶ What did Lenin mean by 'the October episode'?
▶ Why was this document important in Russia in the 1920s?
▶ Why is it important to historians today?

Facts and figures

The postscript was added after Lenin heard that Stalin had been rude to his wife, Krupskaya, on the telephone.

Lenin and Stalin

Other evidence indicates that Lenin had lost confidence in Stalin.

● **The Georgian affair**

In 1920 Georgia, dominated by the Mensheviks, had been recognized as independent by Lenin's government. However, in February 1921 the Red Army invaded and Georgia was quickly conquered. However, the Central Committee of the Georgian Communist Party rejected total integration with Russia. This led to a confrontation and a physical assault by Ordzhonikidze upon a Georgian Communist. The whole Georgian Central Committee resigned in protest. Stalin – as Commissar of Nationalities this was his area of responsibility – defended Ordzhonikidze, but Lenin asked his secretaries to gather more information. He sent notes to Trotsky for him to use against Stalin. On 6 March 1923 he dictated this letter to the Georgian party leaders:

> **Note**
>
> Serge Ordzhonikidze was a Georgian Bolshevik and a close ally of Stalin.

> **Source 6**
>
> To Comrades Mdivani, Makharadze and others (copy to comrades Trotsky and Kamenev)
> Esteemed Comrades, I follow your affairs with all my heart. I am enraged at the rudeness of Ordzhonikidze and the connivance of Stalin and Dzerzhinsky. I am preparing for you notes and a speech.
> With esteem
> Lenin

On 7 March Lenin had another stroke which left him speechless.

● **Lenin's last articles, 1923**

Lenin wrote five articles, which were published in *Pravda* before his stroke in March. One of these concerned Rabkrin, the Workers' and Peasants' Inspectorate. Lenin called for its total overhaul, saying 'no other institution is worse organized'. Stalin had been head of Rabkrin since its formation. Lenin also called for a cut in the bureaucracy of the party, headed by Stalin, and the government.

> **Facts and figures**
>
> Rabkrin had been set up by Lenin to supervise the work of the government and to prevent corruption.

Conquest (in his book *Stalin*) concludes that 'Lenin was working hard at his political plans until the last moment. Stalin was saved, in fact, by luck.'

Lenin's funeral

Lenin's death shocked the Russian people. Here is how Figes describes the scene in *A People's Tragedy*:

> **Source 7**
>
> The announcement [of Lenin's death] was made to the delegates of the Eleventh Soviet Congress. There were screams and sobbing noises from the hall. The public showed signs of genuine grief: theatres and shops closed down for a week; portraits of Lenin, draped in red and black ribbons, were displayed in many windows; thousands of mourners braved the arctic temperatures to line the streets of Moscow, where Lenin's body was brought to lie in state. Over the next three days half a million people queued for several hours to file past the bier [where his body lay].

Source 8

◄ Lenin's coffin in Red Square as crowds queue in the snow to pay their last respects.

So many soldiers volunteered to stand guard round the body that they had to increase the guard from 8 to 24 and change it every 3 minutes! Lenin's funeral would be the event of the decade in the Soviet Union. Trotsky was absent for reasons which are not entirely clear, although he did claim that Stalin told him the wrong day and this prevented him from returning from convalescence by the Black Sea.

Stalin led the mourners and gave the funeral speech over the body – a powerful image for the rest of the population when they contemplated who might later take Lenin's place. Here is a brief excerpt from the speech he gave:

Source 9

In leaving us, Comrade Lenin ordered us to keep the unity of our party as the apple of our eye. We swear to thee, Comrade Lenin, to honour thy command.

In leaving us, Comrade Lenin ordered us to maintain and strengthen the dictatorship of the proletariat. We swear to thee, Comrade Lenin, to exert our full strength in honouring thy command.

In leaving us, Comrade Lenin ordered us to strengthen with all our might the union of workers and peasants. We swear to thee, Comrade Lenin, to honour thy command.

■ **Think about**

▶ What kind of language is Stalin using here?

▶ What was Stalin trying to achieve in this speech?

▶ Do you think the speech was effective?

The Lenin cult

After his death the Politburo set up an Immortalization Commission to preserve Lenin's memory. The decision was taken, against his wife's wishes, to preserve his body and place it in a mausoleum on Red Square, the historic heart of Russia. Every city soon had Lenin's statue and the old capital was renamed Leningrad. Many ordinary citizens named their children after the Communist leader. Thousands of workers responded to the party's call to join the party in the Lenin Enrolment.

Facts and figures

In 1922 Tutankhamen's tomb was discovered, and this perhaps in part inspired the decision to embalm Lenin.

What kind of party ruled Russia in 1924?

When Lenin died, Russia was a one-party state: the Communist Party ruled without challenge. If we are to understand how and why Stalin became the most influential figure in Russian politics, we must first understand the Communist Party. In theory the Communist government was supposed to be a dictatorship of the proletariat, but by the end of the Civil War there was virtually no proletariat. Most workers had either been recruited into the army or had fled into the countryside to seek food and employment. They returned to the cities after 1921, but a dictatorship of the Communist Party was now in place.

Party membership

Before 1917 middle-class, professional revolutionaries had led the 10,000 Bolsheviks. By 1924 the party was much changed. It had grown to 472,000 on Lenin's death. However, many of the new recruits were not workers but bureaucrats, and managers. For a party claiming to be the 'vanguard of the proletariat' this was embarrassing. Some of the recruits were what Trotsky called 'radishes' – openly 'red' but retaining 'white' loyalties under the skin. Party membership brought benefits: improved rations and health-care, access to foreign goods, holidays, superior accommodation etc. According to Figes, under Lenin 5000 Bolsheviks with their families lived a privileged existence in the Kremlin, eating food cooked by chefs trained in France, taking saunas and using a fleet of cars to whisk them away to the theatre. Now that many Communists had comfortable positions they wanted to preserve them. They were more likely to support someone who was, like them, inside the party machine and was seen as a safe pair of hands.

After Lenin's death there was a huge recruitment drive – the Lenin Enrolment. Many more of these new recruits were, or had been, ordinary workers. Some historians have argued that these new members found it easier to identify with Stalin, from his lowly origins, than with the intellectuals in the leadership.

Decision-making in the party

In theory the Communist Party was democratic (see Source 10 below). Ordinary party members elected local committees. They in turn elected regional party groups, who chose delegates to the national party congress. This congress elected a Central Committee, which then chose the leaders, who sat in the Political Bureau (Politburo) and decided matters of policy. They also elected the Orgburo, which supervised the administration of the party.

In fact almost all officials in the party were appointments from above. This was a tradition begun when the party was an underground revolutionary organization and its leaders lived in exile, running it on almost military lines. In the Civil War elections had not always been possible. The party now worked through an elaborate system of patronage. Party officials at all levels made appointments and built up clients on whose support they would rely in elections. At the Twelfth Party Congress 85 per cent of the delegates were party employees, so their jobs and privileges were dependent on their loyalty to the party line or their party patron. Stalin, as head of the party secretariat, was best positioned to influence party appointments and build up a base of support throughout the party. It was said that anyone in the party was simply a telephone call away from Stalin.

Facts and figures

Party members by social class

	1919
Workers	52%
Peasants	15%
Managerial	18%
Intellectual	14%
	1923
Workers	43%
Peasants	26%
Managerial	29%

Facts and figures

Party membership 1924–1929

1924	472,000
1925	801,804
1929	1,535,362
1927	86% under 50
	54% under 30

Of 430,000 members in 1920 only 135,000 were still party members in 1927.

Quotation

The bureaucratization of the party has developed to unheard-of proportions as a result of secretarial selection. There has been created a very broad stratum of party workers, who completely renounce their own opinions.

Trotsky to the
Central Committee in 1923

Source 10

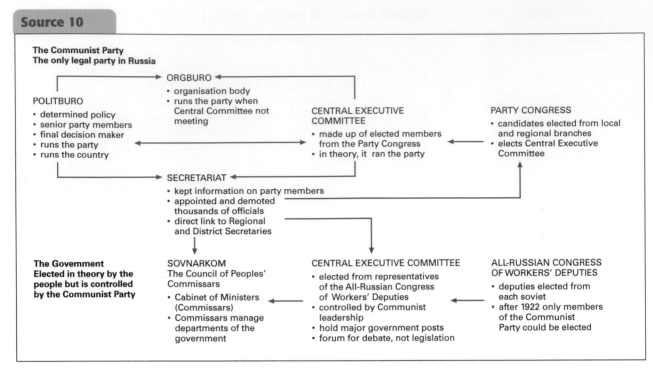

In practice, after 1919, important party and government decisions were made in the Politburo of the party. Ministers often did not attend Sovnarkom (cabinet) meetings in person, but they rarely missed Politburo meetings. Lenin often signed decrees without consulting even the Politburo, and many others followed his example. Pipes summed it up:

▲ Power in Russia and the Communist Party in the 1920s.

Source 11

The Bolsheviks were not like any western party. They were more like a ruling class.

Disputes in the party before Lenin's death

The Civil War years had created a party that had grown accustomed to the need for accepting orders from above. Orders from Moscow had to be obeyed if the Bolsheviks were to stay in power. This had not prevented important disagreements between the members.

- In 1918 **Left Communists**, including Bukharin, had denounced the Treaty of Brest-Litovsk.
- In 1920 **Democratic Centralists** demanded more open debate within the party and more democratic control by ordinary members of the party leadership and its decisions.
- In 1920 **The Workers Opposition** campaigned for greater involvement by trade unions in the running of the economy.
- In 1921 Lenin persuaded the party to accept **The Decree on Party Unity**. He hoped it would bring to an end the debates within the party. It failed to do so.
- In 1923 **Trotsky** spoke out for a greater emphasis on industrialization and changes in the NEP.

Who were the principal contenders for power?

If one man was to dominate Russia on Lenin's death, he would probably emerge from the members of the Politburo in 1924.

Source 12

▶ The politburo in 1924. Working clockwise from the top left, they are Kamenev, Stalin, Trotsky, Rykov, Bukharin and Zinoviev together, and Tomsky.

Cross reference

You can read more about Socialism in One Country on page 152

Note

The Communist International (Comintern) was set up in March 1918 to spread Communism overseas – believed at the time to be essential for the survival of the Bolshevik regime.

Bukharin

Born in 1888 he was the youngest member of the Politburo, a candidate member in March 1919 and a full member in 1924 after Lenin's death. His parents were teachers in Moscow and he went on to study economics there at university. He joined the Bolsheviks in 1906 when still a teenager. He was arrested and exiled to the Arctic Circle, but escaped and lived abroad until February 1917. He played a major part in the October Revolution in Moscow. Though he was close to Lenin, he had opposed the Brest-Litovsk Treaty, believing that revolution would spread if the war continued. He became an enthusiastic supporter of the NEP when he realized that international revolution was not imminent. He probably first coined the expression 'Socialism in One Country'. As editor of *Pravda* from 1918 he had control over the whole Soviet press. Lenin called him 'the party's best theoretician'. He co-wrote the best-selling *ABC of Communism* in 1919 and became Chairman of Comintern in 1925.

Kamenev

Born in 1883 into a Jewish family, he studied law in Moscow. He married Trotsky's sister. Before the First World War he was in exile with Lenin, with whom he edited Bolshevik publications. He returned to St Petersburg in 1914 and was arrested. Released after the February Revolution, he was one of the first Bolshevik leaders to return to the capital. There he urged co-operation with the Provisional Government and a closer working relationship with the Mensheviks. He believed that Russia was not ready for a socialist revolution and criticized Lenin's *April Theses*. When the party took the decision to plan a *coup d'etat*, he openly criticized the decision in the newspapers! After the October Revolution he resigned his chairmanship of the Central Executive Committee of Soviets when Lenin refused to form a broad left coalition, though he kept his control of the Moscow Soviet. However, he soon found himself deputizing for Lenin at meetings of Sovnarkom. In 1922 he formed a triumvirate with Zinoviev and Stalin to prevent Trotsky becoming more powerful.

Rykov

Born in 1881 into a peasant family, he was regarded as a moderate in the party. He spent the years before 1914 in Russia, escaping from Siberia seven times. With a reputation as a good administrator, he acted as People's Commissar of the Interior 1917–1918 and Chairman of the Supreme Council of the National Economy in 1918–1920 and 1923–1924. He was elected to succeed Lenin as the Chairman of Sovnarkom and Prime Minister of the USSR.

Stalin

Born into a poor family in Georgia in 1879, he was sent to a school for training priests. After he was expelled for truancy, he was drawn into underground politics. He joined the RSDLP and worked as an agitator and fundraiser. This meant robbing banks, including a famous raid in Tiflis in 1907. He was sent to Siberia many times, escaping each time. Lenin personally asked that 'that wonderful Georgian' be elected to the party Central Committee in April 1917.

He was made Commissar for Nationalities after the Revolution. This was not a glamorous post for the Communist Party, since it involved supervising the 'backward' peoples of the RSFSR. It did give wide powers to appoint people to senior positions within the regions of Russia. He supported Lenin's line on most matters. During the Civil War he organized food supplies in the south, and had conflicts with Trotsky.

In 1919 he was made head of Rabkrin. This organization was set up to check on the work of those in the government service. It gave Stalin powers to inspect all government departments. He was the only Politburo member to be also a member of the Orgburo, which supervised party affairs. In 1922 he was asked to become General Secretary of the Party, though he tried to decline the offer at first. The post of General Secretary gave Stalin the responsibility of administering the whole Communist Party, another position carrying great powers of patronage. Did he use it to build a strong group of supporters within the party? When Lenin had his first stroke he was part of the unofficial 'triumvirate'. Because of his many posts in the bureaucracy, he was nicknamed 'Comrade Card Index' in the party. He did not have a reputation as a great Marxist theoretician.

Trotsky

Born in 1883 he was a gifted Jewish writer and orator. He was widely travelled and well educated. He criticized Lenin's centralization of the party, and set up his own group Mezhraionka. He was Chairman of the St Petersburg Soviet in 1905, after which he was arrested many times. He returned to Petrograd in May 1917 and soon merged his group with the Bolsheviks. He chaired the Military Revolutionary Committee of the Petrograd Soviet, which seized power in October. As Commissar for Foreign Affairs he negotiated the Treaty of Brest-Litovsk, though he disagreed strongly with Lenin. In March 1918 he was made Commissar for War, creating the Red Army from virtually nothing. His determination and energy played an important role in the defeat of the Whites. He was elected to the Politburo in 1919. Always a reluctant supporter of the NEP, in 1923 he spoke out openly against it. He also urged the party to concentrate more on international revolution. He had had bitter disputes with Stalin, though he acknowledged to a colleague in 1924 that he thought Stalin would emerge as 'the dictator of the USSR'.

Zinoviev

Born into a Jewish farming family, he was a passionate orator. He joined the RSDLP in 1901 and remained close to Lenin after the party split in 1903. He spent the next 14 years in exile with Lenin working on the party newspapers. On his return to Petrograd he opposed the October *coup*, co-writing an article in the press criticizing the *coup* before it had happened. He then resigned from the Bolshevik government when Lenin refused to coalesce with other socialist parties. He was quickly rehabilitated and was the first Chairman of Comintern in 1919. In 1922 he formed the triumvirate to combat Trotsky's influence in the party and was Chairman of the Petrograd Party.

■ Activity

Copy out and fill in this chart using the information in this chapter.
Each of the Politburo members had great influence in the party.
Each had difficulties in his position or in his past record in the party.
Who do you think was best placed to become the dominant figure in the party after Lenin's death?

	Bukharin	Kamenev	Rykov	Stalin	Trotsky	Zinoviev
Character						
Connection to Lenin						
Party popularity						
Powers of patronage						
Service to the party						
Marxist theory						
Links with other Politburo members						
Government experience						

The battleground

Who would become the dominant figure in Russian politics would not only be determined by what these individuals had done in the past, there were also important policy considerations for the future.

Who was the true disciple of Lenin?

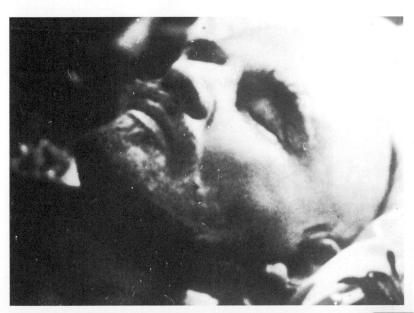

▶ The embalmed body of Lenin in his mausoleum.

The sometimes bitter debates in the party did not cease with Lenin's death; in fact they intensified. The so-called 'Literary War' saw each leader trying to prove to the party he was the best interpreter of Lenin, while criticizing the position of others. Each politician strove to take on Lenin's mantle – to identify himself as Lenin's closest comrade and most faithful disciple. But as you know Lenin had altered his policies from time to time. What, therefore, was Leninism?

Economic Policy

The New Economic Policy was not popular in the Communist Party. It was a great defeat for the world's first Communist government to have to reintroduce capitalist competition and private ownership back into the Russian economy. Walter Durranty, the American journalist, in 1923 described the result:

Source 14

Lenin's New Economic policy has put a severe strain on...many members of the Communist Party...there is now staying in the Moscow Guest House a certain Urquhart, who before the Revolution was the head of a huge Anglo-Russian copper corporation in the Urals. He is credited with having been the chief supporter of Kolchak and Denikin. For Communists he has come to personify the arch-fiend of capitalism, but now they see him negotiating concessions with the Soviet government on apparently friendly terms.

■ **Think about**

▶ Why were some party members unhappy about the NEP?

Lenin told the party that this was a temporary measure: 'We must take one step back in order to take two steps forward'.

But what was temporary? A few months? A few years? A few decades? Should the party abandon the New Economic Policy? If so, when?

Russia's relations with the rest of the world

Lenin had believed that communism could only survive in Russia if it was supported by other Communist countries. Even when Russians were starving in 1921 the government sent scarce resources to overseas parties to start a revolution abroad.

During the First World War Lenin looked to the soldiers in the western armies to bring about a revolution, spurred on by the Russian example. Later in 1920, during the Polish war, he hoped to march communism into Europe on the points of Russian bayonets. By 1922 the immediate prospects of revolution elsewhere appeared hopeless. How should the Communist government react to this? There were two main approaches:

● **'Permanent Revolution'**
Trotsky and others on the left of the party believed that the Soviet Union could not achieve communism without help from other socialist states. In Trotsky's words: 'There is not enough proletarian yeast in our peasant dough'. The first priority of the government, therefore, should be to foster revolutions overseas.

■ **Think about**

▶ What did Trotsky mean by this?

● **'Socialism in One Country'**
Stalin put forward this different view at the end of 1924. Now that the last attempt at revolution had failed in Germany in 1923, spreading revolution

■ **Think about**

▶ Why might Stalin's views have won more support in the party?

overseas looked more and more unlikely. Stalin, therefore, argued that the Soviet Union could achieve communism by its own efforts, without external help.

How should the Communist Party govern?

One of the prices paid for victory in the Civil War was greater party discipline. Not only had all other political parties been banned but also, when faced with calls for more democracy in the party in 1920 and 1921 by such groups as The Workers' Opposition, Lenin had persuaded the party at the Tenth Party Congress in 1921 to ban separate factions within the party. This gave huge power to the Party Secretariat and the bureaucracy, especially Stalin. Some members, especially Trotsky, called for more open discussion within the party.

By far the longest and most important debate was on the economy.

'Left' and 'Right' Communists.
What should be done about industry?

All Russian Communists believed that industrialization was crucial to the building of a socialist society. As Marxists they believed that true communism could not be achieved until mass production had created a surplus of goods, so that 'From each according to his ability, to each according to his needs could be met'. The problem was how to achieve this.

The party was divided fundamentally on the issue. The two wings of the party which debated these economic differences were called at the time 'Right' and 'Left' Communists.

'Right' Communists

They believed that, after the economic collapse of the war years, Russia needed time to recover and consolidate. Bukharin said:

Source 15

We tried to take on ourselves the organization of everything – even the organization of the peasants and the small producers…From the viewpoint of economic rationality this was madness.

For them any talk of achieving socialism in the foreseeable future was out of the question. Bukharin talked of decades. He believed that the best way to socialism was by allowing the peasants to improve their farms:

Source 16

Enrich yourselves [To the peasants] We shall ride to socialism at the speed of the peasant nag.

This would not only provide more crops, such as cotton, for industry, but also more and cheaper food for the cities. Surpluses would also provide food exports abroad. With the foreign currency this earned, and rising taxes from successful farmers and Nepmen, there would be capital to invest in industrial expansion.

In this way Russia would become a modern industrialized country.

Note

Nepmen was the party's name for private traders.

Source 17

Expanded industrial growth

Private investment

More Nepmen?

But

State investment

Greater demand for manufactured goods

More grain to sell abroad

Foreign currency

Increased production

More Kulaks?

But

More tax revenue

Higher peasant income

The Government

High food prices for industrial workers

Sets

High agricultural prices

But

◀ Bukharin's path to industrialization

'Left' Communists

These believed that the NEP was an obstacle to socialism. If it had been necessary in 1921, it was now time for a change. They thought the NEP was creating a new bourgeoisie in the countryside, the so-called *kulaks*, and in the towns in the form of Nepmen. The USSR was also becoming an industrialized society far too slowly.

Source 18

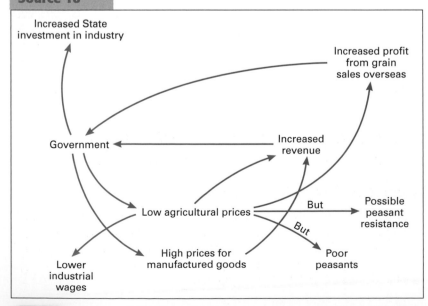

Increased State investment in industry

Increased profit from grain sales overseas

Government

Increased revenue

Low agricultural prices

But

Possible peasant resistance

But

Lower industrial wages

High prices for manufactured goods

Poor peasants

◀ Primitive socialist accumulation

Note

Smychka was the alliance Lenin called for between workers and peasants.

Note

Vesenkha was The Supreme Council for National Economy. Communists believed that the direction of the economy should be decided by the government.

'Primitive socialist accumulation' was the policy desired by many on the left. Preobrazhensky, a friend of Trotsky, thought the price of grain paid to the peasants should be reduced and as much grain as possible should be sold abroad to raise the capital to buy machines and machine tools. A national economic plan should be made to achieve rapid industrialization. The peasants would have to bear the burden of this transformation. This would mean turning away from Lenin's *smychka*.

Economic planning

Vesenkha was set up to plan the economy in 1917. In 1926 a new head was appointed, Kuibyshev, who wanted to expand industry more quickly. In 1921 Vesenkha set up Gosplan to collect statistics. Gosplan also produced a plan to industrialize Russia. At the end of the 1920s these two organizations produced ambitious targets for the economy. Historian J.N. Westwood in 1980 described the economic situation as follows:

Source 19

The situation after 1925 was this: the fast rate of economic improvement of the preceding years was in danger of petering out, for it had been obtained by the relatively easy restoration of pre-war productive assets and future increments could be gained only by investing in completely new plant.

Westwood, *Russia since 1917*, 1980

■ Activity

Divide yourselves up into pairs. One from each pair should take on the role of 'Left', and the other of 'Right' Communists. Write a short speech explaining why you think your approach to industrializing the USSR is the right one. You can then debate this with your class.

When you have finished, note down what were the key differences between 'Left' and 'Right' Communists.

■ Think about

▶ Had Lenin given a firm direction for the party on this important question?

▶ Which of the two groups in the party do you think was likely to win the argument? Why?

To find the answer read on…

The battle for dominance 1922–1929

The struggle for power can be divided into three distinct stages.

Stage One. The defeat of Trotsky

■ Think about

▶ What party organizations did Kamenev, Zinoviev and Stalin control?

Trotsky was popular in the Red Army, but he lacked a power-base in the party. Kamenev, Zinoviev and Stalin headed the important party organizations. When they co-operated with each other in the so-called Triumvirate, they were able to outvote Trotsky and his few supporters decisively in the Politburo, the Central Committee and the Party Congresses.

Lenin had given Trotsky advice, especially on the Georgian question, on how to attack Stalin, but he declined to do so. Trotsky's most potent weapon was Lenin's *Political Testament*, which had been so critical of Stalin. However, when the *Testament* was discussed by the party in 1924, Zinoviev and Kamenev spoke for Stalin. The Central Committee after Lenin's death decided that the *Testament* should remain secret.

Trotsky made difficulties for himself. In October 1923 he had criticized the Central Committee for their conduct of economic policy and complained of 'the incorrect and unhealthy regime in the party'. He complained that appointment had replaced election within the party, 'a secretarial apparatus from above'. The Party Congress, almost to a man, rejected Trotsky's view. He was also accused of factionalism, since he had persuaded 45 other members of the party to sign his criticisms. It began a concerted attack by Stalin, Zinoviev and Kamenev on Trotsky's record.

At this crucial time Trotsky was continually ill. He failed to attend Lenin's funeral. He said afterwards that Stalin had told him the wrong day! Perhaps this failure illustrates Trotsky's lack of political sensitivity.

The death of Lenin was followed by the 'Literary War'. Stalin in *On the Foundations of Leninism* attacked Trotsky's criticisms of, and disloyalty to, Lenin. The arguments grew very bitter. Trotsky replied in *Lessons of October* with a detailed attack on Zinoviev and Kamenev for their actions in opposing Lenin in 1917. Kamenev, Stalin and Bukharin continued the attacks. Stalin published *Comrade Trotsky's Theory of Permanent Revolution*. Denunciations of Trotsky at many party meetings became routine.

The result of these attacks was that Trotsky was replaced as Commissar for War by his deputy, Frunze, in January 1925. Trotsky made no moves to use his command of the Red Army to protect his position. Perhaps he accepted the fact that Stalin would become dominant in the party. Trotsky is reported to have said to Smirnov in 1924:

Source 20

[Stalin] is needed by all of them; by the tired radicals, by the bureaucrats, by the Nepmen, the upstarts, by all the worms that are crawling out of the upturned soil of the manured revolution. He knows how to meet them on their own ground, he speaks their language and he knows how to lead them. He has the deserved reputation of an old revolutionary.

Stage Two. The defeat of the Left

Once Trotsky's influence had been eclipsed, Zinoviev and Kamenev grew uneasy about the influence that Stalin increasingly had over the party. They were also unhappy about the conduct of policy to the peasants.

After allowing many concessions to the peasants, the result had been greater difficulty for the government in the purchase of grain, despite a good harvest. Zinoviev called in December 1925 for a change of policy to the peasants and in foreign policy. Kamenev criticized the idea that there should be 'one leader' and again attacked Stalin's authority in the party.

■ **Think about**
▶ Why do you think the Party Congress rejected Trotsky's criticisms?
▶ What does this episode suggest about Trotsky as a politician?

■ **Think about**
What does this quote tell us about:
▶ the situation in the USSR?
▶ Trotsky?

Facts and figures

The Politburo in Dec 1924
Bukharin, Kamenev, Rykov, Stalin, Trotsky, Zinoviev

The Politburo in Dec 1926
Bukharin, Kuibyshev, Molotov, Rudzutak, Rykov, Stalin, Tomsky, Voroshilov

In 1926, party meetings in Leningrad and Moscow were addressed by critics of Zinoviev and Kamenev. Elections to the city committees put new 'loyal' members in control of these two key cities – and Zinoviev and Kamenev were removed as Secretaries of the local parties.

The size of the Politburo was increased by adding close political allies of Stalin, Voroshilov, Rudzutak, Molotov and Kuibyshev. In 1926 Trotsky, Kamenev and Zinoviev finally joined together in the 'United Opposition'. They attacked the NEP and the lack of free debate in the party. It was too late. The party removed Zinoviev and Kamenev from the Politburo in 1926 and then, with Trotsky, from the party in 1927.

In October 1927 the United Opposition, together with Krupskaya (Lenin's widow) held a demonstration in Moscow's Red Square. There were more police present than followers. It was the last organized effort by the Left.

Stalin and Bukharin now appeared the twin giants of the party. In 1928 Trotsky was exiled to Kazakhstan, and then in January 1929 expelled from the USSR.

Stage Three. The defeat of the Right

Bukharin, Tomsky and Rykov argued that the NEP must continue for many years. The *smychka* must be preserved.

In 1927 there was a crisis of grain supplies – once again after a good harvest. The party, with Stalin's support, passed a number of new measures, including:

● Soldiers were to be sent into the countryside to requisition grain
● All hoarded grain was to be confiscated
● Hoarding grain was made a crime (Article 107).

In 1928 Stalin took a special interest in the Shakhty affair, a trial of so-called saboteurs in Russian mines allegedly acting in league with foreign spies.

Bukharin wrote a withering attack on the new policy to the peasants in *Notes of an Economist* in September 1928. Now it was those on the Right who were denounced as factionalists. They were slowly removed from their positions. In 1929 Bukharin lost his presidency of Comintern, editorship of *Pravda* and his seat on the Politburo. Tomsky was sacked as head of trade unions. In 1930 he and Rykov were removed from the Politburo. Stalin was now the dominant figure in the party and the Soviet Union.

■ Historical debate

This summary of events gives an outline of how many of the prominent figures in the 1920s lost their political positions. Historians do not agree on why this happened. Some see Stalin as a devious, cold and calculating man, without any political convictions, who manoeuvred in the party debates so that he could oust possible rivals. Others see Stalin as the moderate figure in the party, holding it together while others broke away and attacked the party line. For some the real divisions in the Soviet Union were about personalities; for others they were about principle.

To find out more, turn to Chapter 12 'Historians and Stalin.'

> **Quotation**
>
> We have internal enemies. We have external enemies. This, comrades, must not be forgotten for a single moment.
>
> Stalin, 1928

Spotlight

Was the NEP working?

In industry

Monthly Wages of Urban Workers

In roubles (reckoned on the basis of the 1913 value of the rouble)

1913	30.5
1920–1	10.1
1922–3	15.9
1924–5	25.2
1925–6	28.6

Industrial Production

	1913	1920	1921	1923	1924	1926
Factory production (millions of roubles)	10251	1410	2004	4005	7739	11083
Coal (millions of tons)	29.0	8.7	8.9	13.7	16.1	27.6
Electricity (millions of kWh)	1945	–	520	1146	1562	3508
Steel (thousands of tons)	4231	–	183	709	1140	3141
Cotton (millions of metres)	2582	–	105	691	963	2286

Urban unemployment

Under the NEP State-run factories were expected to increase productivity. Workers were laid off as a result.

1922	160,000 unemployed
1929	1,741,000 unemployed

In 1924–1925, according to the historian Nove, 18 private companies employed between 200 and 1000 workers each.

Nepmen

According to the historian Andrle only 25% of licensed traders under NEP had their own premises. The rest were market stall-holders and pedlars.

Source 21

▲ An anti-Nepmen cartoon from 1927.

■ Questions

1 Why were wages paid in kind in 1921?

2 Did the life of ordinary factory workers improve after 1922?

3 To what extent had industry recovered from the Civil Wars by 1926?

4 What kinds of people were most 'Nepmen?'

5 Does the evidence here suggest that the party wholeheartedly supported the NEP?

Some changes made to the NEP before 1928

- 1926 Nepmen had to pay a new tax on 'superprofits.'
- In 1926 penalties of three years' imprisonment were imposed for 'evil-intentioned increases in price'.

Wages in kind (goods and food)

1921	7% of wages in money The rest in kind
1923	Rationing stopped
1924	All wages paid in money

Government declarations before 1928

- 1926 Party Congress demanded 'the strengthening of the economic leadership of large-scale socialist industry over the entire economy of the country.'
- 1927 Sovnarkom Decree called for 'a united all-union plan...which would facilitate the maximum development of economic regions...and the maximum utilization of their resources for the purpose of industrialization of the country.'

In agriculture

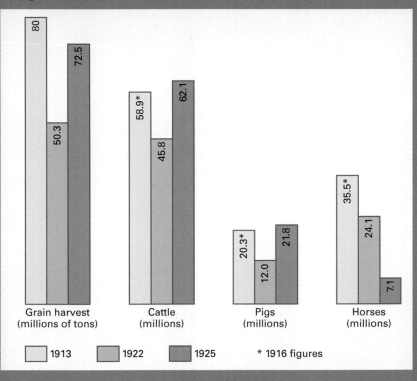

Grain harvest (millions of tons)	Cattle (millions)	Pigs (millions)	Horses (millions)
80 / 50.3 / 72.5	58.9* / 45.8 / 62.1	20.3* / 12.0 / 21.8	35.5* / 24.1 / 7.1

1913   1922   1925   * 1916 figures

% of farm types according to sown area in 1927	
State farms	1.1
Collective farms	0.6
Peasant holdings	98.3

Farming Methods in Russia in 1928

Most of the 350,000 villages divided up their land in three large fields according to the strip system.
20% of peasants still farmed with a wooden plough.
50% of the harvest was cut by hand.

In 1925 a party conference:
- Reduced agricultural taxes
- Allowed peasants to hire labour
- Allowed peasants to lease land from other peasants.

All these measures benefited the richer peasants.

State farm prices

In 1926 the State cut the prices paid to peasants by an average of 6%. The cut in grain prices was 25%.

Result

At the end of 1927 the State had been able to buy at the lower fixed price only 50% of what it had bought by December 1926. The harvest had been excellent.

International comparisons

Gross domestic product per head in constant $

	1913	1928
Japan	800	1150
Russia (USSR)	900	900
Italy	1550	1780
Germany	1960	2280
France	2000	2550
USA	3790	4690
UK	2970	3110

In transport

Number of road vehicles in the Soviet Union in 1925

Cars	7448
Lorries	5500
Buses	263

1917–21 Because of inflation public transport was free
1921 Charges on public transport were reintroduced
1926–7 Railways carried more traffic than in 1913
1926 The party imposed high rail tariffs on private traders.

■ Questions

1 Was the State closer to meeting the food needs of the working population in the cities in 1927 than it had been in 1920?

2 Why did the government find it difficult to buy grain after the 1926 harvest?

3 What might a 'Right Communist' have suggested was the best way to tackle this problem?

4 What do international comparisons suggest about the achievements of the world's first Communist government at this time? What would party members have felt about this?

5 Was public transport more in keeping with a Communist society in 1927 than in 1920?

Was the USSR closer to socialism in 1927 than in 1920?

What would a Marxist socialist society be like in terms of its a) agriculture, b) industry c) social and political organisation?

Collect together all the information you can find about the USSR in 1920 and 1927. Then make a presentation to your group, using at least one visual image.

The crisis of 1927–1928

In 1927–1928 the USSR once again found itself facing major problems. These came on two fronts – domestic and foreign.

At home

The grain harvest of 1927 was not as good as the bumper harvest of 1926, but it was still more than enough to feed the cities. However, by December the State had managed to buy from the peasants only half of what it had bought by the same month the previous year. The industrial population was threatened again by starvation. Why had this happened?

The State lowered the prices offered to peasants. As a result they had less incentive to sell.

Much of Russia's surplus grain before 1917 had come from the large estates, which produced for the market for profit. After the Revolution these estates had been replaced by peasant farmers, who consumed a larger proportion of their produce themselves.

There was a real shortage in the towns of goods for the peasant farmers to buy. What was the point in selling grain to the State in return for money with which you could buy nothing? Much better to eat it yourself or feed it to your animals.

There were fewer private traders (Nepmen) because Article 107 of the Criminal Code had made them liable to arrest and imprisonment.

How should the problem be solved?

Here there was genuine disagreement between those on the left and the right in the party.

The 1927 Party Congress agreed in December to encourage farmers to join collective farms to compete with private farmers, though Molotov urged harsh controls for *kulaks* and 'large scale collectivization.' After the Congress, party leaders went into the countryside to supervise grain collections. Stalin went to western Siberia, where requisitioning as in 1918 was used to collect grain. The party used force, rather than persuasion or higher prices, to encourage peasants to release surpluses.

The 'extraordinary measures' worked and enough food was found, but it left a legacy of bitterness in the countryside. This was called the 'Urals-Siberian method.'

In 1928 State grain prices were raised by 20 per cent to tempt farmers to sell their grain, but, despite an adequate harvest, food supplies to the government fell again. Private traders toured the countryside offering double the State prices for grain. Rationing had to be reintroduced into Moscow and Leningrad.

All this meant a crisis in industry too. Instead of exporting grain, the government was forced to buy grain from abroad to feed the cities. This threatened the Five Year Plan for industrial development which had just been agreed.

Abroad

The NEP began a short period of easier relations with the West. In 1922 only Germany had good relations with the USSR, but in 1924 the British and Italian governments recognized the USSR. However, events took a turn for the worse when Germany entered the League of Nations in 1926, leaving the USSR isolated again. In the same year Marshal Pilsudski seized power in Poland. Pilsudski had led the forces that defeated the Red armies in Poland in 1920 and he was violently anti-Communist.

In 1927 British police raided the offices of the Soviet trade delegation in London, claiming to find documents which showed the USSR was working secretly to bring about a Marxist revolution in the UK. Britain broke off diplomatic relations with the USSR. Meanwhile in China, Communists were slaughtered by their former allies the Kuomintang.

The international situation caused great anxiety, and Russia was seized by a war scare. Were all these events a sign of a forthcoming united attack by capitalist powers on the world's only Marxist state? Were the wars of foreign intervention of 1918–1920 to be repeated? If so, how would the industrially backward USSR survive? In Stalin's famous words of 1931 (see Source 22).

The end of the NEP

These events had a profound effect on Russian politics. The party became convinced it was faced with enemies within and outside the USSR. The NEP, they believed, was not a solution either to the State's agricultural needs or to its need for rapid industrialization. It, therefore, abandoned private trading and began a whole-scale collectivization of peasant farms. This left turn did not go unopposed. Bukharin, Rykov and Tomsky spoke out against it. They were denounced as 'factionalists' and were gradually removed from their positions of influence. Trotsky was expelled from the USSR.

■ Source 22

We are fifty or a hundred years behind the advanced countries. We must make good this distance in ten years. Either we do it, or we shall be crushed.

■ Think about

▶ Who did party members believe were the enemies within? Why?

■ Further reading

A. Bullock, *Hitler and Stalin: Parallel Lives*, 1991
E.H. Carr, *The Russian Revolution from Lenin to Stalin, 1917-29*
R. Conquest, *Stalin*, 1991
S. Fitzpatrick, *The Russian Revolution*, 1982
R. McNeal, *Stalin: Man and Ruler*, 1988
A. Nove, *An Economic History of the USSR*, 1992
R. Pipes, *Three Whys of the Russian Revolution*, 1998
R. Tucker, *Stalin as Revolutionary*, 1974
C. Ward, *Stalin's Russia*, 1993

■ Activity

Stalin has been called the party's 'arch-mediocrity' and a 'grey blur.' Others called him a 'shrewd tactician' 'with judgement and analytical power'. Look back at this chapter. What evidence can you find to support these two differing views of Stalin in the events of 1922–1929?

● Did Stalin change his attitude to the central issues facing the Communist government?
● Which of the leading politicians in the 1920s remained consistent in his policies for the Russian economy?
● Make a list of all the reasons why Stalin emerged as the dominant figure in Soviet politics by 1929.

Conclusions

By the end of 1928 Stalin was a dominant figure in the Communist Party and, therefore, the State. Lenin's death was followed by intense debates about party policy, and especially about the future of the NEP. These debates provided the essential ideological backdrop for the personal ambitions of individual leaders. Stalin appears to have been either extremely cunning or simply the beneficiary of the mistakes of others as the leading figures, one after another, put themselves out on a limb against party policy. Whatever the reason, the end of the NEP heralded a new period when the party would try not just to stay in power, but would also try to build a Communist society in the USSR, a paradise on earth.

Chapter 9

Building Paradise

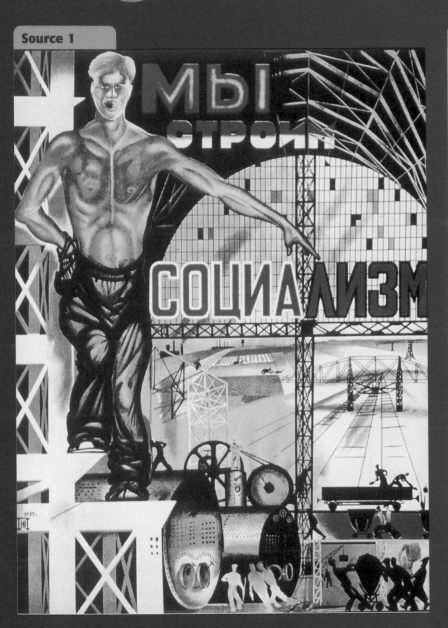

Lathe operators measured 'precision' grinding with their fingers because they had no instruments. Tractors suffered cracked blocks and stripped gears because the peasants who drove them 'knew no more than that when you pushed the pedal the tractor moved – matters such as lubrication and timing were completely beyond them.'…Overmanning was rife…Vast numbers were absorbed into office work…Politics and class origin were more important to promotion than ability.

Moynahan, *The Russian Century*, 1994

■ Think about

▶ How does this poster suggest socialism should be built?

▶ This is a government poster. Does this limit its usefulness to historians?

◀ A Communist poster from 1927. It says 'We are building socialism'.

Introduction

The 1930s saw a remarkable transformation in the Soviet Union. At the end of the 1920s the Soviet Union remained a backward state in comparison with other major powers. Twelve years of Communist rule had restored the country to roughly the same economic position that she had occupied in 1913. This may perhaps be regarded as a great achievement in view of the appalling cost of the First World War and the following period of civil war. It was not, however, what Russian Marxists hoped to achieve. From 1928 onwards the cautious pragmatism of the NEP years was thrown aside and the whole population was plunged into a concerted drive to industrialize and modernize the USSR – a 'Second Revolution.' Lenin's revolution had been to put the Communist Party in power; Stalin's would build the Communist Utopia in the Soviet Union.

Note

Pragmatism means that there was less emphasis on ideology and more on gaining practical results.

The methods chosen to carry out this 'Second Revolution' were extraordinary. The peasants were driven into collective farms, largely against their will. So-called *kulaks* were shot or driven into exile in an effort to create a classless, socialist society in the countryside and modernize the primitive state of Soviet agriculture. Meanwhile, three Five Year Plans set impossible targets for industrial enterprises. Huge power plants, new canals and railways, vast new industrial complexes were all constructed from scratch, often in the most inhospitable climate and terrain. In order to complete at least partially these great transformations, the party believed a new culture with different attitudes had to be built. Those who did not actively support the new objectives set for the Soviet people were now seen as 'enemies of the people,' whether they were party members or not. The secret police, the OGPU or later NKVD, filled the labour camps which appeared across the Soviet Union with those who were regarded as an obstacle to socialist progress.

Key questions

- Why and how were the farms of the USSR collectivized?
- How successful were the collective farms?
- Why and how did the USSR become more industrialized?
- How successful was the industrialization drive in the USSR?

Although historians disagree about many of these questions, what is not in doubt is the turmoil into which the country was plunged and the suffering which the population had to bear.

Building socialism in the countryside?

As we have seen in the last chapter the NEP was in crisis in the late 1920s. The most urgent problem was to provide food for the cities.

Why were farms collectivized?

1. To achieve socialism in the countryside

From 1925 onwards, private traders and entrepreneurs in the cities and industrialized regions had to face increasingly harsh taxes and even arrest. It was, therefore, a growing contradiction to allow private farmers greater freedom to make profits in the countryside. For all members of the party socialized farming meant collective farms. Lenin had set up the first of these, hoping other peasants would follow the example of their success. However, less than 2 per cent of farmers were in collective farms in 1928, and even 'Right' Communists, like Bukharin, were disappointed by this. The 1927 Party Congress approved a target of 20 per cent of farmers to be in collectivized farms by 1933.

Facts and figures

There were two types of collective farm. In both land was pooled and worked together.
1. A *sovkhoz* was run directly by the State. The peasants were paid wages like factory workers.
2. A *kolkhoz* was organized by the farmers themselves. They were given a share of the surplus production of the collective farm after the State had taken its quota.
Stalin favoured the *sovkhoz*, but most farms were of the *kolkhoz* type.

2. To control and transform 'the backward peasantry'

For many forward-thinking Russians the peasantry had always represented the biggest obstacle to progress. Alexander II, Witte and Stolypin had all tried to modernize agriculture and change the ingrained habits of the conservative peasantry. For Communists the desire to transform rural life was even stronger. The peasantry was seen as primitive and uneducated. The proletariat was the class of the future. There was only 1 Communist in every 125 peasant households. Peasant ignorance, they believed, made them easy prey to *kulak* propaganda and religious superstition. They would always be, therefore, a potential source of opposition to the Communist regime.

After collectivization the party hoped to control the peasants, and to 'raise' by education their cultural level to support Communist ideals.

3. To solve the problems of food supply

In 1927 and 1928 the government had great difficulty in purchasing grain to feed the urban population. It resorted to seizing grain, just as Lenin's government had done during the years of civil war. As Marxists, who believed all history was determined by class struggle, the Communist government expected to be opposed by its class enemies. Since the harvest had been good, for them the only sensible explanation of food shortages was that grain was being hoarded by the better-off peasants, the *kulaks*. Collectivization would mean that the State would manage agriculture and guarantee the food supply in future.

4. To raise revenue for industrialization

The new, larger collectivized farms, bringing economies of scale and using modern equipment, would produce more. Large surpluses would then be sold abroad to pay for the import of machinery to build an industrialized society.

5. To destroy political rivals

In 1928 Stalin shared power with the Right: Bukharin, Tomsky and Rykov. A move to forced collectivization would isolate them and enable Stalin to emerge as the dominant figure in the Soviet Union.

6. To prove the success of Communism to the Russian people and the rest of the world

Source 3

We are leaving behind us our age old backward Russian past and when we motorize the USSR and put the peasant on a tractor, then let them try to catch us up – those respected Capitalists with their much vaunted civilization.

Stalin in 1929

How was collectivization achieved?

Policy towards the peasants did not change immediately. At first the party hoped for voluntary collectivization. It drifted toward forcing peasants into collective farms over a period of two years. It began with the grain crisis you have read about in the previous chapter.

Timeline

Nov 1929 25,000-ers into the villages
Dec 1929 Attack on *kulaks* begins
Jan 1930 All-out collectivisation drive begins
March 1930 Stalin's 'Dizzy with success' speech
1932 Peasants allowed to trade 'The Five Stalks Law' Internal passports introduced
1932–4 Famine in principal grain areas
1935 New *Kolkhoz* Charter

Stage One: Emergency measures

In January 1928 the Politburo voted unanimously for 'emergency measures'. In practice this meant confiscating grain by force. Historian Stephen Cohen called this 'a pivotal event,' signalling an end to the *smychka*, the partnership between workers and peasantry. In the summer of 1928 over 100,000 party workers, Komsomol members and factory workers went out into the farms to help with the harvest.

Stage Two: The Urals-Siberian method

This method of collecting grain was approved by the Central Committee in November 1928 and used during the 1928–1929 winter. Village meetings were called and the poorer peasants were asked to point out those *kulak* families hoarding grain. They were offered a reward of 25 per cent of any grain confiscated. This produced some of the grain needed for the cities, but was not a permanent solution to the problems of a secure grain supply in the future.

Stage Three (i): Forced collectivization

In summer 1929 the Collective Farm Centre was set up. Some regional party committees announced plans to collectivize farms in their areas. The Central Committee in November decided on 'a further speed-up of the processes of collectivization' and 25,000 more party workers from the factories were sent into the villages to organize the peasants into collective farms. In January 1929 Stalin had called for the collectivization of all grain-producing areas by autumn 1930. There was now a headlong rush to collectivize and almost 60 per cent of all farms were collectivized between November 1929 and March 1930. In theory peasants were supposed to vote for the creation of collective farms, but there was widespread opposition. Individuals who objected to the new policy ran great risks: in particular of being branded a *kulak* and transported or worse.

Source 4

▶ Peasants voting to join the collective farm.

■ Think about

▶ How enthusiastic were the peasants in this picture about entering the collective farm?

▶ Why were they voting for collectivization?

Stage Three (ii): Dekulakization

Source 5

The world had seemed simple to me. The worker was the ideal, the repository of the highest morality. The *kulak* was a beast, an evil-doer, a criminal.

From the memoirs of General P. Grigorenko, exiled to the USA after Stalin's death

For the party the richer peasants had always been the biggest obstacles to collectivization, and therefore they had to be removed. A separate Politburo committee was set up to make recommendations about the *kulaks*. It divided them into three categories. The most dangerous *kulaks* were to be imprisoned or shot. Category two were to be transported to the North or beyond the Urals. The third group was to be given marginal (poor) land outside the collective farms. Targets were set for dekulakization for each district and village. Peasants were again invited to denounce the *kulaks* in their village. The number of *kulak* families affected by these measures was over 1 million. Probably about one-third of these were transported, according to the historian L. Viola.

Stage Three (iii): Peasant opposition

Although the concept of *kulak* made sense in Marxist theory, it was almost meaningless in terms of the realities of village life. The party assumed that 3 per cent of the peasants were *kulaks*, about 1 million families. Quotas of *kulak* families to be identified were set for each area, but on the ground so-called *kulak* families were difficult to identify. At first there were no definitions for party workers to follow. When the orders finally arrived, they were often found to fit no members of the village. Villages had a complex web of inter-relationships. Richer and poorer families worked together, prayed together, and married each other. 'We have no *kulaks* here' was a common reply when the collectivization squads arrived in villages.

It did not stop many brigades from realizing their quotas, as V. Kravchenko remembered in *I Chose Freedom* published in Britain in 1947.

> ### Source 6
>
> So this was the 'liquidation of the *kulaks* as a class!' A lot of simple peasants being torn from their native soil, stripped of all their worldly goods, and shipped to some distant lumber camps or irrigation works. For some reasons most of the families were left behind…As I stood there, I heard a woman shouting in an unearthly voice…The woman, her hair streaming, held a flaming sheaf of grain in her hands…She tossed the burning sheaf onto the thatched roof of the house. 'Infidels! Murderers! We worked all our lives for our house. You won't have it. The flames will have it!'

Some of the collectivization brigades interpreted their briefs very widely, and tried to collectivize all peasant possessions and property, including goats, chickens, tools and gardens. Many brigades were accompanied by youngsters from the League of the Militant Godless, who also set about attacking the churches, burning icons, taking down church bells and deporting the priests. There was a determined effort to break the culture of the peasants. Churches were transformed into barns, socialist clubs and libraries. Holidays based on the Church calendar were renamed: Easter was now 'The day of the first furrow', the 'Day of Elijah' was now the 'Day of Electrification.' Even villages were renamed 'The Red Ploughman, Red Dawn etc.

This attack on culture, and the deaths accompanying it, reminded many peasants of the Coming of the Antichrist with his Four Horsemen of the Apocalypse. The Communist government was linked to the Antichrist. Priests preached that collectivization was against God's will. It was also associated in the peasant mind with immorality – there were widespread rumours about sharing wives and beds.

> ### Quotation
>
> We must break down the resistance of the *kulaks* and deprive this class of its existence. We must eliminate the *kulaks* as a class. We must smash the *kulaks*…we must strike at the *kulaks* so hard as to prevent them rising to their feet again.
>
> **Stalin to the Party Congress in December 1929**

> ### Quotation
>
> *Kulak* status was in the eye of the beholder.
>
> **L. Viola,** *Peasant Rebels under Stalin*, **1996**

> ### ■ Think about
>
> ▶ What is Kravchenko's attitude to dekulakization?

> ### Facts and figures
>
> The League of the Militant Godless was set up in 1925 to destroy religious belief. Marxists regarded all religion as ignorance and superstition. Many of its members were also members of Komsomol, the youth branch of the Communist Party.

▶ The looting of the Simonov Monastery by Red Army soldiers in 1927.

■ **Think about**

▶ Why do you think this photograph was taken?

▶ In what ways is this photograph useful to a historian?

Quotation

The successes of our collective farm policy are due…to the fact that it rests on the voluntary character of the collective farm movement… Collective farms should not be imposed by force.

Stalin in *Pravda*
on 2 March 1930

There was an explosion of opposition in many areas of the Soviet Union. There were individual acts of terror and murder against collectivizers. More common was spontaneous village action to prevent the removal of a *kulak* family, the disruption of collective farm meetings, breaking open farm stores to take back their grain and tools. Women took the lead in many of these actions, and it was more difficult for the brigades and OGPU troops to use violence against them. Many peasants slaughtered and ate or sold their animals rather than hand them over to the new collective farms. March 1930, in L. Viola's words, saw 'a massive peasant rebellion.'

Stage Four: The party retreats

On 2 March 1930 *Pravda* carried an article written by Stalin under the headline 'Dizzy with success'. This article explained that some party workers had been too enthusiastic and had forced the pace. They were criticized for collectivizing village livestock, closing churches and 'bureaucratic methods'. The article called for the return of unjustly dekulakized peasants and a purge of overzealous officials. The paper sold out quickly and was read throughout the countryside. From a total of 60 per cent of peasants collectivized in February 1930 the figure fell to about 20 per cent by August as peasants left the *kolkhozy* in droves.

Why this sudden retreat? The regime was certainly shocked by the widespread opposition. If the spring sowing of cereal crops was not completed, rationing and perhaps starvation would be inevitable. As events were quickly to show, the party had not abandoned its policies.

Stage Five: Collectivization resumed

As soon as the grain was collected in from the good harvest of 1930, collectivization began afresh. By 1931 more than half of peasant families were in *kolkhozy* again. By 1937 the figure had reached 93 per cent. This time many peasants were allowed to keep small plots and some of their animals. Farms were controlled through a series of motor-tractor stations (MTS) set up all over the country. Each MTS covered about 40 farms. This organization distributed seed and collected the grain. It also decided how much a farm could keep for its own subsistence and how much money should be given as payment to collective farmers. This was very little. Most farmers were now worse off than their fathers and grandfathers had been as serfs.

However, a few collectives, called 'Potemkin Villages', received extra government help. They acted as the showcases for collectivization, appearing in the newsreels and being shown to foreign visitors.

Stage Six: Famine 1932–1934

In January 1933 Stalin spoke thus to the Central Committee:

Source 8

The collective farm regime has destroyed pauperism and poverty in the village…Under the old regime the peasants were working for the benefit of the landlords, *kulaks* and speculators…working and leading a life of hunger.

As Stalin spoke these words, large areas of the Soviet Union were in the grip of famine. Kravchenko described what he found when he stopped overnight in a peasant hut in the Ukraine.

Source 9

Our hostess was a pleasant young peasant woman. All feeling…seemed to have been drained from her starved features. They were a mask of living death…'I will not tell you about the dead,' she said…'the half-dead, the nearly dead, are even worse. There are hundreds of people bloated with hunger. I don't know how many die every day. Many are so weak that they no longer come out of their houses. A wagon goes round…to pick up the corpses. We've eaten everything we could lay hands on…The trees have been stripped of their bark…and the horse manure has been eaten…We fight over it. Sometimes there are whole grains in it.'

V. Kravchenko, *I Chose Freedom*, 1947

■ Think about

Kravchenko became a senior Communist Party official who later defected to the West. His book *I Chose Freedom* was published in the West in 1947.

▶ What value do you place on his testimony?

Families died lying outside warehouses full of grain but under armed guard. The exact numbers of those who died of famine is still a matter of debate, as with all figures from the Communist period, but 4–5 million seems likely. The deaths were ironically concentrated in the richest farming areas, the Ukraine and the Volga regions.

Why did such a severe famine affect the richest farming districts in the Soviet Union?

Source 10

	1928	1930	1931	1932	1933	1934	1935
Grain harvest	73.3	83.5	69.5	69.6	68.4	67.6	75.0
State procurement	10.8	22.2	22.8	18.8	23.3	26.3	28.4
Exports	0.3	4.8	5.1	1.8	1.7	0.8	1.5
Remainder	62.5	61.3	46.7	50.8	45.1	41.3	46.6

(All figures are in millions of tons)

'The Five Stalks Law' 1932

Savage penalties were imposed on *kolkhozniks* who stole or damaged *kolkhoz* property. Farmers were arrested for 'hairdressing' – cutting individual ears of corn in the fields. Hence the popular title for the law.

Facts and figures

To disguise the grain shortages, crop yields were calculated in biological yields. Yields were calculated on crops in the field, rather than crops actually harvested. They were an overestimate by about 20 per cent, compared to the yield.

■ **Think about**

▶ Why might a supposedly impartial western journalist have described the Ukraine in this way when we now know millions were dead or dying?

The harvests of 1931 and for the next three years were poor because of the weather. These would have been difficult years under any economic system. They became impossible because of the heavy procurements collectivized farms had to hand over to the State. Since the urban population had grown from 26 to 40 million between 1930 and 1932, the higher procurements seemed essential to the government.

The consistent shortages in the farms year after year meant disaster for millions. Peasants were forced to give up the grain they needed for their own families. If they stole from the fields they were punished. Some collective farms collapsed because no one was left to work them. Robert Conquest sees this as a deliberate policy to destroy any Ukrainian national feeling. He also calls it 'Stalin's revenge on the peasants'.

Officially the famine was denied. It was made an offence punishable by five years in prison simply to refer to it. The State took severe measures to ensure that no starving peasants were able to buy train tickets to the cities. OGPU officials checked all the trains. Even some westerners visiting the Soviet Union were persuaded that all was well on the collective farms. Walter Durranty wrote in September 1933:

Source 11

I have just completed a 200 mile automobile trip through the heart of the Ukraine and can say positively that the harvest is splendid and all talk of famine is ridiculous....Collectivization may now be said to have been established on a solid foundation, with enormous benefits to the Russian countryside.

W. Durranty, *Russia Reported*, 1934

There were dramatic falls in the number of animals in the Soviet Union. Many peasants chose to kill or sell their animals rather than hand them over to the collective farms. With grain supplies so low, they did not have enough to feed them through the winter. The drop in the number of horses was probably critical, since horses were needed for the many tasks of agricultural work. The new tractors were not plentiful enough to fill the gap and were expensive to hire – perhaps only 4 per cent of what was needed.

Source 12

	1928	1929	1930	1931	1932	1933	1934	1935
Cattle	70.5	76.1	52.5	47.9	40.7	38.4	42.4	49.3
Pigs	26.0	20.4	13.6	14.4	11.6	12.1	17.4	22.6
Sheep and Goats	146.7	147.0	108.8	77.7	52.1	50.2	51.9	61.1
Horses		34.0				17.0		

(Figures in millions of head)

Stage Seven: Consolidation

In 1935 a special Party Congress was called to approve a new model charter for collective farms. This laid down rules for the payment of *kolkhozniks* and for the relations between the *kolkhoz* and the MTS. It also formally legalized private plots of about half a hectare or less for each *kolkoznik* household and recognized the right of every household to own one cow, one sow, four sheep and an unrestricted number of poultry and rabbits. The result of this charter can be seen in the following figures for January 1938:

Source 13

	State/collective farms	Private farms
Cows	5.5	17.2
Sheep and goats	29.3	37.3
Pigs	8.8	16.9

(Figures in millions of head)

The State and collective farms continued to produce low crop yields compared to the private plots. These by the end of the 1930s were producing the vast bulk of the nation's eggs, milk and meat. Most of this was contracted to the State, but any surplus could be sold on a restricted free market to provide income for the hard-pressed peasants.

Document exercise: views of collective farms

Source A

◀ A cartoon showing a peasant working on his private plot, being watched by two peasants from the collective farm.

Source B

Look back at Source 9

Source C

A joke from the 1930s

Stalin complained to a colleague in the Kremlin that his office was infested by mice and that nothing, including traps and poison, had succeeded in getting rid of them.
'No problem!' the colleague replied. 'Just declare that your office is a collective farm. Half the mice will run away and the other half will die of starvation!'

Source D

ДЕНЬ УРОЖАЯ И КОЛЛЕКТИВИЗАЦИИ

КОЛХОЗ БЕЗБОЖНИК

▲ A poster from 1930 showing the success of collectivisation, compared to the old ways.

■ Examination-style questions

1 Comprehension in context
What is the point that is being made in Source A?

2 Comparing the sources
Does Source B give the same impression of the collective farms?

3 Assessing the sources
How useful would a historian find Source C? Explain your answer by close reference to the source.

4 Making judgements
Using the sources and your own knowledge, explain why peasants often had a different view of the collective farms from that of the government (Source D).

■ Activity

1 Few writers outside Russia have shown sympathy with collectivization and dekulakization. Would the Communist Party in the 1930s have regarded it as a failure?
Look back at the reasons given earlier in the chapter why the party adopted this policy.
In pairs, taking each reason in turn, draw up a list of points to assess whether each objective had been met wholly, in part or not at all.
What is your verdict? Was collectivization a failure?

2 It would be tempting to think that everything changed in the countryside. Much recent writing, however, stresses the failure of collectivization to change life on the farm.
Working with a partner, draw up a list of ways in which rural life changed, and ways in which it did not.

3 'The Communists simply didn't understand peasants.'
Does the evidence in this chapter support this conclusion?

Life in the collectivized village

Source 14

I read about the achievements of the collective farms, but that's all window-dressing…If you compare workers in factories, they live much better than *kolkhozniks*…You can make 15 roubles and more at the factory; you can buy cloth and other goods too, as much as you want… But just let the *kolkhoznik* try to buy something where *he* lives – you can't buy cloth here and the *kolkhozniks* go round badly dressed…You can't get any lower than the village.

A letter to Kalinin 'the all-union peasant elder' in the 1930s. Thousands of such letters were sent to party leaders in the 1930s.

Facts and figures

The 1937 census shows there were 18 women to every 10 men on the *kolkhozy*.

Facts and figures

The 1937 census showed there were 19 million peasant households in the USSR compared to 26 million in 1929.

Source 15

When Kirov was killed,
They allowed free trade in bread.
When Stalin is killed,
They will disband all the *kolkhozy*.

From secret police archives in Smolensk, Ukraine. When Kirov, a party leader, was killed, this was a popular ditty

Source 16

Oh brothers! Oh, sisters! Don't go into the collective farm
Antichrist will lay his mark upon you three times.
Once on the hand,
The second on the forehead for all to see,
And the third on the breast.
If you believe in God, don't join the collective farm.
And if you are in the collective farm, oh sisters, leave.

A popular rhyme in 1930

Source 17

At a meeting the *kolkhoz* director announces prizes for the best *shock workers*. One milkmaid is given a radio, another gets a gramophone, and a third gets a bicycle. Everyone claps, and the milkmaids are happy. The director announces: "And now comrades, we award the first prize to the best shock worker, who is politically conscious, worked without taking days off or holidays, and set a record for raising pigs; she is an example for everyone. I hereby present our leading pig-tender with the complete works of our beloved comrade Stalin." The meeting fell silent. A voice from the back said: "Just what the bitch deserves".

A joke from the 1930s

Source 18

They change the chairmen of the *kolkhoz* every year. That's not long to put *kolkhoz* affairs in order, but its quite long enough to gear up your own household economy – steal yourself a prettier little house, breed some ducks or geese, plant an orchard…They may remove him from his position, but what does he care…he has improved his family's position.

From the novel *Drachuny* by M. Alekseev, Moscow 1982

Source 19

For some time it has become dangerous for *kolkhoz* activists to go out at night…People have been shooting at them from the forest, shooting at the men who exposed class enemies and purged the village of hooligans. Bliunger, the headmaster of the school, has been shot at twice. The secretary of the rural soviet and the veterinarian were saved from death by chance.

Violence in the *kolkhoz* from a national newspaper for teachers

Facts and figures

Education in the villages

Pupils in primary schools
1929	8 million
1933	14 million

Pupils in secondary schools
1932	2.5 million
1939	6.9 million

Facts and figures

Religion in the villages

Number of priests in census: 1926, 79,000; 1937, 31,000
The 1937 census showed 57% of the population as believers, when it was clear that the State was opposed to religion.

Traditional peasant religious festivals were continued and many working days were lost. These festivals were often associated with drunkenness.

Priests were officially banned from *kolkhoz*. Records show some were even paid by the collective farms.

Source 20

▲ A painting from 1935 showing life on a collective farm.

Source 21

You see shrubs planted in front of the houses, orchards, in almost every village now. The cottages are often roofed with iron, whitewashed or smoothly spread with clay, as if plastered. The squares are planted with trees. The windows have white curtains, often lace, and there are flowers on the window-sills.

A 1935 report in *Pravda* from a village in the Volga

■ Activity

These sources give different impressions of life in the villages after collectivization.

1 Divide the sources into official and unofficial sources.
Do all the official sources give the same impression? Why is this the case?
What reservations would a historian have about Sources 15 and 17?

2 Source 14 is a private letter to a party leader.
What does it tell us about collective farms in the 1930s?
Do you think letters, like this one, are a good source for the historian?

3 Source 18 is from a historical novel set in the 1930s.
Can a historical novel like this be of any use to historians?

4 Which of these sources do you think give the most reliable picture of the collective farms?

5 What level of support for collectivization is shown by the sources?

6 What do these sources suggest about the farmers' attitudes to the Communist government?

Building an industrial society

The vision

We are going full steam ahead along the road of industrialization to socialism, leaving behind our century-old Russian backwardness. We are becoming a metallic country, an automotive country, a tractor country.

Stalin, November 1929

To turn their back on the backward Tsarist past and make Soviet Russia the equal of the capitalist West was a vision of the future that many in the Communist Party, and many ordinary Russians too, must have shared for many years. Lenin himself had once, perhaps rather naively, suggested that 'Communism equals Soviet power plus electrification'.

ОРУЖИЕМ МЫ ДОБИЛИ ВРАГА
ТРУДОМ МЫ ДОБУДЕМ ХЛЕБ
ВСЕ ЗА РАБОТУ, ТОВАРИЩИ!

■ Think about

▶ What does Source 23 tell us about the aims of the Soviet government in 1921?

◀ A poster from 1921.

The timing

At first glance the First Five Year Plan of 1928/1929 can be seen as a sudden break with the policies of the NEP. In fact the setting up of Vesenkha after the Revolution was a signal that the party intended to plan the economy in a new way. During War Communism 1919–1921 the government had taken control of the management and direction of the economy, establishing priorities and allocating resources of men and materials. Even though the NEP saw a change of strategy, it did not mean a change of direction. Gosplan in 1924 had begun to announce target figures for industrial production, and in the following year began to sketch longer term plans. In 1927 the Fifteenth Party Congress instructed Gosplan to produce a Five Year Plan for the entire economy. When therefore that plan was published in 1928, it had been in gestation for some time.

Note

Vesenkha was the Supreme Council of National Economy
Gosplan was set up to provide the government with reliable statistical information.

However, the timing of the First Plan was not an accident. There were compelling reasons for its adoption at that time. These were the 'war scare' years (see Chapter 8). Moreover, the Left of the party, who had first proposed rapid industrialization as the highest priority of the government, had now been defeated, making it possible for the party to adopt the Left's policies without putting its principal supporters in power!

Industrialization was also necessary if collectivization was to work. Tractors and agricultural machinery were desperately needed to make the collective farms successful.

The plans

The party had studied industrialization in the west, especially in the USA. It believed that heavy industry, iron and steel, had been the basis of their advance, and decided to imitate this in Russia. The belief that the USSR faced threats from foreign powers was another factor causing the emphasis on heavy industry, since this would provide the basis of an armaments industry. At the outset of the First Five Year Plan fantastic targets for increased production were set by Gosplan for each industry: in coal over 100 per cent, in iron 200 per cent, in electricity 400 per cent. When the first few months appeared to be going well the party adopted even higher 'optimal' targets in 1929. When this seemed to be working, even these 'impossible' figures were raised (see below). Some older and wiser heads disputed the viability of these new targets.

> **Source 24**
>
> 'I cease to be responsible for the planning dept. The plan figure I consider to be purely arbitrary'
> To this a young woman comrade retorted:
> 'We do not doubt the knowledge or goodwill of the professor...but we reject the fetishism of figures which holds him in thrall...We reject the multiplication table as a basis for policy.'

The results for the First Five Year Plan were as follows:

Millions of tons	1927–8 production	1932–3 (optimal target)	1932 (amended target)	1932 actual
Coal	35	75	95–105	64
Oil	11.7	21.7	40–55	21.4
Iron ore	6.7	20.2	24–32	12.1
Pig iron	3.2	10	15–16	6.2

These statistics alone do not tell the whole story. Much of the plant needed to meet these targets did not exist. Whole new towns and factories had to be constructed, often in distant regions. These then had to be linked to other industrial plants and mines by train and road. Labour and power were also needed in these new industrial enterprises, as well as new technology and machine tools, and the staff to manage and use them. To arrange all this required an enormous bureaucracy. Ordzonikidze, for example, headed a new Commissariat of Heavy Industry.

So impossible were the targets that to talk of these as Five-Year 'Plans' is regarded by many as a distortion of language. Just to demand high production targets did not mean there was a rational plan to achieve them!

> **Note**
>
> The leaders of the Left in the mid-1920s were Trotsky, Kamenev and Zinoviev.

> **Note**
>
> **1928–1932** First Five Year Plan (The government declared targets achieved nine months early)
> **1933–1937** Second Five Year Plan
> **1938–1941** Third Five Year Plan (Cut short by the German invasion in 1941)

> **Note**
>
> Intellectuals, managers and academics all came under savage attack as 'bourgeois specialists' when the First Five Year Plan began.

How was this to be achieved?

1. Propaganda

The Five Year Plans were represented as battles in a war to build socialism against capitalist enemies. Workers were urged on to achieve ever greater tasks by propaganda of every kind, posters, factory meetings, radio broadcasts, theatre groups etc.

The propaganda seems to have been at least partly effective. Volunteers flocked to travel to some of the most inhospitable regions of the USSR to help to build an urban Communist society. Not to be forgotten also was the extra help of volunteers from the capitalist West.

Quotation

There is no fortress the Bolsheviks can not take.

A common Bolshevik slogan

Source 25

◀ A 1931 poster showing a woman in a textiles factory.

Source 26

▶ A 1933 poster. Above a capitalist laughs at the First Five Year Plan in 1928, but his reaction is different in 1933.

Source 27

▼ A 1930s poster about Japan, which says 'Let them keep their pig's snout out of our garden'. Japan and the USSR fought border wars in the 1930s.

■ Think about

▶ What themes are stressed in these posters?

▶ Why were these the themes chosen by the Communist Party?

▶ Do you think that the posters were just propaganda, or are they a real indication of the objectives of the Communist government?

2. Forced labour

Since there was little money available to buy construction equipment abroad, much of the work had to be done by hand. This demanded millions of hands to work often in extreme conditions. Volunteers alone would not fill the need: forced labour was the answer and it was very cheap and easily replaced. The millions of transported *kulaks* provided a great part of this forced labour, but it also comprised other 'enemies of the State', such as members of various religious groups and former members of the bourgeoisie. These forced workers were found all over the new industrial regions and along the great transport projects, such as the Belomor Canal. Deaths seem to have been commonplace.

Facts and figures

Population in millions

	Urban	Rural
1920	20.8	110.0
1929	27.6	126.7
1933	40.3	125.4
1939	56.1	114.5

Cross reference

You can find out more about the use of forced labour in Chapter 10.

Workers examine targets during the First Five Year Plan.

■ Think about

▶ Why were these figures so prominently displayed?

▶ Does this photograph prove they made an impact in Soviet Russia?

Facts and figures

Jasny, an expert on Russian economic data estimates wages as follows:

1928	100
1932	49
1937	60
1940	56

3. Socialist competition

In capitalist countries the pursuit of profit was what motivated managers and workers to work harder and produce more. The USSR was not supposed to believe in this. Instead 'socialist competition' was introduced – a kind of race between factories, mines etc. to produce the most possible. Regular meetings were held to urge workers on to equal the achievements of a similar factory down the road. Whether it was successful as a method is difficult to judge.

4. Stakhanovites and shock workers

During the First Five Year Plan targets were not only being set for factories and construction teams, but also for individual workers. In one Moscow factory there were over half a million norms set for different tasks! Wages were decided by a worker's success or failure to reach these norms. During a single nightshift in August 1935 Alexei Stakhanov cut 102 tons from a coal seam in the Donbass region. This remarkable achievement was 14 times the quota or norm set for a shift! In a few months Stakhanov was a household name in the USSR; thousands tried to emulate him in every sector of the economy, even apparently waiters!

This was no doubt encouraged by the party, but within a year almost one-quarter of industrial workers were classed as Stakhanovites, with as many others graded as shock workers, a slightly lower but honoured category. The planners were then able to increase industrial norms by between 10 and 15 per cent in 1936. The rapid spread of Stakhanovism does suggest to some historians a great level of commitment to the government's vision of the future. More cynical observers argue that workers simply wanted the benefits the status brought.

5. Low wages

Robert Service suggests that average real pay in 1932 was only half of what it had been at the end of the NEP because of rising inflation. Jasny calculated that even in 1940 the average Russian consumed in food and goods 7 per cent less than in 1928. This disguised what had happened to wages, because now many women were working as well as men, and they were often working longer hours. Workers, in other words, subsidized these achievements by their own lower living standards.

6. Fear

Managers and technicians were made personally responsible for their work. Failure to meet targets could be serious. The period of the Plans was punctuated by a series of industrial trials in which managerial and technical staff were accused of sabotage and wrecking. Since they had often held senior positions before the Revolution or had parents from a bourgeois background, they were easy targets.

The first of these was the famous Shakhty trial in 1928. Fifty-five engineers in the Donbass were found guilty of co-operating with foreign powers to hold back Soviet production. 'Death to the wreckers!' appeared in the headlines as their trial began in Moscow. One of the defendants was denounced by his 12-year-old son! The only evidence in the trial was the confessions of some of the accused. Some of these tried to withdraw them in the trial, explaining they had been gained by threats and ill treatment in prison. Eleven were sentenced to death, and five were eventually executed.

In December 1933 Stalin introduced a law to hold directors and managers responsible for substandard or incomplete goods. Procurators (legal officers) toured factories to educate workers and check on production. However, this led to an immediate wave of arrests, and this of course disrupted production even more. Ordzhonikidze, the Commissar for Heavy Industry, received thousands of written complaints from factories about the arrests, and he in turn sent hundreds of petitions for release to the procurators. By the autumn of 1934 the arrests of managers had slowed almost to a halt.

7. Education

The ambitious Plans required a whole new class of people to run them, and the State began a vast programme of technical education to provide them. They were especially necessary because of the baiting of 'bourgeois specialists' that the party had encouraged since 1928 in a new outburst of revolutionary enthusiasm. Academic learning, as we saw in Source 25, was no longer respected. As Stalin said to the Central Committee in April 1929, 'Wrecking by the bourgeois intelligentsia is one of the most dangerous forces of opposition to developing socialism'.

Until the new personnel were ready, skilled tasks were often done by semi-trained ex-peasants. The First Five Year Plan saw 1.5 million workers promoted to managerial positions. There was a campaign throughout the 1930s to eliminate illiteracy. Foreign help was also bought in; Ford for example supervised the building of a giant automobile plant.

Were the Five Year Plans successful?

There has been a fierce debate between economic historians about this. R.W. Davies in his book *Soviet Economic Development from Lenin to Khrushchev* gives the following estimates for what the USSR produced over the period of the three Five Year Plans.

Note

There are many sets of statistics available, and they are all different.

Source 29

	1928	1937	1940
Gross National Product	100	172	203

This corresponds to an annual compound growth rate of between 5 and 6 per cent, significantly more than was being achieved in most western countries, which had been plunged into depression after the Wall Street Crash. However, the production increases were very uneven. The biggest gains were achieved in heavy industry, which the planners thought was the priority.

Source 30

	1927	1930	1932	1935	1937	1940
Coal (million tons)	35	60	64	100	128	150
Steel (million tons)	3	5	6	13	18	18
Oil (million tons)	12	17	21	24	26	26
Electricity (million kWth)	18	22	20	45	80	90

Huge projects were completed. The Dneiper dam and hydro-electric power station was one of these, the biggest in Europe. Agricultural machinery complexes were built at Stalingrad and Kharkov. A huge iron and steel plant was built at Magnitogorsk (see pp. 182–186). There was also a significant shift of industry to the Urals and beyond, thought to be out of range of any foreign attack. These would also exploit the rich mineral resources of Asia.

Cross reference

See maps on pages 19 and 47.

Source 31

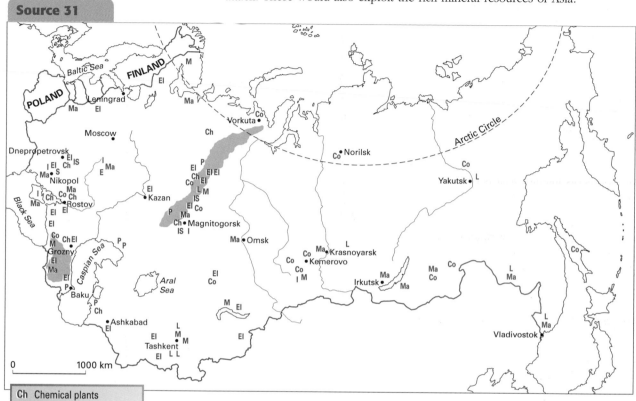

Ch	Chemical plants
Co	Coal mines
El	Electricity power stations
L	Lignite mining
M	Metal industries (not iron)
I	Iron mines
IS	Iron and steel complexes
P	Petroleum extraction
S	Steel plants

▲ Industrial expansion during the Five Year Plans

Measuring output in the USSR does not always tell the whole story. Meeting targets was the main priority and very often quality suffered. Between 1928 and 1941 8,000 huge new enterprises were built. The difficulty of planning a whole economy as vast as that of the USSR meant all kinds of problems. Spare parts were often unavailable, so that once a tiny component needed replacing production stopped or machines became useless. Lewin argued that 'The First Five Year Plan…landed the country in such chaos that it took at least two years to straighten things out.' Of course, some of the vast projects were wrong-headed from the start. The Belomor Canal, built to connect the Baltic and the White Sea was built at enormous human cost, but in fact was too shallow to take any of the warships for which it was designed!

Bureaucracy destroyed individual initiative. It was more important to have a legitimate reason why targets were not met than to think of a way of overcoming the problems. One of the administration's responses to blockages and problems was to by-pass their own bureaucrats and to send high-ranking officials or party members to try to find a solution. When the Donbass coal-mines, despite heavy investment, produced less not more coal, the Politburo threw out three plans to improve the situation from the Commissariat of Heavy Industry and invited ordinary miners to Moscow in 1933 to discuss matters. A census in 1934 found that one-quarter of the new coal cutting machines was not being used, and one-third of the new pneumatic drills. This was presumably either because miners had not been trained to use them or because they were broken and no one knew how to repair them.

Another response to difficulties was 'storming.' This called on workers and party comrades to put in extra hours to overcome problems. Kravchenko wrote of the new metal plants at Nikopol:

Source 32

Nikopol, I thought, was symbolic of the whole industrialization effort – prodigal in spending life and substance, barbarous in its inefficiency, yet somehow moving forward.

V. Kravchenko, *I Chose Freedom*, 1946

The engineer and writer Antonov gives a similar verdict on the Moscow Metro:

Source 33

By the [engineers']...estimates the construction would be completed by 1937 at the earliest. Stalin lost patience, did not study the estimates of the engineers, and ordered that the first line should start up on November 7, 1934. Naturally there could be no objections. Feverish work got under way. Moscow young Communists were mobilized to dig tunnels. They dug day and night by hand. The timetables for organizing the work lost all sense. The draughtsmen could not keep up with the diggers. The Arbat station had to be redone three times. And the trains on the first circle of the Metro started, not on November 7 1934, but on May 15, 1935. This was a striking record, achieved contrary to engineering science. How many extra million roubles were spent to achieve this record is another matter.

■ **Think about**

▶ In what ways does Antonov criticize the way the Metro was built?

▶ Does Antonov's evidence support that of Kravchenko in Source 32?

We have already suggested that most Russians were no better off at the end of 1940 than they were in 1928 before the Five Year Plans. There were, however, some important exceptions, which might strike you as odd. Marx had after all written, 'From each according to his ability, to each according to his need.' Stalin criticized the equalization of wages in a famous speech in 1931, insisting that workers be paid in accordance with their responsibilities and skills. Stalin argued that equality of pay would only be possible when true communism had been achieved. Technicians and managers, therefore, were now able to earn up to four times more than ordinary workers.

Cross reference

You will read more about equality of pay in Chapter 11.

Millions more paid a heavier price for the Soviet Union's industrialization – the prison camp population. Before Soviet archives had been opened up, some historians estimated that as many as 9 million people were to be found in labour camps. Now the number is generally assessed as between 2.5 and 3.4 million people, the majority of them men. These men made a significant contribution to the success of the plans, especially in the major construction projects. Twelve per cent of timber was produced by the gulag population, and they also mined most of the nation's gold.

Note

There were over 100 gulags (forced labour camps) spread throughout the USSR in the 1930s.

Perhaps the best testament to the success of the USSR is to compare its victory in the Second World War with Russia's defeat in the First World War. It is difficult to see how the USSR of the 1920s could have withstood the violence of the Nazi *blitzkrieg* and emerged victorious.

Document exercise: The Five Year Plans

Source A

As a result of the successful fulfilment of the Second Five Year Plan [1933–1937], the basic historic task of the Second Five Year Plan has been solved in the USSR: all exploiting classes have been definitely liquidated and the causes of the exploitation of man by man and the division of society into exploiters and exploited have been completely destroyed…

The victory of socialism in the USSR assured a historically unprecedented inner moral and political unity of the working people under the banner of the Communist Party and Soviet authorities that was …capable of finishing with the remnants of hostile classes, with their alien influences' and of delivering a rebuff to all manner of hostile incursions from the outside…

From a Resolution of the 18th Party Congress, 20 March 1939

Source B

You are told of the achievements of the USSR but you must see the realities in order to value at their true worth the achievements of Comrade Stalin. You cannot buy bread at the market; it is forbidden, and other foodstuffs are so dear that a worker's wage for a month is only enough for five days.

An anonymous letter from a worker in Saratov in 1932

Source C

While the economies of the capitalist countries were sinking ever deeper into recession, the Soviet economy was booming. The laying of a firm foundation for a socialist economy created favourable conditions for the further progress of the country's national economy in the Second Five Year Plan period, 1933–7…

The country's working class continued to grow… By the mid-1930s, Soviet industry, saturated with up-to-date equipment and machinery, had an adequate army of skilled workers. The material and cultural level of the workers had risen, as had their level of political awareness.

Kukushkin, *History of the USSR,* published in Russia in 1981

■ Examination-style questions

1 **Comprehension in context**
   What is meant by 'the victory of socialism' in Source A?

2 **Comparing the sources**
   In what ways does Source B present a different picture of the Soviet Union in the 1930s from that given in Source A?

3 **Assessing the sources**
   How reliable do you consider Source C to be for the student of twentieth-century Russia?

4 **Making judgements**
   Using the sources and your own knowledge, how successful do you consider the Five Year Plans of 1928–1941 to have been?

Magnitogorsk

Background information

In 1929, on the banks of the Ural river, the building began of a new industrial city, Magnitogorsk. It was situated here to take advantage of the local magnetite (iron ore) deposits. By 1933 it had a population of over 200,000 people.

Source 34

▶ Magnitogorsk in production.

Gigantomania

means unnatural obsession with massive projects.

John Scott

Scott was an American volunteer at Magnitogorsk. A trained metalworker, he became disillusioned with America during the depression and sailed to Russia to create a better society. He was working for the American Arthur Mackee Corporation, who supervised the construction of this massive project. In 1942, back in America, he wrote *Behind the Urals* from which these quotations have been taken. He seems to have been affected by the same 'gigantomania' which affected the government.

Source 35

Within several years, half a billion cubic feet of excavation was done, forty-two million cubic feet of reinforced concrete poured, five million cubic feet of fire bricks laid, a quarter of a million tons of structured steel erected. This was done without sufficient labour, without necessary quantities of the most elementary materials. Brigades of young enthusiasts from every corner of the Soviet Union arrived in the summer of 1930…Later groups of local peasants and herdsmen came…because of bad conditions in the villages, due to collectivization…About three-quarters of the new arrivals came of their own free will seeking work, bread cards, better conditions. The rest came under compulsion.

He describes the hardship suffered:

Source 36

Men froze, hungered and suffered, but the construction work went on with a disregard for individuals and a mass heroism seldom paralleled in history…Tens of thousands of people were enduring the most intense hardships to build blast furnaces. I would wager that Russia's battle of ferrous metallurgy alone involved more casualties than the battle of the Marne.

In early April it was still bitter cold, everything was frozen solid. By May the ground had thawed and the city was swimming in mud. Bubonic plague had broken out in three places nearby. The resistance of the population was very low because of under-nourishment during the winter and consistent overwork. Sanitary conditions were apalling. Within two weeks the sun was upon us. By the middle of May the heat was intolerable. In the barracks we were consumed by bedbugs and other vermin…It was a varied gang, Russians, Ukrainians, Tartars, Mongols, Jews, mostly young and almost all peasants. The Tartar Khaibulin had never seen a staircase, a locomotive or an electric light until he arrived in Magnitogorsk.

Scott described the room he shared with a Russian worker:

Source 37

The room was about six feet by ten and had one small window, which was pasted over with newspaper to keep the cold out. There was a small table, a little brick stove, and one three-legged stool. The two iron bedsteads were rickety and narrow. There were no springs, just thin planks across the iron frame…The barrack block housed 80 people…One of the rooms was the Red Corner. Here hung the barrack room newspaper…here was a 200 book library. Twice a week classes for the illiterates were held here…At about 6 o'clock a dozen or so workers, men and women, gathered in the Red Corner with a couple of balalaikas and a guitar…And they sang! Workers' revolutionary songs, folk tunes and old Russian romantic lyrics.

Source 38

▲ Living quarters in a tent for Magnitogorsk workers.

The 'specials' were even worse off living for a long time in tents through the Russian winter. Scott describes his lunch in the canteen:

The 'specials' were those forced into labour camps, mainly deported *kulaks*.

Source 39

It wasn't bad soup. There were some cabbages in it, traces of potatoes and buckwheat, and an occasional bone. It was hot, that was the main thing. The workers ate with relish, some of them having put mustard in it for flavour...[The second course] consisted of a soup plate filled with potatoes covered in thin gravy, and a small piece of meat on the top.

The 'specials' received much less, sometimes with tragic results, as workers fell to their deaths:

Source 40

The riggers were mostly ploughboys who had no idea of being careful. At thirty-five below without any breakfast in you, you didn't pay as much attention as you should.

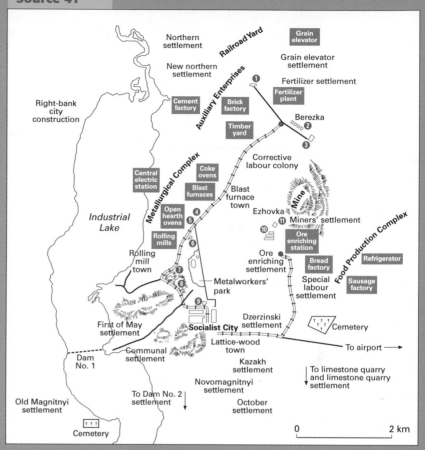

Key:

1. Train station
2. Houses of the elite
3. Miners' club
4. Central hotel
5. Factory administration
6. Party committee
7. NKVD
8. Central market
9. Theatre and metalworkers' club
10. Hospital barracks
11. Mining and metallurgical institute
+++++ Tramline
▨ Location of industrial activity

▶ The layout of Magnitogorsk

Source 41

The foreigners lived in a separate area, which was nicknamed 'American City.' Berezka was home to the local party secretary, OGPU officials and factory directors.

Source 42

▲ Not all workers lived in tents.

Americans and privileged Russians shopped at the Insnad (restricted) store for:

Source 43

caviar, Caucasian wines, imported cloth and materials, shoes, suits, books and food at a tenth of Russian prices…The size of the pay envelope, the number of bank notes under the mattress, no longer determined living standards. What one ate or wore depended almost exclusively on what there was in the particular store to which one was attached.

Workers even sought opportunities for self-improvement.

Source 44

Many workers went to night school after an eight hour day to study mechanics…He felt he would have more next year. His children were going to school. He was secure against sickness, as were his children. Unemployment had been forgotten…School expenses, lighting, heating, teachers' salaries and sometimes even books and paper for the students were met from the large fund for training…The students paid nothing. They even got special privileges, longer vacations, time off for work during excavations.

When the whole country was mobilized by the state to root out 'wreckers', Scott reports only one deported *kulak*, who filled a turbine with ground glass. Of the 'specials' he wrote:

Source 45

Very frequently the 'specials' worked better than average, since they were usually the most energetic elements of the village.

Scott's verdict on Magnitogorsk includes these two passages:

Source 46

The Magnitogorsk I left in early 1938 was producing upward of 5000 tons of steel daily…The town was full of rough and earnest young Russians…They were also writing poetry, going to see remarkably good performances of *Othello*, learning to play violins and tennis. All this out in the middle of a steppe, where ten years before, only a few hundred impoverished herders had lived.

Stalin's indomitable will and his ruthless tenacity were responsible for the construction of Magnitogorsk and the entire Ural and Western Siberian industrial area. Without Stalin the job would never have been done.

■ Activity

How reliable as a witness was John Scott?

1 What impression does Scott give:
   a) of life in Magnitogorsk?
   b) of the attitudes of the people in Magnitogorsk?
   c) of the success or otherwise of Magnitogorsk?

2 How useful is *Behind the Urals* to historians studying the USSR in the 1930s? Consider the following:

   ● Was Scott in a position to know the truth about Magnitogorsk and its inhabitants?
   ● Why did Scott go to the USSR? How might this have affected what he wrote?
   ● Does Scott give a balanced account, or are these extracts largely one-sided?
   ● How would a historian set about checking the truth of Scott's statements?

3 Do these sources suggest that Magnitogorsk was a success for the Communist government?

■ Further reading

Magnetic Mountain by S. Kotkin is a more recent book about Magnitogorsk.

Prepare a report which presents all the costs and benefits of the economic policies of the 1930s. Use visual materials, maps, timelines, pictures, to illustrate your points from more than one electronic source and create a new way of presenting statistical information in your report. Email your fellow students with your ideas and exchange any sources you think are particularly helpful. You might find a comparison between the achievements of the Soviet economy with that of the Nazi economy at the same time helpful. Prepare materials to present your views to the class.

You are now in a position to debate/discuss in your class the following questions:

1 Did the achievements of collectivization and the Five Year Plans justify the suffering they caused?

2 Would the New Economic Policy have provided a better way forward to achieving an industrialized society? How different would that society have been?

3 Write an essay 'How successful were the agricultural and industrial policies pursued in the USSR in the 1930s?'

Conclusion

In the 1930s a gigantic experiment in the organization of human society took place in the Soviet Union, one that attracted great interest far outside her borders from both the detractors and the supporters of Marxism. Her traditional farming communities were transformed into supposedly model collectives and her industrial capacity was vastly increased.

There is still debate as to whether this could have been achieved more effectively by other methods; whether the enormous cost in death and human misery could have been avoided. It is difficult to make a case for the changes in the countryside, where millions died callously ignored by their own government without achieving any improvements in production. Indeed farming continued to be a problem area for the Soviet government long after Stalin was in his grave. It seemed almost impossible to boost levels of production to match those achieved in the West. Looking at the changes in government policy, it is possible to argue that the peasants secured important concessions from the government.

The legacy of the industrialization of the 1930s is with Russia still. The 'produce at any price' philosophy resulted in poor quality though increased quantity of goods. It left Russia with a legacy of inefficiency, which meant that it was unable to compete with the West once the Iron Curtain was removed. However, in the short term it gave Russia the capacity to produce the military equipment to defeat its enemies in the Second World War.

If the 'Second Revolution' was to be fully successful, it demanded not just higher growth rates. It also needed a change of heart in the Soviet people themselves. Would the population be willing to forego increases in their own standard of living indefinitely to meet the targets set by the government? Would Soviet citizens be able to find a new work ethic which did not depend on the individual profit motive, but on working for the good of the wider community instead? This is the subject of Chapter 11.

As we have seen one method employed by the government to spur on their citizens to greater efforts was to raise the spectacle of 'enemies within'. Soviet citizens were told that as they approached communism, capitalist countries and class enemies would try even harder to overthrow their 'successful' system. Vigilance and self-criticism was demanded of everyone. The next chapter will examine how this affected the USSR in the 1930s.

■ **Further reading**

V. Andrle, *A Social History of Twentieth Century Russia*
R. Conquest, *The Harvest of Sorrow*, 1986
R.W. Davies, *The industrialisation of Soviet Russia*
S. Fitzpatrick, *Stalin's Peasants*, 1994
S. Kotkin, *Magnetic Mountain*, 1995
V. Kravchenko, *I Chose Freedom*, 1947
A. Nove, *An Economic History of the USSR*
J. Scott, *Behind the Urals*
L. Siegelbaum, *Stakhanovism and the Politics of Productivity in the USSR 1935-41*, 1988

Chapter 10

The Terror

◀ Stalin with six year old Engelsina Chezkova. Engelsina's father was shot as a spy and her mother died after being denounced as 'an enemy of the people'.

Source 2

He [Stalin] helped draft the indictments of Marshal Tukhachevski and his fellow military defendants…and personally ordered death sentences for them. [Indeed he signed numerous death sentences, including a record 3167 on 12 December 1938.]….He sponsored the persecution of his enemies' innocent family members. In the fall of 1937, he approved a plan to summarily shoot tens of thousands of 'anti-Soviet elements' and to establish target figures for the shootings by province.

Arch Getty 'The politics of repression revisited', in *Stalinist Terror: New Perspectives*, 1993

■ Think about

▶ Why was this picture often reproduced in the USSR?

Introduction

By the end of the 1930s images of Stalin were to be seen everywhere throughout the Soviet Union. Source 1 is a famous image of the *vozhd* (the boss) as he was known at the time. Cities had been renamed in his honour, for example Stalingrad and Stalino. His birthday was celebrated as a major national event. The press and the propaganda machine of the State produced from 1935 onwards 'a saturation of visual images of Stalin physically close to the people' (S. Davies, *Popular Opinion in Stalin's Russia*). Much evidence points to the fact that Stalin was both genuinely respected and popular amongst many ordinary people, not simply members of the Communist Party.

However, in Source 2 Arch Getty lists some examples of Stalin's known personal involvement in the murder of his own people. In 1937–1938 alone perhaps as many as 1 million Russians were shot without proper trial, many drawn from the ranks of the party but also including some more senior figures. Others were investigated and 'purged' from the party. Many former leaders of the party were subjected to staged show trials in which they confessed to 'impossible' crimes, such as the murder of Lenin and plotting to overthrow the USSR with Germany and other capitalist countries. For some historians these two images of Stalin are easy to explain. While patiently destroying his own enemies and establishing a personal dictatorship, Stalin tried to maintain the support of the population by a propaganda campaign, presenting himself as the benign father of the nation.

Key questions

- Why were there repeated purges in the Communist Party?
- Was there real opposition to the regime in the 1930s?
- Who killed Sergei Kirov?
- Why did the regime put on trial some of its leading figures?
- Why did the 'great purge' happen in 1937–1938?
- Who was responsible for 'the purges'

Why did the party purge its members?

Purging, expelling unsuitable members from the party, was not a new phenomenon in the time of Stalin's leadership of the USSR. As we have seen in earlier chapters, party members enjoyed considerable benefits; membership was the only way individuals could hope to have any influence on the policies of the government either at local or national level. Inevitably, therefore, the party attracted many people who were not really committed Communists. Trotsky had called these people 'radishes,' red on the outside but white inside. Since it was accepted that the party had a historic role to play in the development of communism, not only in Russia but also throughout the world, the leadership had to ensure that its members were loyal, committed and set a suitable example to the rest of the population. The first major purge (*chistka*) of the party had happened in 1921, when the Civil War had been won but the party still faced opposition in the country. One-quarter of party members was expelled at this time.

Historians fundamentally disagree about what purging was about. For some, purging was ridding the party of undesirables, lazy members, drunks etc. For them, this was simply good housekeeping. Others think that purging was one of the methods Stalin, like Lenin before him, used to rid himself of critics, potential rivals and their supporters. It is possible, of course, that both these views might be correct!

> **Note**
>
> The word 'purge' is not recognized in Russia. Instead the Russians describe these events as '*chistki*,' (singular *chistka*) literally cleansings.

Stalin's purges

The 1924 Lenin Enrolment (begun after his death) brought about a great expansion of the party. The CPSU under the NEP had accepted some measure of capitalism. In 1928 the policy of the government changed, and the attack on *kulaks* and nepmen began; the class war was sharpened. It was not surprising, in view of this radical change of direction, that it should be accompanied by another purge of the party. This also of course coincided with the final defeat and removal from influence of the leaders of the Left, Trotsky, Zinoviev and Kamenev, as well as the first attacks on the Right, Bukharin, Rykov and Tomsky.

The *chistka* of 1928–1930 was run by local party branches. Each member had to justify his membership after a process of self-criticism before his colleagues.

Source 3

◀ A chistka on an Uzbek collective farm in 1930.

■ **Think about**

▶ What impression does this photograph give of the atmosphere in a local *chistka* meeting?

As a result, about 11 per cent of members were 'cleansed' from the party. Evidence of dissent within the party surfaced in 1932. Therefore, in 1933 the party began a second *chistka*, which was to last two years. This time it was administered from Moscow by a Party Control Commission under Politburo member Kaganovitch, a sign of the importance with which the party viewed the matter. Here Victor Kravchenko describes the purge procedure he experienced in 1933:

Source 4

The Commission members sat behind a red-draped table on a platform decorated with portraits of Politburo members and slogans; a bust of Stalin, banked with flowers, held the most prominent position. The Communist to be examined was called to the platform. He handed over his party card to the Chairman and began a recital of his life history. It was a political and spiritual strip act … It was always better to bring up errors yourself….. 'concealing' anything from the party compounded the gravity of the crime concealed. After the confessional, the purgee was questioned by members of the Commission and by people in the audience. He was reminded of omissions and tricked into contradictions. Comrades spoke up in his favour or against him.

Kravchenko, *I Chose Freedom*, 1947

■ **Think about**

▶ What was Kravchenko's opinion of the purge procedure?

NB. Kravchenko fled the USSR in the Second World War and wrote his book in exile.

▶ Does this procedure seem to you unfair?

By 1935 a further 20 per cent had been ejected from the party. But this process also showed that local records were in a total shambles, so the party ordered that all party documents should be checked again. The 1935 Party Plenum (a full meeting of the Central Committee) allowed new admissions into the party, which it had earlier stopped:

Think about

▶ What does Source 5 suggest was the Central Committee's main concern in the *chistki*?

▶ Does this source support the view that the *chistki* were primarily intended to remove political enemies?

Source 5

…as long as such a shameful chaos prevails in the registration of party members, until order has been established in our party house…In so doing the plenum of the Central Committee once again warns all party organizations…that in admitting each new member the party rules are to be strictly observed, and that bearing in mind the errors revealed during the verification of party documents, the party ranks are not to be clogged up with persons who have been admitted at random.

In 1936, as a last attempt to restore some kind of order, all party members were required in person to exchange their cards for new ones. While this process was taking place, hundreds of party officials were examined and many expelled. Moscow obviously did not believe that these officials were carrying out their orders.

This resulted in 9 per cent more party members being ousted. The reasons given are instructive (see Source 6).

This meant that about 40,000 party members had been expelled for political opposition, past or present. How many of these were real critics of the regime in the 1930s is very much open to question. The Party Control Commission called on all members to be more vigilant, and to check future would-be members more closely.

Source 6

Non-political reasons	76%
Being spies or linked to spies	1%
Being Zinovievites	3%
Being former White Guards or *kulaks*	20%

Activity

1 How do you think this continuous purging appeared to a rank and file party member?

2 How do you think the purges appeared to a member of the Party Control Commission?

Was there real opposition to Stalin's authority?

Historians are divided as to whether there was real, organized opposition or whether this existed only in the lurid imaginings of Stalin and his police.

There was widespread grumbling about the regime. Given the harshness of collectivization and the Five Year Plans, it would have been amazing if it had been otherwise. We have seen earlier that those attempting to force peasants into the collective farms were sometimes met with violence. However, this opposition was episodic and at a low level; it was not directed at the central government, though it obviously worried the party leadership.

Source 7

Dinner for the workers
First course – kerosene soup
Second course – fresh moss
Third course – suede pudding

Sign in the Kirov works in October 1935

Timeline

'Industrial' trials 1928–1934

Shakhty	1928
'The Industrial Party'	1930
Mensheviks	1931
Metro-Vickers	1933

Industrial sabotage

There was a series of industrial trials, in which engineers and technicians were charged with sabotage and wrecking. The first and most famous of these was the Shakhty trial of 1928. More than 50 were arrested and put on trial for alleged sabotage and spying in the Shakhty mines in the Ukraine. The only evidence was the prisoners' own confessions. Events in the courtroom revealed that these had been gained only after severe pressure. Eleven were sentenced to death, though six had their sentences commuted for co-operating with the police. As we saw in the previous chapter, in 1933 the government made it a criminal offence for a factory to produce substandard goods and imprisoned managers and directors of plants as a result. Those responsible were accused, as in the Shakhty trial, of sabotage and wrecking.

Do these arrests and the later industrial trials provide us with evidence of real opposition? Certainly at a time when the Soviet Union was pushing to meet new and impossible targets in production, persecuting 'bourgeois experts' does seem counter-productive. It now seems clear that these trials were designed for propaganda purposes – to ensure vigilance, to inspire greater efforts and to unite the people behind the regime. It is perhaps more indicative of the state of mind and anxieties of the leadership than an indication of Soviet reality.

Political opposition

The 1920s had been a time of division and dispute from the Politburo right down to the rank and file members. By 1930, however, all the former members of Lenin's Politburo other than Stalin had been squeezed out. They had all since recanted their former views and been to some extent rehabilitated. Only Trotsky remained a distant threat, living in exile. On the face of it there seemed a greater degree of solidarity within the party than at any time since 1917. Did the realities inside the party match up to this apparent atmosphere of calm and shared ambitions for the future?

Since Trotsky's exile in January 1929 he had not remained silent on Russian affairs. He began his own Russian magazine, the *Bulletin of the Opposition*, copies of which found their way into Russia. The *Bulletin* was strongly critical of the regime and of Stalin, and was read by the Politburo. In November 1932 the *Bulletin* carried a top secret Soviet report on the USSR economy. Trotsky still had many former political friends and supporters inside the Soviet Union – and in the upper echelons of the Communist Party. We now know that Trotsky was still in touch with some of them. His son, Lev Sedov, acted for him in Berlin and in 1932 wrote to his father that an anti-Stalin bloc had been set up, explaining 'it embraces the Zinovievites, the Sten-Lominadze group and the Trotskyites'. Trotsky himself wrote to the Politburo asking to be readmitted into the USSR, threatening agitation inside the party if he was not.

In 1932 OGPU, the secret police, discovered another attack on the direction of policy and of Stalin in particular. 'The Riutin Platform' was a 200 page document which was secretly passed around amongst some of the party leaders. In it Riutin, a former member of the party Central Committee, attacked the forced collectivization programme and demanded more openness and toleration in the party. The document, properly called 'Stalin and the Crisis of the Proletarian Dictatorship', claimed to be the manifesto of the League of Marxists-Leninists.

Note

The Politburo in 1924

Bukharin, Kamenev, Stalin, Rykov, Trotsky, Zinoviev

Note

Lominadze had been regional secretary for the Trans-Caucasus, but was expelled from the Central Committee for 'right-opposition'. He committed suicide in 1935.

Source 8

A regime of unheard of terror and colossal spying, achieved through an extraordinarily centralized and ramified gigantic apparatus, concentrating in its hands all the material resources…this is the main basis of Stalin's dictatorship…[Stalin] has placed himself on a pedestal like an infallible pope and cannot admit either the criminality of his policies or even the slightest mistake…The most evil enemy of the party and the proletarian dictatorship, the most evil counter-revolutionary and provocateur could not have carried out the work of destroying the party and socialist construction better than Stalin has done…the leadership of Stalin must be finished as quickly as possible.

■ Think about

▶ What did Riutin mean by 'socialist construction'?

▶ Why might many in the leadership of the party have been shocked by this document?

NB Consider what was happening in the USSR at the time.

Sergei Kirov

Kirov was head of the Azerbaijani Central Committee in 1920. He became a candidate member of the USSR Central Committee in 1922 and a full member in 1923. In 1926 he became First Secretary of the Leningrad Party after Zinoviev's removal and a Politburo member. He voted against the death penalty for Riutin in 1932. Some said he had good looks and charisma as well as liberal views.

■ Further reading

The evidence about Kirov's death and events that followed is contradictory. Thurston, in *Life and Terror in Stalin's Russia*, 1996, gives a thorough and interesting analysis of the evidence.

■ Think about

▶ Why did the NKVD link Trotsky with Zinoviev and Kamenev?

Clue – look back at the events of the 1920s in Chapter 8.

In 1934 there are some indications of further resistance to Stalin's authority. According to some sources, pressure was put on Kirov to take over Stalin's post as General Secretary of the Communist Party. It is argued that Kirov was a moderate in the party leadership and opposed the worst excesses of collectivization and the Five Year Plans. When he declined the offer, the Congress then abolished the post of General Secretary, making Stalin one of four secretaries. When the elections were held for the party Central Committee, allegedly 166 out of over 1200 delegates did not vote for Stalin. This was allegedly covered up by destroying the offending ballot papers.

Kirov's assassination?

On 1 December 1934 the CPSU was thrown into a frenzy of anxiety. Outside his office in the party headquarters at the Smolny Institute in Leningrad, Politburo member and Leningrad party boss Sergei Kirov was shot dead. The assassin was immediately apprehended, Leonid Nikolaev, a disgruntled party member. How had he managed to evade the strict security surrounding party leaders? Was he acting alone or with others?

Stalin acted with great speed on hearing of the assassination. A decree was announced on 1 December giving the NKVD sweeping powers to deal with 'terrorist organizations and terrorist acts':

Source 9

Emergency decree summary

1 Investigations to be completed in 10 days.
2 Military tribunals to try the suspects.
3 No defence or prosecution lawyers allowed.
4 No appeals were permitted.
5 Executions were to be carried out immediately.

Stalin went by overnight train with senior figures from Moscow to Leningrad, and personally interrogated Nikolaev. The assassin was shot without trial, and Kirov's bodyguard was killed in a traffic accident while being taken for questioning. The NKVD announced the existence of a Trotskyite centre in Leningrad. Party members were ordered to guard against Trotskyites and Zinovievites. Many were arrested and deported from Leningrad, some of them Kirov's closest supporters. Zinoviev and Kamenev were arrested in January 1935 and charged with organizing a 'Moscow Centre' to murder Kirov. They pleaded guilty to 'political and moral responsibility,' though denying any involvement in the murder itself, and were sentenced to long prison sentences. In 1935 the Society of Old Bolsheviks and the Society of Former Political Prisoners were both disbanded. Both these organizations enjoyed considerable status in the CPSU.

Who killed Kirov?

The death of Kirov is a key incident for understanding events in the USSR in the 1930s. If Stalin was behind the murder of one of his closest associates, the view that Stalin was the main motive force behind all the other deaths of the decade seems plausible.

If on the other hand Kirov, a member of the Politburo, was assassinated by a malcontent in the party, then perhaps the purges in the party and country appear logical and justified. The evidence is not absolutely conclusive. What do you think?

Source 10

The latest attempt to come to grips with the Kirov assassination was the work of Iakovlev's Politburo Commission ...the working team concluded that 'in this affair, no materials objectively support Stalin's participation or NKVD participation in the organization and carrying out of Kirov's murder.' The team's report opened some rather large holes in the popular version. According to oral tradition, Leningrad NKVD Deputy Chief Zaporozhets had approached Nikolaev, put him up to the crime, and provided the weapon and bullets. It now seems Zaporozhets had not been in Leningrad for months before the killing and that he never met Nikolaev. Nikolaev had owned the revolver...since 1918...he had purchased the bullets used in the crime legally...Nikolaev was not detained three times while carrying a gun and following Kirov. Actually he had been stopped only once...A frustrated *apparatchik* [civil servant] with delusions of grandeur and lifelong chronic medical problems, Nikolaev wrote in his diary that he wanted to be a great revolutionary... Anyone with a party card could be admitted to the third floor [of the Smolny HQ – Nikolaev had one]. Neither the bodyguard nor his closest collaborators expected Kirov to come to Smolny that day; he had telephoned and said he was staying at home. Kirov arrived unexpectedly and ran into the...assassin, who was in Smolny...to secure a pass to the upcoming party meeting. The assassin and his victim met by accident in Smolny; Nikolaev was not stalking Kirov.

Arch Getty, *The Politics of Repression Revisited*, 1993

Source 11

Kirov, a member of the Politburo and virtual dictator of North Russia, fell dead... Stalin and Voroshilov rushed to Leningrad. According to stories circulated in Party circles, Stalin personally supervised the intensive cross-examination. No outsider, of course, could know what he learned, but from his subsequent behaviour it can be surmised that Stalin was alarmed to the point of panic.

Kravchenko, *I Chose Freedom*, 1947

Source 12

Kirov was an obstacle, and he represented a mood hostile to any increase in Stalin's power...Stalin's decision was that Kirov had to be killed...Nikolaev had made two previous attempts to get suspiciously close to Kirov, had been arrested and found to have a revolver in his briefcase, and had then been released. On 1 December, Nikolaev was able to get, with his revolver (and cartridges from the local NKVD sports club), into the third floor of the Smolny Institute in Leningrad, where Kirov worked. He waited for some hours. When Kirov arrived, his personal bodyguard Borisov was detained at the front door, and Kirov was unprotected when the assassin fired. Borisov was to be killed in the back of a truck by two NKVD men two days later, when they brought him to testify at the inquiry into the crime. The Leningrad NKVD chiefs were given short sentences for 'criminal neglect' of their duties. They were shot in 1937–1938.

Conquest, *Stalin, Breaker of Nations*, 1993

Source 13

Kirov, was among those who inspired and carried through the notoriously ruthless measures against the peasants and the wiping out of the *kulaks*. The Kem and Murmansk coasts, with their prison camps, were under his jurisdiction. Furthermore, he was in charge of the construction of the Baltic-White Sea Canal... It looked at first the continued terror was only a belated and exaggerated aftermath of Nikolaev's shot.

Nikolaevsky, *Letters of an Old Bolshevik*, allegedly based on conversations with Bukharin in Paris, 1936

■ Think about

▶ What are the key points made by Conquest? Which are specifically refuted by Arch Getty?

▶ What does Arch Getty imply about Nikolaev's character and motives? How does this differ from Conquest's view?

Source 14

Kirov used to live in our house. He was one of us, an old colleague and a friend. Kirov spent the summer of 1934 with us. He was closer to us than any of his colleagues, and my father needed him. I will never believe that my father was involved in his death. Wouldn't it be more logical to link his killing with the name of Beria? (Beria was a prominent member and later head of the NKVD.)

From *20 Letters to a Friend* by Svetlana Alliluyeva, Stalin's daughter. Much of her teens was spent with Stalin in his dacha (holiday home) where she met all the senior party figures. This book was written in 1963, 10 years after her father's death.

Source 15

I am guilty of nothing, nothing, nothing before the party, before the Central Committee and before you personally. I swear to you by everything that is sacred to a Bolshevik. I swear to you on Lenin's memory. I cannot even imagine what could have aroused suspicion against me. I beg you to believe my word of honour. I am shaken to the depths of my soul.

Zinoviev to Stalin, 1935

Source 16

SECRET

THE FACTS

1. The villainous murder was committed by the Leningrad group of Zinoviev followers calling themselves the Leningrad Centre.
2. Ideologically and politically, the Leningrad Centre was under the leadership of the Moscow Centre of Zinoviev followers, which apparently did not know of the preparations for the murder of Comrade Kirov.
3. …These two centres constituted one entity, being united by one common worn-out, jaded Trotsky-Zinoviev platform.

Letter from the Central Committee January 1935 to all party organizations. The letter also urged party leaders to read it to their groups and discuss its contents.

Source 17

I must be blind. I have reached the age of fifty but have never seen this 'centre' of which it appears I have been a member.

Kamenev in his trial in 1935. He was accused of being a member of a 'Moscow Centre'

Source 18

The November issue of *Za Rossiyu* the White Guard newspaper of Belgrade…deliberately called for the removal of Kirov in Leningrad, as well as Kaganovitch in Moscow, observing of Stalin that he was too well guarded; a specific incitement to murder which is said to have been repeated in other journals of the emigrés [Russian exiles].

From *Soviet Communism* by S. and B. Webb, 1935 (British visitors to Russia in 1934)

Source 19

300 NKVD workers in Leningrad were fired or transferred to other work. Ezhov reported to Stalin that, although the Leningrad NKVD had in the city more than 21,000 informers controlled by 2000 special informers, it was incompetent…Although in the two-and-a-half months following the assassination 843 former Zinovievists were arrested in Leningrad, most of them were exiled to remote regions.

Arch Getty and Naumov, *The Road to Terror*, 1999

■ Activity

1 The view that Stalin had Kirov murdered is based on the idea that Kirov was more liberal, and therefore more popular in the party – a rival to Stalin's authority. Is this view supported by Sources 11, 13, and 14?

2 For what reasons may some historians find these sources unreliable?

3 How did Stalin and the Politburo react to Kirov's death? Did they use it for their own political ends?

4 Read through all the sources and the background.

Draw up a balance sheet of all the evidence suggesting Stalin was behind Kirov's death, and of all the evidence suggesting he was not. Discuss or debate your own conclusions with those of other students.

Is there enough evidence for us to be sure what really happened?

Who killed Kirov?

Look at what two different authors have to say on this subject. Present a short talk to members of your group, using at least once image (eg spidergram, table etc), in which you compare and make judgements about the views of the historians you have read. Use this as the basis of a group discussion.

A relaxation of tension?

The years 1934–6 were successful years economically for the USSR. Many of the new plants were now producing goods. Rationing of food was ended in 1935, which was a very popular measure. The rural famine was over. The 1934 Party Congress was nicknamed 'The Congress of Victors', because so much progress toward socialism had been made. The number of arrests also declined:

Source 20

Arrests by Security Police 1930–1936

	All crimes	Counter-Rev crimes	Executions
1930	331,544	266,679	20,201
1931	479,000	344,700	10,651
1932	410,000	196,000	2,738
1933	505,300	283,000	2,154
1934	205,000	90,000	2,056
1935	193,000	109,000	1,229
1936	131,168	91,127	1,118

■ **Think about**

▶ Why did the security police arrest so many between 1930 and 1933?

In 1935 the party decided to introduce a new constitution, one that was more fitting for a socialist society where there were no longer any class differences. The most prominent member of the committee drafting the constitution was Bukharin, now apparently completely rehabilitated. The 'Stalin Constitution', introduced in November 1936, made the USSR appear the most democratic state in the world, giving to all the right of employment at a time when millions were unemployed in Europe and the USA. Freedom of religion, the press and assembly were all guaranteed. Even ex-*kulaks* and priests were given back the right to vote. This calmer period did not last long.

Quotation

People will have more room. They can no longer be pushed aside

Bukharin, quoted in B. Nikolaevsky, *Letters of an Old Bolshevik*, 1936

The show trials

In August 1936 Zinoviev and Kamenev with 14 others were put on trial again for complicity with Trotsky in plots to kill Stalin and other members of the Politburo. Out of these, 14 confessed, including Kamenev and Zinoviev. In these confessions, obtained by promising the accused their lives if they were 'helpful', other old comrades were mentioned and implicated in their plots. These others included Rykov, Tomsky, Piatakov and Bukharin. All the accused were found guilty, after a hate campaign in the press and newsreels, and shot shortly afterwards.

The sad story is told of Zinoviev begging for his life on his knees before his executioners. This was apparently re-enacted to Stalin at a dinner for the secret police. He was so delighted with the performance that he asked to see it again, but had to beg it to stop because he was laughing so much.

No sooner was the trial over when in September 1936 Stalin and Zhdanov, on holiday together by the Black Sea, sent a telegram to the Politburo (Source 21).

■ **Biography**

G.L.Piatakov
Born 1890.
1915 edited *Kommunist* magazine.
1924 opposed NEP; close to Trotsky.
1931–6, Deputy Commissar for Heavy Industry.
1937 executed.

■ **Biography**

G. Yagoda
Joined Cheka in 1920.
Deputy Head of OGPU at time of Riutin Platform 1932.
Head of NKVD 1934–36. (This replaced OGPU.)

Source 21

We deem it absolutely necessary and urgent that Comrade Ezhov be nominated to the post of People's Commissar for Internal Affairs. Yagoda has definitely proved himself to be incapable of unmasking the Trotskyite-Zinovievite bloc. The OGPU is four years behind in this matter.

In January 1937 a second show trial followed. Piatakov's wife pleaded with him to plead guilty to save the life of their child. He pleaded guilty. Here is an excerpt from the verdict against them:

Source 22

In 1933, in accordance with direct instructions given by the enemy of the people, L. Trotsky...there was formed in Moscow...an underground parallel anti-Soviet Trotskyite centre...The principal aim...was to overthrow the Soviet power...and to restore capitalism and the power of the bourgeoisie by means of wrecking, diversive, espionage and terrorist activities to undermine the economic and military power of the Soviet Union...The enemy of the people, L. Trotsky, undertook...to liquidate State farms, to dissolve the collective farms, to renounce the policy of industrialization of the country and to restore...the social relations of capitalist society.

■ **Think about**

▶ Do you think party leaders believed these charges?

▶ How might the verdict against Piatakov be useful to historians today?

Note

Ordzhonokidze had been, since 1932, Commissar for Heavy Industry, a key role in the Five Year Plans.

All the accused were found guilty. Radek and another of the accused were sentenced to imprisonment, but the rest were condemned to death – not however before they had all implicated Bukharin and others in their plots. Shortly after the trial Piatakov's boss, Politburo member Ordzhonikidze, died, probably having committed suicide. Ordzhonikidze's brother had already been shot by the NKVD and he himself is known to have had several long telephone calls with Stalin before his death. His death was announced to the world as a heart attack, presumably to save the party embarrassment.

The last of the three major show trials was held in Moscow in March 1938. The accused included Bukharin, Yagoda, and Rykov. Their colleague Tomsky had committed suicide when he was first linked to the investigation. Bukharin admitted his guilt in court in order to save his wife and children, but spent the trial refuting all the specific accusations made against him. Vyshinsky, the State Prosecutor, concluded his summing up with this statement:

Source 23

Our whole country is awaiting and demanding one thing. The traitors and spies who were selling our country must be shot like dirty dogs. Our people are demanding one thing. Crush the accursed reptile. Time will pass. The graves of the hateful traitors will grow over with weeds and thistles. But over us, over our happy country, our sun will shine with its luminous rays as bright and joyous as before. Over the road cleared of the last scum and filth of the past, we, with our beloved leader and teacher, the great Stalin, at our head, will march as before onwards and onwards, towards Communism.

■ **Think about**

▶ Who do you think Vyshinsky's speech was intended for?

▶ How effective do you think it is as a speech?

Bukharin and the other accused were shot. Bukharin wrote a final letter to Stalin asking for mercy, but curiously also admitting that he had attended a meeting in 1932 when some of his younger followers had talked about Stalin's death!

Why the *Ezhovschina* – the 'Great Purge'?

The period between the second and third show trials mentioned above saw a surge in the numbers arrested, imprisoned and shot. Mass graves located across the USSR testify to the number of victims. This period, the 'great Purge' has been called by Russians the '*Ezhovschina*', the Ezhov phenomenon, after the head of the NKVD 1936–1938.

In February 1937 a full meeting of the Central Committee of the Communist Party met in Moscow. It must have been a difficult meeting for it lasted 11 days, much longer than the usual 4 or 5. The main point of dispute was how to deal with opposition in the party and with Trotskyites in particular. Speaker after speaker described their success in weeding out Trotskyites in their own districts. Stalin believed, however, that many in the party were protecting members from criticism and attacked the 'families' in the local parties as follows:

Source 24

What does it mean if you drag a whole group of pals along with yourself? It means you've acquired a certain independence from local organizations and, if you like, a certain independence from the Central Committee.

Zhdanov put forward a conciliatory view that members needed better education and that secret elections would put a stop to corruption and nepotism. Molotov and Ezhov wanted a more aggressive policy towards suspected oppositionists. No final resolution, however, was published. It was during this meeting that Bukharin was denounced and expelled from the party. The Central Committee agreed finally to set up a special commission of five Politburo members to investigate opposition within the party and to act on its behalf.

When the meeting dispersed, the NKVD moved quickly. It first fell on the army leadership. Trotsky had, of course, been Commissar for War, so many leading officers had enjoyed his confidence. April and May saw the arrest of many generals, including Marshal Tukhachevski, the hero of the Civil War. They were accused of plotting with foreign powers, especially Germany, to overthrow Stalin. Physical torture was certainly used. For example, Tukhachevski's 'confession' was splattered with blood. By December 1938 the leadership of the Soviet armed forces had been devastated. Only two out five marshals remained in place and about two-thirds of senior officers had been arrested or shot. The precise impact on the armed forces is disputed. According to Thurston only 6.9 per cent of officers in the army in 1936 were dismissed but not re-appointed by 1940. Other estimates have been as high as half of the officer corps removed permanently. Whatever the figures, the USSR's international situation, with Hitler successfully flouting the Versailles peace terms and Germany's rapid rearmament, was growing more desperate each month. In this light the attack on the Red Army seems difficult to explain, unless the leadership genuinely thought there was a plot being hatched to threaten the Communist regime in the USSR.

It was not only the Red Army that was affected. The Politburo legalized torture in August 1937, just after receiving a report from Ezhov that he proposed to arrest over 250,000 before the year's end. Targets were set for each district. 28 per cent would be shot; the rest were to be detained.

The targets for these arrests and executions were laid down by the Politburo – returning *kulaks* and political prisoners who were inspiring sabotage and other

■ Biography

Ezhov

His nickname was the 'bloody dwarf.' He was rumoured to have shot his former boss Yagoda personally. In March 1939 he was arrested by his own former employees and disappeared.

■ Think about

▶ What does this suggest Stalin believed was wrong with the CPSU?

■ Historical debate

The so-called 'Generals' Plot' has caused another disagreement between historians. Thurston suggests there is evidence supporting the idea of a plot. Segeev maintains that the plot was a fiction of the Germans to create instability in the Red Army. To others it was simply all an invention of Ezhov or Stalin to purge the army of possible oppositionists.

'anti-Soviet' crimes. Ezhov added to the list priests, former members of political parties, nationalists, former Whites and so on. Was there a pattern to the arrests? It seems to have hit party members most savagely – particularly those in the higher and middle ranks. Only about 3 per cent of the delegates to the 1934 Party Congress were elected to the Party Congress in 1939. Only 16 out of 71 members of the 1934 Central Committee were alive in 1939.

Source 25

Arrests and executions 1936–1938

	Total arrests	Arrests for counter-revolutionary crimes	Convictions	Executions
1936	131,000	91,000	275,000	1118
1937	936,000	779,000	791,000	353,000
1938	639,000	593,000	554,000	329,000

Was this all a sinister plot by Stalin to remove everyone who might even pose a possible threat to his authority? According to Stephen Cohen, speaking on the ITV documentary series Stalin, the arrests were almost arbitrary. 'No one was guilty, therefore no one was innocent'. According to some authorities the whole Russian people lived under the threat of arbitrary arrest. Thurston, however, argues that many groups were almost totally unaffected by the 'great purge'. According to Service, however, 'The impact of the Great Terror was deep and wide and was not limited to specific political, administrative, military, cultural, religious and national groups'.

Was Stalin personally involved in the purges?

There can be little doubt that Stalin was involved in the show trials and the purges. Before the trials the interrogators reported to Stalin each day on the 'progress' they were making with their investigations. Stalin said to a NKVD official in July 1936:

Source 26

Now then, don't tell me any more that Kamenev, or this or that prisoner, is able to withstand that pressure. Don't come to report to me until you have in this briefcase the confession of Kamenev!

At the trial of Bukharin Stalin was momentarily revealed by a trick of the light while secretly listening behind a curtain to the proceedings in the courtroom. Source 2 showed how many death sentences Stalin approved personally. A scribbled note to Ezhov at about the same time says simply, 'Shoot all 138 of them'.

However, it must also be true that, of the million or so shot by the NKVD during the *Ezhovschina*, few of the victims can have been personally known to Stalin. Although Stalin signed the documents which authorized mass killings, others selected those sent to their deaths. The NKVD in each area was set a quota for arrests and executions. At the very least there were many thousands within the police system and within the party who were deeply involved in the arrests and the killings.

Cross reference

You will find more on this historical debate in Chapter 12.

■ **Think about**

▶ What can we learn about Stalin's role in the trials from Source 26?

▶ What can we learn about his attitude to the accused?

Document exercise: images of Stalin

Source A

◀ A painting entitled 'Unforgettable moment'.

▼ A cartoon published by Russian exiles in France in 1939.

Source B

Poem by Lebedev-Kumach 1937

And so – everywhere. In the
  workshops, in the mines,
In the Red Army, the kindergarten
He is watching.
You look at his portrait and it's as if he
  knows
Your work and weighs it;
You've worked badly – his brows
  lower.
But when you've worked well, he
  smiles in his moustache.

Source C

Pravda describes the 7th Party Congress in January 1935

At 6.15 Comrade Stalin appears. All the
delegates rise as one man and greet
him with a stormy and prolonged
ovation. From all parts of the hall come
the shouts of 'Long live the Great
Stalin', Long Live our Vozhd'. A new
outburst of applause and greetings.
Comrade Kalinin…reminds the
audience that it is Comrade Stalin who
is 'the instigator, inspirer, and organizer'
of the whole gigantic work of the
Soviet Union. A new storm of applause
passing into an endless ovation.

Source D

Examination-style questions

1 **Comprehension in context**
   What image of Stalin is presented in Source A?

2 **Comparing the sources**
   To what extent do Sources B and D present a similar image of Stalin?

3 **Assessing the sources**
   How useful would Source C be to a historian studying Stalin's role in the USSR?

4 **Making judgements**
   Using the sources and your own knowledge in your answer, would you agree that Stalin was genuinely popular in the USSR in the 1930s?

▶ Prisoners building the Belomor Canal in 1933.

Think about

▶ Were conditions in the gulag much worse than those Russians suffered outside?

Think about

▶ Why was Shukhov content with his day?

▶ What image does Solzhenitsyn present of gulag life in this excerpt?

▶ Shukhov is a fictitious character. Does this affect the usefulness of the book to historians?

Further reading

One Day in the Life of Ivan Denisovitch can be taken as a simple description of the life of a gulag inmate. It can also be seen as a metaphor for Stalin's Russia as a whole.

Life in the gulags

In 1939 almost 3 million people were in labour camps (gulags) in the USSR. Life in the labour camps is perhaps best described in the novels of Alexander Solzhenitsyn, who spent eight years in them. A grinding routine of hard physical work in extreme temperatures, a struggle simply to survive another day seemed to be the norm.

The labour camps produced most of Russia's gold and much of its timber. Prisoners were also involved in building the new cities and transport links.

Source 27

Source 28

Shukhov went to sleep fully content. He'd had many strokes of luck that day: they hadn't put him in the cells; they hadn't sent the team to the settlement [where there was no cover from the subzero temperature]; he'd pinched a bowl of kasha [a kind of porridge] at dinner; the team-leader had fixed the rates [of work] well; he'd built a wall and enjoyed doing it; he'd smuggled that hacksaw blade through; he'd earned something from Tsezar in the evening; he'd bought that tobacco. And he hadn't fallen ill. He'd got over it.

A day without a dark cloud. Almost a happy day.

There were three thousand six hundred and fifty-three days like that in his stretch. From the first clang of the rail to the last clang of the rail.

The three extra days were for leap years.

The end of *One Day in the Life of Ivan Denisovitch*, a novel written by A. Solzhenitsyn who himself spent many years inside gulags

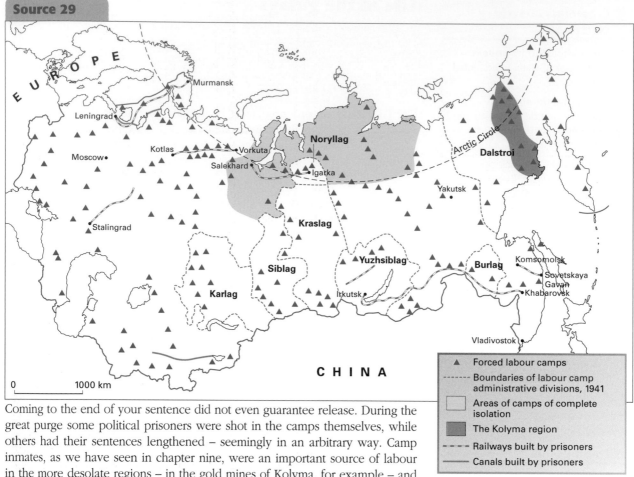

▲ The location of the gulags in the USSR.

Coming to the end of your sentence did not even guarantee release. During the great purge some political prisoners were shot in the camps themselves, while others had their sentences lengthened – seemingly in an arbitrary way. Camp inmates, as we have seen in chapter nine, were an important source of labour in the more desolate regions – in the gold mines of Kolyma, for example – and in many of the vast construction works of the Five Year Plans. Life expectancy must have been very low, especially for the 'politicals' who seem to have been most harshly treated. It is important to remember that many of the inmates, whose bodies were wrecked by this savage regime, in a former life had been intellectuals, writers, engineers etc. At a time when the whole of the country was involved in trying to bring about 'socialist construction', this was perhaps not the best use of their talents.

'Normality' is resumed

In April 1939 Ezhov, the principal agent in the 'great purge' was himself arrested. This is now seen as a signal for the end of the wave of arrests and executions. Ezhov was replaced as head of the NKVD by his deputy Beria.

In March 1939 the first Party Congress since 1934 met. Stalin set the new tone:

It cannot be said that the cleansings were not accompanied by grave mistakes. There were unfortunately more mistakes than might have been expected. Undoubtedly, we shall have no further need to resort to the method of mass cleansings. Nevertheless, the cleansings of 1933–36 were unavoidable and their results, on the whole, were beneficial.

This marked an end to the waves of mass arrests. Quotas for arrests were abandoned and thousands released from the gulags. Many more were restored

■ Think about

▶ What does the location of these camps suggest about their purpose?

■ Think about

▶ What does Source 30 suggest about Stalin's attitude to the cleansings?

to their party membership and positions. Amongst the last to suffer were some of the secret police who had carried out the purges, Ezhov himself being shot in 1940. In truth party purges never really stopped; they simply continued at a slower pace and were resumed after the war with even greater intensity. From the outbreak of war in Europe in September 1939, the government had other preoccupations, although Hitler did not attack the USSR until 1941.

Timeline

'The Terror'

1928	Shakhty	Engineers
1928	Collectivization	Kulaks
1928	Chistka	Local party members

■ Further reading

J. Arch Getty, *Origins of the great Purges,* 1985

S. F. Cohen, *Bukharin and the Russian Revolution,* 1974

R. Conquest, *Stalin: Breaker of Nations,* 1993

R. Conquest, *The Great Terror: A Reassessment,* 1990

R. Daniels, *The Stalin revolution,* 1990

R.W. Thurston, *Life and terror in Stalin's Russia 1934-41,* 1996

D. Volkogonov, *Stalin: Triumph and Tragedy,* 1991

C. Ward, *Stalin's Russia,* 1993

Quotation

1937 was essential. Remnants of various kinds of enemies still existed, and in view of the fascist threat, they might have united.

> Molotov, Foreign Minister in the 1930s, in an interview in 1970

▶ Do you think this Molotov quotation is a reliable source for us today?

■ Activity

'The terror' is a complex issue. One good way to master it is to draw up a timeline of the main events like the one begun in the margin. Start with the Shakhty Trial and end with the outbreak of war on 1 September 1939. Mark on all the important events in this chapter, and any you can remember from the previous one, and state which groups in the USSR were affected by each.

Also mark on periods when the situation seemed to become calmer. Does your timeline suggest the terror was a continuous phenomenon? Does it suggest these events were part of a planned campaign?

Conclusion – Why did the terror happen?

We have seen that the terror had many different aspects – the industrial trials, the political show trials, the cleansing of the party and the *Ezhovschina*, a process of arrests and executions which went far beyond party members. Why these events took place is still argued between historians. The term 'the purges', used by some historians to describe all these events, assumes that all of these different phenomena are in some way connected. They are seen as part of a sinister programme by Stalin to establish a personal dictatorship in the USSR, and to remove anyone either in the past, present or future who presented/might present a threat to that dictatorship. According to this view, the Russian people and members of the Communist Party themselves at the time were totally cowed into submission, terrified that any random remark would lead to their own arrest, imprisonment or worse. A good example of this point of view is reflected in the novel *Children of the Arbat* by A. Rybakov.

Another western view is to blame the Stalinist excesses on Lenin. He set up the first camps and he urged ruthlessness at every stage after the revolution. Stalin was simply solving problems in the way that Lenin had begun. Stalin was Lenin's truest disciple. Alternatively others place the responsibility on Marxist theory. Dictatorship was what all Marxist theoreticians were led to expect after the revolution.

'Revisionist' historians reject this view of Stalin's decisive role in the 1930s. They argue that this 'totalitarian' explanation is too simplistic, and depends largely on deterministic history – that is that the events of the 1930s were in some sense predictable and the logical outcome of previous situations and thinking. For them 'the purges' are a series of unconnected events, which do not have a simple logic to them. Instead they are the result of the chaos which prevailed in the USSR. They represent not the calculated methods by which a totalitarian government dominated its people, but instead the weakness of that government and its total failure to control even its own followers, let alone those who were opposed or apathetic towards politics.

Many historians fall between these two viewpoints. The 'facts' of the case have been interpreted to support both points of view. This debate is the focus of part of Chapter 12 of this book.

Chapter 11

Society and culture in Stalin's Russia

▲ A poster from 1937 celebrating twenty years of socialism in Russia.

One afternoon the head of the port administration sent for me. He was Trotsky's brother. Passing through an ante-room I stepped into an opulent suite – embossed tables, malachite urns, settees and couches upholstered with costly brocade. Everything matched. An added luxury were two polar-bear skins on the polished parquet floor. A table was covered with a snow-white cloth and laden with platters of jellied veal, cold turkey, juicy, sliced pink sturgeon and fruit in cut-glass bowls. Two bottles of champagne reclined in silver ice buckets. Why were these privileges allowed in hungry Leningrad?

From *A Soviet Odyssey* by Canadian Communist Suzanne Rosenberg, describing an incident shortly after arriving in Russia in 1931

Introduction

Marxists envisaged a future society where inequalities of wealth and power had been swept away in a new spirit of egalitarianism and freedom. All would contribute to society in any way they could, working for the common good, as shown in Source 1. How close was Russia in the 1930s to reaching this goal? Was the talked of socialist society simply a propaganda image to conceal a new class system, based on political privilege, as many historians in the 1950s and 1960s suggested? Suzanne Rosenberg, herself a Communist, seems to have been shocked by what she experienced on reaching the Soviet Union (Source 2).

In this chapter we will look more closely at the realities of society and the values it sought to encourage in its people.

Key questions

- What happened to religious faith?
- How was family life affected?
- What changes were made to schools and education?
- Was it possible to improve your position in life?
- Did people support the regime?
- What kind of cultural life was there in the USSR?

Moving into the cities

By far the biggest change in the life of many Soviet citizens came when they left the collective farms for the cities. Between 1929 and 1941 18.5 million made this journey. Until the introduction of the internal passport in 1932, there were no restrictions on movement. After collectivization those who remained on the *kolkhoz* were destined to a life of poverty and near-serfdom. However, the demand for labour during these years offered many opportunities for those prepared to take the risk of digging up their roots. Those who had specialized skills must have found the move easiest. Tractor and combine drivers, for example, once they were trained by the MTS, could easily find employment in construction and mining.

Leaving all family contacts and the rural life they had been brought up to must have been a profound shock for many people.

Religion

'Religion is the opium of the people', wrote Karl Marx. All Bolsheviks believed that religion was an invention to distract the poor and oppressed from trying to remedy their situation on earth by offering them the prospect of perfect happiness after death. If a Communist society was to be achieved, the shackles of religious belief needed to be shattered.

The attack on religion had begun under Lenin and it continued throughout the 1920s. Lenin had ordered the execution of several bishops, ostensibly because they refused to sell church gold and silver to help those affected by the famine in 1922, but as the NEP developed it saw a decline in religious persecution, especially of some of the non-orthodox congregations. None the less, 117 out of 160 Orthodox bishops had been arrested during this period of relative toleration, which ended dramatically with the First Five Year Plan.

The collectivization of villages was accompanied by widespread attacks on religion. Many churches were closed and their priests were deported. Church buildings were either pulled down or converted to secular purposes, as barns,

■ Think about

Symbols, as we have seen before, were very important in Soviet Russia.
▶ What powerful symbols are used in Source 1?
▶ What are being presented as the most important achievements of the regime?

Note

MTS are Motor Tractor Stations. See Chapter 9 'Building Paradise'.

schools etc. In 1930 there were 30,000 Orthodox congregations, but by 1939 only 1 in 40 churches was still functioning and only seven bishops were still active in the whole of the Soviet Union. Worship could only take place in licensed premises by congregations registered with the government. Many congregations had to apply to use religious vestments and silver from the local authorities and return them after use.

Source 3

◀ A monastery is blown up in 1930 to make way for a cultural centre.

■ **Think about**

▶ What is the attitude of the artist to the destruction of religious buildings in the USSR?

▶ Do you think this is a reliable picture for the historian?

In Moscow church buildings suffered even more. Churches, such as the famous Chapel of the Iberian Virgin by Red Square, were knocked down around the Kremlin to allow the passage of parades of armed vehicles. The Cathedral of Christ the Saviour, built in the nineteenth century to commemorate the defeat of Napoleon, was dynamited to make way for what was planned to be the world's tallest construction, the Palace of Soviets. This was to be crowned by a statue of Lenin, though in fact the Palace was never built because the foundations were unsound.

Source 4

◀ The Cathedral of Christ the Saviour in the heart of Moscow. Stalin ordered its destruction in 1931.

The 1937 design for the Palace of Soviets, which was never built.

Source 5

■ **Think about**

▶ How do Sources 4 and 5 reflect the priorities of the two regimes?

▶ Why do you think Stalin chose this spot for his Palace of Soviets?

In the old capital, St Petersburg, which was now known as Leningrad, the authorities seemed to have a macabre sense of humour. The famous Kazan Cathedral was converted into a museum of atheism, while the Monastery of Alexander Nevsky, where formerly famous Russians musicians were buried, became the place of burial for prominent anti-religious figures.

The Communists also attacked Islam, the second largest religious community in the USSR. Only 1300 mosques were still operating in 1941 as against 26,000 in 1917.

However, there is much evidence that the party's campaign against Christianity was not very successful. Many congregations continued to meet in private houses, despite the lack of ordained priests to take services. The party tried to prevent the observance of religious holy days, but was singularly unsuccessful. Some *kolkhoz* chairmen complained to their bosses that peasants were observing even more religious holidays than before collectivization. Perhaps religion here was a good excuse to resist the demands of the hated *kolkhoz*. Apparently some *kolkhoz* chairmen later in the 1930s were actually churchwardens.

Note

The League of the Militant Godless was set up in the 1920s to fight against organized religion. It consisted mainly of younger people, especially Komsomol, the party's youth organization.

■ **Think about**

▶ Why do you think religious belief persisted in the face of this attack by the State?

The 1937 census showed that despite the official campaigns and activities of the League of the Militant Godless, 57 per cent of Russians said they were still believers. The percentage was even higher for the older generation. Clearly the regime had not managed to dislodge religious belief and the view of the world which it represented amongst the majority of Russians. In fact the tide seemed to be turning in the opposite direction. The League of the Militant Godless lost three-quarters of its members between 1932 and 1938. Its Leningrad branch was closed down for lack of members in 1936.

Educating for the future

Building roads, railways and factories of itself would not create communism. All Marxists believed that a change in political consciousness was also necessary, and that would need to be taught. Education also served other purposes. It was self-evident that a modern economy needed a literate and numerate workforce.

Primary education was made compulsory for all in 1930 for four years. During the 1930s this term was extended, until each child spent seven compulsory years at school by 1939. Even illiterate adults were encouraged to attend school or evening classes. The results were striking; by 1939 illiteracy had declined to just 4 per cent of the male and 18 per cent of the female population. This meant a huge expansion in the number of teachers, though, especially in the rural areas, they were often not well-treated. The onus was put on the *kolkhoz* to find the money for schools, and particularly in the harsh years of the early and mid-1930s money was in very short supply. Feeding the community was a higher priority than teaching them to write.

There were interesting changes in teaching and learning styles. The Revolution had introduced some progressive ideas into schools. Exams had been denounced as 'bourgeois'. Similarly activities which emphasized competition, e.g. sports, were downplayed. Traditional academic education was replaced by a heavy emphasis on vocational training. In 1928 there was an attack on 'bourgeois intellectuals' both in the economy and in education. Many professors were removed from universities, and a proletarian background became compulsory to pursue a university education as a student or to teach at any level. Many universities were broken up and handed over to Vesenkha. Between 1928 and 1934 '900 specialist departments and 566 institutes' (Ward, *Stalin's Russia*, 1993) were set up. Instead of a broad academic higher education, students now passed through narrow specialist courses which prepared them for their future role in completing the Five Year Plans.

Some of the changes in teaching were seen to be counter-productive; by 1935 a more traditional approach was reintroduced. Tests and examinations became compulsory, uniforms were imposed, with pig-tails for girls, and traditional academic subjects were once again studied by all pupils as well as, of course, Marxism-Leninism. The attack on academics slowed. By 1936 the insistence on a proletarian background for higher education was removed. As the number of students in higher education expanded, in 1940 the State introduced fees for higher education, as in Britain in the 1990s. These were also introduced for the last three years of secondary schooling. Here is how one anonymous student reacted:

Facts and figures

Number of schools in USSR	
1927	118,558
1933	166,275

Source 6

Again we're going backwards. Before a boss wouldn't let a worker squeak, and now workers are repressed. Before children of capitalists studied in universities and now workers' children have only one route – to die at the bench like their parents.

■ Think about

▶ What does the author feel about the changes in the USSR since the Revolution?

Literacy was, however, of little use if there was little to read. *Pravda* and *Izvestia* were widely distributed, and sold for only 10 kopeks.

Quotation

'The press should grow not by the day, but by the hour, for it is the sharpest and most powerful weapon of our people.' Stalin

▶ What does this quote tell us about the motives behind the literacy drive?

Facts and figures

Komsomol membership

1929	2.9 million
1940	10.2 million

■ Think about

▶ What impression does this photograph give of the children?

▶ Does this photograph prove that the young supported the regime?

Source 7

USSR newspapers

	1913	1928	1939
Number of Russian papers	775	861	6475
Number of others	84	336	2294
Total circulation (millions)	2.7	9.4	38.0

Publishing houses turned out copies of the classics of Russian and foreign literature at very low prices. Even in the barrack blocks, in which the first workers at the new city of Magnitogorsk lived, there was always a daily paper provided and a small library, although the barracks leaked and were infested by bedbugs. 70,000 libraries were built across Russia.

Children and adults were bombarded with propaganda inside and outside school. The young were encouraged to join party groups, the Young Pioneers, up to 14 years, and then Komsomol, until they were 28. As young Communists they were expected to set an example to their peers: party rules, for example, forbade them to smoke or drink. Most then went on to become full members of the Communist Party. The Communist future, they were told, would be theirs, but they must do their part to build it. And build it they did, volunteering for many of the most grandiose projects of the Five Year Plans, and for the party's biggest prestige project in the capital – the Moscow Metro.

Source 8

▲ Komsomol members parade behind their band.

They were also given idols of their own age group to admire. Source 9 shows Pavlik Morozov, the Young Pioneer who denounced his own father for maintaining ties with *kulaks*. He was murdered as a result by other members of his own family while picking berries in the woods.

Source 9

◀ A statue of
Pavlik Morozov

■ **Think about**

▶ Why were statues put up to Morozov?

▶ What image of the dead boy does the statue present?

Family life

Marriage as an institution did not at first win the favour of all Bolsheviks. For many women through the centuries their experience of marriage had been child-bearing, hard work and brutality at the hands of a drunken husband. Some Communists, including senior diplomat Alexandra Kollontai, went so far as to call marriage a 'bourgeois institution', which gave men the legal framework to exploit the female under-class. Her solution was to dissolve the institution altogether. Both sexes, she thought, should be able to choose to have sexual relations with whomever they wished. As for children, some Communists argued that bringing them up was best left to State-run children's homes rather than to parents at home. This would instil in children the proper social attitudes and destroy any divisions between social groups.

After the Revolution a number of reforms had been passed to try to give greater equality to women. Divorce was made cheap and very easy. All that had to be done was to visit a judge and sign the necessary papers. Abortion was also legalized, though not encouraged. Many people lived together in unregistered partnerships, though marriage was still the norm. Government propaganda, even in the 1920s, emphasized the role of women workers as well as homemakers. Childcare at the workplace was common, though extended families also took on these arrangements themselves.

'The Great Change' put a huge strain on the family and the institution of marriage. The arrest and deportation of over a million *kulaks* often meant their wives went with them. Many families tried to leave children with relatives or friends. As we have seen, for those who remained life on the new collective farms was difficult; young men in particular often could see no future for themselves. They left their villages in millions, with or without the necessary permission, to look for work in the nearest city or industrial region. Many seem to have abandoned their family obligations, often starting up a second family in their new surroundings. Fathers were bound by law to pay maintenance for their children, but, in the chaotic circumstances of the time, it was impossible to track fathers down and they could easily move on if detection looked likely. Factories were desperate for workers, especially if they had special skills. The 1934 famine, which devastated large parts of Russia, left many thousands of orphans. Desperate villagers, without enough food for themselves, sent them off to the nearest town.

For families living together in the cities and towns, life was also harsh. Even party leaders were not exempt from the conditions, long before the rapid movement of people which accompanied the Five Year Plans. Here Khrushchev, the future Soviet leader, reflects in his memoirs, about being a delegate to the 14th Party Congress in 1925:

Source 10

We lived in the House of Soviets…Our quarters were very simple and crowded. We slept on plank beds, and we were stacked together like logs.

Khrushchev, Khrushchev Remembers, 1971

Of course, Khrushchev and his comrades did not have to suffer these conditions for more than a few days. Families often lived together in extremely claustrophobic conditions. Housing was desperately short and families of three generations, grandma, parents and children, lived in rooms of 11 square metres. In this room they ate, washed and slept. Where new blocks of flats were erected in the 1930s, the 'socialist' plan of communal bathrooms and kitchens (*kommunalki*) was often followed. This gross overcrowding must have put enormous strain on family relationships at all levels. Husbands and wives deserted their families and children ran away from unhappy homes. Desperate parents put their children into orphanages and abandoned them there. There were, therefore, an increasingly large number of children being brought up away from their parents. The State orphanages were creaking under the weight of new admissions.

The result of many of these pressures was gangs of street-children in the cities living lives on the margins of society, stealing, scrounging and begging.

Note

High status families were somewhat better off. In 1928 an apartment block, Government House, was begun containing 566 furnished flats with telephones, constant hot water and many other modern amenities.

Facts and figures

Average space per resident in Leningrad

1927	8.5 sq m
1935	5.8 sq m

Juvenile crime became a major problem for the government, absorbing the time of all levels of government – even the Politburo.

What should the government do about this? Juvenile offenders had at first been treated sympathetically by the courts. Social circumstances were held to be responsible for their problems, and education and care the best solution. Now attitudes hardened and, in 1935, a new harsh law was passed by the Politburo. The law in future was to treat all those aged twelve and over as adults, even imposing the death penalty if it was felt to be appropriate. Parents of hooligans were also made liable to fines. Troublesome children could be removed from their parents to State orphanages and parents would have to pay for their upkeep.

In 1936 the government introduced new measures to strengthen family life. The law made abortion illegal, despite much public debate and opposition. Newspapers afterwards carried many stories about the punishment of doctors and illegal abortionists, as well as husbands who forced wives to have illegal abortions, to discourage the practice. The birth rate did increase substantially from 25 to 31 per thousand as a result, but it would appear that illegal abortionists were still kept busy. The same law also made divorce much more difficult, requiring the presence of both parties in the court, and making it considerably more expensive. Absent parents also had to contribute a higher proportion of their wages to the upkeep of children, which was a strong disincentive to divorce. Homosexuality was also banned.

The State also implemented a system to reward mothers who had six or more children. For five years they received 2000 roubles per year, which was a large sum of money for working families. These reforms and payments did not lead to a decline in the number of working women. In Leningrad they rose from 44 per cent to 50 per cent of the workforce between 1935 and 1937. To encourage women back to work after giving birth, almost all large factories set up creches to care for their children. In Moscow in the central Gorky Park was a Children's Village where in suitable weather the creches brought the children for healthy games and outdoor exercise.

When men were mobilized into the army, this percentage continued to grow. However, women still suffered discrimination at the workplace, usually occupying mainly lower positions. Between 50 and 60 per cent of doctors were women, but only 4 women were chief doctors in Leningrad. Illiteracy was also higher amongst women than men.

■ **Think about**

Britain has faced similar problems.
▶ What have recent governments done to try to deal with them?
▶ Have their efforts been successful?

Facts and figures

318 male factory directors in Leningrad.
20 female factory directors in Leningrad.
▶ What does this tell us about sexual equality in the USSR?

Source 11

◀ Women express milk in a Moscow factory in 1930.

■ **Think about**

▶ Why did women express milk in the factory?

What does Source 11 tell us about
▶ the wishes of the State?
▶ the wishes of mothers?

Source 12

Today is a clear day
Merry children
Play and dance
Know no cares
But at home mummy
Toils and knows not
What to cook them
For dinner
How to clothe and shoe
Her own children
Mummy doesn't know
Where to get shoes
They need coats
They need boots
Worries
Poor mother.

The pressure felt by women
is reflected in this poem written
by schoolchildren in 1935

■ Think about

▶ What does Source 12 tell us about the role of women in the USSR?

▶ Do you think it is a reliable source for a historian?

Were people better off in the 1930s?

Not even Stalin claimed that the USSR had become a Communist society in the 1930s. Scarcity of goods and services meant that this was as yet an impossible dream. But exactly how were these scarce resources distributed amongst the Russian population? Did all have equal access?

Workers

Cross reference

See Chapter 9 for more detail about the quality of life in the 1930s.

As far as industrial wages were concerned, the tendency to equalization after 1917 was reversed. In 1931 wage differentials had been sharply increased and many workers were paid on the basis of piecework, that is how much they produced. Jasny's estimates of real wages (what wages could buy) is that they fell by over a half during the First Five Year Plan, and only rose to 56 per cent of their 1928 level by 1940. Many workers, therefore, ate most meals in communal canteens and did not cook. It is also important to remember that luxury goods were only available in shops restricted to party functionaries and managers. Ironically prices were often lower here. There were perpetual shortages in the State shops, and this meant endless queueing and a culture of 'in case' string bags. These were carried all the time to take advantage of any goods suddenly available. Queues formed outside food shops at 2 a.m. in midwinter when temperatures were 20 degrees below freezing. The average married worker in Moscow ate virtually no fat and very little milk or fruit. He ate one-fifth of the meat and fish that was eaten in 1900. Even bread consumption was down by 50 per cent compared to 1900.

Cross reference

You can read more about what the canteen meals were like in the Spotlight on Magnitogorsk on page 184.

Quality of life

Note

NB The situation in the early 1930s was much worse in the countryside. See pp. 168–73.

The whole urban and rural environment also deteriorated. Paint was impossible to find, unless you had the right contacts, so repair and maintenance of homes was very difficult. As the house no longer belonged to you, what was the point in 'wasting' money on it? You could not sell it on to anyone else afterwards. Overcrowding, as we have seen, was a terrible problem for almost all families in towns and cities. The government saw its first priority as the building of

Facts and figures

Average living space per person in Moscow	
in 1930	5.5sq m
in 1940	4 sq m

industrial plant rather than accommodation, which would divert scarce resources. The only clothes the poor could obtain were drab and identical to those worn by millions of others. They were also shoddily made, and thread to repair them was virtually impossible to buy. Such essential items as boots and shoes were also unobtainable at many times.

However, parks were laid out in the cities. The government also put a large emphasis on the health of its citizens.

Source 13

Hospitals and clinics were built across the country. Even in remote rural districts 'flying teams' visited the local people with mobile dental and medical facilities. In the cities 90 per cent of children were born in hospital.

Sir A. Newsholme, a prominent British doctor, toured the USSR and wrote this in 1934 in *Red Medicine*:

Source 14

When a Russian becomes ill, the government does something about it...The Soviet Union is the one nation in the world which has undertaken to set up and operate a complete organization designed to provide preventive and curative medical care for every man, woman and child within its borders.

Farmers

Farmers saw a collapse in their living standards. Collectivization caused the terrible famine which killed millions of farmers in the richest farming regions. By the end of the 1930s the farmers' lot had improved considerably, chiefly because they were allowed their own plots on which to grow food for themselves or to sell on the open market. Mechanization at last did begin to make some impact on their working lives, but still the grain harvest in 1940 at best only equalled that of 1913. Although they knew of the problems of life in the cities from relatives who wrote back, millions fled there, where at least there was a chance to build a new life.

Facts and figures

In Moscow, Gorky Park, formerly the Park of Culture and Rest, had open air dance floors, bowling alleys and a Ferris wheel.

◀ A Moscow health centre in 1934.

■ Think about

▶ What evidence can you find in this picture that the USSR had an effective healthcare system?

Note

Chapter 9 deals more fully with the effects of collectivization

New opportunities

In the cities and new industrial areas some saw their life chances transformed. For some Stakhanovites life did improve. Sheila Fitzpatrick quotes a Magnitogorsk newspaper:

Source 15

Aleksei Tischenko…had arrived in Magnitogorsk in 1933 with all their possessions in a single home-made suitcase. By 1936 the couple owned furniture, including a couch and a wardrobe, as well as dress clothes, including two overcoats, some women's dresses, men's suits, shoes…His prizes included a hunting gun, a gramophone, money and a motorcycle.

However, research has revealed that most Stakhanovites and shock-workers actually benefited very little. Few had new flats and holidays; most had to be satisfied with much less than advertised in Source 15.

None the less, industrialization created literally millions of new opportunities for those with the education, skills, drive or, perhaps most important, the connections to take advantage of them. A new class of foremen, supervisors, technicians, fitters, electricians as well as managers was needed to build and run the new industrial enterprises. A whole army of bureaucrats was needed to administer the Plans, to set and check targets, to order materials, to run the transport system.

Servants made life for the better off much easier. A factory buyer, who had left the USSR, later told an American interviewer in the 1970s that servants were cheap, but difficult to find. It was necessary to negotiate with a *kolkhoz* director for a suitable girl. It is clear that these negotiations involved the exchange of money or favours. He paid his girl servant 18 roubles a month plus board and lodging, while his wife earned 300 roubles per month as a typist! This growing difference between social groups was commented upon by many visitors to the country.

Source 16

One of the noteworthy developments in Moscow life during the past year or so is the emergence…of a new urban bourgeois class. They are…obviously better-fed, and well and are smartly dressed…They frequent the more expensive, if still modest, native restaurants. They live, by our standards, plainly, but in this country it is luxury to have enough.

A British diplomat writing to London in 1931

Sports facilities

The Soviet government set a high value on shared social and cultural activities. Stadia were built in all the large towns and cities to accommodate ice hockey, athletics and football. Teams were supported by government funds, and matches attracted large crowds of spectators.

Source 17

For organized sports the city [Moscow] has about a 100 grounds, besides the new Dynamo Sport Club Stadium…Over the entrance to the stadium is a huge legend reading 'Be Ready for Labour and Defence'.

Newsholme, *Red Medicine*, 1934

■ **Think about**

▶ Why might the employment of house servants seem odd to many commentators of Stalin's Russia?

▶ What can we learn from this about the USSR society of the 1930s?

Chess players and gymnasts were given considerable State support and coaching. They were also given a high public profile. Russian grandmasters dominated the world chess scene, much as they still do today. Physical exercise was emphasized in the schools and mass displays were a feature of the rituals of Soviet life. Mayakovsky, who became almost an official poet (after his suicide) wrote that bronzed muscles and fresh skin were the best clothes in the world.

Source 18

◀ A mass display to commemorate the October Revolution.

■ **Think about**

▶ Why might the government have felt displays like the one shown in Source 18 were needed?

Soviet culture

The government's attempts to win the hearts and minds of the Soviet people knew no limits. By the 1930s the radio occupied an increasingly important place in everyday life. Though there were only 3.5 million radios in the country, loudspeakers were set up about towns and cities so government announcements could be heard by the urban population. A minority of villages was linked to an electricity supply before the Second World War. Workers in the State radio service were left in no doubt about their important role:

Source 19

The Soviet Radio…carries to the masses the inspired word of Bolshevik truth, aids the people in its struggle for the full victory of Communism in our country, summons them to heroic deeds in the name of the further strengthening of the power, of the economic and cultural prosperity of the USSR.

From *USSR Speaking*, a manual for radio workers

■ **Think about**

▶ How did the Soviet government view the role of broadcasting?

▶ How would we in a democracy see the role differently?

The cinema, as in Europe and the USA, was becoming, in the cities at least, the most popular form of entertainment. The themes of the films reflected the concerns of the regime. By the later 1930s, as Nazi Germany threatened, films were increasingly patriotic in tone, and based on real historical figures, such as Ivan the Terrible.

In all the arts the government looked for Soviet stars, instead of the bourgeois figures of the past. The 1920s had seen experimentation in art, music and literature. Marxist theory said that a socialist economic system would produce socialist art. What precisely was the new proletarian art supposed to be like? The prevailing artistic tendencies, not just in the Soviet Union, were towards the abstract, both in art and music.

Literature also served the needs of the regime. Stalin called on writers to be 'engineers of human souls'. Mayakovsky, once the leader of the avant-garde, wrote propaganda pieces, such as *The March of the Shock Brigades* to inspire readers to even greater efforts. However, he also wrote plays, like *The Bath House*, which criticized the callous behaviour of Stalinist bureaucrats. After his suicide in 1930, caused by the hounding of The Russian Association of Proletarian Writers (RAPP) for his play *The Bedbug*, he was honoured by the Communist Party, which he had once supported. A Moscow Metro station was named after him. The regime needed its new stars, even if it had to distort reality to create them. Dead heroes were better than live ones; they were unable to tarnish their image by independent thinking!

'Socialist realism' became the new approved way of writing. Novels during the First Five Year Plan glorified the ordinary worker, under the lead of RAPP. Production was what mattered and it was the job of literature to support this drive. RAPP launched an appeal for 'shock worker writers', for shock workers to try their hand at writing. The result was 5 million roubles spent on commissioning books, but almost all were so poor as to be unprintable! *Time, Forward* by Kataev is an example of the literature approved by RAPP.

In June 1931 Stalin made a dramatic keynote speech, 'New circumstances and new tasks'. 'Bourgeois specialists' were rehabilitated, to restore some order to the chaos into which the Plans had thrown the country. He called for an end to the attack on experts, just because of their class background. Immediately writers felt the change; the approved heroes were now skilled engineers. *Time, Forward* was criticized for its 'concrete hysteria', production at all costs. RAPP was broken up and all writers joined the Union of Russian Writers. It was not compulsory, but only its members could have their work published! Stalin managed to persuade playwright Maxim Gorky, a former critical friend of Lenin, to return to the USSR to head this organization. Propaganda *coups* like this helped to bolster the image of the regime.

Here is an extract from Gorky's speech to the Union's first Congress in 1934:

> ### Note
>
> RAPP led the assault on 'bourgeois' art and literature – forcing the closure of plays.

> ### Note
>
> An excerpt from *Time, Forward* (Source 32 on p. 221) will give you some idea of the kind of novels that were favoured during the early 1930s. Kataev spent months living in Magnitogorsk to research his book, to ensure its 'socialist realism'.

> ### Note
>
> Komsomol denounced RAPP for its slogan 'Overtake and surpass the classics'. Proletarian writers, they argued, must automatically be in advance of 'landlord literature'.

> ### ■ Think about
>
> ▶ Why did Gorky think that Soviet authors were important?
>
> ▶ How would this view be received in the West today?

> ### Source 20
>
> The proletarian state must educate thousands of first-class 'craftsmen of culture', 'engineers of the soul'...in order to restore to the whole mass of the working people the right to develop their intelligence, talents and faculties – a right of which they have been deprived everywhere else in the world....This places us not only in the position, traditional to realist literature, of 'judges of the world and men', 'critics of life', but gives us the right to participate directly in the construction of a new life, in the process of 'changing the world'.

Art followed a similar path.

■ Activity

1 What are the (not very hidden!) messages being conveyed by Sources 21 and 22? Do you think Stalin would have approved of them?

2 Collect together other pieces of 'socialist realism' art. Now look at the art that was favoured in Nazi Germany. What are the similarities between them? Why do you think they are so similar?

3 You may like to contrast these works with other art being produced elsewhere in the 'free' world. Picasso's famous picture of Guernica was also a product of the 1930s, and had a political message. How does it differ from the two 'socialist realism' pictures shown here?

■ Further research

You will find more 'socialist realist' art on these websites:
www.ii.nl/exhibitions/chairman/sovintro.html
www.poster.s.cz/listy/russ8.htm
www.maniichuk.com/gallery.html
www.medicalnet.art/horvath/soc.htm
www.russianartgallery.com/socialrealism.htm

Source 21

▲ A 1930s painting entitled 'Higher and Higher'.

Source 22

◀ A 1930s painting showing lunch on the collective farm.

Dmitri Shostakovitch

Dmitri Shostakovitch

■ Further reading

Shostakovitch was not unique. Find out how other artists were affected in the 1930s:
E.g. Pasternak, Mandelstam

Source 23

The atmosphere was highly charged, the hall was filled – as they say, all the best people were there, and all the worst too. It was definitely a critical situation, and not only for me. Which way would the wind blow?

■ Think about

▶ Why was the atmosphere in the hall so 'highly charged'?

The life and career of Dmitri Shostakovitch illustrate the problems which artists and composers faced in their professional life. Even though he became the most respected Soviet composer and was given a State funeral, there were times when it seemed his very life was in the balance.

Shostakovitch entered the Petrograd Conservatoire of Music in 1919, two years after the Revolution, when the regime was looking for new Soviet composers. His First Symphony was given its first performance in 1926, when the composer was only 20, to great popular applause. His career seemed destined for great things.

In 1934 his opera *Lady Macbeth of Mtsensk* was also well received by the audiences and the press. Unusually it received premier performances in Leningrad and Moscow on the same day. Two years later it was still being regularly performed. The composer intended the opera to be the first of four on the theme of women in society. The plot concerned Katerina Ismailova, who was a triple murderess, and walled up her husband in a cellar! The music and the staging graphically portrayed Katerina making love to her servant. Act three is set in a police station, however, while the finale is in Siberia amongst convicts. Perhaps it was the setting rather than the music itself, which annoyed Stalin when he went to see it in January 1936. At any rate he walked out of the performance.

Shortly afterwards *Pravda* carried a leading article entitled 'Muddle instead of Music'. Shostakovitch's music was described as 'cacophonous' and 'pornographic,' and *Pravda* threatened that the composer 'could end very badly', if he did not mend his ways.

The opera was immediately withdrawn. Shostakovitch was summoned to a meeting of the Composers' Union, which denounced his music as 'incomprehensible', 'formalist' and 'against the proletariat'. The attack on Shostakovich did not suddenly end. *Pravda* boasted that it had 'caught off guard the masked defenders of decadent bourgeois music'. Like many other prominent figures, Shostakovitch packed a small case with warm clothes and boots, and kept it ready, in case the NKVD arrived without notice.

At this time the composer was already completing his Fourth Symphony, a work largely pessimistic in mood. The Union of Soviet Composers now expected that music would be easy on the ear and optimistic in tone. When it was being rehearsed, Shostakovitch suddenly withdrew it, obviously terrified that it would not be well received. Instead he wrote his famous Fifth Symphony, which bore the subtitle 'A Soviet Artist's Practical Creative Reply to Just Criticism'. This ended with blaring trumpets and contained folk tunes. Shostakovitch described the first performance in Leningrad in November 1937 in his 'Testimony', which he dictated to a friend before his death (Source 23). He need not have worried. The symphony was a popular and critical success. Shostakovitch no longer needed his suitcase.

Between 1936 and 1941 the State organized 10 festivals designed to celebrate the cultural life and language of each USSR republic, each lasting 10 days. This was perhaps an attempt to counterbalance the increasing Russification of education and the media.

Music also suffered badly during the 1930s. Composers sought to present the ideologically correct party line. As we have seen this altered from time to time, so it was not always possible to keep up with the latest trend. Mayakovsky wrote his Twelfth Symphony, subtitled 'The Collective Farm', but it was still rejected by Proletkult.

How successfully did the regime mould public opinion?

Source 24

I want to earn even more – two thousand, three-and-a-half, because our Soviet power gives us the chance to work well, earn a lot and live a cultural life. Can't I wear a good Boston suit, buy good cigarettes? I can. Some comrades envy me, but what's that to me?

A Stakhanovite speaking in November 1935

Source 25

For a happy, cultured, joyful life!
How life has changed! Gone are the times when the worker only thought about his daily bread.

Leningrad Pravda, a newspaper, January 1934

Source 26

But a person arrives at suicide because he is afraid that everything will be revealed and he does not want to witness his own public disgrace.... There you have one of the last sharp and easiest means that, before death, leaving this world, one can for the last time spit on the party, betray the party.

Stalin speaking at the December Plenum, 1936

Source 27

Life has become better. Life has become merrier.

Stalin in 1936

Source 28

I want to share my feelings: I live very well and think that I will live even better. Why? Because I live in the Stalin epoch. May Stalin live longer than me! ... All my children had and we are having education thanks to the State and, I would say, thanks to the party, and especially comrade Stalin, for he along with Lenin, opened the way for us simple people...I myself, an old woman, am ready to die for Stalin and the Bolshevik cause.

A letter to President Kalinin from an old woman in 1939

Source 29

I beg you not to cry for me, but be happy. Now he who is born must cry about this life, and he who dies must rejoice. Mummy, I'm sorry, but I cannot live on this earth any longer...No one in our family has ever been put on trial, even long ago, and I can't stand it.

A worker's suicide note in 1940

Source 30

The speeches are good, but there's no bread.

There are not enough food and goods. When will we live to see the end of it? It's time to start getting worried about it.

Comments on a speech by Stalin 1935 at factory meetings

Source 31

The May Day demonstration in 1937 encountered a marked lack of enthusiasm. People questioned why they should go to the demonstration when there was nothing to eat, and meetings at factories to celebrate the day attracted little support. At the Kirov factory, only 30 of the 500 workers from the first shift came to the meeting, and 60 of the 2000 from the second shift. Only 20 of the 1000 workers of the Fifth hydro-Electric Power Station turned up to their meeting.

Davies, *Popular Opinion in Stalin's Russia*, 1997

Source 32

The ore would go into the blast furnaces. The coke would be lighted. Molten iron would flow. The molten iron would be boiled into steel. They would make rails, wagons, saws, axes, ploughs, machines.

And all this would be for the needs, for the happiness of 'him'.

To make life happy, it was not enough to say good words. It was not enough. One needed steel, steel, steel, steel. With steel, there will be a new, happy life, a life that has never been before, a life that has never been seen before!

And all this was for 'him'. And 'he' – that is I. And 'he' and 'I' – are we. And we – that is life!

Now Ishchenko opened his eyes, and, for the first time in his life, looked down the entire length of time. It flowed too slowly. But it flowed for him. The past flowed for the future.

And it lay securely in his hands.

Oh, how good life was, after all!

Time, Forward, a novel by V. Kataev, 1934

Source 33

Soviet acronyms were mimicked by ordinary people. These don't work so well in translation!

OGPU = 'O Lord, help us to flee.
CCCP = Stalin's death will save Russia
VKP (CPSU) = Second serfdom

Source 35

More than 200,000 collective farms and 5,000 State farms have been organized, with new district centres and industrial centres serving them...Unemployment, that scourge of the working class, has disappeared...With the disappearance of *kulak* bondage, poverty in the countryside has disappeared...

Now that the correctness of the party's political line has been confirmed by the experience of a number of years, and that there is no longer any doubt as to the readiness of the workers and peasants to support this line...

Stalin to the 17th Party Congress, January 1934

Source 36

What are people discontented about? In the first place, that the worker is hungry, he has no fats, the bread is *ersatz* [artificial] which is impossible to eat...It's a common thing that the wife of a worker stands the whole day in line, her husband comes home from work, and dinner is not prepared, and everyone curses Soviet power. In the lines there is noise, shouting and fights, curses at the expense of Soviet power.

Pravda's summary of readers' letters, August 1930 for party leaders

Source 34

◀ Stalin delivers a speech in 1936.

■ Activity

Look at each of Sources 24–36 and work out whether they do or do not support the view that Russians supported the Communist government. Draw a table like the one below for recording your results. In the middle column, state how reliable you think the evidence is.

Evidence for	Reliability?	Evidence against

How useful do you think novels like *Time, Forward* are to the historian?

Which of the sources are likely to be typical of what ordinary Russians felt?

Does the evidence suggest the Russian people were afraid to express their true opinions? Were they a cowed population?

Look back at this chapter and Chapters 9 and 10. Is it possible to be certain from the evidence in these chapters how most Russian people viewed the regime?

Rebuilding Moscow

The world's first Communist state should be a beacon of excellence to the rest of the world, an example to inspire the proletariat of other countries. The regime to this end began to build vast new projects in the capital. We have already seen some of these mentioned, the sports stadia and the Palace of

Source 37

◀ The Foreign Ministry building in Moscow.

■ Think about

▶ Why was this style called the 'wedding cake'?

▶ Why did the Communists favour this style of building?

▲ A bronze statue and carvings at the entrance to a Moscow Metro station.

▲ A ceiling mosaic from the Moscow Metro.

Soviets. The Communist 'gigantomania' referred to in the Five Year Plans can also be seen again here. The Russians wanted to build monuments to equal anything in the capitalist world. Stalin's preferred architectural style has been satirized as 'the wedding cake' style, or 'Stalinist baroque.' He planned a series of great buildings to dominate the Moscow skyline, such as the Foreign Ministry.

Most impressive of all was the Moscow Metro. Even today one cannot but be impressed by this monument to socialist realism. Chandeliers light the platforms, and stained glass, mosaics and bronze statues decorate the platforms and corridors. These too had political messages. The Kiev station, built while the Ukrainians were suffering from the worst famine in Russian history, shows mosaics of happy peasants gathering in their plentiful harvest.

Conclusion

No one can have been unaffected by the enormous changes in the 1930s. One historian said the USSR became a 'quicksand society', because people disappeared into it all the time – either because they had been arrested or because they had engineered their own disappearance – to avoid child maintenance, to get a better job, to escape justice etc. Only half the criminals sentenced in Leningrad ever served their sentences.

Some benefited from the changes and rose up the ladder. Sometimes this was by their own efforts, by working hard (Stakhanovites), by improving their level of education. Often, however, it was because of their connections. This was always more important than cash in hand in a society of scarcity. For women, opportunities were available as never before, but few had a real choice as to whether to stay at home and bring up their children or continue to work. The falling real wages of the 1930s forced all but a few wives and mothers to stay at work. For those who did work the evidence shows that few were able to rise to the top of their chosen professions.

Many endured real hardship. Though medical care undoubtedly improved considerably, especially in the towns, the falling standard of living brought a decline in life expectancy. Suicides increased. Workers returned home to unbelievably cramped accommodation with often shared facilities, making 'normal' family life virtually impossible. Even the solace of religion was more difficult to find. Grumbling, shown in the jokes and the memoirs of the period, must have been common. For outspoken dissidents, things turned out much worse.

However, despite all these difficulties there does seem to have been, in at least some of the community, a sense of optimism – a shared sense of struggle to build the world's first Communist society, to build that paradise on earth that Marx had prophesied. Partly, no doubt, as well, this was because of the all-pervasive indoctrination, which affected the arts, the press, schools and the workplace.

For most people, like Shukov at the end of *One day in the life of Ivan Denisovitch* perhaps it was enough to have survived and live to see another day.

■ **Further reading**

V. Andrle, *A Social History of Twentieth Century Russia*
S.A. Davies, *Popular Opinion in Stalin's Russia*, 1997
A. Inkeles and R. A. Bauer, *The Soviet Citizen*, 1959
A. Rybakov, *Children of the Arbat* (novel)
C. Ward, *Stalin's Russia*, 1993

Chapter 12

Historians and Stalin

For the first time ever, the [1936] Constitution made provision for socio-economic rights: the right to work, rest and leisure, maintenance in old age or in cases of disablement...For the first time such personal rights and freedoms were proclaimed as the inviolability of the person* and the home, and the privacy of correspondence. Special attention was paid to material, institutional, political and legal guarantees of rights and freedoms.

Kuritsyn, *The Development of Rights and Freedoms in the Soviet State*, published in Moscow, 1983

*   This meant no one had the right to arrest or imprison someone without proper legal procedures, or invade his/her home.

◄ A British cartoon from *Punch*, published in December 1937. It is entitled 'The Moscow Purge' and the Russian Bear is saying to Stalin 'Must I really take this, after dancing for you so faithfully?'.

Introduction

In the 1930s, at the time of the Five Year Plans in the USSR, people outside looked on either in amazement at the staggering achievement or in horror at the sufferings of the people. This was nicely captured in 1934 in a poem in the *New Statesman and Nation* by MacFlecknoe, who reflected on the differing verdicts delivered by westerners after visiting the USSR.

■ Think about

Look back at Source 1.

▶ What point is the cartoonist making about the USSR?

▶ Do you think, in the light of who drew it and when and where it was drawn, it is a reliable source for us studying Stalin's Russia today?

▶ Does Source 2 give the same impression of Russia in the 1930s?

▶ Why do you think they differ?

■ Think about

▶ What is the poet trying to say in Source 3 about why contemporaries differed in their verdict on the USSR?

Source 3

The sights that X selected
Bore out what he expected -
Great factories rising;
An enthusiasm surprising
For welfare and education;
A New World in formation
Much better than the Old –
Just as he had foretold.

Mr Y saw what he expected –
Breakdown in transportation;
A growing indignation
With the Communist
oppression;
A steady retrogression
To chaos, bloody and red –
Just as he had always said.

■ Activity

Can you find evidence to support the arguments of Mr X and Mr Y in the poem? Divide yourselves into pairs. One from each pair should now look for evidence to support the statements made by Mr X, and the other those of Mr Y. Use earlier chapters in this book and any other sources in your school library and elsewhere.

When you have collected all your evidence, either as a pair or as a class, work out between yourselves whether you think Mr X or Mr Y was closer to the truth about the USSR in the 1930s?

Why do historians differ?

Neither the fictitious Mr X or Mr Y were historians. They were simply observers of the political scene who went to Russia and found there what their prejudices had suggested they would find. However, we expect better of historians – we expect them to be objective, that is to try to write impartially, without prejudice. If historians do not try to be objective, what they write would be no better than propaganda, very much like this view of Stalin produced in the USSR while he was alive:

Definition

Implacable here means that he was totally committed to their destruction

Source 4

Stalin is the brilliant leader and teacher of the Party, the great strategist of the Socialist Revolution, military commander and guide of the Soviet State. An implacable* attitude towards the enemies of Socialism, profound fidelity to principle, a combination of clear revolutionary perspective and clarity of purpose with extraordinary firmness and persistence in the pursuit of aims, wise and practical leadership and intimate contact with the masses – such are the characteristic features of Stalin's style. Never have our villages such contentment known...

Stalin is the worthy continuer of the cause of Lenin, or, as is said in the Party: 'Stalin is the Lenin of today'.

Alexandrov, *Joseph Stalin: A Short Biography*, 1947

However, no matter how hard we might try, it is impossible for any student of history to distance himself completely from his own ideas or preconceptions.

Source 5

Memory fades and distorts, materials reveal nothing without the exercise of disciplined imagination, and in any event all our efforts are refracted through our own times and personality.

Ward, *Stalin's Russia*, 1993

The problems of evidence

In Source 5 Dr Ward suggests some of the problems which prevent the historian from arriving at the 'truth' in explaining what happened in the past. His first comments relate to the problems of evidence. Evidence itself is neutral. It is historians who give it some meaning. But evidence, as we know, may be interpreted in more than one way. Source 4 describes Stalin. Did Alexandrov believe his own propaganda? Did the majority of Russians agree with its sentiments or were they simply too afraid to object? What did other members of the ruling elite think about gushing praise of this kind? Could they have stopped it, if they had wished? Did propaganda of this type serve a purpose for the government as a whole? Precisely what weight does a historian give to this type of evidence?

While Stalin was alive, practically all the information coming from the USSR was officially controlled. Western historians knew what the regime allowed them to know. Movement inside Russia was restricted for foreigners as it was for Russians. Archive departments, such as the Lenin Archive, were closed. We have seen in Chapter 9 that the published economic statistics of the regime were notoriously unreliable.

There were other sources of information about the USSR during Stalin's lifetime, and you have come across some of these too in the previous chapters. One important source came from foreign visitors, such as Walter Durranty (Chapter 9 Source 11 page 169). The poem at the beginning of this chapter suggests why some of this evidence may not be as reliable as the historian would wish. Another source derives from exiles, those who either left the USSR involuntarily, like Trotsky, or fled, perhaps to escape persecution or because they disapproved of the regime. Perhaps some were 'economic migrants', seeking a better standard of living. In all cases what they said and wrote may contain special pleading in defence of their decision to quit the land of their birth. Can we trust, for example, Trotsky when he writes about Stalin?

Source 6

Lenin's relations with Stalin are officially characterized as a close friendship. As a matter of fact these two political figures were widely separated not only by the ten years' difference in their ages, but by the very size of their respective personalities. There could be no friendship between the two.

Trotsky, *Stalin*, 1941

■ **Think about**

▶ Why did Trotsky write this of Stalin?

After the Second World War historians were also able to examine the Smolensk archive, Russian archives captured first by advancing German troops in 1941 and then by American forces in 1945. Dr Ward writes that it 'has profoundly influenced our understanding of the party's structure, the chain of command and relations between Moscow and the provinces'. In particular the Smolensk archive alerted historians to the fact that the USSR was not the streamlined hierarchical society, which at first it appeared. Instead there was a tension between what the party leaders in Moscow decided and what was done at the local level. Party officials often had a different agenda from that of the party bosses in the Kremlin.

Source 7

Despite apparently precise directions and instructions, many authorities went their own way, interpreting the *kulak* category broadly to embrace middle, and even poor, peasants who were opposed to collectivization [and] evicting *kulak* families who had Red Army connections... Certain members of the working brigades and officials... deprived members of *kulak* and middle-peasant households of their clothes and warm underwear, directly from their body, confiscated headwear from children's heads and removed shoes from people's feet.

From the Smolensk archive

Note

Mikhail Gorbachev was elected General Secretary of the Communist Party in 1985. He began a policy of *glasnost*, literally 'openness', which resulted in the opening of many hitherto secret archives to the public and to historians.

Since *glasnost*, when Gorbachev opened up the Soviet archives to Russian and western historians, many more archival sources have been open to historians, but only a fraction have yet been examined. These have enabled some historians to take a 'bottom-up' view of events in the Soviet Union. Instead of concentrating on the high politics of decisions in the Kremlin, historians have to some extent been able to see how these were received and interpreted in the regions – and also how ordinary people were affected by the outcome and how they reacted to government initiatives. Chapters 9, 10, and 11 are full of evidence which would not have been available to historians writing only 15 years ago. It is probably true to say that *glasnost* has affected the writing of history more than any other single development.

Political attitudes

Whether the achievements of the 1930s were to be applauded or not is another cause of debate amongst historians. The most significant cause of this divergence is the political stance of the historian. A historian's political attitudes are not simply a reflection of his own individual personality but they also show the enormous influence of the environment in which the historian has been reared and is writing.

The 1930s was, for some, a time when the evils of fascism threatened Europe in the shape of Hitler and Mussolini. Communist Russia was seen by some as the strongest bulwark against fascism. During the Second World War, for example, Stalin became 'Uncle Joe' to the British public, our loyal ally. British diplomats in Russia who witnessed the tremendous sufferings and heroism of the Russian people wrote favourably of the regime's achievements. For them Stalin's determination alone built the USSR into a modern state. He made the USSR capable of withstanding and then defeating the attacks of Europe's most modern and best-equipped army. Some western historians, therefore, writing about the USSR at this time, show respect for Stalin's achievements.

Source 8

[The Second World War] was in a real sense [Stalin's] victory. It could not have been won without his industrialisation campaign... Collectivisation had contributed to victory by enabling the government to stockpile food and raw materials and to prevent paralysis in industry and famine in the towns. But also collectivisation, with its machine-tractor stations, had given the peasants their first training in the use of tractors and other machines. Collectivised farming had been the peasants' preparatory school for mechanised warfare.

Grey, *Stalin – Man of History*, 1979

■ **Think about**

▶ Grey had been a naval intelligence officer in Russia during the Second World War. How do you think this may have helped to colour his judgement of Stalin?

Later, after Russian troops had occupied Eastern Europe and had imposed Communist regimes there, the USSR became the enemy of the 'Free World', the 'evil empire' (US President Ronald Reagan). Communism was something to be opposed wherever it appeared. The 'domino theory' advocated fighting Communist parties all over the world, for if one state fell, like dominoes others would follow. Some American historians were brought up in the era of Senator McCarthy's Un-American Activities Committee. This carried out witch-hunts for socialists and liberals in an atmosphere of anti-Communist hysteria in the early 1950s. The Russian regime at this time became an important area for historians – to reveal to the world how the Bolsheviks set up their dictatorship and how the Communist Party was able to impose its will on an enslaved population.

Source 9

The fundamental problem of Stalinism...was one of lies and of the terror by which the lie was destined to be turned into the truth. Just as the system based on the lie and on terror had been brought to a very high degree of perfection by the determination of one single human being, Stalin, the breaches opened in this system were to be the fruit of the intuitions...of another single human being, Khrushchev.

Carrere D'Encausse, *Stalin: Order through Terror*, 1981

Since the partial collapse of the Soviet Empire perhaps we shall see in the future historians looking back with nostalgia on the stability that Stalin brought to the world's largest state, as some Russians already do. On the other hand, in the light of its industrial and economic collapse, perhaps Stalin will be seen as the root cause of Russia's current difficulties.

Marxist historians

For Marxists or Marxist-sympathizers Stalin has been a problem. Should they approve a regime whose avowed aims were Marxist, though they often disapproved of some of its features? For the exiled Trotsky this was doubly difficult, since he had played such an important part himself in creating and consolidating the Bolshevik regime. Moreover, in the 1920s he had advocated policies of industrial development which were not a million miles from those Stalin introduced himself. For all Marxists the French Revolution was an important event. They derived their own ideas about revolution and history from it. The French Revolution resulted in a military dictatorship under Napoleon. This was called Thermidor, after the time it occurred. The French revolutionaries tore up the traditional calendar and renamed all the months anew.

Note

Marxist historians are those who accept Marx's analysis of social and economic development. They emphasize in all periods of history the struggle between classes.

■ **Think about**

▶ What is Trotsky saying about Stalin and the USSR in this source?

Source 10

Stalin is the living embodiment of a bureaucratic Thermidor. Today it is impossible to overlook the fact that in the Soviet Revolution also a shift to the right took place a long time ago, a shift entirely analogous [similar] to Thermidor, although much slower in tempo…The poverty and cultural backwardness of the masses has again become incarnate in the malignant figure of the ruler with a great club in his hand. The deposed and abused bureaucracy, from being a servant of society, has again become its lord.

Trotsky on Stalin

Within the Soviet Union, of course, everyone followed the party line until Stalin's death. He was hailed as the man who took forward Lenin's revolution. Stalin 'succeeded' Lenin because he had drive and vision and was supported by the party. Trotsky, Zinoviev, Kamenev, Rykov and Bukharin, all later executed as enemies of the Revolution, were rejected by the party, 'the vanguard of the proletariat'. There were dissidents but they either kept their counsel or they 'were disappeared'.

In 1956 Khrushchev made a famous attack on Stalin, who by now was dead. It must have been a huge shock coming as it did from one of Stalin's most trusted henchmen. It was such political dynamite that it was given behind closed doors to only the party's highest officials. After this, as the perceived excesses of the Stalin regime were exposed more and more to the public gaze, Soviet historians increasingly blamed any shortcomings in Russia on Stalin's personal desire for power. As Marxists they could not blame the party or its ideology. In his memoirs, written after being deposed, Khrushchev wrote this about Stalin:

■ **Think about**

▶ Why does Khrushchev both praise and criticize Stalin in this speech?

Source 11

He really was a man of outstanding skill and intelligence. He truly did tower over everyone around him. … Stalin's vengeance against his own enemies, whom he claimed were enemies of the party, cost us incalculable losses.

Khrushchev, *Khrushchev Remembers*, 1971

Schools of history

Quotation

The history of the world is but the biography of great men.

Thomas Carlyle

No historians share exactly the same view of the events covered by this book. However, they may share the same perspective or general approach. They may share the same assumptions about what brings about historical change. Which, for example, is more important in historical development, the role played by prominent individuals and leaders or the role played by classes? When they do agree on certain fundamentals, we can group them together and we call these groups schools. We can identify the following amongst the main schools when looking at the history of this period:

- Stalinist historians – those who follow the line of the Communist Party during Stalin's lifetime.
- Totalitarian historians – those who see the USSR as a totalitarian state controlled from above by Stalin. These historians see Marxist and Bolshevik ideology as a fundamental cause of the nature of the regime and Stalin's dictatorship.
- Trotskyite historians – these blame Stalin for perverting the work of Lenin and the party after the Revolution.

- Revisionist historians – those historians who turn their attention away from the personality of Stalin and the apparatus of terror. Instead they tend to concentrate on the structures inside the Soviet Union, the groups which supported the regime, the difficulties the regime faced in carrying out important policies. Much of their research has resulted in major revision, for example, of how many died at the hands of the secret police in the 1930s.

We shall concentrate on four main issues of debate:

- Why did Stalin become the most powerful figure in the Soviet Union?
- What were the reasons for the Terror?
- How successful were the economic policies of the 1930s?
- How far did Stalin build on the foundations of Lenin?

Why did Stalin become the leading figure in Russia?

Stalin at the beginning of the 1920s was seen by many as the most unlikely figure to emerge as head of the Russian Communist Party. Trotsky seemed to be the most talented and the one who had accomplished most for the Communist cause. Stalin was the most recent Bolshevik to join the upper echelon of the party, the Central Committee.

Historians have laid particular stress on these key factors in their different interpretations.

Stalin the bureaucrat

Stalin came to power because he was the ultimate bureaucrat at a time when the State was even more bureaucratic than in Tsarist times. He had a flair for administration. His nickname in the 1920s in the party was 'Comrade Card Index'. When one sees the positions he occupied, this is easy to believe. As Commissar for Nationalities until 1923, his first position in the government, he had to administer all the non-Russian territories. Therefore, he appointed thousands within the party to positions of authority. These people then owed him a debt of loyalty. He would be able to count on their support in the future.

As head of Rabkrin 1920–1922 Stalin had the power to examine the work of all State officials throughout the Soviet Union. Rabkrin compiled files and reports and could recommend dismissal.

> **Note**
>
> Rabkrin was the Workers' and Peasants' Inspectorate, set up by Lenin to check on the work of the government and to stop corruption.

By far the most important position he held was that of General Secretary of the Party from 1922 onwards. After the Revolution the Communist Party controlled the life of Russia. Whoever controlled the party would therefore control the government. Stalin was in the best position to do this. He was a telephone call away from any party official anywhere in the Soviet Union. No one else in the party had such a strong position within the party apparatus and the government. According to one view, it gave Stalin the power to manipulate votes in the Central Committee and Congresses of the party. As a result he was able to destroy his rivals one by one. For some this was an accident, for others it was deliberate and a long term strategy.

Stalin's character

Stalin is supposed to have said even before Lenin's death:

Source 12

To choose one's victim, to prepare one's plans minutely, to slake an implacable vengeance, and then to go to bed.... there is nothing sweeter in the world.

Trotsky, in his book *Stalin*, published in 1941 after his murder on Stalin's orders, wrote:

Source 13

It is impossible to understand Stalin and his latter-day success without understanding the mainspring of his personality: love of power, ambition, envy – active, never-slumbering envy of all who are more gifted, more powerful, rank higher than he.

According to this view Stalin was consumed by personal ambition and carefully planned his rise to power, abandoning friends and principles whenever it was convenient. He was fortunate to be at the nerve centre and had the talents to exploit his position.

The party

Some emphasize the experiences of the party in the Civil War. Robert Conquest wrote:

Source 14

It transformed the new mass party into a hardened and experienced machine in which loyalty to the organization came before any other consideration...In destroying the 'democratic tendency' within the Communist Party, Lenin in effect threw the game to the manipulators of the party machine. Henceforward, the apparatus was to be first the most powerful and later the only force within the party.

Lenin's demand for a ban on party 'factionalism' in 1921 strengthened the hand of those who stood for the status quo and prevented the formation of any groups who could then threaten Stalin's growing power in the party.

The nature of Marxism-Leninism

Some historians have argued that Lenin's reinterpretation of Marxism was the real cause of Stalin's rise. For Marx communism would be achieved in an industrialized society, where it was possible for the principle 'From each according to his ability, to each according to his need' to be realized. Lenin's view that the Communist Party could act as 'the vanguard of the proletariat' and drive Russia forward towards communism, even though the proletariat itself was tiny, meant that the party would always be surrounded by a sea of opposition. This would mean the maintenance of a strong centralized totalitarian government. This would prevent the achievement of their ultimately libertarian goals – a society free of exploitation where all would find fulfilment. It was not civil war which made the party totalitarian: it was the nature of

Lenin's ideas. As Lenin's most loyal disciple, Stalin was therefore his natural successor; indeed Lenin had granted him all the posts he occupied on his death in 1924. According to Pipes, Stalin was Lenin's closest working colleague in the last years of his life.

Good fortune

Another view of these events is to see Stalin's rise as accidental. He was lucky that:

1. Lenin was incapacitated when he was on the point of taking action against him over the Georgian affair and his rudeness to his wife.
2. Trotsky seemed unwilling to rock the Communist boat even when Lenin gave him the ammunition.
3. Zinoviev and Kamenev were more preoccupied with fears of Trotsky than with Stalin's growing authority.
4. When he tried to turn down the offer of the General Secretary post, his attempt to turn it down was declined.

■ Activity

Look at the four schools of history mentioned on pages 229–230.

Which of these five factors are likely to be stressed by historians from each school:

1 Stalin's position in the bureaucracy?

2 Stalin's character?

3 The nature of the party?

4 The nature of Marxism-Leninism?

5 Good fortune?

How responsible was Stalin for the Terror?

Interpretations of the Terror follow very similar lines. Totalitarian historians emphasize Stalin's personality as a key cause of the Terror, as in Source 12 above – his morbid fear of opposition. They may also emphasize the acceptance of Lenin's view of the role of the party and the Marxist view that class struggle was inevitable. As Stalin himself said, the nearer the USSR approached communism, the more bitter would be the battle put up by communism's enemies. The Terror, therefore, was also the result of the way Communists saw the world. All these historians treat the economic trials, the *chistki*, the Show Trials and the arrests and deaths carried out by the OGPU and the NKVD as part of one process – as Stalin tightened his grasp of power.

Revisionist historians, while not denying Stalin's importance in this process, emphasize other factors. They point out that the evidence of Stalin's involvement in some of these events is not proven. In Chapter 10 we looked at the evidence linking Kirov's death with Stalin. They would emphasize the dynamic situation in the USSR – i.e. that not everything was decided from above. The trials, *chistki* and arrests are, for revisionists, unconnected events, arising for different reasons. The purging process in the party was a result of lower-rank party members denouncing those in comfortable positions above them. The purging of the party ranks was necessary because too many self-servers had joined the party who had no real interest in the Marxist cause. They might also claim that the NKVD in the *Ezhovschina* was really out of the control of Stalin or the party. Instead it was used to settle old scores. For revisionists the events of the 1930s are a complex process, which defeat any simple explanation. There were significant divisions of opinion at the highest levels, as in the Party Plenum of 1937. The general public was not completely cowed, as is seen in the letters of complaint to prominent members of the government, especially to Kalinin. As S. Davies puts it:

Source 15

The new sources indicate that the Stalinist propaganda machine failed to extinguish an autonomous current of popular opinion. The machine itself was far from omnipotent, lacking sufficient resources and personnel to make it fully effective. Whole regions and social groups remained excluded from its influence at various times.

Davies, *Popular Opinion in Stalin's Russia 1934–41*, 1997

For Trotskyites bureaucrats trying to consolidate their position carried out the Terror. Stalin as the head of the bureaucracy played a dominant role. At least one historian with Trotskyite sympathies, Isaac Deutscher, has suggested that Stalin's attack on his party was a rational attempt to ensure that the USSR was fully united when the inevitable assault from Germany began.

For orthodox Stalinists the purge was necessary because there were real enemies inside the USSR. As the Five Year Plans brought their successes, the enemies of the USSR intensified their activities and the State had to destroy them or be destroyed itself. Revisionist historians, especially J. Arch Getty, have also emphasized the dissent within the Soviet Union.

How successful were the economic policies of the 1930s?

This question has raised important debates between historians. Everyone is agreed that the USSR was a backward economy in comparison with the economies of the USA, Britain and Germany in 1928. But would the NEP successfully although slowly have transformed the USSR into a modern power? Would agricultural and industrial development have been more successful if left to the work of market forces? These kinds of debates do not fit easily into the totalitarian/revisionist divide. A great deal also hangs on interpretation of figures, about whose accuracy we are still uneasy.

Source 16

Percentage fulfilment of the goals of the Five Year Plans

Industrial Production	First Five Year Plan 1928–1932	Second Five Year Plan 1933–1937
Official Soviet estimate measured in 1926–1927 prices	100.7	103.0
Estimate by Jasny	69.9	81.2
Estimate by Nutter	59.7	93.1
Estimate by Kaplan and Moorsten	65.3	75.7

A big debate still rages about whether collectivization robbed agriculture so that investment could be made in industry. Some have argued that there was a net inflow of money into farming, when all the MTS are taken into account.

All historians agree on the terrible cost in lives of the collectivization and dekulakization programme. Its success or otherwise is largely dependent on whether it is thought to have been necessary. All Marxist historians would accept the desirability of the ideal of collective farming. It is important to remember that collectivization was not just about increasing production; it was also about social engineering, destroying the profit motive and individualism and building a new kind of society. No one expected this would be easy or that hearts and minds could be altered overnight. From the perspective of the post-war period Russia's farming remained unproductive.

This debate is mirrored when industrialization is studied. There is some disagreement about how much was achieved in economic growth. Could this have been achieved more successfully by other means? Historians have also disagreed about the central control of the Five Year Plans. The setting of targets for industries did not constitute rational planning. In this sense the use of the term 'Five Year Plans' is a misnomer. In fact the combination of impossible targets and heavy-handed policing meant that a culture of covering one's own back and 'blat' and developed within the economy. It became, as has been said earlier, more important to *appear* to have met targets rather than actually to have achieved them.

The social effects of these policies are also to some extent a matter of debate. Did they produce a more egalitarian society or one which was more divided than ever before? Was a new self-perpetuating elite formed – an elite which lived in better accommodation, enjoyed better health care and holidays, and whose children also enjoyed higher education and an early step into a good career, denied to millions of other Russians? Totalitarian historians tend to argue that the USSR simply replaced one class system with another more ugly version. Revisionists tend to emphasize that millions were able to benefit from new opportunities, and that there was therefore considerable support for the regime as a result. Others would point out that in the 1930s no one could feel safe; those with some position to protect were even more likely to receive a visit from the secret police. This tends to make the idea of self-perpetuating classes ridiculous.

Did Stalin simply continue Lenin's work?

For totalitarians Lenin laid the foundations on which Stalin built. Lenin laid down the direction of the new regime in all its fundamentals. Under Lenin Cheka was created, the first prison camps for political dissidents were set up, the first attacks on *kulaks* during the Civil War took place. It was Lenin who set up the one-party state. He too forced through the decree on factionalism in the party, which Stalin was to use against 'deviationists' of the Left and Right.

> **Note**
>
> Motor tractor stations and the equipment they managed, though still inadequate for the needs of collectives before 1939, marked a considerable net investment in agriculture.

> **Note**
>
> 'Blat' was the unofficial network of personal contacts, bribery and black market, which enabled people to acquire what they needed/wanted. 'Blat is higher than Stalin' was a popular saying.

> **Cross reference**
>
> Look back at Chapter 11 for more on the social changes in the 1930s.

Source 17

They were entirely right to use the iron fist to repress any opposition...But, of course, if political life in the country is extinguished, the Soviets will also not be able to avoid progressive paralysis. Without general elections, freedom of the press and assembly, and a free conflict of opinions, the life of any social institution will die away, and become a mere form, and bureaucracy will become the only active element.

Rosa Luxemburg, a German Marxist

Others reject this view:

Cross reference

This is also touched on in Chapter 7.

Source 18

Stalin's rule differed from Lenin's in its greater degree of totalitarian despotism. During Lenin's time some form of institutional rule by party and government survived...Stalin's was the first truly personal despotism to have existed in a modern state.

Schapiro, *The Communist Party of the Soviet Union*, 1960

Source 19

It is hard to imagine Lenin, however, carrying out a terror upon his own party. Nor was he likely to have insisted on the physical and psychological degradation of those arrested by the political police. In short Lenin would have been horrified by the scale and methods of the Great Terror.

Service, *A History of Twentieth Century Russia*, 1997

If Stalin built on Lenin's work, it was in a way of which Lenin would not have approved. Indeed some authorities, e.g. Lewin in *Lenin's Last Struggle*, would point out that Lenin substantially revised his own views on how the USSR should proceed. There are enough contradictions in Lenin's own pronouncements to indicate that he himself was not absolutely clear which policies were the best for Russia. If we cannot be clear about Lenin's own intentions, then it is unlikely that there will ever be any consensus on this issue. When we remember that Stalin himself on many occasions made strategic and tactical changes of direction, then the issue becomes very uncertain indeed.

Conclusion

The debate about Stalin's role in the government and the developments in the USSR in the 1930s shows no signs of coming to an end. More research will no doubt be used to bolster every point of view, but as long as historians write and are able to express their own opinions, unlike those in the former Soviet Union, they will continue to disagree. Perhaps it is best to recognize the merits of all sides:

■ Further reading

J. Arch Getty, *Origins of the great Purges*, 1985
A. Bullock, *Parallel Lives*, 1991
R. Conquest, *Stalin: Breaker of Nations*, 1993
R. Conquest, *The Great Terror: A Reassessment*, 1990
R. Daniels, *The Stalin revolution*, 1990
I. Deutscher, *Stalin*, 1966
R. Medvedev, *Let History Judge*, 1971
R .W. Thurston, *Life and terror in Stalin's Russia 1934-41*, 1996
D. Volkogonov, *Stalin: Triumph and Tragedy*, 1991

Source 20

If he was not as omnipotent and omniscient as his cult alleged, he was for many years extremely powerful. While there is some justification for attributing to Stalin responsibility for a wide range of policies and events, it is possible to exaggerate his personal role...

McNeal, *Stalin: Man and Ruler*, 1988

Interpretations exercise: Stalinist politics

Read these four extracts and then answer the questions on page 237.

Source A

At every stage Stalin remained several stages ahead of the other players in the grim political game which was played out in Russia between 1934 and 1939, constantly surprising them by the subtlety of his calculation, the depth of his duplicity and above all by the lengths to which he was prepared to go in ruthlessness. In fact the paranoid tendencies which were his most distinctive psychological characteristic were highly functional in such a situation making it easier for him to satisfy both his political and psychological needs at the same time, reinforcing each other.

His political needs were threefold. The first was to overcome the opposition to and criticism of his policies within the party...Stalin saw his second need to...attack and root out the source of opposition and criticism in the collegial structure of the party leadership and the tradition of intra-party democracy...The logical conclusion of this was to move from a single-party to a single-ruler state. This was a conclusion from which Stalin did not draw back...The third and ultimate stage of Stalin's programme, therefore, was to get rid of all...hindrances and govern alone.

Bullock, *Hitler and Stalin: Parallel Lives*, 1992

■ Think about

▶ Which school of history does this source best 'fit'?

Source B

This book argues that Stalin was not guilty of mass first-degree murder from 1934 to 1941 and did not plan or carry out a systematic campaign to crush the nation. This view is not one of absolution, however: his policies did help to engender real plots, lies, and threats to his position. Then this fear-ridden man reacted, and over-reacted, to events. All the while, he could not control the flow of people within the country, job turnover, or illegal acts by managers and many others. He was sitting at the peak of a pyramid of lies and incomplete information, and he must have known it. His power was constrained in fundamental ways, which contributed to his anxiety and tendency to govern by hit-and-run methods. His attitudes and deeds must be situated in a context of vast, popular suspicion generated in part by the First World War and the Russian Civil War. Several conclusions follow: Stalin becomes more human than others have portrayed him. And his regime becomes less malevolent but possessed of greater popular support than is usually argued.

Thurston, *Life and Terror in Stalin's Russia*, 1996

■ Think about

▶ Which school of history does this source best 'fit'?

Source C

[After Kirov's death] the trend was…toward intensification of the terror inside the party to its logical conclusion, to the stage of *physical extermination of all those whose party past might make them opponents of Stalin or aspirants to his power.* Today I have not the slightest doubt that it was at that very period…that Stalin made his decision and mapped out his plan of 'reforms'… The determining reason for Stalin's decision was his realization, arrived at on the basis of reports and information reaching him, that *the mood of the majority of the old party workers was really one of bitterness and hostility toward him…* As Stalin perceived it, the reasons for the hostility toward him lay in the basic psychology of the *Old Bolsheviks.* Having grown up under the conditions of revolutionary struggle against the old regime, we had all been trained in the psychology of oppositionists, of irreconcilable nonconformists.

Letters of an Old Bolshevik, the alleged report of Bukharin's discussions on a visit to Paris with a Menshevik historian, Nicolaevsky, published in 1938

Source D

Lenin used severe methods only in the most necessary cases, when the exploiting classes were still in existence and were vigorously opposing the Revolution, when the struggle for survival was decidedly assuming the sharpest forms, even including a civil war.

Stalin, on the other hand, used extreme methods and mass repressions at a time when the Revolution was already victorious, when the soviet state was strengthened, when the exploiting classes were already liquidated…It is clear that Stalin showed in a whole series of cases his intolerance, his brutality and his abuse of power. Instead of proving his political correctness and mobilizing the masses, he often chose the path of repression and physical annihilation, not only against actual enemies, but also against individuals who had not committed any crimes against the party and the Soviet government…He considered that this should be done in the interests of the party, of the working masses, in name of the defence of the Revolution's gains. In this lies the whole tragedy.

Khrushchev's secret speech to the Twentieth Party Congress 1956

Cross reference

Look at page 258 for the circumstances in which Khrushchev's speech was made.

■ Further reading

C. Ward, *Stalin's Russia,* 1993
C, Ward, *The Stalinist Dictatorship,* 1998 (carries extracts of many historians)

■ Questions

1 What impression does Bullock in Source A give of Stalin's character and motives?

2 How does Thurston in Source B disagree with Bullock about:
a) Stalin's character?
b) Stalin's motives?

3 Do Bullock and Thurston have any areas of agreement?

4 Would Bullock or Thurston best be able to use the evidence of Source C? Explain your answer by careful reference to all the sources and the attitudes of the historians behind them?

5 This report of Nicolaevsky has been questioned by many historians of the Soviet period. Can you suggest some reasons why they have questioned its reliability?

6 How useful would a historian studying Stalin find Khrushchev's speech?

7 Bullock's and Thurston's books were written only four years apart from each other. Why do you think they have such a different viewpoint?

Chapter 13

Stalin – the final years

▲ Refugees return to the burnt ruins of their town after the Germans have retreated. All that is left is the brick chimney stacks.

◀ Stalin, Roosevelt and Churchill at Teheran in December 1943.

Introduction

Stalin's final years in power saw the Soviet Union claim a place as one of the world's two super-powers. On his death in 1953 it sat like a colossus across Eastern and Central Europe. Lenin had hoped to bring communism to Europe on the point of Russian bayonets: it was finally ushered in by Stalin's T-34 tanks. The cost of the Second World War to the Russian people was horrendous, as suggested in Source 1. Roughly half of all the casualties of the war were Russian. Over half of these were civilians caught up in the conflict in one way or another. The devastation to the fabric of Russia's agriculture, industries and transport systems was just as great. The people of the USSR at the end of the war no doubt hoped that their sacrifice would bring them some tangible rewards and perhaps a gradual easing of the political climate.

Stalin was presented as the great architect of Russian victory and the Generalissimo of the war with an unchallenged position in Soviet politics. Would the regime now steer a new course?

Key questions

- How and why did the USSR emerge victorious in the war?
- What were the results of the war for the USSR?
- What changes were made after the war in the USSR's planned economy?
- What changes were made to the political life of the nation after the Second World War?

The Great Patriotic War 1941–1945

The Soviet Union and Germany in the 1930s

Trotsky described his policy as the first Commissar for Foreign Affairs as the issuing of declarations to incite revolution and then closing down Russia's foreign ministry. At first Russian Communists had hoped to have nothing to do with capitalist countries, believing that the revolution would sweep them all away. This was replaced by a new policy of expediency, dealing with other countries on the basis of what was best for the USSR and the cause of international communism.

Hitler's rise to become Chancellor of Germany in 1933 forced Stalin's government to adopt a more active policy. Hitler cancelled a long-standing agreement between Germany and the USSR for military co-operation in the training of men and the development of new technology. In 1934 the USSR applied to join the League of Nations, once called the 'robbers' den' by Lenin. Her Commissar for Foreign Affairs, Maxim Litvinov, tried between 1934 and 1939 to organize a European alliance to prevent German expansion. However, the nations of Europe, especially Poland and Britain, were reluctant to become involved in an alliance with Communist Russia. Instead the policy of appeasement saw Hitler first break the controls placed on Germany at Versailles and then annex Austria and Czechoslovakia, while France and Great Britain took no action except to condemn Hitler's invasions. Negotiations with Britain and France were resumed in the summer of 1939 but made little progress.

In April 1939 Litvinov, a Jew and a respecter of western culture, was replaced by Molotov, a hard-nosed bureaucrat. The frosty relationship between the USSR and Germany began to thaw, ending in the signing of the Nazi-Soviet Pact in August 1939. The unlikely event of two states with diametrically opposed social and political systems making a treaty of friendship shocked the whole world.

Think about

▶ What image does Source 2 give of Stalin personally and the USSR's role in world affairs?

Note

Russians remembered how they had suffered at the hands of the Germans at the Treaty of Brest-Litovsk. Hitler had written in *Mein Kampf* about his intention to seek 'living space' once again in Eastern Europe.

Timeline

Jan 1933 Hitler becomes Chancellor of Germany

September 1934 USSR joins the League of Nations

1935 Hitler announces rearmament plans

March 1936 Hitler reoccupies the Rhineland

November 1936 Germany and Japan sign Anti-Comintern Pact

September 1937 Soviet troops occupy Manchuria

March 1938 Hitler occupies Austria

July 1938 Japanese attack Soviet Army near Vladivostok

September 1938 Hitler wins the Sudetenland from Czechoslovakia

March 1939 Hitler invades Czechoslovakia

April 1939 Litvinov replaced by Molotov

August 1939 Nazi-Soviet Pact

September 1939 German invasion of Poland

Hitler after all had persecuted the German Communists, while Stalin had publicly denounced fascism on many occasions and sent money, arms and men to help the Spanish in their Civil War against the forces of the Right. This famous British cartoon captures this mood:

RENDEZVOUS

Source 3

◀ A British cartoon published on 20 September 1939

■ Think about

▶ What does this cartoon suggest about the chances of success of the Nazi-Soviet Pact?

▶ Do you think Russian Communists would have shared this view of the agreement?

Russia's border wars

The Nazi-Soviet Pact was a ten-year non-aggression treaty, in which both parties promised not to attack the other for at least ten years. A secret clause divided Poland into German and Russian zones, and also recognized Finland, Estonia, Latvia, Lithuania and Bessarabia as inside the USSR's sphere of influence. German troops invaded Poland on 1 September 1939, followed by Russian troops a fortnight later. Poland ceased to exist. In 1940 Russia formally occupied the Baltic States of Estonia, Latvia and Lithuania, having forced their governments to accept Russian bases on their territory the previous year. They became new republics of the USSR. Bessarabian territory became part of the new republic of Moldavia.

At the end of November 1939 war broke out with Finland when the Finns found it impossible to accept Russian demands for territory close to Leningrad. The Winter War did finally end in Russian victory but only after the Finns had inflicted humiliating defeats on more numerous Russian forces. Russian deaths approached 200,000 until a peace treaty was signed in March 1940. Russia's poor showing convinced Hitler that the officer deaths during the *Ezhovschina* had fatally weakened the Red Army, and made him confident that the USSR would crumble if attacked by German forces, who by the summer of 1940 had taken over almost all of Western Europe.

Cross reference

For more details of the *Ezhovschina* see page 198.

Russia had also faced war in the East. Japanese forces had occupied Manchuria in 1932 and attacked China in 1937. Japan also signed the Anti-Comintern Pact in 1936 with Germany, and later Italy, promising to co-operate against international communism. In the summer of 1939, after many border skirmishes with Manchurian forces, the Red Army finally annihilated their army and an uneasy peace in the East followed.

The Finnish War forced the Red Army to change much of its organization. Voroshilov was replaced as Commissar for Defence by Timoshenko and harsher discipline and training was introduced, together with privileges for the senior officers. Officers, who had proved their ability against the Finnish and Japanese, were promoted. Zkukov was made the new Chief of Staff.

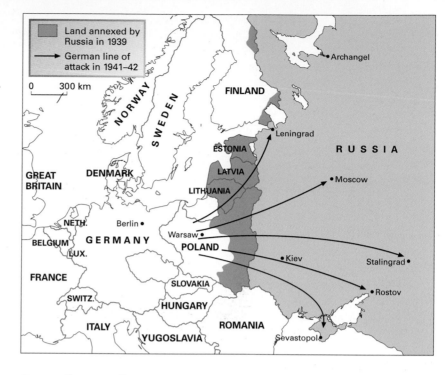

Source 4

▶ Russian gains under the Nazi-Soviet Pact and the direction of the German advances in Russia, 1941-42.

Map legend: Land annexed by Russia in 1939 · German line of attack in 1941–42 · 0   300 km

Facts and figures

The German invasion army was the largest ever assembled including:
5.5 million men
almost 5000 planes
2800 tanks

Timeline

1941 June German attack on the USSR
July Stalin orders 'Scorched Earth' policy
September Leningrad surrounded Kiev captured
October Attack on Moscow begins
December Russian counter-attack
1942 May German offensive begins
August Battle of Stalingrad begins
November Soviet forces surround Stalingrad
1943 February German army surrenders at Stalingrad
July Russian victory at Kursk November Kiev recaptured
1944 January Siege of Leningrad ended
June Operation Bagration (Soviet offensive) begins
1945 January Warsaw captured
April Vienna captured Battle for Berlin
May German forces surrender

Operation Barbarossa

There was growing evidence in the spring of 1941 that Hitler was intending to attack Russia with a huge offensive. German planes violated Russian airspace, deserters reported German plans, even Churchill sent warnings of the impending onslaught, but Stalin refused to believe that Hitler would break his word. As a result when the German offensive, code-named Barbarossa, began on 22 June 1941, Soviet armies were overrun and their air forces destroyed on the ground. Stalin for a few days disappeared altogether from the public eye, leaving Molotov to make the necessary announcement of war to the Russian people.

The German advance carried on at speed. All the territory gained from the Nazi-Soviet Pact was quickly lost and the government in Moscow began to evacuate documents, artistic treasures and even Lenin's body. Government departments were relocated to Kuibyshev and Stalin himself prepared to leave the capital. However, the German forces were held at the outskirts of the city. They had expected all serious resistance to be over when the winter arrived. Their troops had no winter clothing and the tanks became unusable as diesel froze. Harried by partisans behind their lines and Zhukov's forces at the front, they were compelled to retreat as Russian troops counter-attacked. Leningrad was surrounded and cut off from the rest of the country for over two years. The Russian army had lost almost 5 million dead or taken prisoner, and enormous amounts of military equipment, which would be difficult to replace.

The next year Hitler concentrated his forces in an all-out attack towards the Caucasus to gain the oilfields there. The advance was at first brilliantly successful, but ground to a halt in the streets of Stalingrad. There, in February 1943, General Von Paulus' army was trapped and forced to surrender by a powerful Russian counter-attack. The Germans had overstretched themselves. They were trying to hold a front over 2000 miles long with impossibly long lines of supply, which deprived their soldiers of spare parts, food and ammunition.

The siege of Leningrad

On 8 September 1941 advancing German forces completely surrounded Leningrad. For 900 days the city remained cut off – the only, hazardous, supply route lay across Lake Lagoda by night and within range of German guns. They were, however, unable to capture the city. The sufferings and endurance of the people were remarkable.

Source 5

The snow had come early that year [1941]. The first flakes fell on 14 October and by 31 October the city was blanketed in snow at least four inches deep. 'There was no running water, no electricity and no heat,' wrote Priotrovsky. 'People were using furniture and parquet floors for firewood…Their water supply came from the [River] Neva – the staff [of the Hermitage Museum] made a hole in the ice which froze again every night…

Norman, *The Hermitage*, 1997

Source 7

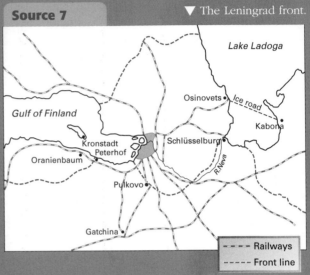

▼ The Leningrad front.

Source 6

▲ Actresses try to keep warm at a Leningrad theatre, winter 1942. The show must go on.

Source 8

Bris Piotrovsky records having a birthday feast on 14 February 1942. His brother came back from the front bringing with him a slice of bread, which had turned to crumbs in the frost. Orbeli gave him a small bottle of eau de cologne (100% proof) with which to wash it down and allowed him a ration of furniture glue which the Hermitage staff had learned to serve up as jelly… The restorer's drying oil was also used for frying appetizing morsels like potato peelings.

Norman, *The Hermitage*, 1997

Source 9

People walked and fell, stood and toppled. The streets were littered with corpses. In pharmacies, doorways, entries, landings and thresholds there were bodies…The janitors swept them out in the morning like rubbish…It was a flood of death that no one could handle. The hospitals were crammed with mountains of thousands of corpses, blue, emaciated, horrible. People pulled bodies silently down the street on sleds.

Volkov, *St Petersburg*, 1996

Source 10

Zhenya died 28 December at 12.30 a.m. 1941
Grandmother died 25 January at 3 p.m. 1942
Lyoka died 17 March at 5 a.m. 1942
Uncle Vasya died 13 April at 2 a.m. 1942
Uncle Lyosha 10 May at 4 p.m. 1942
Mama 13 May at 7.30 a.m. 1942
The Savichevs are dead. Everyone is dead. Only
Tanya remains.

The diary of Tanya Savicheva, aged 12. [Tanya herself died of malnutrition in 1944.]

Source 11

The Germans bombed the city ruthlessly from the air and bombarded it with heavy artillery from the surrounding territory…

Along with other Leningraders, the teachers and students of the conservatory, including Shostakovitch, dug anti-tank ditches around the city. Then Shostakovitch…was drafted into the fire brigade that kept watch from the conservatory roof. He also wrote songs and musical arrangements to entertain soldiers at the front.

Volkov, *St Petersburg*, 1996

Source 12

Dmitri Shostakovitch has written a symphony that calls for struggle and affirms faith in victory. The very performance of the Seventh Symphony in besieged Leningrad is evidence of the inextinguishable patriotic spirit of the Leningraders, their stalwarts, faith in victory, readiness to fight for the last drop, and to win victory over the enemy. Listen, comrades.

The announcement before the broadcast of the Leningrad premiere of Shostakovitch's Seventh Symphony, composed largely in Leningrad. So important was this event as optimistic propaganda for the regime that the Russian army spent weeks before the broadcast identifying the location of German artillery. Therefore, on the day of the concert, Russian guns were able to put them out of action so that the broadcast would not be interrupted.

Source 13

The entire able-bodied population of Leningrad [and surrounding districts are] to work on reconstruction, with the following work periods: for workers and employees with an 8-hour working day and those employed by military units: 30 hours a month; for workers and employees with a longer working day, and for students and schoolchildren: 10 hours a month; for citizens not working…60 hours a month. Workers and employees are to work outside their usual working hours.

Decree of the Leningrad Soviet 1944

Source 14

At the corner of Rastannaya and Ligovka streets a shell burst near the truck [carrying bread]. The driver had been killed by a shell splinter; all around it was dark. The situation could hardly have been better for theft. Yet having seen the unguarded bread, passers by…surrounded the spot and did not leave until a second truck arrived with the delivery manager of the bread plant.

A survivor recalls one incident during the siege

Source 15

The enemy is trying to break into Leningrad. He wants to destroy our homes, steal the people's wealth, flood the streets and squares with blood of innocent victims, rape the peaceful populace, and enslave the free sons of our homeland.

Zhdanov, Leningrad Party boss, appeals to the city on 21 August 1941

■ Questions

The Stalinist government liked to suggest that the suffering endured and determination to resist during the siege of Leningrad showed how much the people were devoted to the Communist regime.

How far do you agree with this view of the Leningrad siege?

Stalin's victory

In 1943 the Germans and their allies could mount only one major attack at Kursk, the biggest tank battle of the war. Here too they were thrown back. In 1944, however, called in Russia 'The Year of the Ten Victories', Russian forces pushed the enemy steadily back. In January 1945 Russian troops began the final push to Berlin bringing the war to a conclusion when Hitler committed suicide in his bunker.

Why did the USSR emerge victorious?

The single most important factor in Germany's defeat must be the seemingly unlimited capacity of the Russian people to endure the worst possible disaster and still to struggle on. It is well caught in this extract:

Source 17

> The whole organization…was caught in the mighty surge of patriotism that came up from the profoundest depths of Russian history and the Russian soul… At the core of the nation there is a hard, eternal and unconquerable element – it was that was bared in Stalingrad, that survived bloodletting and disaster on a horrifying scale. It had nothing to do with Karl Marx and Stalin.
>
> Kravchenko, *I Chose Freedom*, 1947

Quotation

Russians could identify themselves with their government, their party, and their Stalin in the common struggle.

Westwood, *Endurance and Endeavour*, 1980

The Russian people were convinced by every possible form of propaganda that the fight was worthwhile and would end in victory. All Leningraders and Muscovites went out to dig anti-tank ditches to hold back attacks in 1941. The government even relaxed its attitude to the Orthodox Church. Stalin met with Church leaders and allowed the appointment of a new Patriarch Sergius. The Holy Synod was reinstated and some training colleges for priests were reopened. Similar concessions were made to other religious groups. The new Patriarch described Stalin in November 1942 in *Pravda* as 'the God-chosen leader of our military and cultural forces…'

■ Think about

▶ Why did Orthodox priests make comments like this about Stalin, who had acted brutally against them in the past?

Stalin's own image was boosted by comparison with Ivan the Terrible in Eisenstein's film of that name. Many aspects of censorship were relaxed allowing Russians more freedom to write and read than they had had since the early years of the Revolution. To encourage food production, limits on the sizes of the private plots of collective farmers were removed. Posters all over the country exorted everyone to give everything to the common struggle.

▶ A recruitment poster for the Red Army from 1941.

Source 18

■ **Think about**

▶ How does this poster try to win new recruits for the army?

Quotation

If it had not been for Hitler's fanatical racism, the USSR would not have won the struggle on the Eastern Front. Stalin's repressiveness towards his own citizens would have cost him the war against Nazi Germany, and the post-war history of the Soviet Union and the world would have been fundamentally different.

Service, *A History of Twentieth Century Russia*, 1997

NB. However, if the Nazis had not been racist, they would not have invaded the USSR at all!

Facts and figures

Zoya Kosmodemyanskaya was caught by Germans while she was setting fire to stables. She was tortured and shot. Her body was found hanging from a gallows by a Russian counter-attack outside Moscow. In January 1942 her heroism was described in *Pravda*.

The German army had a golden opportunity to win the support of at least some of the people they had conquered. Many Ukrainians, who had survived the famine of 1932–1933, welcomed the Germans initially. Some captured Russian soldiers under General Vlasov were even recruited into the so-called Russian Liberation Army. However, German atrocities – approximately 11 million died during the German occupation – drove many Russians who might otherwise have been sympathetic to a 'liberating' army, into opposition. They were repulsed by the activities of the *Einsatzgruppen* who arrested and shot hundreds of thousands in the occupied regions. Jews and known Communists were the most common targets. To Hitler Slavs were '*untermenschen*', sub-human, and only of value if they could perform services for the Reich. He planned to settle Aryan Germans in the territories of western Russia. Accordingly millions of conquered Russians were sent west to work in labour camps. Even savage reprisals by the occupying army were unable to prevent support for the Russian partisans who operated behind German lines. There were about 250,000 active at the peak of the war, who attacked German units and their lines of supply. The Soviet propaganda machine was able to make heroes of those Russians tortured and killed by the enemy to inspire others to follow their example.

War production played a critical part in victory. When the government had regained its composure after the initial German attacks, they quickly organized the wholesale dismantling and removal of factories in western Russia to the Urals and beyond. Over 10 million people were evacuated from vulnerable districts to these same areas where they rebuilt their factories. In 1942 production of tanks and planes exceeded the figures achieved in 1941. New weapons poured off the production lines – T-34 tanks, Katyusha rockets and Yak fighter planes. Working hours were extended to 12 hours per day, and the working week became 6 days. By 1943 the USSR produced more war materials than Germany. None the less, the Russians could not have achieved all this on their own. Allied help played a crucial part – especially in the supply of lorries; over 400,000 were supplied by the United States during the war. Russian soldiers also marched in 14 million pairs of US boots. In 1945 Soviet exports were valued at 1433 million roubles. Imports were 14,805 million roubles.

Force and the threat of force cannot have been far from any Russian mind. The consequences of appearing to be critical of the regime were severe. NKVD officials shot suspects in prisons before they abandoned them in retreat. Penal battalions were sent into battle before regular troops to detonate minefields and draw enemy fire. In the Red Army SMERSH units of the NKVD were deployed behind Russian armies to 'encourage' them not to retreat.

> **Note**
>
> In Russian, SMERSH stands for 'Death To Spies'.

Above all else, as in 1812, the Russian winter and the Russian mud acted as the USSR's best allies. The huge distances involved rendered Hitler's thoughts of a quick victory impossible. The huge resources of the USSR, strengthened in the Five Year Plans of the 1930s, meant that in 1944 the German armies were outgunned and outnumbered. For the historian Isaac Deutscher, Stalin should be given credit for much of what was achieved:

Source 19

He had solidly armed his country and reorganized its military forces. His practical mind had not been wedded to any one-sided strategic dogma. He had not lulled the Red Army into a false sense of security behind any Russian variety of the Maginot Line...He could rely on Russia's vast spaces and severe climate. No body of men could now dispute his leadership. He had achieved absolute unity of command, the dream of the modern strategist.

Deutscher, *Stalin*, 1966

■ Activity

KEY SKILLS

Some view the Russians' victory over Germany as almost accidental – the product of German mistakes and the geography and climate of the USSR. For others it was a product of Stalin's leadership and the strength of the Communist system. Others regard the dogged determination of the Russian people as the key factor.

1 What evidence can you find to support these different theses?

2 Would the German armies have been successful if Russia had not been Communist?

Present a short talk to members of your group, using at least once image (e.g. spidergram, table etc) and use this as the basis of a group discussion.

The legacy of war

The Russians endured unimaginable suffering. The cold figures below represented innumerable personal tragedies and at the same time a huge challenge to the regime when the war was over. The task of rebuilding was bound to be the priority.

- Civilian deaths   19 million
- Soldiers killed   9 million
- Towns destroyed   1200
- Villages destroyed   70,000
- Railway destroyed   65,000 kms
- Hospitals destroyed   40,000
- *Kolkhozy* wasted   100,000

Much of the territory re-conquered from 1943 onwards had been scoured of anything of value: the retreating German armies destroyed even houses. Over half of Kiev, capital of the Ukraine, had been reduced to rubble. Millions were living in holes in the ground as the war ended.

Scores remained to be settled when the fighting was over. General Vlasov, leader of the pro-German army of Russians, was publicly hanged in Red Square. The regime was deeply suspicious of anyone who had come into contact with the enemy during the war. The NKVD was very active in the liberated territories. Returning POWs were not welcomed back to their families as heroes, but instead most found themselves taken straight to labour camps, tainted even as prisoners by their contact with foreign capitalism. Some of the smaller national groups had also been transported from their home regions on the outbreak of the war. The Germans of the Volga had their own republic but in 1941 were transported east as enemies of the State. Other national groups followed, including Kalmyks, Chechens and Tartars. They were transported by cattle-truck to Kazakhstan and abandoned there. There were further deportations when the war was won. Over 400,000 Lithuanians, Latvians and Estonians were transported, because they were thought to have collaborated with the Nazis. The numbers in labour camps rose from 1.6 million in 1942 to 4.7 million in 1947, most working in mines in the most uninviting areas of north-eastern Siberia.

The USSR and the Cold War

The USSR, for long a relative bystander in international diplomacy, now occupied centre stage. Lenin in 1920 had talked of taking Communism into Europe on the point of Russian bayonets. Communist regimes were now installed in many of the liberated territories, backed by Soviet armies of occupation. In Yugoslavia Communists had led the resistance to German forces and they set up their own government in Belgrade.

Source 20

▶ The Soviet sphere of influence in Europe after the Second World War.

USSR in 1938
Acquired by USSR 1939–45
Soviet satellite states
Communist but not Soviet satellite

It is not difficult to understand why Soviet troops stayed on after 1945. German armies had invaded Russia twice in 27 years. Though the USA, France, and Britain had fought alongside the USSR in the struggle against Nazism, in 1918 and 1919 all these states had sent troops to assist White armies in the Civil War. Soviet Marxists continued to believe that there was an inevitable rivalry and conflict between capitalist and socialist societies. Accordingly the USSR had to do what was necessary for self-defence and it tightened its control over the 'satellite states', the government of Czechoslovakia finally becoming totally Communist in 1948. In February 1946, Churchill in a famous speech in the USA, said 'an iron curtain has descended across the continent' (Europe).

If Russian armies dominated Eastern Europe, American forces in 1945 were to be found in Western Europe and in East Asia. The dropping of the atomic bombs at Hiroshima and Nagasaki shocked Stalin. When the USA refused to share its atomic knowledge with the USSR, he committed the Soviet Union to yet another vast project to compete with the capitalists. This also placed an extra financial burden on the people. There were attempts made in the United Nations to limit atomic weapons' development by establishing international control of uranium, but the proposed Baruch plan would have left the USA alone with the capability to build atomic weapons.

The political divisions in Europe were strengthened by economic developments. Europe after the war faced enormous financial and economic problems. In 1947 the USA made available under the Marshall Plan over $13 billion in loans and grants to European states. Stalin blocked American money to the USSR's satellites, fearing this was a threat to its own sphere of influence, and set up the Communist Information Bureau (Cominform) to counter the propaganda from the West. American plans to revitalize the German economy were particularly abhorrent to Stalin.

The Americans, however, believed that they detected the hand of the Soviet Union in almost every trouble spot around the world. A civil war in Greece, in which the Greek Communists were fighting for power, caused US President Truman to declare in 1947 that the United States would support 'free peoples…resisting attempted subjugation by armed minorities or outside pressure' – the so-called Truman Doctrine. In fact Stalin had instructed the Greek Communists to exercise caution, and was also keen to prevent Italian Communists from creating a domestic crisis. An atmosphere bordering on hysteria grew in the United States, and this was intensified when in 1949 the USSR exploded its own atomic device.

Berlin played a crucial role in intensifying divisions in Europe. In 1945 it had been decided that it, like the rest of Germany, would be divided between the four victorious allies, France, Great Britain, the USA and the USSR. It lay, however, about 180 km inside Soviet occupied East Germany. In June 1948 a new currency was introduced into the three western zones of Germany, despite opposition from the USSR. The next day the Soviet government cut all communications with West Berlin. Only an airlift lasting 11 months kept the people of West Berlin supplied with their daily needs. Though the crisis eventually came to an end, it made European leaders aware of their military dependence on the United States and their vulnerability in the face of an imagined Soviet attack. As a result, the North American Treaty Organization (NATO) was signed to bring about greater military co-operation between the USA and Western Europe.

Timeline

1945 Potsdam Conference divides Europe
1946 Churchill's 'iron curtain' speech
1947 The Marshall Plan
Cominform set up
The Truman Doctrine
1948 Czech Communist Party seize power in Prague
Berlin Blockade begins
1949 NATO set up
USSR explodes atom bomb
People's Republic of China established
1950 Korean War breaks out
1953 Stalin dies

■ Further research

Find out more about the mood in the USA by reading about Senator Joseph McCarthy.

The NATO alliance forced the USSR, as in the past, to look even more to its own defences. However, she was now no longer the only Communist state in Europe (see map on page 247) and in 1949 Mao Tse Tung established another Communist regime in China. Soon the Cold War extended to Asia. In 1950 Communist North Korean forces invaded the non-Communist South and a 'hot' war broke out, though it was a war in which there was no direct Soviet involvement. The Truman Doctrine brought United Nations' forces to the assistance of South Korea. To the USSR this must have appeared a particularly threatening time. General Macarthur openly called for a nuclear attack on China who, unlike the USSR, did support North Korea. For the Soviet Union, the need to maintain her defences in the face of what must have appeared to her as American imperialism, placed huge strains on an economy struggling to rebuild the ruins of 'The Great Patriotic War'.

Rebuilding and recovery

Because of the international situation the USSR had huge defence budgets to maintain. Over 100 army divisions were stationed in Europe when in February 1946 Stalin announced the first of three new Five Year Plans. The targets of the Fourth Plan (i.e. the first of the post-war plans) were concentrated on heavy industry and transport. As a result the urban workforce increased from 67 to 77 million in the immediate post-war period. The casualties of war meant the recruitment of many more women into the industrial workforce. The working week remained at its war peak, up to twelve hours per day in a six-day week. The methods of the 1930s were reintroduced. Wage differentials were maintained, Stakhanovites were lauded in the press, targets were set and workers were transferred across the USSR, wherever their skills were needed. Rations, which had been at starvation levels for all but the party bosses during the war, were maintained long after the war. The harvest of 1945 produced less than 60 per cent of the pre-war harvests. In 1946 the USSR was hit by a nationwide drought, worse than the terrible drought in the Volga region of 1921. The collective farms had been robbed by the war of their strongest workers, leaving women, children and the old to manage on their own. In the western regions they had also lost most of their livestock. Deutscher described the industrial scene:

Facts and figures

Women for example made up a third of the workers in building.

Quotation

I firmly believed that after victory everything would suddenly change…everybody expected that once victory was won, people would know real happiness.

The War 1941–5 by I. Ehrenburg, a later critic of Stalin, published in 1965

Source 21

Engineering plants were worked by adolescent semi-skilled labour. People were dressed in rags; many were barefoot. It seemed almost a mockery to urge them to 'catch up' with the United States.

Deutscher, *Stalin*, 1966

In the light of all these difficulties the achievements of the Fourth Plan were considerable. Machinery looted from East Germany supplemented the resources of the USSR, while Moskvitch cars were made in Moscow in what had been the German Opel factory. The Zeiss optical works was also moved to the Moscow region. By 1950 the industrial fabric of the USSR was much stronger than before the war, despite the usual failures in central planning and the resulting bottlenecks in production. However, workers were worse off at the end of the Fourth Plan than in 1928. A devaluation of the rouble by 90 per cent in 1947 affected the savings of everyone. Consumer goods were in very short supply, even if one had the money, but the USSR was now second only to the USA in its industrial capacity.

Source 22

	1940	1945	1950 (Plan target)	1950 actual
Total farm production	100	60	127	99
Coal (millions of tons)	166	149	250	261
Oil (millions of tons)	31	19	35	38
Steel (millions of tons)	18	12	25	27
Leather footwear (millions of pairs)	211	63	240	203
Electricity (billion kWh)	48	43	82	91

The government faced extraordinary problems in the agricultural sector. The number of collective farmers was perhaps only one third of that at the start of the war, and most machines had been destroyed. Horses were also very scarce. The peasants again paid the heaviest price for the industrial advance of the USSR. They faced government interference in every area of their lives. They were forced to give up the extra land they had taken over during the war. Moscow told them which crops to grow and which seed to use. They also set higher and higher procurements for the collective farms in grain and livestock, which meant it was common for peasants to have to buy flour and other foodstuffs in the towns. In addition, Stalin in 1948 announced a plan 'for the transformation of nature', which called on peasants to plant forests, often in unsuitable areas, and dig canals and irrigation ditches. Wages on the collective farms were very low, amounting to less than 20 per cent of average industrial wages even 10 years after the end of the war. In 1949 a poor quality suit cost more than one year's average agricultural earnings. Even farmers without cows were asked to deliver milk, forcing them to 'beg, borrow or buy' (Nove) the milk. Taxes increased, including a tax on fruit trees on private plots.

Agriculture emerged as one of the main challenges for the regime, though the crisis was not obvious in published figures, because the government still counted 'biological yield' not what was actually harvested. To bring economies of scale collective farms were forced to amalgamate, but it brought no benefits. Khrushchev put forward an idealistic scheme to settle peasants in modern 'agrocities' in the countryside, treating farmers as simply an agricultural proletariat. It was criticized in the press and the party.

Politics in the post-war years

You have read in Chapters 10 and 12 of the debate concerning Stalin's power and authority in the USSR in the 1930s. There was for a long time less argument about his position after the war, and it was accepted that Stalin was now absolute, having striven for many years to put himself in this position. A so-called 'mature dictatorship' had been reached.

At first glance it is easy to see why there was more unanimity. The Politburo and Central Committee did not meet at all between 1947 and 1952. Stalin himself retired from the public limelight, giving only one important speech after 1948, but his suspicious nature was reflected in the arrests of members of his own family and friends. Molotov's wife, for example, was arrested, as were the sons of Mikoyan, both described by Conquest as 'veteran Stalinists'. After the death in 1948 of Zhdanov, the Leningrad Party leader and Politburo member, there was a wide-ranging purge of the Leningrad Party in 1949, carried out by the secret police under Beria. This led to the arrest of thousands, including the rising stars Voznesensky a close political ally of Zhdanov and head of Gosplan,

■ Think about

▶ Why were the results in agriculture so much worse than those in industry?

Cross reference

For biological yields see page 169.

Quotation

He saw enemies everywhere…it was all a result of being lonely and desolate.

Alliluyeva
Twenty Letters to a Friend, 1967

and Kuzntesov, the Secretary of the Central Committee in charge of supervision of Beria's secret police. The number of prisoners in labour camps in 1953 was almost 2.5 million. In addition there were 300,000 more in prison and 2.75 million others in special settlements in Central Asia and Siberia. In 1952 he persuaded the Central Committee to replace the Politburo with a larger Praesidium, now seen as a step to reduce the influence of the old guard of the party, Molotov and Mikoyan.

Censorship grew even tighter. The composer Shostakovitch once again found his works were not performed. The novelist Pasternak had his pregnant partner arrested and treated so badly that she lost their child. There was a campaign against bourgeois influence, probably inspired by the tense international atmosphere of the Cold War. It became a crime to tune in to foreign radio stations and jamming stations were built along the frontiers to ensure they were not heard. The biologist Lysenko, who challenged modern genetics, was praised and honoured, though in the West he was regarded as a charlatan.

At the 19th Party Congress in 1952 Stalin remained almost silent, but sat to receive the adulations of the party leadership. His image was even more omnipresent than before.

Timeline

1945 Zhukov removed from positions of influence
1946 Fourth Five Year Plan begins Tightening of censorship
1947 Rouble devalued
1948 Plan for the transformation of nature
1949 Purge of the Leningrad Party
1950 Fifth Five Year Plan begins
1951 Mingrelian Case
1952 Plans to resettle many Jews in Siberia
1953 The so-called Doctors' Plot Death of Stalin

Source 23

▶ The front cover of a Soviet magazine published in 1949 to celebrate Stalin's 70th birthday.

■ Think about

▶ How is Stalin presented in this picture?

▶ Does this prove that he held the public's love and admiration?

However, many historians find the view of the post-war USSR shown in Source 23 as problematic as the totalitarian view of the 1920s and 1930s. At the very least there continued to be great differences between the leading figures in the party about how the affairs of the Soviet Union should be conducted. One such was the continuing debate about the relative importance of capital as opposed to consumer goods in the Fourth Five Year Plan. According to Service, these same individuals 'had to compete for Stalin's approval.' The virtual annihilation of the Leningrad Party leadership in 1949 reflected the bitter rivalries within the ruling elite, as each tried to strengthen his own position and those of his associates. Malenkov and Beria allegedly used the affair to dislodge rivals from positions of authority. Conquest claims that Stalin had talked openly of nominating Voznesensky and Kuznetsov to succeed after his death.

The so-called Mingrelian Case also seems to suggest that Stalin himself believed that Beria was becoming too powerful. Mingrelia, a region of Georgia, was Beria's birthplace, and in 1951 a number of high-ranking Mingrelians were arrested. Ironically Beria was put in charge of the investigation.

The army was another potential threat to Stalin's authority and, during the war, army leaders had enjoyed considerably more latitude than before 1941. Marshal Zhukov in particular, Stalin's military deputy in the war, had emerged with a considerable reputation. Now he was demoted, removed from the Central Committee and from Moscow. During the war, control over some aspects of life had been loosened, the Russian Orthodox Church for example. The re-imposition of tight censorship can therefore be interpreted as a sign of weakness by a regime struggling to reimpose itself against 'society' just as a failing leader also struggled to regain authority over his juniors.

Chris Ward describes Stalin's position in the USSR thus:

Cross reference

Look back at chapter 8. What happened to Trotsky after his success leading the Red Army in the Civil War?

Source 24

This was no self-confident tyrant in charge of a smoothly functioning totalitarian machine, but a sickly old man; unpredictable, dangerous, lied to by terrified subordinates, presiding over a ramshackle bureaucracy and raging, like Lear, against failure and mortality.

Ward, *Stalin's Russia*, 1993

Russian chauvinism continued in the treatment meted out to the minority peoples of the Soviet Union, as we have seen earlier in the chapter with the transplantation of whole populations. As under the Tsars, non-Russian languages, eg Estonian and Rumanian, faced official discrimination. Worst treated of all were the Jews. Anti-Semitism became a feature of policy after the warm reception given by Moscow Jews to the Israeli ambassador when she visited the Moscow Synagogue in 1948. Here was another group that was not allegedly wholeheartedly committed to the Soviet cause. Jewish politicians were imprisoned. Stalin denounced them as 'rootless'. In 1952 he ordered Kaganovitch, himself Jewish, to prepare a list of Jews to resettle in the Jewish republic in Birobidzhan on the Chinese border. *Pravda* announced in January 1953 the discovery of a Doctors' Plot in a Moscow hospital. Most of the arrested were Jewish, and the announcement inspired many isolated attacks on Jews across the USSR. Many historians believe that the Doctors' Plot would have begun another series of party purges including some at the highest level, had Stalin not died before it could be implemented. The 19th Party Congress in October 1952 was dominated by calls for vigilance by comrades, in a similar way to the mood preceding the *Ezhovschina*.

During all of this Stalin personally continued to live a simple life, in the Kremlin or, increasingly, at his *dacha* in the countryside. His daughter described his life at this time:

Source 25

I couldn't make the adjustment to his mixed-up schedule of sleeping half the day, having a meal at three in the afternoon and dinner at ten in the evening, and then sitting up half the night at the dinner table with his colleagues…The whole crowd would come for dinner, Beria, Malenkov, Zhdanov, Bulganin and the rest. I found it dull and exhausting…listening to the same old stories as if there were no news and nothing whatever going on in the world!

Svetlana Alliluyeva, *Twenty Letters to a Friend*, 1967

On 1 March 1953 Stalin collapsed at his *dacha*. He had been drinking the previous night until the early hours with four friends. He ordered tea but gave no orders for it to be brought in. It was only hours later that nervous servants found him lying on the floor of his bedroom. The Soviet leaders argued amongst themselves before calling for medical attention. They may even have deliberately decided to delay medical assistance for fear of being held responsible if Stalin made a recovery! He was finally declared dead on 5 March; a long and terrible death as his daughter described it. The news was announced on the radio the following day. His body, like that of Lenin, was embalmed and interred, after a funeral in Red Square, in the renamed Lenin-Stalin Mausoleum. In the queues outside, dozens died in the crush to see the dead leader.

However, in the labour camps there were revolts by the inmates, hopeful of freedom now Stalin was no more. Troops had to be sent in to quell the most serious of these.

Source 26

▶ The reaction of workers in a factory to the death of Stalin.

■ Think about

▶ Why do you think this photograph was taken?

▶ Does it prove that Stalin was genuinely mourned by the Russian people?

Document exercise: late Stalinism

Source A

After the war...Stalin became even more capricious, irritable and brutal...His persecution mania reached unbelievable dimensions...He decided everything alone, without any consideration for anyone or anything.

The...provocateur and vile enemy, Beria, who had murdered thousands of Communists and loyal Soviet people, cleverly took advantage of this incredible suspicion...Stalin personally supervised the 'Leningrad Case'...When Stalin received certain materials from Beria...he ordered an investigation of the 'case' of Voznesensky and Kuznetsov. With this their fate was sealed.

From Khrushchev's speech to the Central Committee on 25 February 1956 (after Beria's execution) in which he denounced some features of Stalin's regime

Source B

The political repression of 1948–52 did not destroy the potential forces of destabilization...The repression saved the regime for a while from the pressures of criticism from below, but they could not prevent the slide of the country down the slope of crisis...The mood of the masses was dominated by the syndrome of expectancy. The only way of overcoming the crisis was the path of reform from above.

Zubkova, *From Russia after the War*, 1998

Source C

On Stalin's order, and with the active participation of Beria and Malenkov... nearly the entire staff of the Leningrad district was arrested, and many of them died in solitary confinement...Many of the officials who were cut down in 1949–52 belonged to the new generation of leaders who rose to prominence after 1936–7 and distinguished themselves during the war...The rigid framework of Stalin's cult was too confining for the most capable of them. Sooner or later they were bound to become a nuisance to Stalin as people who might diminish his own authority.

Medvedev, *Let History Judge*, 1971.
Medvedev's father was a victim of the purges of 1937–8

Source D

Although he performed his task of leader of the party and the people with consummate skill and enjoyed the unreserved support of the entire Soviet people, Stalin never allowed his work to be marred by the slightest hint of vanity, conceit or self-adulation.

Inserted, according to Khrushchev, by Stalin into the 1948 edition of *Stalin's Short Biography*, which was full of praise of Stalin

Source E

Yes, we were kids of 17, 18 years of age, and those were terrible years, 1946 and 1947. People swelled up from hunger and died, not only in the hamlets and the villages, but in cities...destroyed by the war...The disgusting thing was to read in the newspapers of the happy life of Soviet people. That is what made us heartsick.

A. Zhigulin remembers his youth in the USSR

■ Examination-style questions

1 Comprehension in context
According to Source A, why was there a 'Leningrad Case'?

2 Comparing the sources
In what ways do the authors of Sources B and C differ in their explanation of the repression from the view expressed in Source A?

3 Assessing the Sources
Of what value is Source D to a historian trying to understand Soviet politics after the Second World War?

4 Making judgements
Using the sources and your own knowledge, why do you think there was there renewed political tension in the USSR after the Second World War?

■ Activity
Writing Stalin's obituary

Quotation

Stalin found Russia working with a wooden plough and left her equipped with atomic piles.

From Stalin's obituary in the *Manchester Guardian*, 1953

Quotation

The better part of Stalin's work is as certain to outlast Stalin himself as the better works of Cromwell and Napoleon have outlasted them.

Deutscher, *Stalin*, 1966

Further reading

J. Keep, *Last of the Empires*, 1995
R. Service, *A History of Twentieth-Century Russia*, 1997
W. G. Hale, *Postwar Soviet Politics*, 1982

Source 27

Deranged or not, Stalin remains a towering figure in world history. He had galvanized the forces that built a new form of society, presided over an ultimately triumphant war, and by careful diplomacy had made Russia the second greatest power on earth. He had destroyed the country ways, thrown down old gods, decimated muzhiks [poor peasants] and mullahs, priests and intellectuals, engineers and writers. He died as he had lived, a remote, cruel deity, but for many a deity all the same.

Kochan and Abraham, *The Making of Modern Russia*, 1983

When any prominent political figure dies, all the papers carry obituaries summarizing his life and achievement. Before you write your own obituary of Stalin, look at a broadsheet newspaper and read one of the obituaries to give you some idea of the kind of thing to include. Usually they give a summary of his/her career and character, highlight some particular achievements and then give an assessment of his/her overall impact on his/her times. You may like to consider these questions amongst others:

● Were Russians materially better off in 1953 than in 1928?
● Had Stalin solved the perennial problem of feeding the Russian people?
● Had Stalin advanced the work of Lenin?
● Had the regime reached a solution to the national question?
● Did the USSR now have a sound industrial base?
● Had the Communist regime gained the support of the masses?
● Was the USSR now safe from capitalist encirclement?

You should use visual materials, maps, timelines, pictures, to illustrate your points from more than one electronic source and create a new way of presenting statistical information in your report. Make sure you consult and make notes from more than one written source.

Conclusion

Stalin dominated Soviet politics for almost 30 years. During that time the USSR emerged victorious from 'The Great War for the Fatherland' and became a world power. Stalin could perhaps claim to have guided the USSR and the world closer to his and Lenin's vision of a better Communist future. The USSR had been transformed from a peasant country into an industrial giant surpassed only by the USA. At the same time communism had spread beyond the borders of the USSR into Eastern Europe and China.

However, the price of victory had been terrible and the nature of the regime seems to have been little changed by the experiences of war. The command economy remained, with its strengths and weaknesses. The Communist Party retained a monopoly of political power, and the Gulag Archipelago described by Solzhenitsyn still contained millions of unfortunate men and women. Agriculture was in crisis, though the solutions advocated before Stalin's death were largely reinventions of policies which had already failed. National aspirations had been suppressed, often ruthlessly, and the regime continued, rightly, to be suspicious about its own place in the public's affections.

Now that Stalin was dead, would a new chapter in Russian history be opened? How capable of reform was the system that was Stalin's legacy?

Chapter 14

Khrushchev and de-Stalinization

▲ A battered statue of Stalin in Budapest in Hungary in 1956, during the uprising there.

Source 2

I am old and tired. I've done the main thing. Relations among us, the style of leadership, has changed drastically…The fear's gone. That's my contribution.

Khrushchev

Introduction

Stalin left no instructions or guidance about the future government of the USSR. In the shocked atmosphere after his death the Politburo met and spoke of collective leadership. The 'cult of the individual' was now frowned upon. For 30 years Stalin had dominated Soviet political life, but soon his statues were pulled down all over the USSR and Eastern Europe, as in Source 1. As you have seen in the previous chapter, the country still faced huge problems. How would the Communist Party and its leaders meet the challenges facing them? Would they break out in a new direction or simply follow the course laid out by Stalin for the last 30 years? Is Khrushchev's claim (Source 2) to have changed for ever the political scene accurate?

Key questions

- Why did Khrushchev emerge as the dominant figure in the USSR?
- How and why did Khrushchev attack Stalin's time in office?
- How did Khrushchev try to improve Russian agriculture and industry?
- How did Khrushchev alter the relationships between the USSR and the rest of the world?
- Was Khrushchev more liberal than his predecessors?
- Why was Khrushchev removed from office?

The struggle for power 1953–1956

A joint meeting after Stalin's death of the Council of Ministers, the Party Central Committee and the USSR Supreme Soviet agreed that Stalin's Praesidium of the Central Committee should be reduced to ten members. These ten were the major figures in the party, from whom emerged three main rivals, Malenkov, Beria and Khrushchev. Malenkov became Chairman of the Council of Ministers and the head of the government. Beria became Minister of Internal Affairs including control of the whole security police apparatus. Khrushchev held no ministry but was a Secretary of the Central Committee of the Communist Party. Soon Khrushchev was the dominant figure in the party, and the party proved to be a much more important power base than positions in the government. Between 1953 and 1956 over half of the secretaries of the republic and regional party committees were replaced. When the Central Committee met in 1956 over one-third were new members. These newly promoted personnel all owed Khrushchev some debt of gratitude.

Beria seemed the biggest threat, and he had a reputation for unscrupulousness. Even his closest colleagues were afraid of him and his many MVD (Ministry for Internal Affairs) troops in the capital. It was not long before they acted. He was undermined when those accused in the Doctors' Plot (See page 252) were released. The MVD were accused of extorting false information by torture and their torturers were arrested. The army, who no doubt remembered his key role in the army purge before the war, finally arrested Beria. He and six associates were tried in secret and shot.

Vigorous debates followed, as in the 1920s, about the best course for the USSR. Malenkov advocated a greater emphasis on consumer industry and a more relaxed relationship with the West and with the countries of Eastern Europe. Khrushchev advocated a new policy to plant the 'virgin lands' of Kazakhstan and western Siberia. Good harvests in 1954 and 1955 strengthened Khrushchev's position. In February 1955 Malenkov was forced to resign as head of government, being replaced by an associate of Khrushchev's, Bulganin. Khrushchev was now the dominant figure in the country, though, as we shall see, not by any means a dictator.

■ Think about

▶ What reasons might we have to doubt Khrushchev's words in Source 2?

■ Biography

Nikita Khrushchev

1894 Born, son of a Ukrainian peasant

1899–1917 Various jobs in the Donbass industrial area

1917 Elected to local soviet

1918 Became Bolshevik and political commissar in the Red Army

1922–9 Party worker in the Ukraine

1929 Student at the Industrial Academy in Moscow

1935–8 First Secretary of Moscow Party – supervised the Metro construction

1938 First Secretary of the Ukraine Party

1941 Principal political commissar on the Southern Front, especially Stalingrad

1944 Prime Minister of Ukraine

1949 First Secretary of Moscow Party and a Secretary to the Central Committee

De-Stalinization

The horrors of Stalin's time were slowly becoming known, but only to a few of the party hierarchy. The political atmosphere had begun to relax. Labour camp inmates were returning home, novels critical of Stalinism were being published, notably *The Thaw* by Ehrenburg. However, to publicly denounce Stalin and all his works was still unthinkable in 1956. Khrushchev was granted the right to deliver a speech to a closed session of the 20th Party Congress on the subject of 'The Cult of the Individual and its Consequences'. This speech, delivered over four hours, was a 'turning-point in the USSR's politics' (Service). It was a gamble because many of those in the audience had risen through the party under Stalin. The speech described what Lenin had said about Stalin in his *Political Testament*, and then pointed the finger at Stalin for not having made the USSR ready for the German attack in 1941. The speech then contained a long list of Stalin's crimes against the party.

Source 3

Stalin acted not through persuasion, but by imposing his concepts and demanding absolute submission to his opinion. Whoever opposed this concept was doomed to physical annihilation. Mass arrests and deportations of thousands of people, execution without trial, created conditions of insecurity and fear, even desperation...Stalin was a very distrustful man; sickly suspicious...Everywhere and in everything he saw 'enemies', 'two facers', and 'spies'...And how is it possible that a person confesses to a crime that he has not committed? Only in one way – because of the application of physical measures of pressurizing him, tortures bringing him to a state of unconsciousness, deprivation of his judgement...The majority of Politburo members did not, at the time, know all the circumstances in these matters and therefore could not intervene.

His speech was greeted at some times with gasps of disbelief, applause and shouts. Copies of the speech were given to Communist leaders abroad, and party leaders went back to their committees to discuss it with colleagues. According to one source, at a later meeting someone shouted out, 'Where were you when these crimes were committed?' 'Who said that?', Khrushchev demanded. There was no reply. 'There's your answer: then, too, we were scared'. The criticism of someone who was genuinely admired by some in the party caused a backlash. Molotov, Kaganovitch and Malenkov won a decision from the Praesidium to abolish the post of First Secretary, the base of Khrushchev's power. Khrushchev's appointments in the party then came to his rescue. He insisted that only the Central Committee could abolish the position. When the Central Committee met, the decision was easily overturned. Molotov, Malenkov and Kaganovitch were removed from the Praesidium.

What were Khrushchev's motives for this attack on the hand that had reared him? Perhaps it was partly defensive. If he did not draw a line under Stalin's regime, then someone else would launch the attack and Khrushchev may be tarnished as one of Stalin's henchmen. Others point out that Khrushchev was a genuine idealist, who was probably personally shocked when he discovered the extent of Stalin's terror. Certainly Khrushchev, like all party leaders, knew

■ Think about

▶ What similarities can you see between the period following Lenin's death and that following Stalin's?

■ Think about

▶ What are Khrushchev's criticisms of Stalin in this passage?

▶ Khrushchev had been implicated in the Terror personally. How does he try to escape blame for this?

Timeline

1953 Beria executed
USSR explodes hydrogen bomb
1954 *The Thaw* published
The Virgin Lands project begins
1955 Malenkov resigns as PM
1956 Khrushchev's secret attack on Stalin
Russian troops crush Hungarian rising
1957 Khrushchev announces decentralisation of the economy
Malenkov, Molotov and Kaganovitch removed from influence
1958 Pasternak declines Nobel Prize for Literature
1961 The Berlin Wall is built
1962 The Cuban Missile Crisis
1963 Nuclear Test Ban Treaty
1964 October Khrushchev removed from power

that there had to be major reform of the industry and agriculture of the USSR. Attacking Stalin would enable them to set a new course.

Within a year the labour camps were opened and millions of people had convictions quashed. Sadly most of these were already dead. It was to be five more years before Stalin's name began to disappear from the map of Russia. Stalingrad was renamed Volgograd. The 22nd Congress decided that Stalin's body should be removed from Lenin's mausoleum. It was removed by soldiers at night and buried in a deep pit filled with concrete.

Six years after Stalin's death a new official history of the party was approved, which criticized the excesses of the 1930s. Writers found a new freedom in their criticism of the Soviet past, but this was very much a stop–go affair. Novels critical of Stalinism appeared; however, there were limits. Boris Pasternak was heavily criticized for having his novel *Dr Zhivago*, set in the years of the Revolution and the Civil War, published outside the USSR, and had to refuse the Nobel Prize for Literature when it was awarded. Other writers met a similar fate, including Solzhenitsyn and Yevtushenko, the latter for daring to write a poem about the Holocaust. However, the days of 'socialist realism' seemed to be slowly passing away. When modern works of art were brutally attacked by Khrushchev personally on a visit to a Moscow art gallery in 1962, there was a lively debate amongst the Party Committee before the new tendencies were criticized.

Khrushchev's leadership did not bring an easing of the pressure on religious groups – rather, in fact, the reverse. Orthodox churches were demolished in great numbers, leaving only 7500 as places of worship. Muslim and Jewish places of worship also met the same treatment.

The denunciation of Stalin led inevitably to demands from other Communist states for greater independence and self-determination. Khrushchev showed his support for the independent Communist government in Yugoslavia under Tito, which had refused to enter the Warsaw Pact. A wave of strikes broke out in Poland, resulting in the freeing of Gomulka, the ex-Head of State and a critic of Stalinism, from the camps and his promotion to head of the Polish government in 1956. A more liberal Communist, Imre Nagy, became head of the Hungarian government. When anti-Soviet demonstrations broke out in Budapest and Nagy announced his intention to leave the Warsaw Pact, Khrushchev sent tanks into Hungary. Clearly de-Stalinization did not mean any greater independence for Communist states that might threaten the security of the USSR.

Although Khrushchev was a Ukrainian, de-Stalinization did not bring greater self-government for the nationalities within the USSR. A growing number of Russian nationals settled in the non-Russian areas. These, being situated on the edges of the USSR, were of obvious strategic importance. The USSR was not prepared to relinquish its tight control while the atmosphere of Cold War existed.

Note

Khrushchev thought *Dr Zhivago* too critical of the Bolsheviks in the Revolution and Civil War

Cross reference

You can read the end of Solzhenitsyn's novel *One Day in the Life of Ivan Denisovitch* on page 201.

Facts and figures

The Warsaw Pact was set up in 1955 and included all the Communist states of Eastern Europe except Yugoslavia. It was formed in retaliation to NATO and its decision to allow West Germany to rearm.

The Thaw

Source 4

These momentous changes worked a profound influence on Soviet culture, high and low, and created a climate called the thaw... It is easy to underestimate the euphoria that gripped the younger generation in the Khrushchev years.

These words by the historian R. Stites in his book Soviet Popular Culture *explain the excitement felt by many in the USSR when the process of de-Stalinisation began*

Source 5

He may advocate a boycott of the Communist dining room, instead of joining the commission for improving the food. He may demand the discussion of some problem and then participate not in order to clarify the subject, but to cause disturbance and spread confusion. He tends to shirk lectures, and at the same time complains about the unsatisfactory state of teaching.

From an editorial of Komsomolskaya Pravda *(Komsomol Truth) on 15 December 1956 criticising student demagogues*

Source 6

The main attention of the participants... should be turned towards a profound and all-embracing projection of the culture of Soviet man, in the full many-sidedness of his work, his social and individual life in their indissoluble unity. The artists are called upon to create clear, typical patterns, displaying the rich spiritual world of the Soviet people..., the leading figures of the working class, innovators in production, toilers in Soviet agriculture, the Soviet intelligentsia.

Instructions to artists wishing to have work displayed in an exhibition in 1957

Source 7

Source 8

◄ ▲ Russians adopt Western dress in the 1960s.

Source 9

A man was arrested after running outside the Kremlin walls shouting at the top of his voice, "Khrushchev is an idiot." He was tried and sentenced to six months imprisonment for disturbing the peace… and 19 and a half years for revealing State secrets!

Khrushchev used to tell this joke which was going the rounds in Moscow

Boris Pasternak

Dr Zhivago was finished in 1955. Pasternak submitted it to two Russian literary magazines for it to be published. When it was not printed he smuggled it to Italy where it was published without permission. In 1958 he was awarded the Nobel Prize for Literature. When he said he would accept the prize, he was denounced and expelled from the Union of Soviet Writers. Pasternak wrote an apology in *Pravda*, but died shortly afterwards.

Source 10

Nikita Sergeevich, we thank you for finding in yourself the courage to tell the truth to the whole people and to reveal facts that give us grounds for trusting you and the government. We hold Lenin and his teachings in holy esteem… If your speech and respect for Lenin are not hypocritical, then send us the government's guarantee that the police and security agents will not bother us…

A letter sent to Khrushchev by a worker in an electrical power plant near Archangel. He was arrested for anti-Soviet activities. Khrushchev never saw the letter

Source 11

1. Shouted out by a captured soldier before he was shot by Red partisans in the Civil War:
'Don't humble yourself! Your protest will not reach them. These new oprichniki*, these master craftsmen of the new torture chambers will never understand you! But don't lose heart. History will tell the truth. Posterity will nail the Bourbons (Former French royal family) of the commissarocracy to a pillar of shame, it will pillory their dark deeds.'
**oprichniki were the secret police of Ivan the Terrible.*

2. Take your red banner. You think it is a flag, isn't that what you think? Well, it isn't a flag. It's the purple kerchief of the death woman… She waves it and she nods and winks and entices young men to come and be killed to death, then she sends famine and plague. That's what it is. And you believed her… You thought it was saying: 'Come to me, all ye poor and proletarians of the world.'

Two brief extracts from *Dr Zhivago* by Boris Pasternak

■ Think about

▶ Why in Source 11 are the commissars called 'French Bourbons'?

▶ What impression do these extracts give of the Russian Revolution and its achievement?

■ Activity

How far-reaching was 'The Thaw' in Khrushchev's USSR?

What evidence in this spotlight supports the view that there was a new freedom in the USSR?

What evidence undermines this view?

How would you explain the differences between the evidence?

Why did Khrushchev allow publication of *One Day in the Life of Ivan Denisovich* (See chapter 10) but not *Dr Zhivago*?

Which of these statements would you agree with?

▶ There was simply a change in style not substance after Stalin's death.

▶ There was a change in the leadership but not of institutions or the values they stood for.

▶ The Communist Party had lost control over the youth of the USSR.

The USSR and the world

Stalin had emphasized throughout his time of dominance in the government that the USSR should be on her guard against capitalist attack. In his 1956 'secret speech' Khrushchev explained that conflict between capitalism and communism was not inevitable. He made a point of travelling abroad often, bringing a new easy-going and humorous face to communism. This was a great contrast with the dour foreign minister Molotov, nicknamed 'stone bottom'! It was Khrushchev who pointed out that any conflict between the two power blocks would end up in 'mutually assured destruction' (MAD). An easing of tension would also allow the USSR to reduce her huge standing army. In 1960 this reduction began – from 3.6 million to 2.4 million.

This did not mean that he believed the USSR should relinquish any of its influence in the world, as we have seen in the treatment of those who opposed it in Eastern Europe and with the signing of the Warsaw Pact. In 1960 Russian forces shot down a manned US spy plane over the USSR, capturing the pilot. As thousands of East Germans poured into West Berlin to escape to the West, Khrushchev ordered the building of the Berlin Wall in 1961, cutting West Berlin off completely from East Germany, dividing families and friends whose homes were only a few metres apart.

Source 12

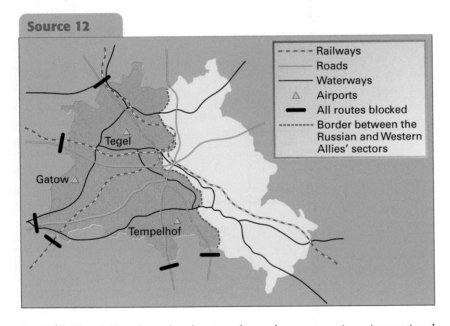

Legend:
- ----- Railways
- ——— Roads
- ▬▬▬ Waterways
- △ Airports
- ▬ All routes blocked
- - - - - Border between the Russian and Western Allies' sectors

Tegel
Gatow △
Tempelhof

◀ The isolation of West Berlin.

In 1962 Khrushchev brought about perhaps the most serious international incident between the super-powers since 1945. The newly Communist Cuba was offered Russian missiles as a protection against America. When the launch-sites were detected, United States President Kennedy set up a naval blockade of Cuba. After a few days of international tension, the USSR agreed to withdraw its missiles in return for a guarantee from the USA not to attack Cuba. Many people saw it as a climb-down by Khrushchev.

In 1963 a sign of improving relations was seen in the signing of the first Test Ban Treaty, which forbade the testing of nuclear weapons in the atmosphere. This agreement drew particularly strong criticism from the People's Republic of China under Mao, who denounced Khrushchev for making agreements with the 'running dogs of capitalism'. Mao even talked about winning a nuclear war, and therefore refused to sign the Test Ban Treaty. The USSR could no longer claim to be the only Marxist authority.

The problems of agriculture

In September 1953 Khrushchev laid out new plans for the failing agricultural sector. He was regarded as something of an agricultural expert, being the son of a peasant. For the first time since the late 1920s there was an honest analysis of the situation:

● there were fewer animals in the USSR than before the Revolution
● farmers' income was far too low because of the low State procurement prices
● productivity was very low
● the party had been deliberately misled by the use of 'biological yields'
● high taxes on farmers were a disincentive to progress

Khrushchev's remedies

Pricing was the first important element to change. It is difficult to generalize about many different crops, but on average procurement prices rose by about 25 per cent between 1953 and 1956. Costs to the *kolkhozy* were cut – such as the cost of transport and the hire of equipment from the MTS. Peasant taxation was reorganized so that it was paid on plot-size rather than for example on fruit trees and livestock. Peasants without livestock were not expected to provide meat. Large increases in the production of fertilizer and farm machinery were announced.

All these measures would take time to show rewards, so Khrushchev then launched his most famous campaign – to cultivate the 'virgin lands' of western Siberia and northern Kazakhstan, 'on the fringes of the area of adequate rainfall' (Nove). After success in the 1954 harvest, the area ploughed was increased. By 1956 an extra 35.9 million hectares were cultivated, equal to the total cultivated area of Canada. To achieve this a great political campaign was launched. Komsomol members flocked out to help in this gigantic experiment. Those who settled had to endure difficult conditions – inadequate housing and other amenities – as well as uncertain crop yields. 1955 was a drought year though it was followed by a good year in 1956.

■ Think about

▶ How does the author of Source 13 show his own opinion of Khrushchev's policies?

Source 13

In the first years the scene of this huge gamble reminded one of nothing so much as the days of the covered wagon as American settlers opened up the West, with hundreds of thousands of men and women, mostly young, torn up from their roots and scattered over the vast steppe in tents, in primitive huts, in dug-outs, freezing through the long cruel darkness of the first winter, seared by the blazing summer sun as they toiled at the first giant harvest over an area the size of France…What Khrushchev dreamed of was the day when these tented settlements…would be transformed into the first of his legendary *agrogoroda*, or agricultural townships, which sooner or later were to supersede everywhere the dark villages with their stubborn traditions and superstitions with a clean, well-regulated, antiseptic paradise.

Crankshaw, *Khrushchev's Russia*, 1959

Other reforms followed. *Kolkhozy* were allowed to set their own production targets, and given more freedom to decide how to use their land. They were told only what they had to deliver to the State. However, the move to amalgamate smaller collectives into larger units continued, the number being roughly halved between 1950 and 1960. The MTS were abolished altogether and repair stations set up instead, for whose services *kolkhozy* had to pay. The machinery was sold off to the farms.

■ **Think about**

▶ Were these methods different from those used by Stalin?

Source 14

▲ Khrushchev visiting a wheatfield on a collective farm in the virgin lands of Kazakhstan in 1959.

Another agricultural failure?

At the 21st Party Congress Khrushchev boasted that the USSR would soon overtake the USA in its production of meat and butter. Agriculture was put at the centre of political debate for a decade and was made a higher priority in investment. The virgin lands experiment was a mixed success. In 1956 they contributed over 50 per cent of the total grain harvest for the USSR. However, erosion by wind proved to be a difficult problem: 13,000 square miles had their topsoil removed in 1960 alone. Results were unpredictable, as the poor harvest of 1963 proved. Khrushchev then had to suffer the humiliation of importing grain from the capitalist West. Khrushchev seemed to be drawn to simple solutions. He urged farmers to grow more maize, which had been successfully grown in the Ukraine, to provide fodder to improve the quality of Soviet livestock. Eighty-five million acres were planted, but only about one-sixth was harvested ripe – a colossal waste of manpower and land. He later began a campaign to increase fertilizer production by 700 per cent, to boost yields from existing fields rather than to convert more marginal land to production. The targets set proved to be impossible to reach in the time.

■ **Think about**

▶ Why do you think this photograph was taken?

▶ Does it prove the 'virgin lands' project was a success?

Note

These figures show a steady average increase, which is misleading. In 1963 the total cereal production was down to 107 million tons. Khrushchev had set a target of 180 million tons. Because of the uncertain climate and lack of rainfall the crops of the 'virgin lands' were particularly variable.

Source 15

Agricultural production in millions of tons

	1952	1953–6 average	1957–60 average	1961–4 average
Cereals (excl. maize)	82	99	120	132
Meat	5.2	6.3	8.2	9.1
Milk	36	42	59	63

Source 16

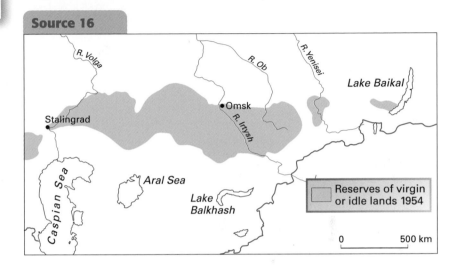

▶ The location of the virgin lands in Kazakhstan.

■ Think about

▶ If collective farms were known to be so inefficient, why did the government persist with them?

The pricing system, despite being a significant improvement on Stalin's time, did little to encourage farmers to grow what was needed. The State altered prices almost at random and the prices offered to farmers were often less than the costs of production. This was the case for eggs, milk and meat. Shortages caused the government to raise the prices of meat and dairy products suddenly in 1962. This caused protests in Novocherkassk, which despite the attempts of Praesidium leaders to calm the crowds, resulted in troops firing on rioters who broke into the city soviet headquarters. Twenty-four were killed, though a news blackout stopped this becoming public knowledge for thirty years.

The sale of produce from private plots provided half of a peasant's income. Despite making up only 3 per cent of the total cultivated area, these produced over 30 per cent of the USSR's produce. There was still little incentive to work hard on the collective fields. Initiative was lacking to improve the farmer's lot. Those who showed some eagerness to better themselves still left the collectives. On top of this there were many ill-conceived government initiatives, such as Khrushchev's own craze for maize, which was grown in land and climate to which it was not suited – with inevitable results.

The closing of the MTS aimed to make *kolkhozy* more independent, but had unfortunate results. There were not the barns on farms to store equipment nor the expertise to maintain them. Mechanics from the former MTS tended to return to industry where living standards and amenities were better. Farm machinery rotted in the fields for want of small spare parts.

The central government proved unable to plan agriculture in the long term, nor would it give farmers economic independence and revert to market trading. As J. Keep put it in *Last of the Empires* (1995), 'By subsidising socialized agriculture the State was ensuring that it remained inefficient'.

Progress in industry?

In 1959 the party launched a Seven Year Plan with more realistic targets than the Five Year Plans of the 1930s. There was again heavy emphasis on power stations. The natural gas, oil and coal reserves of the USSR were to be fully exploited. However, there was also a greater emphasis on consumer goods. The statistics seem to suggest that the Plan was a great success:

Source 17

	1955	1958	1965 plan	1965 actual
Coal (millions of tons)	391	496	600–612	578
Electricity (billion kWh)	170	235	500–520	507
Tractors (thousands)	314	415	–	804
Woollen fabrics (millions of sq.m)	316	385	500	466
TV sets (thousands)	495	979	–	3655
Refrigerators (thousands)	151	360	–	1675
Retail trade inc food (millions of roubles)	50.2	67.2	–	104.8

The system, begun under Stalin, was followed with very little change. Targets were set centrally with little sensitivity to the nation's or industry's real needs. Productivity in the USSR was very low and quality was poor. Meeting the targets was what mattered. At first Khrushchev appeared a reformer here too, setting up 105 regional economic councils to take the place of the national ministries. These would be supervised more closely, it was hoped, by the republic and district party committees. The hope was to avoid waste and red tape and to co-ordinate the work of different branches of production more successfully. All it did was to create another layer of bureaucrats with offices. In a 'command economy' there still needed to be central planning in Moscow, though the State committees that did this were no longer called ministries. A new Supreme Economic Council was also set up in Moscow to co-ordinate the whole apparatus. When Khrushchev was removed, much of this new structure was immediately dismantled.

The standard of living did improve. A minimum wage was introduced in 1956, though most workers earned considerably more. Average household income, according to A. McAuley, grew by over 3 per cent per annum from 1960–1965. The diet of the urban Russian improved considerably, being less dependent on bread and potatoes. Although some items like clothes and footwear were very expensive, other things were much cheaper than in the West, for example books and public transport. By 1968, 50 per cent of Soviet households had a television and a washing machine, though very few had cars and only 10 per cent a telephone. Pensions and other benefits increased.

The substantial increase in the amount of housing constructed meant young married couples could find a place of their own rather than living for years in the overcrowded apartments of their parents. Like consumer goods, the emphasis was on quantity rather than quality and many of the new apartments lacked running water or lifts. These regimented, prefabricated blocks still blot the landscape of Russian cities today, though heating was free and the communal flats of Stalin's day, with shared washing and cooking facilities, were abandoned.

Facts and figures

Meat consumption rose by 55% over the Seven Year Plan.

There were some impressive achievements in transport. Diesel trains were added to Russian railways, and many miles of track were electrified. New lines were opened into the virgin lands to transport grain and agricultural produce. While families in the capitalist West were beginning to acquire cars, the USSR continued to be largely a car-free society, with cars being the perks of the few. In science the USSR made some important breakthroughs.

The Space Race

Khrushchev wanted to prove that the Communist USSR could equal and surpass the Capitalist USA. He had boasted that the USSR would match the USA in agricultural production in three years, though as we have seen this was not achieved. One area in which it appeared the USSR did have a lead over the West was in space exploration, and Khrushchev made the most of the propaganda possibilities this lead presented.

In 1957 Sputnik 1 was launched into orbit, emitting an electronic signal as it went. Russians greeted Americans with 'beep, beep' on the streets of Moscow! Later Sputnik II put the first living creature into space, a dog called Laika, to celebrate the 40th anniversary of the Revolution. However, there was no means at the time for bringing the dog back safely to earth, so she died after a few days in orbit.

> **Note**
>
> ### The USA in space
> **1958** Satellite into orbit
> **1961** Chimpanzee into space
> Commander Shephard into space
> **1962** First US astronaut into orbit
> First telecommunication satellite into orbit
> **1964** Ranger 7 sends back first close-up photographs of the moon
> **1968** US astronauts orbit the moon
> **1969** US land first man on the moon

> ■ **Think about**
>
> ▶ Why did the USSR invest so much in space exploration?

Source 18

▶ Laika the space dog sitting in Sputnik II, before becoming the first living creature to be launched into space from Earth.

In 1959 the USSR went one better, landing a Red Flag on to the moon and, on a later mission, taking photographs of the dark side of the moon, never seen by humans before. After a test flight bringing two dogs back to earth, the first man, Yuri Gagarin, was successfully sent into space in April 1961. On his return he was given a State reception on Lenin's mausoleum. After other flights Valentina Tereshkova became the first woman into space.

The space race had wider implications. Rockets to send men into space could also be used to deliver nuclear warheads against the enemies of the USSR. It also meant a huge investment of scarce resources, which might otherwise have gone into smaller scale, less glamorous projects of immediate benefit to Russian citizens.

Why was Khrushchev removed from power?

In October 1964 Khrushchev went on holiday to the Black Sea. In his absence the Praesidium was summoned to a meeting and Khrushchev was asked to fly back to attend. His leadership was attacked at the meeting, and he was forced at the age of 70 into retirement. Brezhnev took over as First Party Secretary and Kosygin became Chairman of the Council of Ministers.

Source 19

Comrades, forgive me if I'm guilty of anything. We worked together. True we didn't accomplish everything.

Khrushchev

A Central Committee meeting next day confirmed the decisions of the Praesidium, and criticized Khrushchev on many accounts, especially for his 'cult of personality'. *Pravda* carried an article breaking the news to the rest of the population (see Source B on page 270).

Source 20

▲ Yuri Gagarin (the first man in space) toasts Valentina Tereshkova (the first woman in space) at her wedding to Andrian Nikolayev (another Russian astronaut). Khrushchev is prominent in this photograph of these popular Soviet heroes.

■ Think about

▶ Why was Khrushchev a prominent guest at Tereshkova's wedding to a fellow astronaut?

Khrushchev's achievement can best be measured by the fact that he lived in Moscow in retirement until his death in 1971. No longer was there a sweeping purge of a past leader's friends and supporters, and Khrushchev was removed and not shot. This left Khrushchev to record his own memoirs and smuggle them out to the West for publication.

Khrushchev's character, unpredictable and spontaneous, made him engaging for western pressmen, but a difficult colleague. Banging his shoe on the table at a meeting of the United Nations in 1960 embarrassed many. The party was an organization wedded to traditions built up over 40 years. Khrushchev wanted to shake up some of the old ways of thinking. His call for greater devolution annoyed the bureaucrats. His reductions in military expenditure cost him the support of the army. His attack on the certainties of Stalin's day and on Stalin's memory made more enemies, especially amongst those who believed Stalin had played a crucial role in the Second World War. The greater cultural freedom was seen by some as creating weaknesses within the system. De-Stalinization was seen by many as having a dangerous implication for the territorial integrity of the USSR and the Warsaw Pact. Despite their better living conditions even many workers resented the rising food prices.

The diplomatic defeat of the Cuban crisis in 1962 lost Khrushchev the support of some key figures in the armed forces who had stood by him in 1956 and 1957. Above all else the disappointments in agriculture weakened Khrushchev's position. He had made it a high priority, touring the country to talk to and inspire the farmers. When the harvests after 1960 produced less than he had hoped he had laid himself open to criticism, especially after the drought year of 1963. His departure was not mourned by many in the USSR.

Document exercise: Khrushchev's achievement

Source A

The production of grain in our country lags behind the demand…We cannot yet create sufficient grain reserves to permit us to be independent of weather conditions. This task requires high productivity of labour and a scientific approach…We have to give our people more than the capitalist world gives. This is the principal issue. You cannot only promise, you have to deliver. The socialist system is the most progressive, but even after 50 years nowhere is the Communist Party yet able to win in a parliamentary election…The Soviet people have achieved a much better life than before the Revolution; there is no question about that. However, we are not yet a mirror into which the West wants to look…Paradise is a place where people want to end up, not a place they run from! Yet in this country the doors are closed and locked. What kind of socialism is that?…What kind of paradise?

From the last pages of *Khrushchev Remembers*, 1990, smuggled out of the USSR as tapes and published abroad

■ **Think about**

▶ When before in Russian history did liberalization produce more criticism of the government?

Source B

The Leninist Party is the enemy of subjectivism…of hare-brained scheme-making, of half-baked conclusions and hasty decisions and actions taken without regard to realities. Bragging and phrasemongering, bossiness, reluctance to take account of scientific achievement and practical experience are alien to it…It is only on the Leninist principle of collective leadership that it is possible to direct, and develop, the increasing creative initiative of the party.

Pravda, 17 October 1964, justifying Khrushchev's removal from office

Source C

When Khrushchev in 1954 announced the scheme to reclaim and put down to arable farming ninety million acres of virgin or waste agricultural land in Kazakhstan and South-Western Siberia he was concerned quite as much with establishing tight party control over a newly settled area larger than the whole cultivated area of Britain, France, and Spain combined as with increasing food production. For this colossal operation, carried out by half a million 'volunteers' from the Komsomol, from the Army…and from the collectives themselves, was from the beginning centrally controlled. All the drive came from the party supervisors, and the huge new farming units were organized on lines not of the *kolkhoz*, with its old village traditions, but of the State farm.

Crankshaw, *Khrushchev's Russia*, 1959

Source D

It is pleasant now to pass through a village. It used to be different. It used to be as Mamai (one of the Tartar invaders who laid waste to Muscovy) and his horde had only just passed through. Not only were there no new buildings of any kind, but even the old ones were rotting and dilapidated. For most collective farms at that time simply could not afford to build.

Khrushchev speaking in Kiev, April 1959

■ Examination-style questions

1 Comprehension in context
Read Source A. Do you think Khrushchev had abandoned his faith in Marxism after his retirement?

2 Comparing the sources
How and why do Sources A and B disagree about the achievements of the Khrushchev period?

3 Assessing the sources
In view of its content and origins, how much value would a historian place on Source D?

4 Making judgements
Volkogonov called Khrushchev a 'failed reformer'. Looking back on his time as leader of the USSR, do you think this is a fair and accurate assessment?

■ Think about

▶ What are the main criticisms made of Khrushchev in this extract?

▶ Why should a historian be cautious about this statement?

■ Activity   KEY SKILLS

Question 4 provides an opportunity to achieve credit for the key skill of communication. Present a short talk to members of your group, using at least one image (eg spidergram, table etc) and use this as the basis of a group discussion.

Conclusion

Note

Apparat is the party bureaucracy.

Source 21

The Khrushchev years are important if for no other reasons than for the seeds of reform that were then sown which would bear fruit three decades later…Khrushchev's efforts to relax central management and control survived only into the late 1950s. Starting in 1959, the administrative-command style of management began to reassert itself in the form of a revived party apparat. Now it is generally conceded that the five-year period between 1959 and 1964, in which the party reasserted centralised control of the economy, represents a period of serious economic mistakes, particularly in agriculture.

Hart, *The Second Russian Revolution*, 1991

Khrushchev believed in the Communist system to his very core. He had fought for it in the Civil War and the Second World War. He accepted its validity without question. He believed, however, that by shaking up the system he could make it work much more effectively. In fact his economic reforms simply created new bureaucracies which made rational decision-making even more difficult. At the same time, perhaps to bolster his own political position, he made rash promises for the future – in terms of living standards, foreign affairs and above all agriculture. Despite the increased investment, without higher procurement prices Soviet farmers proved to be unable to meet these higher expectations.

However, he did begin 'The Thaw' and artists and intellectuals felt a little freer to present the work they, rather than the party, wished – and this was a lasting legacy. Criticism of the regime became more common and more vocal. At Novocherkassk criticism became violent protest. As Source 10 suggests, Khrushchev was reluctant in the end to abandon the command economy, which Stalin created.

In the end Khrushchev's retirement passed unmourned by the majority of Soviet people, though living standards had begun to improve. His common touch did not save him from the leaders of the party machine who were looking for a more dignified and less unpredictable leader – a safer pair of hands. They found them in Leonid Brezhnev.

Further reading

D. Volkogonov, *The rise and fall of the Soviet Empire*, 1998
J. Keep, *Last of the Empires*
M. McCauley, *Khrushchev and Khrushchevism*, 1987
B. Pasternak, *Dr Zhivago*, 1958
E. Crankshaw, *Khrushchev's Russia*, 1959

Chapter 15

Consolidation and collapse 1964–1991

Source 1

▲ Soviet missiles on parade in Red Square in November 1969 in front of Lenin's mausoleum.

Source 2

Gorbachev was the best thing the Communist Party had to offer. He played the central role in a remarkable chapter of world history, but was forced in the end to go, because in the historical play there was no longer any room for a man who still wanted to be a Communist.

The Wall Street Journal, 27 December 1991

079628

Introduction

Khrushchev had tried to breathe fresh air into the Soviet state and economy. His government had considerable success in raising the living standards of many Russians, in ending arbitrary terror by the security police and in easing the tension of the Cold War. He lost his position as much for the manner of his leadership as for any shortcomings in his policies. The next 20 years of what was called at the time 'developed socialism' were dominated by a series of elderly statesmen, especially Leonid Brezhnev. In 1980 his Politburo, as the Praesidium was once again called, was made up of individuals who were almost all over 70 years old. Commentators have been critical of this page in Russian history – B. Moynahan called it 'The Big Sleep' – seeing the USSR, like its leaders, in terminal decline. When the collapse came it was, however, as unexpected as it was rapid – brought on by Gorbachev, a man who was determined to modernize the communist system and make it work, as described in Source 2.

Key questions

- What was 'developed socialism'?
- What were the causes of the USSR's economic stagnation?
- How did Gorbachev try to reform the USSR?
- Why, when he was so popular in the West, did Gorbachev suffer a coup in 1991?
- Why did the USSR break up?

'Developed socialism'

Khrushchev had maintained that socialism had been attained, and that now the USSR could look forward to reaching communism in 20 years. The new collective leadership, which took over after Khrushchev's removal, abandoned, in public at least, these grand ambitions and concentrated on more practical step-by-step improvements. This was a period of gradual change, rather than the bursts of activity and new initiatives which were common during the Khrushchev period.

Agriculture

Many of Khrushchev's agricultural policies were maintained. Collective farms continued to be increased in size and more and more organized to specialize in one crop. The government to boost production, especially of meat and dairy products, offered higher procurement prices. In order to stop urban discontent which could result from higher prices, this meant heavier subsidies. The campaigns of Khrushchev, e.g. for maize, happened no more. Farmers did see a rising percentage of national wealth going into agricultural investment. Over 25 per cent of all investment was in farming in 1980. At the same time farmers benefited from other changes. Their right to private plots was reaffirmed – Khrushchev had attacked them as contrary to communism – and peasants were able to enlarge them to half a hectare. In 1980 they made up 4 per cent of the USSR's cultivated land, but produced 30 per cent of its food. In 1974 collective farmers were finally given internal passports allowing them to travel freely around the USSR. They also became entitled to State pensions and minimum wages; wages now replaced the labour-day system of payment, where farmers had been paid according to the number of days worked and the productivity of the farm. An increased use of artificial fertilizers saw a steady increase in crops, though these were as ever subject to the vagaries of the harsh climate.

Note

Despite the stagnation of the Brezhnev era, the USSR was indisputably one of the two great world super-powers, as is shown in Source 1.

■ Biography

Leonid Brezhnev (1906–1982)

1906 Born the son of a steelworker
1935 Qualified as an engineer
1939 *apparatchik* in the Ukraine
1941–5 Commissar in the Army – reaching rank of Major-General
1952 First Secretary of the Moldavian Communist Party
1955 Organized the 'Virgin Lands' experiment in Kazakhstan
1956 Secretary to the Central Committee

Facts and figures

Grain harvests (millions of tons)

1962 = 140	1963 = 108
1964 = 152	1965 = 121
1966 = 171	1967 = 148
1968 = 170	1969 = 162
1970 = 187	1971 = 181
1972 = 168	1973 = 222
1974 = 195	1975 = 140
1976 = 224	1977 = 196
1978 = 235	1979 = 179
1980 = 189	1981 = 160

Despite the progress made, the government was very conscious that this sector of the economy was its greatest problem. Agriculture ministers enjoyed only short periods in office unlike almost all other members of the government. Collective farms found it difficult to retain trained technical staff, because they were able to move more easily to the cities to find better paid work and a more interesting life. Agricultural machinery stood rusting still in barns and farmyards because no one knew how to repair it or because spare parts were simply unobtainable. Productivity remained low in comparison to western countries. While total agricultural production was rising by almost 4 per cent per annum in the late 1960s, ten years later it was down to 1.2 per cent, according to J. Keep (*Last of the Empires*, 1995).

Source 3

Growth of agricultural output (5 year averages)

	1966–70	1971–5	1976–80	1981–5
Output in billion roubles	100	114	124	131
Cereals (millions of tons)	168	182	205	181
Meat (millions of tons)	11.6	14	14.8	16.2
Potatoes (millions of tons)	95	90	83	78
Cotton (millions of tons)	6.1	7.7	8.9	9.1

Raising productivity proved extraordinarily difficult; many farmers seemed reluctant workers when not busy on their own private plots. Any new initiatives foundered on the conservatism and reluctance to take risks on the part of the farmers and their managers. One such idea was that of contract brigades, or 'links'. Under this scheme farmers would form teams and negotiate tasks and pay rates according to results. One *sovkhoz*, in the 1960s, demonstrated that grain could be produced for one-third the cost, thereby trebling the income of the team. The *sovkhoz* chairman was arrested and thrown into prison, where he died. His project threatened the whole structure of Soviet agriculture, and seemed to smack of capitalism with its profit incentives to farmers.

In the 1980s the USSR continued to import grain from the USA and Argentina.

Cross reference

Chapter 9 carries more on these problems in Stalin's time.

Industry

Brezhnev's first step was to abolish Khrushchev's regional councils set up to co-ordinate industrial production and to restore central planning and management in Moscow in government ministries. The Politburo resolved to try to make centralized planning and control work. Attempts were made to link managers' bonuses to the profit they returned on their capital. However, managers were not free to make decisions about most of the important aspects of their businesses. Wages and the number of employees were set centrally, and the products they produced and the targets for production were still determined by others. Trade unions were also given slightly more influence than before, which put other pressures on managers *not* to manage but carry on past practices, no matter how inefficient they might be.

Cross reference

For Khrushchev's reforms see Chapter 14.

Note

Compare this with the Five Year Plans under Stalin.

There was also much greater emphasis on consumer goods than ever before. The 9th Five Year Plan (1971–1975) for the first time gave them higher priority than capital goods. However, one very noticeable feature of this entire period was a continual slowing down of industrial growth. The 10th Plan (1976–1980) showed an annual increase in GDP of 2.7 per cent. This was despite very heavy programmes of capital investment. A great deal of this went into defence projects which brought no tangible benefits to the population as a whole.

Source 4

Industrial production – selected items

	1965	1970	1975	1980	1985
Iron ore (millions of tons)	153	197	235	245	248
Steel (millions of tons)	91	116	141	148	155
Coal (millions of tons)	578	624	701	716	726
Cars (thousands)	201	344	1201	1327	1332
Cement (millions of tons)	72	95	122	125	131
Synthetic resins and plastics (thousands of tons)	803	1670	2838	3637	5020
Refrigerators (thousands)	1675	4140	5579	5925	5859
Cameras (thousands)	1053	2045	3031	4255	2090

The slowing down was most obvious in the old staple industries: exactly the same phenomenon was happening in the West. Coal production did not increase because there was increasing reliance on oil and gas supplies, of which the USSR had plenty. With the rising oil prices of the 1970s and 1980s this also provided the USSR with much foreign currency. Nuclear power also contributed a growing percentage of the electricity of the country. Transport received extra funding – with great strides in the electrification of lines. Airline traffic increased, so that Aeroflot, the State airline, carried 100 million passengers in 1980. Cars, though expensive and of poor quality, were more common on the streets. This was largely because of a new plant built by Fiat on the River Volga.

Living standards

Savings in the USSR rose considerably under Brezhnev. The State savings bank held 18.7 billion roubles in 1965 and this had risen to 221 billion roubles in 1985 (Keep). This would normally be taken as a sign of a healthy and vigorous economy with rapidly increasing living standards. This is not true of the USSR. Some goods were of such poor quality and difficult to find that consumers preferred to save their money.

Despite subsidies, the cost of living was high in terms of the wages earned by Russians. The average Russian worker in 1979 had to work for 4.5 hours to earn enough to buy a loaf of bread; his American equivalent only 48 minutes. Housewives queued for hours to buy the bare necessities.

Source 5

◀ A photograph taken secretly in the 1970s and smuggled out of the USSR. It shows pieces of fruit and a cow's head and hooves being sold at a street market.

■ Think about

▶ What can we learn about Soviet life from this photograph?

▶ Why did this photograph need to be taken secretly?

USSR statistics show that households were spending a smaller percentage on food and clothes than earlier, and more on consumer durables. Diet was improving, although slowly. The population was still heavily dependent on bread and potatoes for their staple foods. Statistics conceal also the great regional variations. In Moscow and Leningrad items were usually available that were hardly ever in the shops in the small towns and villages of the outlying regions. Because of the cheap air and rail fares, it was common to see planes and trains full of housewives with packed bags leaving the capital. The State-controlled pricing system produced some very odd results. Airfares were so low that it was profitable for peasants in the Caucasus to fly to Moscow with a bag of lemons or other fruit to sell in the private markets, so scarce and expensive were these products.

However, accommodation was very cheap in comparison to the West, with free heating in the coldest regions. Apartment blocks continued to mushroom all over the USSR. When Brezhnev died, over half of the accommodation in Moscow had been built while he was First Secretary of the Party. Its quality remained as poor as ever. Door frames were not square, roofs leaked, damp spread over walls, lifts did not work – it did not matter provided the construction quota was met. Public transport in the industrial regions was also heavily subsidized.

Living comfortably meant, as it had in the 1930s, 'blat' – using contacts to supply what was needed, whether in goods or services. There was a thriving black ('second') economy in the USSR for imported goods, foreign currency and especially illegally distilled vodka. One-third of private cars were supposedly run on government petrol, because there was also a condoned culture of pilfering from one's place of work. This might be car parts, cloth, processed food, and opera tickets – almost anything. If you needed repairs to any of your electrical appliances, then you approached someone from the 'second economy'. In a sense the 'second economy' made possible the official planned economy, because it filled the gaps of supply. Nor was it confined to the lower echelons of society. Brezhnev's own family was heavily involved in

Note

Of course the 'second economy' is not unknown in Britain too!

underhand dealings. When he died his daughter was being investigated for diamond smuggling, in partnership with the head of the Russian State Circus and a character called 'Boris the Gypsy'!

As ever, the lifestyle of the political leaders was very different from those they served. Brezhnev himself collected foreign cars and had a number of dachas for himself and his friends to relax in when he needed a rest. This encouraged cynicism towards politics and politicians.

Source 6

▶ Leonid Brezhnev enjoys a glass of champagne with President Nixon of the USA. Compare his lifestyle with that of the ordinary Russians in Source 5.

Politics

What did 'developed socialism' mean in political life? On Khrushchev's fall the party spoke always of collective leadership. The government appeared to be led by two men, Brezhnev as head of the party and Kosygin as Chairman of the Council of Ministers. President Podgorny was also an important influence, and of course the military chiefs. However, Brezhnev emerged over the years as the dominant force, and he began to accumulate various other honours, five Orders of Lenin, Marshal of the Soviet Union. In 1977 he took over Podgorny's position as Chairman of the Praesidium of the Supreme Soviet, the USSR's President. Such was his hold on office that he remained in office, like Stalin, right until his death. A team of doctors were in everyday attendance and apparently literally brought him back from the dead on more than one occasion.

Brezhnev's slogan was 'stability of cadres', which meant that few officials were transferred to new posts. Party officials and bureaucrats at all levels therefore tended to remain in place for many years. The whole political system became a cosy world of comrades supporting one another. He surrounded himself in government with friends and past colleagues, and was careful to build up relationships with regional bosses. By avoiding difficult decisions and 'not rocking the boat' he won the support of a majority of the leading figures in the party, which numbered 16 million in 1977. This elite or *nomenklatura* was to some extent self-perpetuating, since they were able to use their influence to advance their families into the best schools and universities and jobs afterwards.

Facts and figures

Under Brezhnev the Central Committee of the Communist Party met only two or three times a year. Power therefore rested with the Party Secretariat.

Note

Despite this cushioned existence, relations between Politburo members, ministers and party secretaries were far from close. They tended to regard each other with suspicion, as potential rivals.

Free discussion was certainly not on the agenda. In 1966 the famous trial of Daniel and Siniavsky, writers who had criticized Stalin's regime, took place. Despite a demonstration in Moscow by students (broken up by the police) they were condemned to long terms of imprisonment. After the trial it became an offence to take part in propaganda 'designed to weaken or subvert Soviet power'. Unofficial publishing, *samizdat*, did not cease; rather it increased, despite the attentions of the security services, arrests and longer prison terms. Some critics were sent to State mental hospitals, because self-evidently they must be mad to attack the 'developed socialism' of the USSR. The whole population was subject to surveillance by the secret police, which was able to make use of modern technology to do this more effectively than ever before. Prison camps contained perhaps a million inmates under Brezhnev.

The campaign for free speech and civil rights had some success, forcing itself into the western press. Under the Helsinki Agreement the USSR agreed to guarantee civil rights, and in 1975 Andrei Sakharov, a leading scientist, was granted the Nobel Peace Prize for his dogged fight against the abuse of the courts by the government. The Brezhnev constitution of 1977 gave the appearance at least of confirming the civil rights of the people and the federal structure of the USSR.

Why wasn't the economy working?

The problems of the Soviet economy were not new and you will have come across them in this book before, even in pre-Soviet times. The economic structure of the country was a mirror of the political structure. There was poor co-ordination between government departments, who jealously tried to protect their own areas of influence. Decisions were made at the top and transmitted down – a command economy. Unfortunately they were decisions that reflected the priorities of the regime and not the needs of ordinary people. Indeed there were no mechanisms by which the wishes of the people could be ascertained. Gosplan assumed what was needed and then planned to produce it. In politics 'democratic centralism' kept the lower ranking party members in line. The primary function of trade unions, almost from the outset, had been, as tools of management, to persuade workers to greater production for the common good.

Poor decisions were the result. The decision-makers were not only out of touch with people; they were also out of touch with the reality of the economy they were supposed to run. The information they had was either inaccurate or incomplete. From Stalin's day onwards, the statistical reports they received were often incorrect and at the worst flights of fancy. There are thousands of examples of this, but one of the most alarming was the discovery made from satellites that whole areas of Uzbekistan, supposedly growing cotton, were in fact uncultivated. The party bureaucracy had siphoned off the funds. Attempts made by stricter supervision and by calling on cadres to expose offenders proved ineffective in holding office-holders to account.

The command economy made sacred cows of the government plans. They had to be achieved come what may. This had a numbing effect on managers at all levels, who would then go to any lengths to achieve their plan. If 3000 tractors were demanded, then 3000 tractors had to be delivered, even if they lacked vital parts, or even if there were no spare parts anywhere to service them when they broke down. It was estimated that despite the huge investment in tractors and other agricultural machinery under Brezhnev that the number of tractors working in the USSR did not increase. As soon as they broke down for whatever reason they were simply abandoned or cannibalized for spare parts.

Facts and figures

In 1964 the poet Joseph Brodsky was put on trial for 'parasitism' – being without a job. He was sent to a mental hospital, where he was given ice-cold baths and then wrapped in a sheet by a radiator. This sheet, as it dried, ripped off his skin.

Cross reference

Chapter 9 deals with Stalin's attempts to transform the Soviet economy.

■ **Think about**

▶ How was corruption on this scale possible?

Quality control did not exist in the USSR. Nor was there any competition from other producers, since foreign goods were virtually unobtainable. Of course, introducing the mechanisms of profit and competition was unthinkable to a communist.

This obsession with completing the plan at all costs also left a terrible legacy for later generations in damage to the environment. Nuclear installations lacking western standards of safety resulted in 1986 in the Chernobyl disaster. Robbing rivers for irrigation schemes to feed cotton fields resulted in the Aral Sea shrinking and becoming officially dead, ruining fishing communities and producing poisonous dust storms covering hundreds of miles.

Source 7

▶ The former fishing harbour of Muynak on the Aral Sea.
The Aral Sea itself is now 95 km from this spot.

■ Research

1 How could the CPSU (Communist Party of the Soviet Union) justify causing such an environmental catastrophe?

2 What other environmental damage was done inside the Soviet Union?

The huge planning apparatus meant that the economy was very inflexible, and could not adapt to new thinking, problems or new technology quickly. The plans were drawn up in advance of their implementation, so change of any kind could take many years. When joint ventures were discussed with representatives from foreign companies, they invariably became exasperated by the inability of anyone to give firm answers to any questions. Although there were efforts to make management more responsive and more responsible by both Khrushchev and Brezhnev, they all failed. The entire mammoth bureaucracy which ran the economy had a built-in interest in maintaining the status quo which would guarantee their comfortable posts and the opportunities they offered. Brezhnev himself acknowledged the problem in his statement that managers feared change 'like the Devil fears incense'!

Source 8

The Central Committee opposes hurried ill-thought-out reorganizations of the managerial structure and of established ways of running the economy.

From Brezhnev's statement to the 25th Party Congress, 1976

Small-scale industry was virtually non-existent in the USSR, but in the West it was this sector which was both the most innovative and most economically buoyant, while the old staple industries were in decline.

There was as a result a crying need to produce better goods and services which people actually wanted. As Gorbachev later famously said:

Source 9

We can send a rocket to Venus, but our fridges don't work.

More work and better value was needed from the ordinary Russian worker and farmer. An obvious lesson could have been learned from the output of the private plots compared to the collective fields, but it was a lesson that the party was unable to contemplate. Workers had little incentive to work harder or produce better goods. Indeed absenteeism was a chronic problem and often alcohol-related. When Andropov, Brezhnev's successor, used the party faithful to identify and seek out those who missed work, the results were alarming. Two generals were found to be using a bathhouse rather than being at their desks. There was a kind of conspiracy involving the whole population, which had become used to the corrupt system. Although short of luxuries and some essentials, workers were under little pressure at work, and accepted a culture of pilfering and skiving which made their lives acceptable. Source 10 is taken from a Russian magazine of the 1970s.

Source 10

'Six Soviet Paradoxes'

1. There's no unemployment, but no one works. 2. No one works, but productivity goes up. 3. Productivity goes up, but there is nothing in the stores. 4. There's nothing in the stores, but at home there is everything. 5. At home there's everything, but no one is satisfied. 6. No one is satisfied, but everybody votes yes.

A shorter version, common in Eastern Europe, was: 'We pretend to work and they pretend to pay us'.

■ Facts and figures

Days lost through absenteeism are estimated at about 10%.

■ A Soviet joke

Three men left work early to visit the barber's, but they found no barbers in the shop. One barber had gone to buy oranges, another to get an appliance repaired and the third to visit the dentist. The barbers returned disappointed, complaining of the poor service. In their chairs they found the grocer, the repairman, and the dentist.

■ Think about

▶ What did these paradoxes mean?

▶ Do you think they were all accurate?

■ Activity

Write down a list of all the different factors which made for stagnation in Brezhnev's USSR. Place them under four headings and see if you can suggest some ways in which these problems might be addressed by Brezhnev's successors.

	Factors	Possible solutions
Problems in the political system		
Problems in the economic system		
Problems caused by past behaviour		
Ideological obstacles		

■ Biography

Mikhail Gorbachev

1931 Born into a peasant family in the Caucasus
1949 Awarded Order of the Red Labour Banner, as a Komsomol leader
1949 Joined CPSU
1950 Law student in Moscow
1953 Married Raisa
1955 Became Komsomol official in Stavropol, his home district
1960 First Komsomol Secretary in Stavropol
1966 First Secretary of Stavropol City Communist Party
1970 First Secretary for the Stavropol region
1971 Member of Central Committee of the CPSU
1978 Head of the Central Committee's Agricultural Section
1980 Full member of the Politburo

▶ What does this outline suggest about Gorbachev?

Source 11

▶ Mikhail and Raisa Gorbachev at Windsor Castle with the Queen during a state visit to Britain.

■ Think about

▶ Which wives of other Communist leaders enjoyed such prominence?

▶ How did the image of the Gorbachevs differ from those of previous Soviet leaders?

Quotation

The whole of life and the entire course of history confirm convincingly the great truth of Leninist teaching. It has been and remains for us a guide to action, a source of inspiration, a true compass for fixing the strategy and tactics of our movement forward.

Gorbachev's Report to the Central Committee, April 1985

The rise of Mikhail Gorbachev

Brezhnev, who died in November 1982, was succeeded as General Secretary of the Party by the 68-year-old KGB head, Andropov (The secret police were reorganized as the KGB after Beria's arrest). He was already a sick man, suffering from kidney failure and needing regular dialysis. Andropov believed that the key to revitalizing the USSR economy was the reintroduction of strict discipline in the work place at all levels. Accordingly checks at work were made to eradicate absenteeism and drunks on the streets faced arrest. Ironically he also introduced a new cheap vodka, promptly nicknamed 'Andropovka'. He began to promote younger and more independent-minded people to posts within the economy and the government. He also used the KGB to root out time-serving and corrupt ministers and party officials. Before much could be achieved, however, he died in 1984.

Chernenko succeeded him as party leader, already 73 years old. He too was a sick man, suffering from emphysema. He was so ill he was unable to deliver the oration at Andropov's funeral. Just over a year later he died. Mikhail Gorbachev, who had been acting First Secretary during Chernenko's illness and had chaired Politburo meetings, was unanimously chosen as General Secretary.

He was 54 years old, and must have appeared as a breath of fresh air for this reason alone after the leaders of the last 20 years. Unlike any of the other previous leaders, except Khrushchev, he was at ease with ordinary people. He was the first leader to appear live on television and toured the country, visiting collective farms and factories. By his side at all times, again unlike any other earlier leaders, was his wife Raisa. She was a striking companion with an eye for her own and her husband's public image.

Despite his affable appearance he was a determined and ruthless politician. However, as all his predecessors since Stalin had done, he needed first to strengthen his political position. In less than 12 months he had transformed the Politburo, advancing new members like Ryzhkov who became a Politburo member in April and Prime Minister in September 1985. Of the 101 government ministers, 39 were sacked and many leading figures in the *nomenklatura* were replaced. His personnel changes were quicker and more wide-ranging even than Stalin's.

How did Gorbachev propose to reform the USSR?

Perestroika and glasnost

The economy that Gorbachev inherited was in decline. Between 1980 and 1985 there was a negative growth rate for the first time under communism in peacetime. The Five Year Plan of 1986–1990 set a target of 25 per cent growth in industrial production and a substantial rise in living standards. The focus was to be in improving industrial productivity by copying the West in automated, advanced production methods. Investment in machine tools was raised. The party knew there was over-manning in many enterprises, and at the same time shortages of labour in others.

Gorbachev believed in the Soviet system, but he believed that the economy needed whole-scale restructuring (*perestroika*). It was necessary to liberate enterprises from the dead hand of central planning and control. They should be free to negotiate with suppliers and customers for goods and services, and have greater control of their own budgets. Employees should also be encouraged to have a more active role in the management of their places of work. The party leadership thought that the workers would respond to these new opportunities by throwing themselves into reorganization and greater production.

> **Note**
>
> Gorbachev first used the terms *perestroika* and *glasnost* in 1984.

The explosion in 1986 at the Chernobyl nuclear power station in the Ukraine had a dramatic impact on Gorbachev's government. News of this, despite the health hazards to the population, was withheld and there was a steady flow of misinformation. It convinced Gorbachev that reform had to be radical and that the secret circles of the party and the government needed opening up to criticism – *glasnost.* 'We need *glasnost* like we need air', Gorbachev said. The heavy hand of censorship was lightened, and magazines and newspapers became more outspoken. The USSR entered into a period of freer discussion and debate than at any time since the summer of 1917. Gorbachev himself talked openly of returning to the real Lenin, lost, he believed, since the late 1920s. Novels denouncing the Stalinist period appeared, most famous of which was *Children of the Arbat*, by A. Rybakov.

> **Source 12**
>
> 'I [Stalin] happened to be going through the Arbat and I noticed young idlers in Western raincoats, laughing. I ask myself: What is more important to them, their Soviet motherland or their Western raincoats?'
>
> 'It is possible to wear a Western raincoat *and* love the Soviet motherland,' said Budyagin.
>
> 'You think so?' Stalin turned and looked at him. 'That's not what *I* think. *My* children don't wear Western raincoats; *my* children are happy with Soviet ones. *My* children couldn't get hold of Western raincoats. I ask myself, where *do* these people get hold of them?'
>
> Rybakov, *Children of the Arbat*, 1988

> ■ **Think about**
>
> ▶ What is Stalin suggesting in the last sentence of this extract?
>
> ▶ What image does this extract give of Stalin?

To show this was a meaningful change, Gorbachev personally telephoned the well-known dissident Andrei Sakharov to invite him back to the capital from internal exile. Jamming BBC broadcasts was ended in 1987.

For historians glasnost was the opening of a new era, allowing archives to be examined for the first time. Gorbachev declared that 'there must be no forgotten names or blank spots'. Enemies of the people were rehabilitated, like Bukharin. Some of the worst crimes committed by Stalin's NKVD were exposed, such as the massacre of Polish officers at Katyn. Though religion was criticized by Gorbachev personally, restrictions on religious groups were lifted. Gorbachev hoped by this policy that the resistance of party officials and government bureaucrats would be swept away. He did not foresee that criticism and open debate might eventually lead to demands for the end to the Soviet system and the Soviet Union itself.

Stepping into the unknown

Economic *perestroika*

To solve the economic problems of the USSR Gorbachev seemed at first, like his predecessors, to put his trust in creating new administrative structures. The Politburo approved a giant new ministry to organize agriculture and food processing. But in the first months of 1987 industrial production began to decline. Radical economic change seemed necessary and it was the subject of much argument in the government and party.

A series of decisions undermined the monolithic economic structures of the USSR. The Decree on State Enterprises passed by the Central Committee agreed that all managers in industries should be elected. At the same time managers were given much more freedom in management decisions to negotiate contracts and set their own wages. Party committees which shadowed the work of ministries were to be merged. Freedom of the press and freedom of speech were guaranteed.

Most party officials and managers did not welcome these decisions. M. McCauley in his biography *Gorbachev* (1998) recalls a joke circulating in Minsk in 1986:

> ### Source 13
>
> Gorbachev, Reagan (US President) and Mitterand (French President) meet and start discussing their problems. Mitterand says he has nine mistresses and one is cheating him. He can't work out which one. Reagan says that this is a minor problem compared to his. He has 50 bodyguards and one is a KGB agent but he can't discover who he is. Gorbachev waves all this aside and complains that his problem is much more serious. He has 100 ministers in his government and one of them is implementing *perestroika* but he doesn't know which one.

Gorbachev had promised the people that they would enjoy higher living standards, but in 1987 industrial production fell by 6 per cent. The defence budget continued to absorb 40 per cent of government spending. There was a worrying government deficit, rising from 37 billion to 57 billion roubles. (Gorbachev had contributed to this himself by stepping up Andropov's campaign against alcohol and destroying grapes in the south. This cut off one of the government's most important and reliable sources of revenue.)

■ **Think about**

▶ In what ways does this remind you of the policies of the 1930s?

■ **Think about**

▶ What is the point it makes about the Soviet government?

▶ How reliable is Source 13 for a historian?

▶ Why might ministers have reacted in this way?

Source 14

◀ A Russian woman drags her drunken disabled husband home on a trolley in 1994.

■ Think about

▶ Why do you think Gorbachev was so keen to eradicate drunkenness in the USSR?

▶ Does this photograph prove he was unsuccessful?

▶ Why do you think this problem was so difficult to deal with?

The drop in world oil and gas prices also cut revenues – oil and gas accounted for 54 per cent of the USSR's exports. To ease the road to *perestroika* the government had declared its willingness to cushion any who lost by the process and increased State benefits. All of the above led to rising inflation, almost 10 per cent by 1989. The government continued, however, to subsidize many prices. Some of those who seized the opportunities to produce privately found that the local party seized their goods and on one occasion smashed greenhouses. The prejudices against private profit were too deeply entrenched to be quickly overthrown. Boris Yeltsin, who had been promoted by Gorbachev, resigned in protest at the inadequacy of the *perestroika* reforms.

In 1989 the economic situation had deteriorated so much that a government commission was set up to recommend a way forward. The proposals amounted to a move to a full market economy, which would involve the withdrawal of the State from the management of the economy. It recommended privatization of companies, the opening of a stock exchange, the leasing of land to farmers and removing price controls. Some ministers could not accept these radical plans, and Prime Minister Ryzhkov put forward a slower more gradual programme. There was more delay while a second commission presented another report.

This new set of reforms was presented to the Supreme Soviet in 1990. It included a recommendation for a 50 per cent increase in most prices. This led to a run on the shops by those who had savings. The Supreme Soviet put off the price rises, which meant a continuation of high subsidies from the State. The government's 1989 plan to deal with the mounting government deficit by cutting welfare benefits and social spending was also rejected. No alternative plan was suggested to deal with the problem.

The Yavlinsky Report urged a crash programme in 400 days in February 1990. Although accepted by Gorbachev, his ministers rejected it. Meanwhile the queues lengthened, and the relatively few independent co-operatives, which had been legalized in 1988, were seen as extorting profits from the public. There was also a wave of strikes, now legal, across the country. A national coalminers' strike was only called off in 1989 when the Prime Minister agreed to a set of demands including an immediate rise in wages. In 1989 7.3 million working days were lost – this went up by 250 per cent in 1990 as workers struggled to maintain their living standards against inflation.

▶ Shopping for food in a nearly empty shop in Moscow in 1990.

Political *perestroika* – 'democratization'

Gorbachev realized that party officials were one of the main obstacles in the achievement of the government's economic goals. Economic and political reforms were thus mutually dependent. Even moderate reform caused bitter debate, let alone the radical ideas of the Yavlinsky Report. *Glasnost*, moreover, had led to free criticism of the privileges enjoyed by the party *nomenklatura*. Because of this Gorbachev began to remove some of their perks. 400,000 lost their Volga cars and chauffeurs. Special shops for party officials were ended.

The conservative wing reacted while Gorbachev was away from Moscow in March 1988 by publishing a letter from a lecturer, Andreeva, criticizing the Gorbachev reforms and praising Stalin's government. It was entitled 'I cannot forgo my principles'. For a short time the future of reform seemed in the balance, and with it Gorbachev's own political position.

The reformers' reply was to call an extraordinary conference of the Communist Party to 'democratize further the life of the party and society'. This conference approved many groundbreaking decisions, including free elections in the party, secret ballots, and an independent judiciary. The Supreme Soviet approved alterations to the constitution. Gorbachev's aim in all this was not to undermine the Communist Party but to strengthen it by making officials and representatives more accountable for their actions. For the first time there were real elections where more than one candidate was put forward by approved organizations for election. In March 1989 elections were held throughout the USSR for the Congress of People's Deputies. The Congress was made up as follows:

```
┌─────────────────────┐
│   Supreme Soviet    │
│    2250 members     │
└─────────────────────┘
```

Made up of:

```
┌──────────────┐  ┌────────────────────────────┐  ┌──────────────┐
│  750 from    │  │  750 from 'Social          │  │  750 from    │
│  Russian     │  │  organizations'            │  │  'national   │
│constituencies│  │  E.g. Academy of Sciences, │  │constituencies'│
│              │  │  trade unions, CPSU        │  │              │
└──────────────┘  └────────────────────────────┘  └──────────────┘
```

Boris Yeltsin was disgraced in 1987 and sacked as party boss of Moscow. He was accused of 'political adventurism' for criticizing the insincerity of many leaders in their attitude to reform, but he still topped the Moscow poll with almost 90 per cent of the vote. In Leningrad the Communist leader was defeated even though he was the only candidate! To be elected it was necessary to win over 50 per cent of the vote cast, and the majority either spoilt their papers or rejected the candidate.

This Congress elected a Supreme Soviet, which sat for two lengthy sessions each year. It was intended to act as a check and scrutinizer of the government, rather than the rubber stamp it had been under earlier Communist governments. Boris Yeltsin succeeded in being elected to the Supreme Soviet when another who had polled more votes withdrew. Gorbachev was elected unopposed as the Chairman of the Supreme Soviet. The proceedings of the Congress were televised, so the public was able to see criticism and questioning of their leaders for the first time. Sakharov called for multi-party elections, the poet Yevtushenko called for the release of all dissidents. It was even suggested that Lenin's body be removed from the Mausoleum, still not accomplished at the time of writing.

The Supreme Soviet proved no less independent. Many of the proposed ministers were rejected. Although almost all elected called themselves communists, they began to arrange themselves into groups. The Inter-Regional Group was formed to press for an 'acceleration of *perestroika*'. The Soyuz (Union) Group wanted to call a halt to further reform – at least for the moment.

The changed political atmosphere resulted in the creation of the first new political groups since the Revolution. The Democratic Union, set up in May 1988, was the first of these. Its leader was arrested 17 times by the police, though she was released on each occasion when she went on hunger strike.

In February 1990 Gorbachev moved further still to satisfy his radical critics by telling the Communist Party Central Committee that they would now need to earn their claim to have the leading role in the USSR. The article of the Soviet constitution that prohibited all parties except the CPSU was repealed in March. At the same time the Congress of Deputies elected him the President of the USSR with sweeping powers to dismiss ministers, issue decrees and also with command of the armed forces.

■ Biography

Boris Yeltsin

1931 Born in Sverdlovsk province
Lost 2 fingers playing with a hand
grenade as a child
Trained as a civil engineer
1976 First Secretary of Sverdlovsk
CPSU
1981 Member of the Central
Committee
1985–7 First Secretary of the
Moscow Party. Began attack on
privileges for party leaders
1986 Candidate member of the
Politburo
1987 Resigned from Politburo
Removed as Moscow Party leader

Perestroika – the nationalities

Perestroika, glasnost and democratization all implied more self-government for the nationalities of the USSR. Gorbachev seems to have failed to understand the national feelings that had lain semi-concealed in many of the nominally self-governing republics. Brezhnev's constitution in 1977 had given these republics the right to secede if they wished.

The first major signs of national tensions were seen in Kazakhstan in 1986. The First Secretary of Kazakhstan, effectively the Prime Minister, was sacked and replaced by a Russian national, which resulted in demonstrations in the capital Alma Ata. The armed forces opened fire killing some of the demonstrators. In the same year came demands from Volga Germans and Crimean Tartars, transported from their home territories during the war by Stalin, to be returned back to their lands. However, Ukrainians and Russians had now taken their lands. A compromise allowed them to return but without their lands or self-government.

The most serious threat to the integrity of the USSR came from the Baltic republics. In 1988 the Estonian government announced its right to veto union legislation. It also declared ownership of all USSR property in Estonia. Lithuania and Latvia followed Estonia's example. Popular fronts were formed of all those, including communists, who wished to see genuine independence. In March 1990 Lithuania finally declared itself independent. Gorbachev placed a trade embargo on Lithuania, cutting off her oil and gas supplies. The declaration of independence was suspended after negotiations, but it began a series of declarations of independence by almost all the republics. The problem was complicated by the presence, in many of the 'fringe' republics, of very large Russian minorities, who did not want to sever links with Moscow, Some of these were in the armed forces, since there were military bases scattered around the borders of the USSR. Politics was therefore often confrontational, the Russians being encouraged to protest by Moscow.

In 1991 Gorbachev sent Russian troops into the Baltic republics and Russian nationalists took to the streets to demand the resignation of the government in Lithuania. Patriotic Lithuanians drove them out of the parliament building in Vilnius. On 10 January Gorbachev used the crisis to demand that Lithuania return to their allegiance to the USSR. On 11 and 12 January Russian troops attacked some government buildings and the television tower, killing 13. The troops, however, did not attack the parliament building where thousands of Lithuanians had gathered to protect their leaders and independence.

A delegation from the Russian Federation, headed by Yeltsin, arrived in Tallinn, the Estonian capital, to broker a settlement. He called on all Russian forces in the Baltic republics to recognize the republican governments. Russia herself recognized the three republics' independence. No further military action was taken against any of the secessionist republics by the government of the USSR, though Ministry of the Interior troops did attack a Latvian government building without instruction.

National feeling produced a crisis in Nagorno-Karabakh, an autonomous region of Azerbaijan, but Armenian by nationality. Here there was inter-communal fighting as Azeris attacked Armenians. There were similar problems in Georgia. Soviet troops used sharpened spades and poison gas to control demonstrations in Tblisi, resulting in 1990 in the election of an anti-communist government in Georgia. Within the Russian Federation itself autonomous areas demanded independence, including Tatarstan and Chechnya.

The USSR was breaking up, but the Russian Federation, the largest republic, administered the kiss of death. Elections in 1990 to the Russian Federation Congress of People's Deputies produced a large following, but not a majority, for the new Democratic Russia Party. Yeltsin won the important election for Chairman of the Russian Supreme Soviet, making him effectively head of the Russian Federation government. Like the other states it declared itself sovereign, making its own ministers and laws superior to those of the Union government.

Perestroika – foreign affairs

Gorbachev's rise to power in the USSR had huge implications for her satellite states in Eastern Europe. Brezhnev had used Soviet troops to maintain hard-line Communist regimes. In 1968 he had destroyed Dubcek's attempt to build socialism with a human face in Czechoslovakia and had installed a military regime in Poland. He had also sent troops in 1979 into Afghanistan where they were trapped in a war against guerrillas which was seen to be unwinnable, and casualties were high.

Gorbachev removed these troops, which brought him great popularity in the short term both in the USSR and in the West. He also made it clear that Soviet troops would no longer be used to bolster unpopular Communist regimes in the satellite states. In Poland there was a non-communist Solidarity government. In 1989 alone Hungary became a multi-party democracy, the Romanian dictator was overthrown by a popular rising and the Berlin Wall came down, paving the way for German reunification. Communism was soon a distant memory in Eastern Europe.

As far as the West was concerned, Gorbachev continued the work of *détente* begun by Brezhnev. This resulted in arms limitation treaties and a final end to the Cold War.

The end of the USSR

The declarations of sovereignty alone did not bring the USSR to a close. The first constitution under Lenin had accepted that the republics were autonomous. Much would depend on the attitude of the leaders of the Russian Federation and the Ukraine as the largest of the republics. What powers would the government of Russia be willing to cede to a newly constituted federal union government? The poor relationship between Gorbachev and Yeltsin in the recent past did not augur well for an agreement.

Gorbachev's actions in the Baltic States to keep the USSR together cost him much support. The reforming President of the USSR now began to look more like a traditional hard-liner. He had already retreated on economic policy, backing a policy which supported central controls of prices, against those who wanted to bring the command economy to an end in 500 days. Yeltsin's Russian Federation decided to back the 500 day plan. Ironically it was Gorbachev who seemed to have deserted *perestroika*.

When it came to the USSR budget, Gorbachev was quickly in difficulties. In the first three months of 1991 Union government spending was 250 per cent more than revenue, because the republics did not pass on their contributions. Gorbachev appeared powerless to do anything about it. The economy was in crisis. Industrial output fell by 18 per cent in 1991, and agriculture by 17 per cent. Gorbachev's government announced large increases in prices. His attempts to gain financial support from the West went largely unheeded.

Timeline

1990 Independence declarations

March	Lithuania, Estonia
May	Latvia
	Azerbaijan
June	Russian Federation
	Uzbekistan, Moldova
July	Belarus, Ukraine,
	Armenia, Turkmenistan
	Tajikistan
October	Kazakhstan
	Kyrgyzstan

Nonetheless, in April 1991 Gorbachev began talks with the leaders of the republics to agree another constitution for the USSR. Leaders of only 9 of the 15 republics attended. Gorbachev called the talks '1+9'; Yeltsin called them significantly '9+1'. On 2 August 1991 Gorbachev announced that a new Union Treaty was ready to be signed. There were no dissenting noises from Yeltsin, who had just won a resounding victory in being elected the first President of the Russian Federation in June.

The 1991 *Coup*

In July the newspaper *Sovetskaya Rossiya* carried this declaration signed by 12 well-known figures, including the commander of the Soviet Army and a member of the Politburo:

Think about

Did the authors of this declaration have any good reason to be fearful?

> **Source 16**
>
> An enormous, unprecedented misfortune has occurred. The Motherland, our country, the great state entrusted to us by history, by nature and by our glorious forebears is perishing, is being broken up, is being plunged into darkness and oblivion.

For some of his colleagues the current predicament of the USSR was entirely the result of Gorbachev's changes and the speed at which they had been introduced. His failure, despite all his many trips abroad, to attract major financial support overseas, also counted against him. Despite being given warnings by the US government, amongst others, Gorbachev went south in August for a vacation on the Black Sea coast. The Union Treaty was due to be signed on 20 August.

Two days before this, however, Gorbachev was put under house arrest and asked to sanction the declaration of a state of emergency. When he refused, he was declared too ill to continue as head of state, and a State Committee for the Emergency was set up, including the Vice-President and Prime Minister. In the past perhaps this would have passed off quietly, but the political atmosphere had changed. The military commander of the Moscow district, General Gravchev, opposed the *coup*, as did President Yeltsin and the Russian government. Yeltsin went straight to the White House, the home of the Russian Supreme Soviet (parliament). From here he called on the plotters to resign and the people of the city to take to the streets to protect democracy. His most famous act was to speak to those who gathered on one of the tanks sent to surround the building.

Source 17

▶ Boris Yeltsin addresses the crowd from a tank outside the Russian parliament building during the attempted coup in 1991.

Think about

▶ Why was this an act of great personal courage?

▶ What does it tell us about Yeltsin's political instincts?

This was quickly surrounded by Soviet troops, and a plan was drawn up by the State Committee to seize it by force. Tanks poured into the capital. Civilians tried heroically to stop them and persuade them to leave. Three were killed in the process. Thousands of Muscovites gathered round the White House to act as a human shield to deter an attack. The great cellist Rostropovitch entertained them with his playing. Would the resolve of the Soviet forces be strong enough to open fire on their fellow countrymen?

The matter was not put to the test. On 21 August some of the conspirators flew out to Gorbachev to explain their case, but he rejected them. They were arrested and Gorbachev flew back to Moscow.

What authority Gorbachev once had was now gone. It was his own ministers and members of his own party, the CPSU, who had tried to overthrow him and end the independence of the republics. None of them were now prepared to sign a Union Treaty which left strong powers in a Union government. Yeltsin banned the CPSU in Russia and in November 1991 the Ukraine refused to sign an economic treaty with the other republics. In December the Ukrainian people voted for independence in a referendum. The rest of the world had already recognized the Baltic States as independent.

On 21 December 11 republics following the lead of Russia, Belarus and the Ukraine agreed to a new Commonwealth of Independent States with its headquarters in Minsk, Belarus. There would be no President, but there would be a common economic zone and some shared military command. Gorbachev spoke on television as President of the USSR for the last time on 25 December:

Source 18

I leave my post in trepidation. But also with hope, with faith in you, in your wisdom and force of spirit. We are the inheritors of a great civilization, and now the burden falls on each and every one that it may be resurrected to a new, modern and worthy life.

On 1 January 1992 the USSR ceased to exist. After almost 75 years the Communist experiment was over. What was its legacy for the peoples of the former Russian Empire? Gorbachev himself recognized the difficulties in his retirement speech:

Source 19

Society now has liberty, it has been emancipated politically and spiritually. And that is the main achievement that we have not fully comprehended, because we have not learned how to use that liberty.

Source 20

▲ The former Soviet Union as it is today.

1 KRASNODAR KRAI
2 ADYGEYA
3 STAVROPOL KRAI
4 ABKHAZIA
5 KARACHAEVO CHERKESSIA
6 Adzharia
7 GEORGIA
8 KABARDINO-BALKARIA
9 NORTH OSSETIA
10 SOUTH OSSETIA
11 INGUSHETIA
12 CHECHNYA
13 DAGESTAN
14 Nagorno-Karabakh A.O.
15 AZERBAIJAN

Document exercise: the achievements of the USSR

Source A

The Soviet Union, then, is on the whole a difficult land in which to live…Undoubtedly one of the advantages which a belief in the principles of Marxism-Leninism, the official creed of the USSR, has brought to its people, or at least its government, is an inherent optimism, a faith that man and his technology can win through despite the enormous problems with which nature confronts them.

Davies (ed.) *The Soviet Union*, 1978

Source B

Per capita consumption by the rural population per annum

	Vodka & alcohol (pints)	Grain (cwt)	Fruit and vegetables (cwt)	Meat and animal products (cwt)	Milk and milk products (cwt)
Early 20th century	5.6	5.04	1.19	0.44	2.20
1940	8.3•	3.98	0.91	0.31	2.80
1968	14.72•	3.39	1.28	0.73	5.28

• urban and rural figures included (1 cwt = about 50 kilos)

Source C

They have to give up [working] entirely at 58 below because machinery breaks down and steel rods snap like twigs in the extreme cold.

What staggered me was that in spite of these conditions, Yakutsk had grown to nearly 120,000 people and included a university, several scientific institutes, a television relay station, a full-scale port on the Lena River...and several dozen small industrial enterprises. Indoor plumbing was a rare luxury...Their water came in the form of huge chunks of ice, sawed mechanically from the frozen surface of the Lena River.

The Russians, written in 1975 by H. Smith, an American newspaper correspondent in Moscow after three years working in the USSR.

Source D

◀ The monument in Moscow to the Soviet space conquerors.

Source E

But many, including Communists, who study its [Soviet Russia's] evolution, especially the key period which began in 1928, might well feel that somewhere in those years there was a wrong turning. And that no one should follow the trail blazed by Stalin, with its terrible sacrifices...It is said that one cannot make omelettes without breaking eggs. In that case, perhaps one should not make omelettes, if the menu happens to provide other choices. Perhaps it is Russia's tragedy that these choices were absent, and a measure of her achievement that, despite all that happened, so much has been built, and not a few cultural values preserved and handed on to a vastly more literate population.

Nove, *An Economic History of the USSR*, 1976

■ **Activity**   **KEY SKILLS**

Question 4 could be planned easily to meet the requirements for the key skills of Communication and Information Technology. You should use visual materials, maps, timelines and pictures to illustrate your points, from more than one electronic source, and create a new way of presenting statistical information in your report. It could also be planned as a group activity if you divide up the topic into sections, such as the situation in Russia at the outbreak of the First World War, Russia in October 1917, Russia under Lenin, the Stalin years, etc.

■ **Examination-style questions**

1 Comprehension in context
What can be deduced from Source B about the quality of Russians' lives in the 20th century?

2 Comparing the sources
Do Sources B, C and D suggest that Russians have overcome 'the enormous problems with which nature presents them'?

3 Assessing the sources
With reference to the source's origins, tone and content, do you think H. Smith is a reliable source for the student of Russian history?

4 Making judgements
Using the sources and your own knowledge, would you agree with Nove in Source E that 'despite all that happened, so much was built' during the Communist period?

Conclusion

The collapse of the USSR had been predicted by some commentators long before it happened. Keeping the Russian Empire intact had been one of the main concerns of the Tsars before the First World War, and the Empire's fragility had been shown in the independence movements during the Civil War. Communists were of course internationalists, who thought nationalism was a tool by which capitalists were able to exploit the working class and the peasantry. It was also used to justify wars of conquest for control of overseas resources and markets. Marxism recognized no international frontiers. Perhaps, therefore, it was understandable that Gorbachev and his supporters would miscalculate the effects of *glasnost* and *perestroika*. They certainly reaped the whirlwind as a result.

Gorbachev remained right up to his fall from power a convinced Leninist. When the Communist Party's monopoly of power was broken, he must have been genuinely astonished at the minority of support the party attracted. There was still, however, a chance that a strong USSR would survive the chaotic economic and political situation of 1990–1991; a new Union Treaty was ready to be signed in August 1991. But this chance was dashed by the 1991 *coup*. This totally discredited the CPSU and persuaded many in the republics that a strong centralized Union would only cause problems in the future. Instead the USSR was replaced by a loose association of independent states, who were none the less economically interdependent. The concentration under communist rule of production in enterprises scattered all over the former USSR proved to be the most powerful force which pulled the republics together.

The creation of the CIS, however, left some questions unanswered. Within the giant Russian Federation were many different national groups, such as the Chechens, whose demands for nationhood were not recognized. Will the Russian Federation itself suffer a disintegration similar to that of the USSR?

Further reading

M. S. Gorbachev *Perestroika*, 1987
M. McCauley *The Soviet Union under Gorbachev*, 1987

Chapter 16

Continuity and change

Source 1

Source 2

The longer I lived in Soviet Russia, the more Russian it seemed to me and the less likely to undergo fundamental change…Gradually, it came through to me that Russians – unlike Westerners – do not take it for granted that Russian dictatorship must inevitably evolve into democracy, for they know its power and its permanence.

Smith, *The Russians*, 1976

◀ A Russian woman collects donations in 1991 to help pay for the rebuilding of the Cathedral of Christ the Saviour, which was blown up by Stalin (see page 206). The new building was fitted with electric lifts.

Introduction

There can be little doubt that the development of the USSR owed much to the traditions inherited from Tsarist Russia. Historians and contemporaries have compared the Soviet leaders with Tsars of the past. Stalin consciously encouraged this by supporting the making of films such as *Ivan the Terrible*. Ivan could be portrayed as a Russian hero who had extended Moscow's authority into Kazan and Astrakhan, opening up the penetration of Siberia, though he had also brutally dealt with what he regarded as treachery from the leading landowners, the boyars. Stalin personally accosted Eisenstein for *Ivan the Terrible*, because he presented the brutal secret police of the time in an unfavourable light, whereas Stalin thought of them as a 'progressive army'. Stalin went on to say:

Source 3

Ivan the terrible was very ruthless. One can show that he was ruthless. But you must show why it was necessary to be ruthless.

In 1855 we read of a Russia economically unable and perhaps unwilling to compete with the leading states in Western Europe and the United States. The economic situation seems to have been very similar in 1991. Did the 1917 Russian Revolution mark any real change in the nature of government and society? Has it been a simple case of 'Plus ça change, plus la meme chose'?

In this chapter we will look at three themes through 140 years

Key themes

- Politics and government
- The economy and society
- The impact of war on change in Russia

Politics and government

Source 4

Russians [have] gloried in the very thing foreigners criticized them for – blind and boundless obedience to the will of the monarch, even when in his most insane flights he trampled underfoot all the laws of justice and humanity.

Karamzin, a nineteenth-century historian

Although written during the nineteenth century this might easily have been an observation of an outsider visiting the USSR in Stalin's time or in the 1970s, as in Source 2. You might like to look again at Stalin's image in the press and the public reaction to his death. There does seem to be a very strong case for arguing that monarchical or autocratic government has been a constant feature of Russia over the period of this book. Here we examine a number of personalities who might be called autocratic, although they represent in the main two very different ideological systems.

How similar was Tsarist and Communist government?

This is a difficult and complex question. You should begin by comparing various features of the two regimes. The following grid should give you some key ideas to examine. Look for and record examples from across the two periods to back up your thoughts.

Features of Russian government 1855–1991		
	Under the Tsars 1855–1917	*Under the Communists 1917–1991*
Who were the decision makers?		
What legitimacy did they have?		
What checks existed on autocratic power?		
Attitude to dissent		
Role of secret police		
Role of bureaucracy		
The government's success in achieving its agenda?		
Responsiveness to the public		

I hope, as you have grappled with this grid, that you have quickly realized that there is at least one serious difficulty – the difficulty of generalizing for all Tsars and all leaders of the CPSU. How was the reign of Alexander III, for example, different from those of both his father and his son? What differences were there between Stalin and the de-Stalinizer Khrushchev? You might have also begun to ask yourself other questions about the seeming similarities between the two periods. Was the Duma of Nicholas II, for example, a better check on his government than the soviets were on the Communist leaders?

However, you should also have drawn some important parallels between the Tsarist and Communist systems of government.

Why do the regimes appear to have so many similarities?

There can be no definitive answer to this question, any more than for most other historical questions. This section is meant only to give you some pointers to pursue. As with the grid above, you should revisit the periods of Russian history you have studied and try to find examples which support, or fail to support, these ideas.

● **Russia's enormous size and the diversity of her peoples and cultures**
  Was some kind of monarchical authority the only way to bind together her peoples? What happened to the USSR when autocratic power was either lost, as in 1917 and the late 1980s, or undermined, as during the Russo-Japanese War?
● **The fear of an external threat**
  Was an autocrat sometimes, or always, necessary to maintain a strong government in the face of a real or perceived threat against Russia's security? Was Russia/the USSR always facing an external threat? How did a Communist regime view the rest of the world?

● **Tradition and ideology**

Did authoritarian government continue because the rulers had been brought up to expect the system to continue? You might look back at the advice given to the future Alexander III, or later perhaps at the respect for Lenin and his writings within the CPSU.

● **The consent or acceptance of the ruled**

Is it possible that, as Smith in Source 2 and Karamzin in Source 4 said, autocracy survived because it suited the needs of the Russian peoples? Or perhaps because many thought any alternative even more unacceptable? There are certainly many in Russia today who look back almost longingly on the certainties of life in Soviet times.

 Communist protestors demand a return to the old regime in 1992.

Source 5

Think about

▶ Why did so many protest in favour of a return to Communism?

Which groups in Russia had a permanent vested interest in the survival of autocratic government?

● **Threats from within**

At what times might Russians have rallied around an authoritarian leader because they felt the regime faced dangerous elements inside its own borders?

● **Repression**

Did authoritarian government continue because the repressive apparatus was so effective that it destroyed or fatally weakened those who chose to oppose it?

Assessment

Why has authoritarian government been such a strong feature of Russia between 1855 and 1953/1956/1964/1991?

How much support have successive governments enjoyed since 1855?

The economy and society

This is how Hedrick Smith described the countryside in the USSR, after his time there as a correspondent for the *New York Times*:

Source 6

It surprised me to see that just ten miles from the Kremlin, near the little village of Little Mytishchi, city life and its modern conveniences simply come to an end. New apartment buildings give way to izbas, squat, low peasant cabins. Side roads are suddenly no longer paved but turn to dirt, often no more than two ruts or footpaths dribbling off among garden fences...Plumbing remains a luxury...Off the main highways, I have seen peasant women doing their wash by hand in the fresh cold waters of country streams, with the onion domes of a church visible over trees.

Smith, *The Russians*, 1976

Cross reference

Compare Source 6 with the picture of rural life in the nineteenth century in Chapter 1.

This statement might just as easily have been taken from the diary of a traveller in Russia 150 years ago. It paints a picture of an almost unchanged rural society, despite the attempts of almost all of Russia's leaders to modernize and close the gap with the West.

What was done to try to close the gap with the West?

Before we start to consider this question, it is important to remember that many in the Russia of the nineteenth century did not wish to follow slavishly every new trend from the West. To survive as a major power, however, and to maintain her Empire some of the Tsars' advisers believed that some controlled introduction of western industry was needed. Control was seen to be necessary because industrialization in the West had also been accompanied by demands for greater governmental accountability and the end of autocratic rule.

How did governments try to 'modernize' the Russian economy?

Filling in the grid below will help you to bring together an overall plan of what was done and how this affected Russia/the USSR. Look out for and record examples in your grid of government actions in three fields – agriculture, industry and transport.

Attempts to 'modernize' the economy 1855–1991			
	Agriculture	Industry	Transport
1855–1881			
1881–1905			
1905–1917			
1917–1922			
1922–1928			
1928–1953			
1953–1964			
1964–1991			

When do you think the most determined efforts were made to transform Russia/the USSR? When do you think the most successful efforts were made to transform Russia/the USSR? Why were these efforts more successful than other attempts? Which sector of the economy was most successfully modernized?

Why was Russia unable to close the gap with the West?

■ **Think about**

▶ What does the joke suggest about the Communist system?

▶ Are the suggestions of the various leaders true representations of their views?

Source 7

The train of communism is trundling across the field of life one day when the engine splutters and dies.

Comrade Stalin wakes up. 'Shoot the driver!' he suggests.

Comrade Khrushchev demurs [hesitates]. 'Rehabilitate the driver!' he argues.

Comrade Brezhnev settles comfortably back in his seat. 'Let's just pull the blinds down, close our eyes and rock from side to side,' he says. 'Then nobody will know the train has stopped.'

Finally Comrade Gorbachev leaps to his feet. 'You've all got it wrong' he shouts. 'What we need to do is get off the train and all shout together: the train isn't working, the train isn't working.'

A Soviet joke of the 1980s

In 1830 Russia's per capita income was 70 per cent of the European average; in 1913 it was only 60 per cent, despite Russia's high growth rate in the 20 years before 1914. Between the wars when many other economies experienced problems, especially after the Wall Street Crash in 1929, Germany and Japan exceeded the USSR's growth rate. After the Second World War there was a period of economic growth, but this slowed down and stopped under Brezhnev. You should remember that the USSR did possess the richest natural resources in the world to help in her pursuit of economic growth and prosperity to equal the West.

What is the most important factor in explaining Russia's seeming inability to close the gap is again a matter of debate, but these key points may help you to work out your own order of priority.

● **Climate and environment**

Russia's cold and dry areas make farming difficult. Much of her soil outside the fertile 'black earth' region is poor. Agriculture is simply more difficult in many parts of Russia than elsewhere. If agriculture is unprofitable there will be less money to invest in industrial development or improvements to the infrastructure, such as roads and housing. How did various governments try to overcome these difficulties?

● **Foreign invasion**

Unlike the UK or the USA, Russia faced occupation and utter devastation at many times in her history, but particularly in the twentieth century. Which war brought the greatest damage to her industries, agriculture and infrastructure?

● **Resistance to change**

All societies to some extent or other resist change. When and how did this reluctance of the population to change damage the attempts to modernize the Russian economy? You should be able to find examples throughout the period covered in this book.

● **The actions of government**

Did the actions of government help to narrow the gap with the West or did they have the opposite effect? Was the dekulakization of the First Five Year Plan an aid to increased agricultural production? What were the effects on food production of the government's refusal to use grain stocks in 1933 to feed the rural population? On the other hand did the MTS help to modernize agricultural production? Was the command economy a successful way of achieving sustainable economic growth?

- **Ideological constraints**

  How did Tsarist suspicion of the middle-class intelligentsia slow economic change? How and when did Marxist views of profit prevent initiative and entrepreneurship? What were the lessons to be learned from the fact that in 1975 27 per cent of total agricultural production came from the less than 1 per cent of land farmed individually by the peasants in their private plots?

- **The failure to develop a consensus or an agreed strategy**

  Government policy tended to shift with the wind under the Tsars and in the USSR. When and why did these shifts take place? What were their effects on economic development?

- **The difficulties of the internal market and trade**

  In the nineteenth century trade was restricted by inadequate transport and a lack of finance for investment. Under Communist rule these problems were inherited. Even under the Tsars much of the investment came from the government or overseas financiers. In the USSR the laws of supply and demand did not apply, at least not officially. Instead government planning agencies decided what should be produced. The quality of management and work was often poor. Consumers had no choice, however, so there was no pressure to maintain high quality standards.

- **Shortage of foreign currency**

  When was this so acute that it contributed to the spread of famine in Russia?

Assessment

How successfully did successive Russian governments deal with the problem of agricultural backwardness?

Why has Russia/the USSR not managed to catch up with the West in industrial development?

How important was war in bringing about change in Russia?

'War is the locomotive of history.'

This famous phrase of Trotsky illustrates another theme running through the history of Russia, as it does through the histories of many other states. In the 140 years covered in this book how often did war have a decisive impact on affairs? We can probably highlight at least seven moments:

- The Crimean War 1854–1855
- The Russo-Japanese War 1904–1905
- The First World War 1914–1918
- The Russian Civil War 1918–1921
- The Second World War 1939–1945
- The Cold War 1945 onwards
- The Afghanistan War 1979–1988

How did each of these conflicts help to bring about change?

What is it about war that has contributed to bringing about rapid change?

> **Note**
>
> Since foreign affairs lie, in the main, outside the scope of this book, you should also consult other sources to support your work on this question.

079628

Was war simply an accelerator to changes that were already under way? Would, for example, Tsar Nicholas II have granted the October Manifesto if there had been no Russo-Japanese War? Would the Bolsheviks have been able to seize control of Russia if the First World War had ended in 1916?

Assessment

Has war been the key factor in precipitating change in Russia since 1855?

Conclusion

At the turn of the Millennium Russia had been a nominally democratic state for nine years. However, many of the problems which governments of all persuasions have battled with over the centuries still persist into the twenty-first century. There is apathy towards politics and distrust of politicians in many areas, representing a huge gulf between rulers and ruled, between the executive and 'society'. Russia has still to find an economic system that will bring the comparative riches of the West to most of her people. Russian industry in many cases has not been able to survive the cold air of international competition. In some areas of the former USSR the average life expectancy is lower than at any other time of peace since 1900. Although some national groups have won their independence in the 1990s, there are still demands for greater autonomy from other areas, such as Chechnya, within the Russian Confederation.

However, Russia can no more be ignored today by the West than she could at any other time in the last 150 years. To understand her present predicament, we must first understand her past.

Index